Arms of the City of New Orleans, 1755

# The Odyssey Continues

*Masterworks from the New Orleans Museum of Art*
*and from Private New Orleans Collections*

Exhibition held for the benefit of the
New Orleans Museum of Art's Katrina Recovery Fund

November 17, 2006 to February 9, 2007

## WILDENSTEIN
19 EAST 64TH STREET
NEW YORK, NY 10021

*This exhibition is held under the High Patronage of His Excellency Jean-David Levitte*
*Ambassador of France to the United States*

ISBN 0-9721956-3-7

Exhibition and catalogue conceived by Joseph Baillio

Design: A. Porter Gillespie

Printing: Capital Offset Company Inc., Concord, New Hampshire

A Wildenstein Publication
19 East 64th Street
New York, NY 10021
212-879-0500
*www.wildenstein.com*

Front cover: Giovanni Battista Tiepolo, *Boy Holding a Book* (cat. no. 27), detail
Back cover: Naum Gabo, *Construction in Space: Suspended* (cat. no. 86)
Frontispiece: Photograph © Alan Karchmer/Esto

# CONTENTS

## ACKNOWLEDGMENTS

We are greatly indebted to the following scholars and museum personnel who have assisted us in one way or another in assembling the exhibition and preparing the catalogue: Lisa Ackerman, Chief Administrative Officer, The Samuel H. Kress Foundation, New York; Julia Armstrong-Totten, The Provenance Index, The Getty Research Institute, Los Angeles; Ida Balboul, Research Associate of Modern Art, The Metropolitan Museum of Art, New York; Carole Blumenfeld, Paris; Richard R. Brettell, Professor of Aesthetic Studies, University of Texas, Dallas; Vivian Bullaudy, Director, Hollis Taggart Galleries, New York; Jason T. Busch, former Assistant Curator of Architecture, Design, Decorative Arts, Craft and Sculpture, The Minneapolis Institute of Arts; Lisa Calden, Registrar, University of California Berkeley Art Museum and Pacific Film Archive, Berkeley; Patricia Chandler, Curator, The Sydney and Walda Besthoff Foundation Collection, New Orleans; Beatrice G. Epstein, Associate Museum Librarian, The Image Library, The Metropolitan Museum of Art, New York; Gail Feigenbaum, Associate Director of Programs, The Getty Research Institute, Los Angeles; Jane Glover, Archives of American Art Affiliated Research Center, M.H. de Young Memorial Museum, American Art Study Center, San Francisco; Susan Grinols, Fine Arts Museums of San Francisco; Anne M. Guité, New York; Mary Lee B. Harris, Director of Development, Ursuline Academy, New Orleans; Ruth Janson, Brooklyn Museum; Laurence B. Kanter, Curator, The Robert Lehman Collection, The Metropolitan Museum of Art, New York; Tom Lanham, Louisiana State Museum; Nina Maruca, Registrar, The Metropolitan Museum of Art, New York; Linda Muehlig, Associate Curator of Painting and Sculpture, Smith College Museum of Art, Northampton, Mass.; Patrick Noon, Chief Curator and Patrick and Aimee Butler Curator of Paintings and Modern Sculpture, The Minneapolis Institute of Arts; Alison Purgiel, Minnesota Historical Society, Saint Paul; Margo Pollins Schab, New York; Nathan Silver, Drawings Department, The J. Paul Getty Museum, Los Angeles; Lorraine Stewart, Archives Department, The Museum of Fine Arts, Houston; Marion C. Stewart, Associate Curator of European Art, The Fine Arts Museums of San Francisco; Gerald Stiebel, Stiebel Ltd., New York; Tom Strider, Newcomb Art Gallery, Tulane University, New Orleans; and Carol Togneri, Chief Curator, Norton Simon Museum, Pasadena, California. We owe a special word of appreciation to John T. Magill of the Williams Research Center at The Historic New Orleans Collection. Without his efforts, the illustration of the introduction would not have been nearly as rich. Moreover, he and his Director, Priscilla Lawrence, graciously waived the reproduction fees.

We also wish to thank a number of private individuals who helped us clarify issues of provenance and provided historical data that went into the drafting of the introduction and the catalogue entries: Jacqueline Buechner, New York; Chen Ing Chang, New York; Cynthia Chin; Véronique Delavenne; Mary Jane Harris, New York; Tricia Perez, New Orleans; Mrs. Richard Rush, North Fort Meyers, Florida; and Bonnie Warren, New Orleans.

Finally, we are pleased to acknowledge the assistance we received from the staff of the Frick Art Reference Library, New York; The New York Public Library, New York; The Thomas J. Watson Library, The Metropolitan Museum of Art, New York; The Library of The Museum of Modern Art, New York; The Library of the Whitney Museum of American Art, New York; and The Morgan Library & Museum, New York.

Joseph Baillio and Eliot W. Rowlands

(cat. no. 10, detail)

On Monday, August 29, 2005, a catastrophe of tremendous magnitude took place in New Orleans. Within a few hours, eighty percent of this beautiful, vibrant, unique city was severely impacted by Hurricane Katrina and the flooding that ensued. Many lives were shattered and families displaced. There were thousands of destroyed or badly damaged houses, businesses and public and private institutions. Moreover, the catastrophe exacted a huge toll on the city's social and cultural fabric.

This tragedy had a profound resonance in France, where people rallied to assist New Orleans, which was founded by the French, and where French culture is an essential part of the city's historic heritage. There was a general feeling that we had to act concretely to contribute to the recovery efforts in New Orleans and the restoration of as much of its former glory as possible.

The first phase of French relief was in the form of financial aid, and it totaled more than $25,000,000. On November 4, 2005, France's Minister of Culture and Communication, Monsieur Renaud Donnedieu de Vabres, visited New Orleans, after which he helped launch a series of programs to benefit Louisiana's French immersion schools, New Orleans musicians and various French-Louisiana cultural projects.

Among the many initiatives that we have taken to achieve these goals, the support of the New Orleans Museum of Art occupies a special place.

On August 29, 2005, NOMA was literally marooned in a sea of chaos and destruction. A guardian angel had protected it from the flood, but the building was totally isolated and exposed to looting. A French insurance company, AXA, which had a contract with NOMA, immediately sent security guards to protect the collections. NOMA's director, John Bullard, worked frenziedly with his staff to bring life back to this cultural flagship. And it was during his visit to New Orleans that Monsieur Donnedieu de Vabres announced that the French National Museums and NOMA will hold a major exhibition of French art in early 2007. The project is moving forward under the supervision of our Ministry of Culture in partnership with the most important museums and cultural institutions in France.

I would like to extend my warmest congratulations to Guy Wildenstein for organizing the present exhibition as a benefit for NOMA. Thanks are also due to John Bullard, who selected numerous masterworks from his museum's collection to be shown in New York and to the private collectors who lent generously. Some of France's greatest artists— among them Claude Lorrain, Boucher, Greuze, Corot, Degas, Braque and Bonnard—are represented here at their best.

Once more, thank you, Guy Wildenstein, for showing us that as life goes on, NOMA will recover just as the city of New Orleans is recovering. The Odyssey continues…

His Excellency Jean-David Levitte
*Ambassador of France to the United States of America*

I was seized with a strange feeling as I sat down to draft this message to an exhibition catalogue that Joseph Baillio was kind enough to ask me to write. It is one that I experience each time I am called on to evoke the story of my direct ancestors in faraway Louisiana, which is part of me and is present in my mind like a paradise lost.

This feeling is saddened by the memory of Hurricane Katrina which overwhelmed New Orleans in August of last year. I was able to gauge the extent of the disaster last December as I took a four-hour flight over the devastated city and the nearby Mississippi delta on board a hydroplane. What I was seeing immediately brought back to my mind the deeply buried impressions I had received when in my childhood I saw the destructions of World War I in the department of l'Aisne (Picardie) where I was born. Those mounds of broken and splintered wood, houses mangled and crushed by the hurling winds and piled one upon another, such an apocalyptic landscape could really only be compared to the ravages of war. I would like to say here to all the inhabitants of the Crescent City how well I understand their suffering and admire their courage.

But this tragic moment is also associated with two wonderful images. That of the staff members of the New Orleans Museum of Art who refused to be evacuated so that the works housed there were not left without surveillance; and that of the museum miraculously spared the unleashing of the elements. I regard this valiant effort and this affection for the works housed in the museum as symbols of the indestructible life of art in the midst of a wrecked city and in the hearts of its citizens.

Now I would be remiss were I not to explain to the readers of this catalogue the reasons for my visceral attachment to New Orleans and its environs. My ancestor, Bernard d'Hauterives, landed in Louisiana only a few years after the founding of New Orleans in 1718. This first in a long line of "American" d'Hauterives had three sons, all military men. One of them commanded France's Arkansas outpost at the confluence of the Mississippi and the Arkansas rivers after the Treaty of Paris in 1763, at a time when the immense colony of Louisiana had been handed over by France to Spain. My ancestor, the Chevalier Jean Antoine Bernard d'Hauterives, a former Captain in the army of Louis XV, was given by the Spanish governor of the province the responsibility of settling the exiled Acadian people then arriving in Louisiana on lands inhabited by the Attakapaw and Opelousa peoples. It was there that he built his house in 1765. It still exists and is located in the Longfellow-Evangeline State Park near the little town of Saint Martinville, and I had occasion to depict it in one of my paintings.

If I am not American and do not have childhood memories of Louisiana—my grandfather left the state around 1870, lived for a while in Spain, where he met my grandmother, and then settled permanently in France—I have always imagined that I somehow belonged there. The first time I visited the state, around the age of thirty, I instinctively sensed that I already knew it. This impression could be considered natural in light of my family's history. I attribute it also to specific qualities of the land, its natural beauty which I immediately found inspirational, the flat tonal nuances of the bayous, the incomparable light of a landscape with large expanses of water, in which colors and the radiance of the sun merge into each other, offering a painter like myself an ideal palette.

And how could one avoid recalling the perennial ties between Louisiana and France? Innumerable events remain impressed on their respective histories, marking the encounters of two geographically divided lands: Louisiana has long fascinated and inspired the French by the beauties of its untamed wilderness, and France has bequeathed a part of its culture and its *art de vivre* to the inhabitants of the state.

It is not the least of the present exhibition's merits that several works in the collections of the New Orleans Museum of Art—most importantly Degas' moving portrait of his sister-in-law, Estelle Musson (cat. no. 50)—remind us of this connection.

Arnaud d'Hauterives
*Secrétaire perpétuel de l'Académie des Beaux-Arts of the Institut de France*

New Orleans is a special city to us in France. It is dear to our hearts, of course, because it reminds us of a lost territory and has the enduring charm of the Ancien Régime, a little corner of home under the blinding sun of America's Deep South. The Louisiana of the Abbé Prévost and the nineteenth-century Utopians was a distant place and a promised land. Sarah Bernhardt made a visit there in 1881 and fell in love with it, for she found the city to be "infinitely delightful," enjoying the diversity of the population, praising the "grace" of the women and the general gaiety. Several years earlier, Degas, who was Louisianian through his mother, had stayed there almost six months to visit his family and seek new subjects for his brush: "Nothing appeals to me as much as the black women of every skin tone holding in their arms little white children, so white against houses with fluted wooden columns and gardens of orange trees and ladies in muslin in front of their little houses and steamboats with two funnels, as high as factory chimneys."

Of that Louisiana, in its contrasts and activity, he will leave us one of his great masterpieces, *Portraits in a Cotton Office (New Orleans)* (figs. 57 and 58), an unforgettable image. He gave this painting—in the rhythmic patterns of its composition—a distinctive, lively, bright and thoroughly modern syncopation, and in so doing created what he understood to be "the art of Louisiana" and a veritable "symphony of the new world." There we are in France *and* in America, just as when we walk through the old streets of the Crescent City or visit the very beautiful New Orleans Museum of Art (once called the Isaac Delgado Museum).

I had the opportunity to discover New Orleans about twenty years ago thanks to my friend George Shackelford, today Curator of the Museum of Fine Arts in Boston. I saw it again, severely impacted, about one year ago in the company of our Minister of Culture and Communications, Renaud Donnedieu de Vabres, who was anxious to make a special trip there to bring France's support to this lovely city so devastated by the hurricane. Soon the French National Museums will join forces to offer a wonderful selection of masterpieces to NOMA.

Today, by organizing the present exhibition, Guy Wildenstein, who works so tirelessly to foster the best Franco-American relations, emphasizes in his own way the indestructible bonds that unite us.

Henri Loyrette
*Président Directeur du Musée du Louvre*

The city of New Orleans has always held a special place in Franco-American relations and in the hearts of the citizens of both nations.

Like most Americans, the French were deeply affected by the tragedy that unfolded in New Orleans in late August of 2005, when we saw threatened or destroyed in a matter of hours numerous vestiges of a fascinating, centuries-old past. Cognizant of the great richness of the cultural heritage in both the public and the private sectors of this famous city, we are delighted at the prospect of its recovery.

AXA was happy to participate in preserving from harm the treasures of the New Orleans Museum of Art, thanks to the remarkable efforts of our colleagues at AXA Art in New York. In constant touch with John Bullard, the museum's Director and his valiant staff, the members of AXA Art's team made sure that the works remained unharmed. The present, wonderfully orchestrated exhibition, marks the beginning of a rebirth for the museum.

The variety of NOMA's collections, its holdings of American art, its Impressionist paintings, notably works by Degas who had family ties with New Orleans, its sculpture garden, as well as the collections of enlightened members of the local community are so many tangible proofs of the city's identity and of the sensibilities of the public that has access to them.

If it is true that works of art are the pillars that support a people's collective memory and culture, then those individuals who—like Guy Wildenstein and his organization—contribute to this rebirth. They align themselves with the founders of the Franco-American compact that was made at the time the United States was created, and they deserve the recognition of future generations.

Henri de Castries
*President of the Administrative Council of AXA*

(cat. no. 14, detail)

(cat. no. 53, detail)

# FOREWORD

On August 29, 2005, Hurricane Katrina hit New Orleans with unprecedented fury, forever altering the lives of its citizens. While the New Orleans Museum of Art is located between the badly flooded Mid-City and Lakeview areas, its placement on a high ridge saved it from the surrounding flood waters. Miraculously, our collection of 40,000 artworks survived unharmed, but our building and adjacent sculpture garden sustained multimillion-dollar damage. This catastrophe had a devastating impact on the Museum's finances, forcing us to close our doors for six months and, far worse, to lay off 85% of our staff.

Although all of our trustees and employees were scattered across the state and around the country after the storm, under the inspiring leadership of Board President S. Stewart Farnet, a three-year financial recovery and stabilization plan was quickly prepared to ensure the Museum's future. Our Katrina Recovery Committee, dynamically headed by trustee Paul J. Leaman, Jr., launched a $15 million campaign, and he and I began traveling the country to solicit foundations, corporations, and individuals. The response to our requests for support was tremendously positive and gratifying and placed the Museum firmly on the road to recovery. Our Besthoff Sculpture Garden reopened on December 10, 2005; laid off workers began to be rehired in January 2006, and the Museum was able to reopen on March 3, first for three days a week and now five days a week. There is still much work to be done. Repairs to the building and garden are just beginning. Our staff now stands at only 40% of its original size and our attendance is only 15% of pre-Katrina levels.

The New Orleans Museum of Art's recovery is the result of the dedication and hard work of its much reduced staff and loyal volunteers, particularly our fully committed trustees. Of equal importance was the sympathy and generosity of people from across the country and abroad who came forward to help our Museum. In this regard I must say that the response from France was immediate and inspiring. Louisiana has long enjoyed a unique relationship with France, both historically and culturally. The French people have always had a deep affection and high regard for the people of Louisiana. These sentiments are beautifully expressed in the "Messages of Hope" in this catalogue.

Our Museum was fortunate to have its collections insured by AXA Art Insurance Corporation, a subsidiary of AXA, the great French financial conglomerate. Just one day after the storm, Christiane Fischer, President of AXA Art Insurance, was in constant communication with me and our staff to devise the best plan to preserve our collection. Ms. Fischer and her staff had an immediate proactive response which made possible the airlifting of a private security force from New York to New Orleans, where they guarded the Museum for over two months. Just as important, once the flood waters subsided, AXA was able to transport to the Museum a large generator and constant fuel supply which enabled us to restart our climate and security systems, which had been inoperable since the storm, due to the city-wide failure of its electrical grid. Later, in the spring of 2006, the New Orleans Museum of Art was invited to present an exhibition of *200 Years of Art in Louisiana,* at the gallery at AXA's New York headquarters where a most successful benefit was held as well.

The French Government's response to Katrina was equally prompt. On November 3, 2005, an official delegation lead by Renaud Donnedieu de Vabres, Minister of Culture and Communications, together with French Ambassador to the United States Jean-David Levitte and President-Director of the Louvre Henri Loyrette, visited New Orleans to assess the damage and discuss French support. For the Museum, this visit resulted in the organization of an extraordinary exhibition from the French National Museums—*Femme, Femme, Femme: Paintings of Woman in French Society from Daumier to Picasso*—to be presented in New Orleans from March 4 to June 3, 2007.

Now the French-founded firm of Wildenstein & Company has graciously agreed to host an exhibition of nearly one hundred European and American paintings, sculptures and drawings from our Museum and a few private New Orleans collections. Of course the emphasis is on the French School, one of the Museum's strengths. We are indeed honored that Wildenstein, long the world's premier art gallery, would deem our collection worthy of exhibition. For this we first are indebted to Guy Wildenstein and to his colleague Joseph Baillio, a distinguished scholar of French art, who happens to be a proud native son of Louisiana. Knowing well our Museum's collection and the post-Katrina challenges we now face, they both responded immediately in the most positive manner and all arrangements were quickly made. To aid our Katrina Recovery Fund, Mr. Wildenstein also offered to open the exhibition with a two-night benefit, which he generously chose to underwrite. The Benefit Committee, chaired by one of our long-time trustees, Mrs. Frederick M. Stafford, have worked deligently to insure the success of both events.

In preparing for the exhibition, several works received conservation treatment in New York. In particular our life-size portrait of Queen Marie Antoinette by Vigée Le Brun (cat. no. 39), the centerpiece of our eighteenth-century French Gallery, was expertly revarnished by David Bull and Teresa Longyear as a generous contribution to our Katrina Recovery Fund. I am tremendously grateful to them.

While engaged in research on the catalogue, Joseph Baillio discovered that a long-missing portrait miniature of Madame Auguste De Gas, née Marie-Célestine Musson (fig. 51), a native of New Orleans and the mother of Edgar Degas, was coming up for auction in Paris. He personally purchased this rare object and has generously donated it to the New Orleans Museum of Art, where it will eventually be displayed near Degas' portrait of her niece, Estelle Musson De Gas (cat. no. 50).

To all of the staff at Wildenstein & Company who made the exhibition and this beautiful catalogue a reality—in addition to Messrs. Wildenstein and Baillio, this includes Eliot Rowlands and Porter Gillespie—I extend the heartfelt appreciation of the trustees and staff of the New Orleans Museum of Art. Our good friends at Wildenstein and those who have supported the benefit events join the growing host of guardian angels who have guaranteed the financial stability and longevity of our Museum. For this we are forever grateful.

E. John Bullard
*The Montine McDaniel Freeman Director*
*New Orleans Museum of Art*

Fig. 1. Hurricane Katrina after Landfall, August 29, 2005. Photograph courtesy of AXA Art Insurance, New York

Fig. 2. Hurricane Katrina after Landfall, August 29, 2005. Photograph courtesy of AXA Art Insurance, New York

On August 29, 2005, Hurricane Katrina (figs. 1 and 2) slammed into the Mississippi Delta, causing an enormous amount of damage and destruction. The following day a monstrous storm surge from the Gulf of Mexico caused major breaches to develop along the levee and drainage and industrial canal system separating the north-eastern part of the city of New Orleans—an area which should never have undergone the massive urban development that occured there in the twentieth century—from Lake Ponchartrain or connecting that huge body of water to the Mississippi River. As there were no adequate locks or floodgates in place to relieve the pressure, there was little to prevent the water from pouring into the most exposed parts of the City that Care Forgot, bringing death and incalculable ruin in its wake. In the worst hit areas of the city, what the storm spared the flood mutilated or left mouldering in a swampy ooze once the waters had receded. A desperate situation was compounded when, on September 24, the winds of Hurricane Rita overtopped levees and created additional flooding through the same breaches.

Among the unnumbered victims of the two events was the venerable New Orleans Museum of Art, one of the United States' major metropolitan cultural institutions, which holds the largest and most comprehensive fine arts collection in the Deep South. Although New Orleans has experienced great hardships and natural catastrophes in its past, none has exacted such a toll or excited more interest and compassion throughout the world. Even those historically preserved areas of the stricken city that were left largely intact because they are built on somewhat higher ground—the French Quarter, much of the Faubourg Marigny, parts of Esplanade Ridge and the Lower and Upper Garden Districts—have been impacted by the disaster, if only in economic terms.

Fortunately, the 1911 Greek Revival building and its expansions sit on a mound of land near the main entrance of City Park, high enough so the inundation did not actually reach its base (fig. 3). But the surroundings were submerged, and a nasty, toxic brew managed to leech its way through fissures in the underlying concrete slab that were created by hydrostatic pressure. Staff offices where records were kept and art storage rooms took on polluted groundwater to a level of three or four inches. The museum's foundations were thus compromised and the concrete slab will eventually have to be replaced. Offices in the basement were invaded and mechanical and electrical systems, including telephone lines, were rendered useless.

Thanks to the vigilance of eight members of the museum's staff and their families that did not immediately leave the building when most New Orleanians were urged to vacate the city by the Federal Emergency Management Agency (FEMA), almost all of the more than 40,000 artworks in its permanent collection remained untouched. However, two pieces in its Sydney and Walda Besthoff Sculpture Garden (fig. 4) were severely impacted (Kenneth Snelson's *Virlane Tower* of 1981 and George Segal's *Three Figures and Four Benches* of 1979), as were a number of art objects kept in an off-site storage location. Within the confines of the city, wholesale looting and vandalism were taking place. Finally, the holdouts were ordered to leave the premises by National Guardsmen and were literally dumped on a highway outside the city.

From their offices in New York, the C.E.O. of the AXA Art Insurance Corporation, Christiane Fischer, and members of her crisis management team quickly assessed the scope of the disaster. They hired the International Investigative Group to send in a team of twelve, heavily armed security guards, most of them former New York City police officers (fig. 5), and they reached City Park in a custom-made amphibious vehicle on September 4.

Their mission was to protect the vulnerable museum and its collections in its direst hour. Later, their company sent in a gigantic emergency generator to restore power for the air-conditioning, pumps, dehydrators, and climate control. It functioned for a period of eight weeks, evacuating 14,000 gallons of water per day. National Guardsmen cleared away debris and broken tree limbs.

The final tally is depressing indeed. According to recent assessments, the flooding inflicted more than $6,000,000 in damage on NOMA's physical plant and its adjacent five-acre landscaped sculpture garden. NOMA's Director E. John Bullard, its Deputy Director Jacqueline Sullivan and their employees now have to cope with an absolute catastrophe in terms of the financing of their daily operations, and every day they are faced with the question of their museum's very survival. Sources of revenue have been drastically curtailed, as the museum can expect little funding from either the municipal government of New Orleans, which has lost a considerable portion of its population and its tax base, or the state of Louisiana. Both are economically overwhelmed by the realities of physical destruction and population displacement.

Fig. 3. View of the New Orleans Museum of Art surrounded by water, September 2005. Photograph by Jackie Sullivan

Some sources of individual and corporate funding have dried up. The museum's membership and its cadre of volunteers are either dispersed or remain inactive. Special events such as exhibitions and docent tours for both adults and children have been seriously curtailed. Even more alarming is the fact that eighty-five percent of the staff of curators, administrative personnel, photographers, art handlers, guards, gardeners and maintenance crews had to be laid off in October of 2005. For a time, NOMA was operating with little more than a skeleton crew. Fortunately, some of the employees have been re-hired. Since March 3 of this year, it has been opening its doors to the public free of charge. However, attendance so far is only 20% of pre-Katrina levels. For the single year of 2005, NOMA incurred a deficit of $700,000, and that type of loss is expected to continue.

To respond to the crisis, the museum has announced a $15,000,000 Katrina Recovery Campaign, the goal of which is to keep NOMA alive and culturally active over the next three years. John Bullard and the museum's thirty-four-member Board of Trustees[1] have organized an international advisory committee, whose membership includes Charles C. Bergman (Chairman of the Pollock-Krasner Foundation), John H. Bryan (retired Chairman and C.E.O of the Sara Lee Corporation), Sir Timothy Clifford (Director-General of the National Galleries of Scotland), James Cuno (President and Director of The Art Institute of Chicago), Christopher Forbes (Vice-Chairman of Forbes, Inc., and President of American Friends of the Louvre), Agnes Gund (President Emerita of The Museum of Modern Art in New York), Kitty Carlisle Hart (a native of New Orleans who serves as Chair Emerita of the New York State Council on the Arts), JoCarole Lauder, Henri Loyrette (President and Director of the Musée du Louvre), Leonard and Susan Bay Nimoy and Richard W. Oldenburg (Honorary Chairman of Sotheby's North and South America).

In this battle for survival, the challenges facing the museum are daunting. Appeals have been made and some have been answered. There has been world-wide interest in the museum's plight. Henri Loyrette, the President-Director of the Louvre, has visited New Orleans and has agreed to sponsor a major exhibition of works of art from the collections of some of France's national museums—the Louvre, the Musée d'Orsay and the Centre Pompidou. It will take place early in 2007. As of February 2006, NOMA had received nearly $3,000,000 in financial grants from organizations, corporations and private donors. The prominent philanthropic contributors include the Zemurray Foundation, the Azby Fund, The Andrew W. Mellon Foundation, the Andy Warhol Foundation for the Visual

Fig. 4. The Sydney and Walda Besthoff Sculpture Garden in the aftermath of the flood, September 2005. Photograph courtesy of the New Orleans Museum of Art

Arts, the Whitehead Foundation, the Benjamin M. Rosen Family Foundation, the Deutsche Bank Americas Foundation, the J. Aron Charitable Foundation, the Elizabeth Cheney Foundation. Moreover, the Association of Art Museum Directors and a number of regional cultural organizations have contributed in one way or another to NOMA's recovery efforts.[2]

Recently, a fund-raising exhibition entitled *The Big Easy to The Big Apple: 200 Years of Art in Louisiana from the Battle of New Orleans to Katrina*[3] was held on the premises of AXA's New York headquarters on 7th Avenue. The fund-raising gala event on April 10—*An Odyssey: An Evening to Benefit the New Orleans Museum of Art*—netted the museum approximately $1,000,000, and that evening the ten members of New York's finest who had stood guard over the museum were suitably honored (fig. 6).

I would like first and foremost to extend my deepest gratitude to the anonymous private lenders without whose participation the exhibition would not be nearly as rich and comprehensive.

I am profoundly honored that His Excellency Jean-David Levitte has agreed to sponsor the exhibition in his official capacity as France's Ambassador to the United States. He was also gracious enough to draft for the catalogue an inspiring statement of his country's pledge to assist in the rebuilding process now going on in New Orleans. And a special word of recognition is due to my friend Michel David-Weill, a member of the Institut de France and President of the Conseil supérieur des Musées nationaux, who kindly agreed to act as an Honorary Chairman of our Benefit Committee. The Weill family has deep roots in Louisiana. They left their native Alsace in the 1840s and set up a business in New Orleans with their cousins the Lazards. With the passage of time, their enterprise grew and developed into Lazard Frères, one of the world's most prestigious financial advisory and asset management firms, of which Monsieur David-Weill is Chairman emeritus.

I am much indebted to Henri Loyrette, the Director and C.E.O. of the Musée du Louvre, Arnaud d'Hauterives, Secrétaire perpétuel de l'Académie des Beaux-Arts at the Institut de France, and Henri de Castries, President of the insurance giant AXA, for their enthusiastic support of the exhibition and for addressing their thoughts of encouragement to the victims of Katrina in New Orleans. The presentation and installation of this exhibition in New York owes much to Christiane Fischer, C.E.O. of the AXA Art Insurance Corporation and her colleague, Vivian L. Ebersman, Director of Fine Art Expertise at AXA Art.

Recognition is also due to John Bullard and his unconquerable staff at the New Orleans Museum of Art—Victoria E. Cooke, Curator of European Painting; John W. Keefe, Curator of Decorative Arts; Paul Tarver, Registrar; Jennifer Ickes, Assistant Registrar; Steven Maklansky, Assistant Director for Art and Curator of Photography; Emma Haas, Executive Assistant—as well as to the outside photographer, Judy Cooper. Despite the problems they have to contend with on a daily basis, they were invariably cooperative in mounting the exhibition and bringing it to New York and in providing information and photography.

My colleague, Joseph Baillio, a native of Louisiana, conceived the idea of the exhibition following Katrina and has written an exemplary catalogue, which includes an informative and entertaining history of the city of New Orleans from the time it was founded by the French until the creation of the museum. In this, he was superbly assisted by Eliot Rowlands. This publication will in future serve as a primary reference source for the works featured in the show.

Fig. 5. Guards on duty at the New Orleans Museum of Art following Hurricane Katrina, September 2006. Photograph courtesy of AXA Art Insurance, New York

Porter Gillespie has designed this elegant book, and he carried out much of the iconographical research through contacts in New Orleans and elsewhere. Matthew Parry was responsible for the superb in-house photography and was closely involved with the color corrections. Jay Stewart, President of Capital Offset Company, has performed with great professionalism and in the timeliest fashion, in spite of delays in the production of the final text. It is a delight working with him and his team in Concord, New Hampshire.

Odile Poncet should be credited for the proofreading of the manuscript, which she carried out with her usual meticulous standards. Elizabeth Lorig was also involved in the proofreading of the text. Ay-Whang Hsia cleared up problems relating to the collection histories of certain works. Donna C. Swartz and Jennifer L. Van Etten were unstinting in the effort they expended during the research process. Anne Sohier, Sophie Pietri, Amélie Naux and Emma Braid-Taylor provided invaluable help in tracking down some of the bibliography and the imagery used to illustrate the Introduction. Joseph Tursellino and Philip J. Dempsey have done yeoman labor by coordinating the crating and shipment to New York of the works in the exhibition and in the planning of the elegant presentation in the gallery rooms. They worked hand in glove with Don Hanford and his staff of Boxart Inc. and David Cohen and his staff at Masterpiece International, Ltd. Raymond Skeeter and his amazing crew—Fernando Echeverri, James Molina, Miguel Riano, Robert Toussaint and Omar Zambrano—worked tirelessly and with good humor as they installed the exhibited works. Greg Schmitt, Mario Giannini and Marcos Lopez of Bavarian Computer Works created a custom software program that allowed us to handle with ease the tremendous amount of data and imagery that went into the making of the catalogue. Finally, Claudine Godts was responsible for the organization and coordination of the opening night events, and for this she deserves my profound thanks.

Fig. 6. Former New York policemen being honored on the evening of April 10, 2006, at the AXA Gallery, New York

All of us at Wildenstein & Co. trust that New Yorkers and out-of-towners alike will enjoy viewing the magnificent works in the exhibition, those from the New Orleans Museum of Art as well as those lent privately. We also sincerely hope that the exhibition will bring the museum's plight to the attention of the widest possible audience, and that the proceeds of the opening night events and the daily admissions will add significantly to its ever growing recovery fund.

Guy Wildenstein

NOTES

1. The membership of NOMA's Board of Trustees is as follows: <u>Officers</u>: S. Stewart Farnet, President; David F. Edwards, Vice President; Mrs. Ludovico Feoli, Vice President; R. Hunter Pierson, Vice President; Mrs. Edward N. George, Secretary; Mrs. Mason Granger, Treasurer. <u>Members</u>: Sydney Besthoff III, J. Herbert Boydstun, Mrs. Kenneth Broadwell, Edgar L. Chase III, Dr. Isidore Cohn, Jr., Timothy Francis, Ms. Tina Freeman, Mrs. James Frischhertz, Lawrence D. Garvey, Mrs. David Groome, Stephen A. Hansel, Edward F. Harold, Dr. Stella Pinkey Jones, Dr. Herbert Kaufman, Paul J. Leaman, Jr., Dr. E. Ralph Lupin, Mrs. Paula L. Maher, Edward C. Mathes, Charles B. Mayer, Mayor Ray Nagin, Dr. Howard J. Osofsky, Dan Packer, Mrs. Robert J. Patrick, Prof. Thomas Reese, Michael J. Siegel, Charles A. Snyder, Mrs. Richard L. Strub, Mrs. James I. Taylor, Mrs. Patrick F. Taylor, Louis A. Wilson, Jr. <u>National Trustees</u>: John H. Bryan III, Mrs. Carmel Cohen, Aaron I. Fleischman, George L. Lindemann, Mrs. James Pierce, Mrs. Benjamin Rosen, Mrs. Robert Shelton, Mrs. Billie Milam Weisman. Honorary <u>Life Members</u>: Russell Albright, M.D., Mrs. Jack R. Aron, Mrs. Edward B. Chase, Jr., Prescott N. Dunbar, Mrs. Richard W. Freeman, Jr., Dr. Kurt A. Gitter, Mrs. H. Lloyd Hawkins, Mrs. Killian Huger, Dr. Richard W. Levy, Mrs. J. Frederick Muller, Mrs. Charles S. Reily, Jr., Mrs. Françoise Billion Richardson, B. Randolph Richmond, Jr., Mrs. Frederick M. Stafford, Harry C. Stahel, Moise S. Steeg, Jr., Dr. Samuel Z. Stone, Mrs. Harold H. Stream and Mrs. John N. Weinstock.

2. Locally, the Louisiana Arts and Science Museum in Baton Rouge (where NOMA's staff set up a temporary operation center until it was able to return to New Orleans) and the Opelousas Museum of Art, and nationally such fellow museums as the North Carolina Museum of Art, the Kimbell Art Museum, the Tampa Museum of Art, the Memphis Brooks Museum of Art, the Cincinnati Museum of Art, the Bass Museum of Art, the Flint Institute of Arts, the Baltimore Museum of Art, the Sterling and Francine Clark Art Institute and the Museum of International Folk Art.

3. The show, which took place between March 10 and May 13, 2006, included works by Diane Arbus, Ernest Bellocq, Henri Cartier-Bresson, Edgar Degas, Walker Evans, Robert Frank, Lee Friedlander, Hyacinthe Laclotte, Clarence John Laughlin, John T. Scott, Edward Weston and William Woodward.

(cat. no. 15, detail)

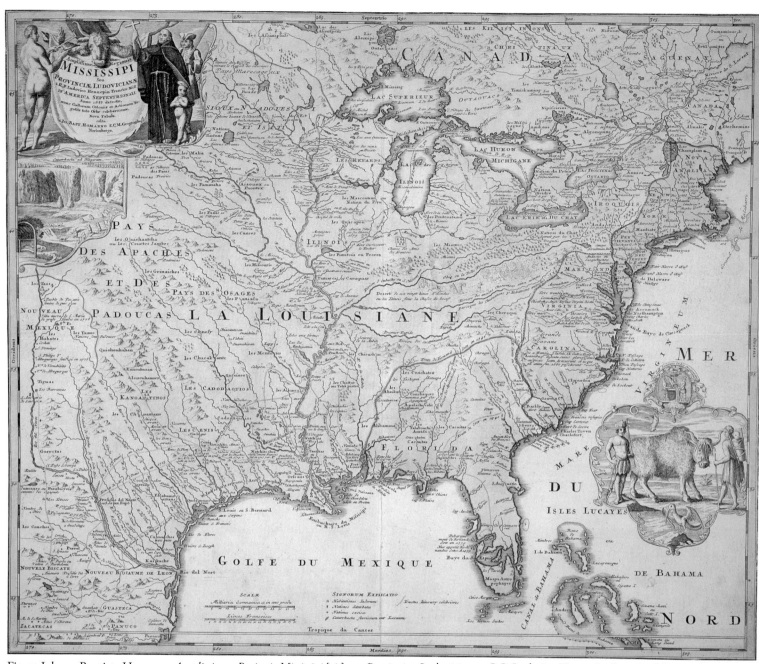

Fig. 7. Johann Baptista Homann. *Amplissimae Regionis Mississipi [sic] seu Provinciae Ludovicinae a R.P. Ludovico Hennepin Francisc. Miss. in America Septentrionali,* 1720. Engraving. Minnesota Historical Society, St. Paul

# NEW ORLEANS, ITS HISTORY AND ITS PEOPLE
## BETWEEN THE XVIIᵗʰ AND THE EARLY XXᵗʰ CENTURIES

BY JOSEPH BAILLIO

Fig. 8. S.R. Sutton. *Aerial View of the City of New Orleans.* Board of Commissioners, Port of New Orleans.

Fig. 9. Philippe de Champaigne. *Portrait of Jean Baptiste Colbert (1619-1683),* 1655. Oil on canvas. The Metropolitan Museum of Art, New York (Gift of the Wildenstein Foundation, Inc.)

The nostalgic "Old South" image that many people have of New Orleans (fig. 8) as a free-wheeling port city on the Mississippi Delta, notable for its mixture of races and cultures, picturesque and musty colonial architecture, lush sub-tropical vegetation, exotic cuisine, quaint folklore and colorful but decadent customs is something of a literary construct[1] given an almost mythical life by a succession of nineteenth- and twentieth-century writers[1] and perpetuated by a host of less gifted imitators. But it has some basis in fact, just as a good deal of historical truth underpins Margaret Mitchell's romanticized depiction of antebellum-, Civil War and post-Civil War Atlanta in *Gone with the Wind*. New Orleans has a past like that of no other metropolis in the United States, one that was conditioned by its geographical position and the ways in which it was settled by the French, the Spanish and the Americans who, each in their turn, have governed it.[2]

## EARLY EXPLORATION OF THE MISSISSIPPI VALLEY

By the late seventeenth century, much of the North American continent had been carved up by explorers on behalf of the major European monarchial powers, Spain, England and France. New Spain was ruled by a viceroy from Mexico City, and it included Central America, Mexico, a large part of Texas and much of the western United States. The king of Great Britain held dominion over a long stretch of colonies extending along the eastern seaboard, each under the rule of a governor. The original colony of Louisiana was for nearly a century an integral part of New France. This huge, mostly undefined area of the present-day continental United States rose in the shape of a funnel from the coast of the Gulf of Mexico into southern Canada (fig. 7), and it comprised all or portions of the following American states, most of which are situated between the Appalachians and the Rocky Mountains: Montana, Wyoming, the two Dakotas, Missouri, Iowa, Minnesota, Nebraska, Kansas, Arkansas, Colorado, New Mexico, Oklahoma, Texas and, of course, Louisiana.

Some of its southernmost regions had been visited via the Gulf of Mexico as early as the second decade of the 1500s, when Alonso Álvarez de Pineda (1494–c. 1520) and the conquistador Pánfilo de Narváez (1470–1528) came upon the mighty Mississippi, which they dubbed *"el Rio del Espíritu Santo."* Around 1541, the area above the delta was explored by Hernando de Soto, who died there the next year, and his corpse was apparently deposited in its waters. However, as they did not find gold or silver deposits to exploit, the Spaniards made no attempt to lay claim to the river and the lands on either side of it for their sovereign.[3] More than one hundred years passed before, in June of 1673, the intrepid French missionaries Jacques Marquette and Louis Joliet entered the Mississippi from the north, and they followed it as far south as the mouth of the Arkansas River before returning to Canada.

## THE FOUNDING OF THE LOUISIANA COLONY

A little less than a decade elapsed before René Robert Cavelier de La Salle (1643–1687) traveled from Canada to the Illinois River and from there descended the Mississippi[4]— then referred by the French as the Fleuve Colbert, in honor of Louis XIV's powerful

Minister of Finances and the Navy, Jean Baptiste Colbert (fig. 9), or the Fleuve Saint-Louis—to the drainage basin in the Gulf of Mexico. The purpose of his expedition was to prevent the English and Spanish from laying claim to land that reached into southern Canada, which the French already occupied. On April 9, 1682, on the west bank of the river, in what is today the state of Louisiana's Plaquemines Parish, La Salle and his party of soldiers, missionaries, northern native American scouts and a notary solemnly took possession of the vast territory for Louis XIV (cat. no. 15), the third French king of the Bourbon dynasty, for whom it was named. This was part of a grand strategy engineered by the absolutist "Sun King" and his council of ministers to insure that the base of their Canadian provinces was protected, that the important trade in furs, lumber and minerals in the upper reaches of the Mississippi and Ohio Valleys had a permanent maritime outlet, and that their ships were given relatively easy commercial and military access to Mexico and the coasts of Middle and South America.

Fig. 10. Alexis Simon Belle. *Portrait of Antoine Crozat (1655-1738) in the Costume of the Order of the Saint-Esprit,* 1715. Oil on canvas. Musée national des Châteaux de Versailles et de Trianon. Réunion des Musées Nationaux

In 1712, Louis XIV granted an exclusive charter for the colonization of Louisiana and the direction of all commerce carried on within its boundaries to the financier Antoine Crozat (fig. 10). Through the latter's appointed governors, Crozat introduced into the territory the pernicious trade in slaves from western equatorial Africa.[5] It soon became well entrenched and formed the basis of the territorial economy. But Crozat's Compagnie de Louisiane, an offshoot of the Compagnie des Indes Occidentales Françaises,[6] did very little to increase the number of French men and women in the territory.[7] This was in sharp contrast with what the English were accomplishing in their North American provinces. In fact, French Louisiana would never be sufficiently populated to create an indissoluble bond between it and the motherland. Moreover, during his tenure as director of the Compagnie de Louisiane, Crozat had never been able to make this overseas venture as profitable as he had anticipated.

The first attempts at settlement along the Gulf coast were commanded by Pierre Le Moyne d'Iberville (fig. 11), the senior member of a large family of French Canadian explorers and naval officers. Soon after the end of the War of the Grand Alliance, he was commissioned by the royal ministry of the navy to journey to the Gulf of Mexico. There he ordered fortifications erected and garrisoned on the Mobile river and on the shore of Biloxi Bay. Thus, original command posts in Louisiana were located further east of the Mississippi at the Île Dauphine, Mobile,[8] the stockaded Fort Saint-Louis de la Mobile and Biloxi. The waters at these locations, however, were not deep enough to provide a harbor for the anchorage of ships of large tonnage, and the French began inspecting the estuary of the big river in search of such a port. With the help of indigenous peoples,[9] d'Iberville led scouting parties in canoes along the coast and into the back country on the west bank of the Mississippi.

### The establishment of the port of New Orleans

The old Louis XIV died in 1715, leaving his throne to his five-year-old great-grandson, the Duc d'Anjou, who would reign as Louis XV (fig. 12). Because of the new king's tender age, the real power was at once vested in a Council of Regency headed by the child's cousin, Philippe II, Duc d'Orléans (fig. 13). It was during the Prince Regent's term as de facto head of the French state that, in March of 1718,[10] one of d'Iberville's younger brothers, Jean Baptiste Le Moyne de Bienville (fig. 14), staked out with a small crew of laborers and soldiers a primitive trading post on the east bank of a deep, crescent-shaped[11] bend in the river. The site on which New Orleans was founded had been previously reconnoitered by Le Moyne d'Iberville as he was exploring the Bayou Tchoupic,[12] which he renamed Bayou Saint-Jean in honor of his patron saint, along a portage used by the indigenous people of the Chitimacha and Acolapissa tribes.[13] It was below sea level and water was everywhere.

Fig. 11. G.D. Warburton, after an unknown French artist. *Portrait of Pierre Le Moyne d'Iberville (1661-1706).* Engraving

Fig. 12. Nicolas de Largillierre. *Commemorative Portrait of Members of the Bourbon Dynasty—Louis XIV, his Son the Grand Dauphin, his Grandson the Duc de Bourgogne, his infant great-grandson, the Duc d'Anjou, the future Louis XV, and Busts of Henri IV and Louis XIII—and the Royal Governess, the Duchesse de Ventadour,* circa 1715-20. Oil on canvas. The Wallace Collection, London

A detachment of workmen—carpenters (among them André Joseph Pénicaut),[14] *voyageurs* or *coureurs des bois* from Canada and the Illinois country, as well as some convicts—cleared away a thick canebrake and growths of trees along the river's edge. They then set about constructing makeshift housing, barracks and a warehouse. As a tribute to the Regent, Bienville named the place "La Nouvelle Orléans" and within a matter of decades it became the major settlement in the Louisiana province.

Bienville chose this location because it was slightly above sea level, and he mistakenly believed that it was relatively safe from hurricanes and flooding. In fulfilment of La Salle's dream, he saw it as an ideal port of transhipment from which to control traffic and commerce on the Mississippi and the tributaries feeding it. Le Moyne de Bienville became governor of all of the Louisiana territory in 1701. New Orleans lay at a point a little more than one hundred miles inland from the mouths of the Mississippi, on the alluvial strip separating it from Lakes Borgne[15] and Ponchartrain. The latter, a huge brakish body of water, and the smaller nearby Lake Maurepas were named for two members of

Fig. 13. Jean Baptiste Santerre. *Philippe II, Duc d'Orléans (1676-1723) and Minerva*, circa 1717-18. Oil on canvas. Musée national des Châteaux de Versailles et de Trianon. Réunion des Musées Nationaux

Fig. 14. After an unknown French artist. *Portrait of Jean Baptiste Le Moyne de Bienville (1680-1767).* Engraving

Fig. 15. Robert Levrac Tournières, *Portrait of Louis Phélypeaux, Comte de Ponchartrain and de Maurepas (1643-1727), Chancellor of France,* circa 1695. Oil on canvas. Musée national des Châteaux de Versailles et de Trianon. Réunion des Musées Nationaux

the Phélypeaux family who served Louis XIV's government as Ministers of the Navy and were thus in charge of the overseas colonies, Louis Phélypeaux (fig. 15) and his son Jérôme (1674–1747).[16] Lakes Borgne and Ponchartrain were connected[17] and provided an entrance to and an exit from the Gulf of Mexico (fig. 16). The river could not be ascended by French galleons and frigates from the Gulf and would only become navigable once engineers had succeeded in dredging away the sandbars that blocked its several entrances in the tidewater passes of the delta. This only occured around 1722, the year the seat of the colonial government was officially transfered from Biloxi to New Orleans.

## THE MISSISSIPPI BUBBLE

By August 1717, Antoine Crozat's largely economic hold on Louisiana had been transferred to another monopoly, the Compagnie d'Occident or Compagnie du Mississippi, a scheme hatched by the Scottish economist John Law (1671–1729), who sold the idea to Regent Orléans. To capitalize his plan for encouraging trade between France and its overseas colonies in the lower part of North America, Law created a royal bank and issued paper money backed by neither coinage nor bullion. As an enticement to attract gullible investors, he advertised Louisiana as an Eldorado where fortunes could be easily realized. The result was rampant speculation, and people clamored to buy bonds and concessions of plantation land in the faraway colony. In the end, Law's system collapsed in the so-called "Mississippi Bubble," and many of those who had invested in it were left with worthless bonds, debt papers and currency or landed estates they were incapable of managing from afar.

Law assiduously fed false information to journalists in Europe in order to make New Orleans appealing for future inhabitants. French language news sheets such as the *Mercure historique et politique*, which was published in The Hague, spoke in hyperbolic terms about the settlement as early as October of 1719, describing it as having six hundred houses, each seated on a plot of one hundred twenty *arpents* of land.

In fact in its first years New Orleans was an assemblage of primitive and mostly squalid hovels covered with bark and reeds sitting on a spongy, reptile- and mosquito-infested swamp land and on sloughs bristling with palmettos. The insalubrious conditions in which the first settlers lived was a natural breeding ground for parasitic or viral diseases such as malaria, cholera, smallpox, plague, leprosy and the dreaded yellow fever.[18] Indeed, epidemics would be a common scourge in New Orleans until measures of hygiene were introduced at the end of the nineteenth century. The below sea level topography and often oppressively hot and humid climate were such that the little enclave was often endangered by flooding from the river and nearby lakes, bayous and cypress swamps, as well as by rain storms and the hurricanes that roared ashore from the Gulf of Mexico. As early as the second year of occupation, New Orleans was completely submerged and large portions of it had to be rebuilt.

## FATHER CHARLEVOIX'S VISIT TO NEW ORLEANS

While visiting the new community, the Jesuit chronicler Pierre François Xavier de Charlevoix (1682–1761) described the place and predicted a glorious future for it in a letter he addressed to the Duchesse de Lesdiguières on January 10, 1722:

> Here I am finally arrived in this famous City that has been named *la Nouvelle Orléans*....This City is the first that one of the largest Rivers in the World has seen built on its banks. If the eight hundred beautiful Houses & the five Parishes that the *Mercure* assigned to it two years ago are still limited today to about one hundred Shacks placed without much order, to a large Warehouse built of wood, to two or three Houses which would not grace a French Village, & to half of a

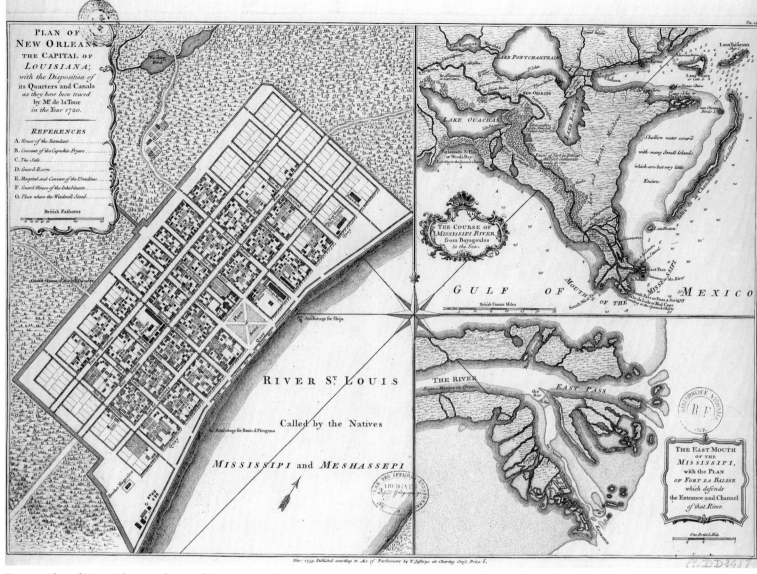

Fig. 16. *Plan of New Orleans and Map of the Estuary of the Mississippi River with Lakes Borgne, Ponchartrain and Maurepas*

pathetic storehouse that was lent to his Lordship[19] and of which he hardly had time to take possession when he had to leave it in order to take shelter under a tent. But on the other hand, what a pleasure to see this future Capital of a beautiful & vast Country growing imperceptibly & to be able to say without sighing, like Virgil's hero referring to his beloved fatherland consumed by flames, *& the fields where once had stood the City of Troy*: but filled with the best founded hope. This wild and deserted place that canebrakes and trees almost entirely cover will one day be, & perhaps this day is not far off, an opulent City & the Metropolis of a large & rich Colony.

You will ask me, Madame, on what I am basing this hope? I base it on the geographical situation of this Town at 23 leagues from the Sea, & on the bank of a navigable river that can be reached in twenty-four hours, on the fertility of the soil, on its temperate and fine climate at thirty degrees of Northern latitude, on the industriousness of its inhabitants, on its proximity to Mexico which can be reached in two weeks by Sea, to Havana which is even closer, to the beautiful islands of America[20] & the English Colonies. Is anything more required to make a flourishing city? Rome & Paris did not have such considerable beginnings, were

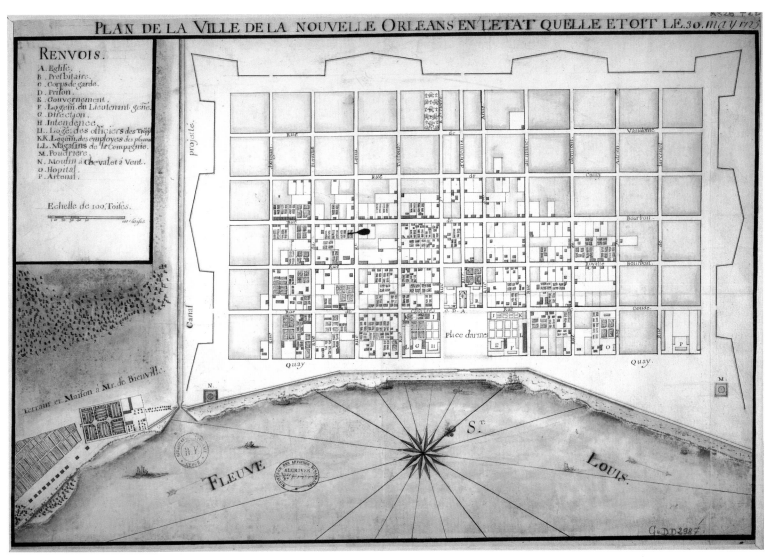

Fig. 17. *PLAN DE LA VILLE DE LA NOUVELLE ORLEANS EN L'ETAT QUELLE ETOIT LE 30 may 1725* (showing the position of Governor Le Moyne de Bienville's house outside the city limits, to the left of the projected canal). Archives nationales de France, Paris (Dépôt des fortifications et des colonies)

not built under such fortunate auspices, & their Founders did not encounter of the Seine & the Tiber the advantages we have found on the Mississippi compared to which those two rivers are no more than streams.[21]

### Le Blond and de Pauger lay out the city (the "Vieux Carré")

By 1724, the land had been carefully surveyed and a real town was being laid out in a grid pattern of forty-four perfectly square blocks, each one of equal dimensions, with eleven plots running horizontally along the river's edge and four deep (figs. 17 and 18). The plan was designed by two civil engineers stationed in Biloxi, Louis Pierre Le Blond de La Tour, who died in 1723 before it could be completed, and his assistant and successor Adrien de Pauger (d. 1726). The streets were assigned the names according to the following system: saints of the Roman Catholic faith (the rues Sainte Anne, Saint Louis and Saint Pierre); members of the ruling family in France (the rues de Bourbon,[22] de Chartres,[23] de Conti,[24] du Maine,[25] Royale[26] and de Toulouse[27]); important public buildings (the rue de l'Arsenal); and the founder of the city and governor of the entire province of Louisiana (the rue de Bienville). As New Orleans expanded into the swamps and more blocks were added, this particular form of nomenclature was adhered to.[28]

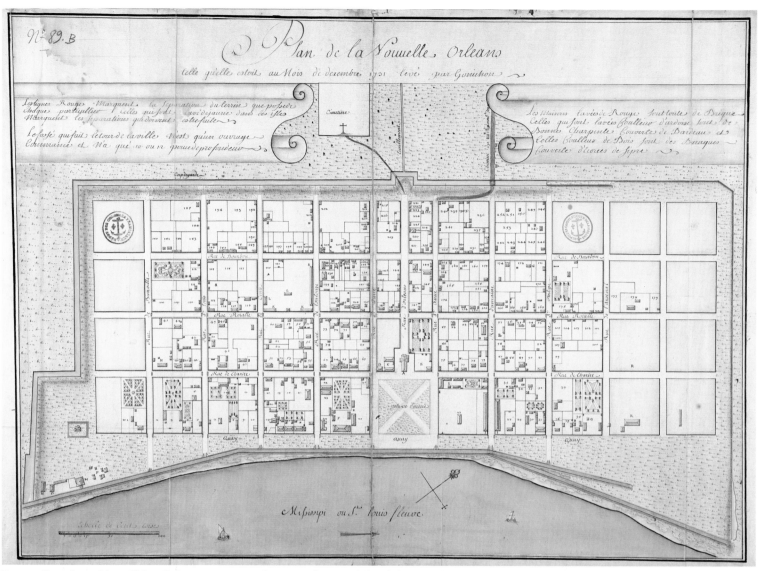

Fig. 18. Gonichon. *Plan of New Orleans as it appeared in December 1731 (Plan de la Nouvelle Orléans telle qu'elle estoit au mois de dexembre [sic] 1731).* Pen and India ink and watercolor on paper. Archives nationales de France, Paris (Dépôt des fortifications et des colonies)

In 1725, Jean Pierre de Lassus de Saint-Geniès (1694–1758) and his brother Joseph de Lassus de Marcilly,[29] natives of the village of Montréjeau in Languedoc, were sent to the settlement as surveyors and topographical draftsmen. The following year Lassus de Saint-Geniès painted a fascinating watercolor (figs. 19 and 20) in which he depicted New Orleans from the opposite side of the Mississippi. The city is hemmed in by a forest and brush. In the center is the Place d'Armes with a church in the distance and barracks on each side. Three large sailing vessels are anchored at the wharf. In the foreground, Amerindians are building a fire, and in one of the large pirogues a native brandishes a pole on which he has stuck the head of a slain enemy.

The area of New Orleans constituting the original city has long been known as the "Vieux Carré" or the French Quarter. It was built around a parade ground, the Place d'Armes or the Place Royale,[30] which faced the riverfront. Parallel to the Mississippi's course, at the center of the far side of this plaza, on the site now occupied by the Cathedral, sat the parish church of Saint-Louis, which was ministered to by priests of the Capuchin order. Placed symmetrically on either side of it were the seat of government where ultimately the Conseil Supérieur and the Intendance would meet and the priory of the Capuchins, known as the Presbytère. Although the square retains to this day its original configuration,

Fig. 19. Jean Pierre de Lassus de Saint-Geniès. *View and Perspective of New Orleans (Veüe et Perspective de la Nouvelle Orléans),* 1726. Pen and India ink and watercolor on paper. Archives nationales de France, Paris (Dépôt des fortifications et des colonies)

during its relatively long history all of the buildings lining three sides of its periphery have undergone radical changes, some of them several times.

Within ten years, New Orleans was home to a constabulary, a municipal *corps de garde*, night police (*veilleurs de nuit*),[31] a prison, a hospital, royal storehouses, an arsenal, a powder magazine, additional barracks for the military, a guardhouse for local militia and two convents. Lots granted to settlers for the construction of individual dwellings were ditched and palisaded. Because of flooding, some houses built in the old Colonial French style were small and relatively simple in their design and could rightly be called cottages. As years went by and fortunes grew, domestic architecture became more and more elaborate and elegant, but the vernacular style was maintained.[32] Behind a number of them were the kitchens and kitchen gardens in which poultry and other small livestock were raised. The little municipality was walled, gated and moated for its own protection, and, because the surrounding terrain was below sea level, networks of crude *levées* (earthen embankments calculated to prevent flooding from the river) were created. Strollers were only able to avoid garbage and slops accumulating in the unpaved streets once gutters and cypress or brick sidewalks called *banquettes* had been put in place. Entire sections of the city were often laid waste by natural disasters and by fire,[33] and each time they were reconstructed along the lines of Le Blond and de Pauger's simple geometrical scheme (fig. 21).[34]

## LOUISIANA'S FRENCH GOVERNORS AND FRICTION WITH THE NATIVE PEOPLES

The work of the first governors assigned to Louisiana,[35] especially Le Moyne de Bienville and Étienne Périer, was complicated by numerous factors. The French royal ministries were reluctant to pay the expenses of maintaining the colony which were regarded as a useless drain on the treasury, population growth was painfully slow and local commissioners, jealous of their prerogatives, were a constant source of annoyance and bickering. Relations with nearby native tribes such as the Natchez and the Chickasaws deteriorated as the French encroached more and more on their lands; a series of wars ensued, the result being the near extinction of the Natchez.[36] Furthermore, there was often unrest among the slave populations of the city and its immediate environs. Droves of settlers preferred to remain within the confines of the city's walls.

## EARLY POPULATION GROWTH IN NEW ORLEANS

The sexual license and criminality that are endemic in the Crescent City have deep historical roots. New Orleans was the exotic place to which the tragic Manon Lescaut

Fig. 20. Detail of fig. 19.

was sent as a common whore in the Abbé Prévost's eponymous novel (1731), and she and her lover the Chevalier Des Grieux were depicted in association with the governor of Louisiana.[37] The plot accords with the factual evidence of the time. Some of the French women in the original colony had been kept in almshouses[38] or prisons for crimes of vagrancy, delinquency and especially prostitution.[39] They were swept up by the police or the *maréchaussée* and forcibly sent to the colony on board the Compagnie du Mississippi's ships that set sail from Atlantic ports.[40]

The Duc de Saint-Simon deplored the practice that the English had conceived for colonizing their overseas possessions, the arbitrary abduction and deportation of people of both sexes, the unwanted, the scourings of the streets and houses of detention:

> By manipulating that Mississippi thing in every way possible, in other words by playing the shell game that was called by that name in imitation of the English, they tried to establish in this vast country some real outposts. For the purpose of populating it, in Paris and throughout the realm, they engaged in abducting the criminal elements and healthy beggars of both sexes along with quantities of street women. If this had been carried out wisely, with discernment and the requisite measures and precautions, it would have fulfilled the proposed objectives and

rid Paris and the provinces of a useless and often dangerous burden. But they went about it in Paris and everywhere else with such violence and even illegalities by sweeping up just about anyone, that there arose considerable discontent. No care had been taken to provide for the subsistence of so many unfortunate souls along the roads or in places designated for their embarkation. They were kept at night in barns with nothing to eat or in whatever holes in the ground they happened to be near and from which they could not get out. They let out cries that elicited pity and indignation. But insufficient charity, as well as the lack of care taken of them by their captors lead to a horrific number of deaths. This inhumanity, added to the agents' barbarity, a violence of a kind until then unknown and the abduction of people who did not fall within the prescribed categories but whom certain individuals wished to get rid of by word of mouth or through bribery of the abductors, led to a huge outcry expressed in such tones that it was decided that this could no longer be tolerated. Some of the soldiery that was sent away was treated no better during the crossing. Those people who remained behind were released and left to their own devices, and the abductions were stopped. Law, regarded as the mastermind behind these practices became generally despised, and the Duc d'Orléans was forced to repent that he had been persuaded to allow this to happen.[41]

When deportees were fortunate enough to survive the grueling voyage—a good percentage of them died at sea of scurvy, dysentery and fevers—once in New Orleans they often had to toil as indentured servants. In 1720, the monopoly granted Law's Compagnie du Mississippi was dissolved and the governance of Louisiana reverted to the Crown.

Fig. 21. Thierry. *Plan of the City of New Orleans, Capital of the Province of Louisiana (PLAN DE LA VILLE / LA NOUVELLE / ORLEANS CAPITALE / DE LA PROVINCE DE LA LOUISIANE), 1755.* Pen and India ink and watercolor on paper. The Historic New Orleans Collection, New Orleans

## Economic and social life in the colony under the French

Military presence in French colonial New Orleans was considerable, and soldiers were mostly quartered in barracks constructed within the confines of the original city. They and their officers were directly responsible to the representatives of the Compagnie du Mississippi, the *Intendants*, who also had under their command the constabulary, the legal courts and the jail that had been instituted to maintain order and administer justice. The work force was in large part made up of the destitute, convicts and, especially, enslaved West Africans who were being imported in ever greater numbers into New Orleans through Biloxi.[42] They toiled on the numerous plantations that surrounded the original city.

Fig. 22. Pierre Dupin, after Jean Antoine Watteau. *Departure for the Islands (Départ pour les Isles).* Engraving

The city was the hub from which French administrative officials, soldiers, new colonizers and missionaries were dispatched to outposts throughout the territory. In 1721, the population of lower Louisiana was increased by an influx of German speakers,[43] who assimilated so well with the French that they soon adopted their language and culture.

The government of the young Louis XV sent to New Orleans groups of impoverished young French women, each of whom was provided with a small chest of money to be used for expenses and as a dowry for a prospective husband. They were called *filles à cassette*, and responsibility for their care and well-being were entrusted to nuns. Few of them actually survived long enough to be betrothed and wed to a suitor, and one wonders if any Louisiana families can actually trace their ancestry back to them. Antoine Watteau's *Départ pour les Isles*, which is known from a print by Pierre Dupin (fig. 22), may well depict their doleful predicament. But as French women continued to be in very short supply in colonial Louisiana, men frequently had children by slave concubines, and thus was produced a racially mixed population that would continue to grow in number as the city became more populous. This custom actually contravened the terms of the odious *Code noir* that was decreed in 1724.[44] By 1732, there may have been as many as five thousand people of different races and racial composition living in or very near New Orleans.

Protestants and Jews were deemed undesirable in New Orleans during the first decades of its existence, so in the city there was a sizeable contingent of the Catholic clergy of various orders sent there by the diocese of Quebec.[45] Their mission was to care for the souls of the members of the community, white and non-white, to educate the children of the French colonists and to convert non-believers to the faith. Nuns tended the sick and invalid and also played an educational role. Prominent among them were sisters of the order of St. Ursula, the Ursulines, whose large convent on the rue de Chartres (fig. 23), constructed in 1745 on orders of Louis XV, is purportedly the oldest surviving building in the entire Mississippi Valley.

Fig. 23. Photograph of the old Ursuline Convent on Chartres Street, 1903

Early Louisianians' principal means of subsistence consisted of hunting, fresh-water and deep-sea fishing, lumbering, trapping and trading in furs and hides, as well as the importation and exportation of various foodstuffs and manufactured goods. By the mid-eighteenth century the southernmost parts of the territory (notably the immediate environs of New Orleans heading northward, along what is today the River Road or to the south, beyond Chalmette) were dotted with plantations on which African slaves performed almost all of the heavy manual labor. On both large estates and small farms, the major crops grown in the fertile soil of Louisiana became cotton, sugar cane, Indian corn, indigo, rice, tobacco and certain fruits. In New Orleans, the French community grew as more and more physicians, apothecaries, lawyers, financiers, importers of luxury items, inn- and cabaret-keepers, horse traders, furniture makers, carriage makers, saddlers, wheelwrights, blacksmiths, butchers, grocers, clothiers, jewelers, gold- and silversmiths and other types of craftsmen and tradesmen arrived.

Fig. 24. François Hubert Drouais. *Portrait of Louis XV,* circa 1773. Oil on canvas. Musée national des Châteaux de Versailles et de Trianon. Erich Lessing/Art Resource, NY

## Cession of the colony of Louisiana to Spain

At the close of the Seven Years War, by the secret Treaty of Fontainebleau of 1762 and the Treaty of Paris of 1763, Louis XV (fig. 24) deeded much of the Louisiana Territory west of the Mississippi, as well as its capital city on the delta, to his Bourbon cousin and ally, Carlos III (fig. 25) of Spain, whose naval fleets had been defeated by the British and who had in the bargain lost both Cuba and the land stretching between the eastern bank of the Mississippi and Florida. But in doing this, Louis prevented the land from falling into the hands of George III. The French colony was now part of New Spain, and "La Nueva Orleáns" became a veritable melting pot. The influx of Spanish-speakers who arrived there under Carlos III and his son, Carlos IV, came for the most part to serve in military or administrative capacities. As for the Catholic Church, the diocese to which New Orleans belonged was transferred from Quebec to Havana.[46]

Fig. 25. Anton Raphael Mengs. *Portrait of Carlos III,* 1761. Oil on canvas. Museo nacional del Prado, Madrid

## The arrival of the Acadians in Louisiana

It was at this juncture that approximately twelve thousand French-speaking Acadians who, during Great Britain's ruthless campaign of ethnic and religious cleansing that their descendants the *Acadiens* (Cajuns) refer to as the *"Grand dérangement,"* began arriving in Louisiana.[47] They had been exiled from their Canadian homeland of Acadie[48] and with France's help relocated to isolated and swampy regions of southern Louisiana that had for so long been the home of the Attakapaw and Opelousa nations.[49] This hinterland, through which ran the slow currents of the freshwater bayous, is the locus of some of the major episodes of Henry Wadsworth Longfellow's *Evangeline, A Tale of Acadie* (fig. 26), which recounts these brave French people's struggle, a poem first published in 1847.

## Spanish governance of Louisiana

Between 1765 and 1803, the Spanish Crown sent a succession of more or less authoritarian governors[50] of its overseas province of "La Gran Luisiana" to New Orleans, where their headquarters were the Casa Capitular or Cabildo[51] on the old Plaza de Armas. Spanish authorities in the city—the Governor General, a Civil Lieutenant, *alcaldes* and twelve *regidores*—presided over official life in settlements in what is now the state of Louisiana and throughout the entire territory. They left an especially large imprint on New Orleans. The first years of Spanish sovereignty were bedeviled by social unrest and even open insurrection on the part of the native New Orleanians, Germans and Acadians, who were used to the relatively mild governance of the French[52] and bristled under the comparative harshness of their new rulers and the restrictive trade policies they enacted. The revolt was quelled when five of the leaders of the rebellion were executed on orders from governor Alejandro O'Reilly, an Irish mercenary in the service of Spain. Others were given long prison sentences in New Orleans or in Havana.

Old French families fiercely clung to their culture. Eventually, a *modus vivendi* was found, the two Latin cultures merged and there gradually evolved in New Orleans a very distinctive Franco-Spanish or "Creole" style of living. The official, administrative language was Spanish, but most people continued to speak French. Some Spaniards in positions of authority even thought it best to assimilate by intermarriage, and they soon were Gallicized. As for the descendants of Africans, those that were able to accumulate enough wealth could buy their freedom but could exercise only limited rights. According to the local caste system, New Orleanians of mixed ethnicity—the product of miscegenation—were categorized according to the gradations of their skin pigmentation,[53] and when for whatever reason they were released from bondage, they were called *"gens de couleur libres"* (free people of color). Having an intermediate status between masters and slaves, some of them consorted freely with their white relatives, received a good education, prospered financially and even owned slaves, while others fared no better than their African ancestors.

Fig. 26. Joseph Rusling Meeker. *Acadians on the Achafalaya River ("Evangeline")*, 1871. Oil on canvas. Brooklyn Museum, New York

## The Spanish side with the American insurgents in Britain's colonies

The last two decades of the eighteenth century were a period of economic prosperity due in large part to the development of international political and commercial interests of which the port of New Orleans was the center. During the American War of Independence, governor Bernardo de Gálvez (for whom the Texas coastal city of Galveston was named), the son of Spain's viceroy in Mexico City and later viceroy himself, won great popularity with the French in New Orleans when he blockaded the Mississippi, allowing access to the river only to Spanish, French and American vessels. He thereby insured the supply of arms, ammunition and food to the embattled colonial American insurgents in the upper reaches of the Mississippi. Later, after Spain declared war on Great Britain, he conducted a campaign against the latter's forces and overwhelmed them at the battles of Baton Rouge, Natchez, Mobile and Pensacola. He even managed to have east and west Florida returned to Spain, and he reinstated trading policies that allowed Americans commercial access to the port of New Orleans following the official end of the revolutionary war in 1783.[54]

Under Governor de Carondelet, the walls and moats protecting New Orleans were strengthened, and fortifications were added in places where the city appeared vulnerable to attack by outsiders or even local citizens converted to the ideals of the French Revolution. These forts were connected by defensive walls (fig. 27). Carondelet also commissioned the digging of the large canal bearing his name that was intended to facilitate the drainage of the swamps in the rear of the city.[55]

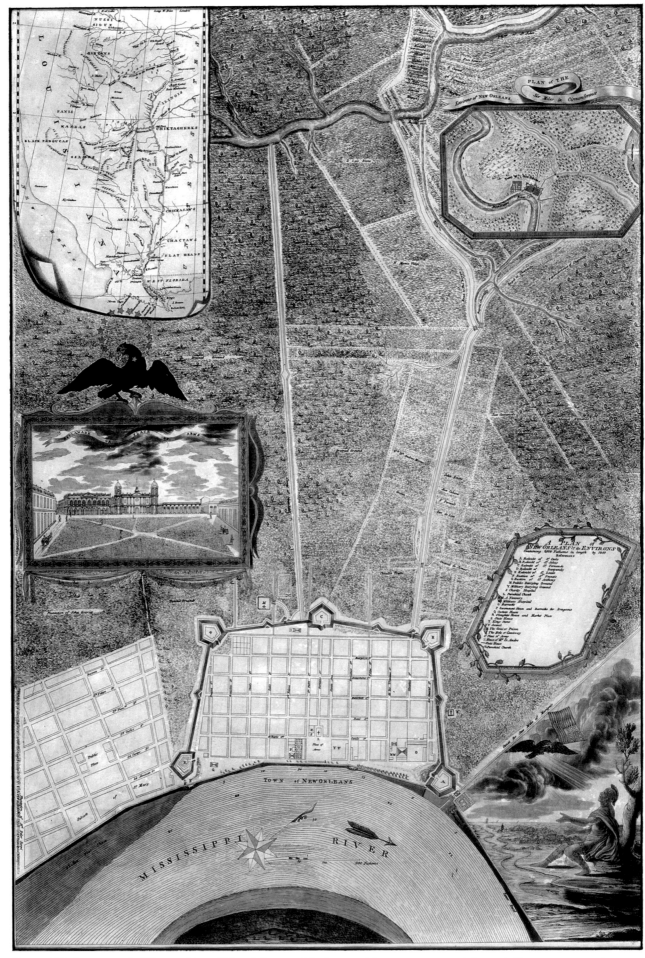

Fig. 27. J.L. Bouqueto de Woiseri. *Map of New Orleans and Its Vicinity*. The Historic New Orleans Collection, New Orleans

Fig. 28. House at 417 Royal Street, constructed in 1795 for Edgar Degas' great-grandfather, Vincent Rillieux, and since 1954 the site of Brennan's Restaurant

## Architectural renovation in Spanish New Orleans

On Good Friday of 1788 a fire engulfed a large area of the Vieux Carré, and among the important buildings that were destroyed were those on the far end of the Plaza de Armas. Another conflagration in early December of 1794 laid waste to large sections of the city. A new type of architecture then took root, which accounts for the particularly Mediterranean or "Spanish Colonial" look of a great many houses in the oldest sectors of New Orleans. The stately, brightly painted mansions of the wealthy, as well as commercial and administrative buildings were provided lush, secluded courtyards planted with exotic vegetation and decorated with columns, basins, statuary and urns. They too were constructed in such a manner as to conform to life in a semi-tropical climate and were characterized by relatively fireproof brick and stuccoed exterior walls which were whitewashed or painted in bright colors, corrugated tile roofs, long corridors, jalousies, heavy locks, bolts and hinges, as well as balconies trimmed with elegant wrought iron lattices.[56] Until the present day, this type of building and exterior ornamentation has been perpetuated, even in the tonier districts of the city. By 1797, there were over two hundred fifty buildings there.

The beautiful brick dwelling at 417 Royal Street (fig. 28) in the Vieux Carré is a perfect example of the New Spanish style. Originally assigned the number 215, the first structure built there belonged to a Baron Hambourg to whom the lot on which it sat had been granted by the Conseil Supérieur. The first sale of the property on record occurred on December 3, 1794, when Gaspard Debuys and Hubert Rémy purchased it from Angèle Monget. On December 8, just five days later, the great fire of that year destroyed the original house. Vincent Rillieux,[57] the great-grandfather of the painter Edgar Degas, bought the land from Debuys and Rémy on January 8, 1795, exactly one month later. The elaborate two-story house as it appears today was built for him that year. Bricks were used in the construction of the mansion, and it had great arched passageways leading into the carriage entrance, or *porte cochère*, which was paved with flagstones and opened at the other end onto a series of garden courtyards.[58]

Fig. 29. José Francisco Xavier de Salazar y Mendoza. *Portrait of Don Andrés Almonester y Roxas (1728-1798),* 1796. Oil on canvas. Courtesy of the Louisiana State Museum, Loaned by the Archdiocese of New Orleans

Spanish entrepreneurs such as the notary Andrés Almonester y Roxas (fig. 29),[59] a member of the minor, impecunious nobility of Andalusia who arrived in New Orleans with Governor O'Reilly in 1769, amassed great wealth. Almonester's was made in real estate speculation, but he is best remembered for his many public-spirited benefactions.[60] He was responsible for the reconstruction of the Church of St. Louis and the buildings on each side of it, the Cabildo (with the *calabosa* facing in its courtyard and opening onto the Calle San Pedro) and the Casa Curial (the Presbytère) after they burned to the ground in 1788 (fig. 30).[61] Moreover, he built a chapel for the Ursuline convent and at great cost provided the city with a charity hospital and a leprosarium.[62] As a reward for his public spiritedness, he was made a knight of the order of Carlos III and an *alférez real.*[63]

Among Almonester's many urbanization projects were two groups of income-producing wooden houses that he had built along the Calles Santa Anna and San Pedro flanking the Plaza de Armas, which had become rather shoddy and sad-looking.[64] They replaced military barracks and residences that until then had stood there. On one corner he had constructed a private townhouse for himself and his much younger French Creole wife, Louise de La Ronde.[65] Upon his death, the old hidalgo bequeathed his properties (which included nearby plantations and slaves) to his soon to be remarried widow[66] and their two young daughters. On Louise Almonester's orders, the twenty-one structures overlooking the Plaza de Armas were rebuilt in brick and elevated on piers or *pilotis* in order to avoid inundation when floods occurred.

Fig. 30. Thomas Williams. *The Place d'Armes* (the Cabildo, St. Louis Cathedral and the Presbytère as they were reconstructed, after the fire, on orders from Almonester), 1845. Lithograph

### A new influx of emigration from France and the Caribbean

In the final decade of the eighteenth century, two waves of French-speakers arrived in New Orleans as a direct result of the Revolution. *Émigrés* allied to the Girondins or other Federalists sought asylum there when the bloody convulsions of the Jacobin reign of terror caused many citizens to flee their native country. Thousands of others of different races and nationalities arrived in the city during the slave uprisings led by Toussaint-L'Ouverture in islands of the West Indies (in particular Saint-Domingue, the present-day Haiti and the Dominican Republic) that had changed ownership several times in the geopolitical game of chess played by the European maritime powers. This was the period during which the sugar industry was put on a firm basis, and New Orleans benefited immensely from the resulting economic surge.

### Retrocession of the Louisiana Territory by Spain to France

In October of 1800, by a clause of the secret Treaty of San Ildefonso that put a temporary halt to warfare between republican France and monarchial Spain, Carlos IV retroceded Louisiana to his enemy, a consular government headed by General Napoléon Bonaparte (fig. 31). However, an expeditionary flotilla commanded by General Victor never actually set sail to retake possession of Louisiana, and by early 1803, it was evident that

Fig. 31. Joseph Chinard. *First Consul Napoléon Bonaparte,* 1801. Plaster. Private collection

Fig. 32. Jean Antoine Houdon. *Bust of Thomas Jefferson,* 1789. Marble. Museum of Fine Arts, Boston. Photograph courtesy of The Wildenstein Institute

Fig. 33. J.L. Bouqueto de Woiseri. *"UNDER MY WINGS EVERYTHING PROSPERS"* (View of New Orleans from the de Marigny Plantation soon after the Louisiana Purchase), circa 1803. Chicago History Museum

the government of the newly founded United States had no intention of allowing the French to control navigation on the Mississippi and commerce in the port city of New Orleans, to which the Spanish had granted them almost unfettered admittance in 1783 and again in 1795.[67] When the armada Bonaparte sent to repress the slave revolt in Saint-Domingue failed, he saw clearly that maintaining a French empire in North America was an impossibility.

### SALE OF THE LOUISIANA TERRITORY TO THE UNITED STATES

Bonaparte was also realistic enough to understand that his troops could not prevent such a huge and sparsely populated land from falling into the hands of his English foes. So he made the reasonable decision to sell to the United States all eight hundred twenty-seven thousand square miles of the largely unmapped wilderness that comprised the Louisiana territory for the absurdly low figure of 80,000,000 francs ($15,000,000). With the Senate's approval, President Thomas Jefferson (fig. 32) appointed James Monroe to join the American envoy to France, Robert Livingston, and finalize the drafting of the Louisiana Purchase document, which was dated April 30, 1803. It was signed and sealed by them and the French representative, François Barbé-Marbois, in Paris on May 2. The treaty was promulgated late that July and was ratified by the American Senate on October 29. On November 30, the transfer of power from Spain to France took place in the Sal Capitular of the Cabildo in New Orleans, with the Spanish monarch represented

Fig. 34. Jacques Tanesse (Surveyor of the City of New Orleans). *PLAN of the City and Suburbs of NEW ORLEANS from an actual Survey made in 1815.* Buildings from left to lower right: The Firehouse (1813), The Seat of Government (1761), The Customs Building (1809), the Théâtre d'Orléans (1813), the Meat Market (1813), the Town Hall (1795), the Parish Church (1794), the Presbytère (1813), the Miliary Hospital and Barracks (1758), the Théâtre Saint-Philippe (1810), the Collège d'Orléans (1812), the Convent of the Ursulines (1735) and the Charity Hospital (1815). The New Orleans Historic Collection, New Orleans

by governor Manuel Juan de Salcedo and Carlos IV's personal envoy, the Marqués de Casa Calvo. Less than a month later, on December 20, authority was handed over to the United States by Pierre Clément de Laussat, the French colonial prefect. The *procès-verbal* was also signed in the Cabildo, then the French Republic's tricolor was lowered from its mast on the Place d'Armes and the stars and stripes were hoisted as salvos were fired from nearby fortifications (fig. 33).

By this action, the United States had more than doubled its geographical surface and made a giant leap in the direction of continental expansion. Americans then began arriving in the Crescent City in droves. The first Anglo-American governor of the "Orleans Territory" during the Federal period of New Orleans history was a Virginian, William Charles Cole Claiborne (1775–1817), who had been present at the ceremony on the Place d'Armes. In order to perform his duties, he had to learn French, and two of his successive wives were native French speakers. A good number of New Orleanians were by then openly referring to themselves as *Créoles* (in Spanish *Criollos*), a word designating them or their forbears as having come to the colony directly from France or Spain or having transited through a Caribbean island like Guadeloupe, Martinique, Saint-Domingue or Cuba.[68] Joséphine Tascher de la Pagerie, the future wife of Napoléon Bonaparte and Empress of the French, was a Creole born in Martinique. In January of 1804, Claiborne sent the following message to President Jefferson:

Fig. 35. Pierre Villain. *Portrait of Bernard-Xavier-Philippe de Marigny de Mandeville (1785-1868),* circa 1820. Engraving

I now embrace a leisure moment to write you inofficially [*sic*] from this City; and to observe that the high expectations I had formed of the value of our new acquisition to the United States, are fully confirmed by my personal observations. The country on the Mississippi is fertile, happily adapted to cultivation, its productions various and abundant, the people wealthy, and in the enjoyment of all the necessaries, and many of the luxuries of life. New-Orleans is a great, and growing City. The commerce of the Western Country concentrates at this place, and there appears to me a moral certainty, that in ten years, it will rival Philadelphia or New-York.[69]

## New Orleanians under American dominion

Having lived under an authoritarian, monarchial form of government, the Creoles had difficulty coming to terms with American representative democracy in all of its complexities. The next two decades saw the development of self-government in Louisiana. The city of New Orleans was incorporated on February 17, 1805, and its first mayor was the planter Jean Étienne de Boré (1740–1820), the father of Louisiana's sugar industry, who was appointed by Claiborne.

The son of Louis de Boré and Thérèse Céleste Carrière de Montbrun, Étienne de Boré descended from a noble family in Normandy. His grandfather, Robert de Boré, had been a member of Louis XIV's privy council. As was the custom in the colony, young de Boré was sent to France to be educated, upon leaving school he entered the royal regiment of Mousquetaires. In 1768 he returned to Louisiana. Finding no inducement to stay in the colony, which was no longer French, he returned to France in 1769. Two years later, he married Marie Marguerite d'Estréhan.[70] In 1776 he returned to Louisiana with his wife, who possessed property bequeathed to her by her father Jean Baptiste d'Estréhan des Tours, a former royal treasurer of Louisiana. He settled on a plantation about six miles above New Orleans, on a site near today's Audubon Park, and there he devoted his time to cultivating indigo. In 1794, he began growing sugar cane on the estate, and the following year he perfected a process for making granulated sugar from cane juice at a considerable profit.[71]

The fifty-year-old de Boré was selected as mayor of the city to placate the French Creoles, but he remained in office for little more than a year. During his administration the Banque de la Louisiane was founded. Until then all transactions had been made with Spanish paper money and Mexican silver coins. De Boré was ill disposed towards Anglo-Americans and did not cooperate with Governor Claiborne in establishing good rapport between his French-speaking compatriots and their aggressive new rulers, whom they correctly saw as intruders and parvenus wishing to supplant them in every domain. He died on his plantation, bequeathing $100,000 to each of his three daughters, one of whom was married to a former Spanish official, Carlos Gayarre. The latter couple later gave birth to the Louisiana historian, Charles Gayarré.[72]

According to the census taken at the time, of the almost eight thousand five hundred inhabitants, three thousand five hundred fifty-one were Caucasian, three thousand five were slaves, one thousand five hundred sixty-six were free people of color and two hundred fifty-three were designated as "other persons." In 1806, when the Aaron Burr conspiracy was foiled,[73] the city went through a period of martial law. It soon had to absorb two new waves of immigrants. The first occurred in 1809, when Spain was at war with Imperial France and refugees who had originally fled Saint-Domingue and sought asylum in Cuba made a swift exodus and headed for New Orleans, which absorbed them with little difficulty. The second influx happened in 1810 at the time of the so-called West

Florida Rebellion. Another contemporaneous event that marked the city's history was a slave insurrection that occured in January 1811, the so-called German Coast Rebellion.[74]

Louisiana's boundaries were defined, and the territory was admitted to statehood on April 30, 1812, with New Orleans as its capital.[75] The elected legislature, which until then had been territorial, subdivided it into seven judicial and administrative districts designated not as counties but as "parishes," the French and Spanish ecclesiastical units. The Crescent City constituted the major portion of Orleans Parish. The state adopted a civil legal system derived from Roman, Spanish and French law; technically, it had features reminiscent of the Napoleonic Code but did not actually replicate it. The criminal laws of Louisiana were entirely based on English Common Law as practiced in the rest of the Union. 1812 was a banner year for New Orleans, because the first steamboat navigating the Mississippi River berthed at one of its wharves.

Fig. 36. After Edward W. Kemble. *Dance on Congo Square.* Hand-colored engraving made for George W. Cable's *Creole Slave Songs* and published in *The Century Magazine,* April 1886. The New Orleans Historic Collection, New Orleans

### EXPANSION OF THE CITY INTO THE "FAUBOURGS"

New Orleans was an American city with a difference. The proud and rather insular French-speakers felt betrayed by Bonaparte's decision to abandon them. By this time, the plantations abutting on three sides of the tightly circumscribed and densely populated Vieux Carré, suburbs called *faubourgs*[76] were springing up (fig. 34), and at length they became chartered communities.[77]

To the northeast lay the Faubourg Marigny, named for the planter and gambler Marigny de Mandeville (fig. 35),[78] who at one time owned nearly a third of the land in the city and its immediate suburbs.[79] Consisting mostly of the latter's estates, it began on land bounded by what is now lower Esplanade Avenue and the Champs-Elysées (Elysian Fields Avenue), a sizeable, wedge-shaped area stretching north from the Mississippi River.[80] The development started in 1805 when the twenty-year-old Marigny divided his plantation on the outskirts of the Vieux Carré into parcels. These he sold piecemeal, but almost exclusively to fellow Creoles, free people of color and newly arrived European immigrants.[81]

Stretching north beyond the old Ramparts[82] was the Faubourg Tremé, named for the plantation of a Frenchman, Claude Tremé, native of Sauvigny in Burgundy who settled in New Orleans in 1783 and made his fortune in hat-making and real estate speculation. After it was created around 1810, the Faubourg's population was made up of free blacks and persons of mixed ethnicity.[83] On its fringe was the Place Congo or Congo Square (fig. 36), the common on which slaves and free people of color congregated on Sundays to transact business, exchange news, sell produce and other goods and to sing and dance to the pulsating rhythms of their African ancestors.[84]

> The great holiday place for the slaves in those days was Congo square, then well outside the city limits. People are yet living who remember what a gala day Sunday was to the negroes, and with what keen anticipations they looked forward to it. On a bright afternoon they would gather in their gay, picturesque finery, by hundreds, even thousands, under the shade of the sycamores, to dance the Bamboula or the Calinda; the music of their Creole songs tuned by the beating of the tam-tam. "Dansez Calinda! Badoum! Badoum!" the children, dancing too on the outskirts, adding their screams and romping to the chorus and movement. A bazaar of refreshments filled the sidewalks around; lemonade, ginger beer, pies, and the ginger cakes called "estomac mulattre," set out on deal tables, screened with cotton awnings, whose variegated streamers danced also in the breeze. White people would promenade by to look at the scene, and the young gentlemen from the College of Orleans, on their way to the theatre,

Fig. 37. David William Moody, after John William Hill and Benjamin Franklin Smith, Jr., *Bird's-eye View of New Orleans, with Boats Moored along the Batture and the City of Algiers to the Left,* 1852. Color lithograph. The Historic New Orleans Collection, New Orleans

always stopped a moment to see the negroes dance "Congo." At nightfall the frolic ceased, the dispersed revellers singing on their way home to another week of slavery and labour: "Bonsoir, dansé, Soleil, couché!"[85]

There people also could observe the rituals of Vodou,[86] a mystic religion originally imported from West Africa via the Caribbean that in New Orleans was an amalgam of the occult, animism and Catholicism. After it was prohibited, it was practiced in secret, and its best known priestess was the legendary Marie Laveau (d. 1881).[87]

Fig. 38. George Caleb Bingham. *Boatmen on the Missouri,* 1846. Oil on canvas. Fine Arts Museums of San Francisco, Gift of Mr. and Mrs. John D. Rockefeller 3rd, 1979.7.15

Finally, to the southwest rose the Faubourg Sainte-Marie, which had originally been laid out in 1778 on orders from the French planter Bernard Gravier (d. 1797). Its size was later increased by his brother Jean Gravier. It was bordered on one side by the Canal des Pêcheurs,[88] and around it were additional *faubourgs* that were eventually absorbed into it.[89] Part of it sat on lands once occupied by plantations operated by the Jesuits,[90] the Ursuline order of nuns and the Livaudais family. Favored by the Anglo-American residents of New Orleans, it grew and morphed into the fashionable Upper and Lower Garden Districts and Carrollton.[91] The river front in this section of the city included the *batture* in front of the levee,[92] the size of which increased in proportion to the ever-growing alluvial deposits left by the Mississippi (fig. 37).

The plan of New Orleans as it stands today—despite the twisting of the Mississippi and excluding the communities on its west bank, such as Algiers and Gretna—is hardly more than an expanded version of this three-pronged layout, but since the mid-nineteenth century it has been divided into numbers of municipal districts and political wards.

Fig. 39. Marie-Adrien Persac. *The Port and City of New Orleans* (viewed from Mandeville Street in the Faubourg Marigny, with the Market in the foreground), circa 1858. Watercolor and gouache on paper. The Historic New Orleans Collection, New Orleans

## LIFE IN NEW ORLEANS AT THE BEGINNING OF THE XIXTH CENTURY

Many inland trade restrictions were lifted by Claiborne, and business in the port of New Orleans surged, as did the city's revenues. A stranger traveling there for the first time under United States dominion would have had a heady experience. For decades to come, it would be a rowdy place in which hard-drinking backwoodsmen, gamblers, stevedores, roustabouts, freebooters and adventurers of all stripes rubbed shoulders or came into conflict with the various strata of the indigenous society. Most of them had floated down the Mississippi in pirogues, keelboats, flatboats (fig. 38), barges or rafts. For Anglo-Saxons, the cultural divide must have seemed unbreachable. The city was alien to them because of its semi-tropical climate, its open markets,[93] its pungent aromas, its distinctive cuisine, its racial diversity, its slave auctions, its dueling fields,[94] its above-ground burial vaults,[95] its Vodou superstitions and rituals, its overwhelming preponderance of Roman Catholics, its pre-Lenten carnival or *Mardi gras* festivities and its relatively lax sexual mores. They would also have been disoriented by the medley of Latin languages spoken there. One of the most prevalent was the Creole *patois*, whose colorful vocabulary, grammar, syntax and speech patterns were heavily influenced by a hybrid form of French that had evolved in islands of the Caribbean.[96] A would-be poet was struck by the almost endless variety of people one came across in the city's streets:

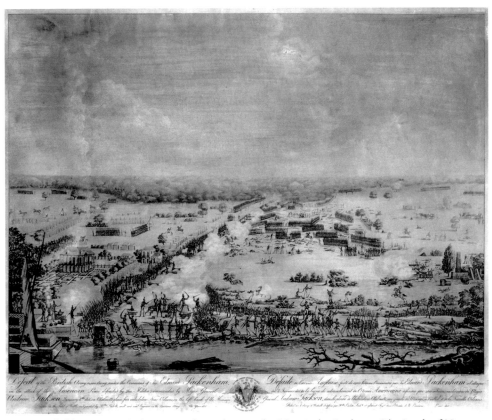

Fig. 40. Philibert Louis Debucourt, after a drawing by Hyacinthe Laclotte. *The Battle of New Orleans* (to the left, the plantation of Edmond Macarty below New Orleans, at Chalmette), circa 1815. Aquatint. The New Orleans Historical Collection, New Orleans.

Have you ever been in New Orleans? If not you'd better go,
It's a nation of a queer place; day and night a show!
Frenchmen, Spaniards, West Indians, Creoles, Mustees,
Yankees, Kentuckians, Tennesseans, lawyers and trustees,
Clergymen, priests, friars, nuns, women of all stains;
Negroes in purple and fine linen, and slaves in rags and chains.
Ships, arks, steamboats, robbers, pirates, alligators,
Assassins, gamblers, drunkards, and cotton speculators;
Sailors, soldiers, pretty girls, and ugly fortune-tellers;
Pimps, imps, shrimps, and all sorts of dirty fellows;
White men with black wives, *et vice-versa* too.
A progeny of all colors—an infernal motley crew![97]

## NEW ORLEANS CUISINE

The food served to Anglo-Saxon or European newcomers to the place was particularly exotic. Early New Orleans cooks had made use of the abundance of game and fish in the area, poultry and meats from other domesticated animals, local fruits and nuts (especially the pecan, from which pralines were made), Indian corn and vegetables grown in tenant farms known as *métairies* on the outskirts of the city and along the Mississippi. Other products that could travel without spoilage, such as wine, had been shipped to the colony from France. The *étouffée* and the *fricassée* were techniques integral to the cuisine of the first French inhabitants. Spaniards had brought with them their own culinary preferences; thus ham, the *chorizo* and their derivatives, *tasso* and the spicy *andouille* sausage,[98] became staples on New Orleans tables. Louisiana *jambalaya*,[99] a relative latecomer to Creole cuisine, is said to be an adaptation of Spain's *paella*. The African and native American populations of the city also introduced into the kitchens in which they worked their cooking techniques and key elements of their diets such as rice, dried beans, sweet and fiery peppers, savory spices and the fragrant seasoning *filé*.[100] Africans were certainly the inventors of what is the oldest and best known of Louisiana dishes, *gumbo*.[101] As New Orleans was surrounded by water, oysters and shellfish, especially Gulf shrimp and crabs, as well as crawfish and terrapins from the bayous, became essential ingredients in Creole cookery; they were abundant and relatively inexpensive.

All of these products were available in the public market that grew up along the levee near the Place d'Armes (fig. 39).[102]

Fig. 41. Rembrandt Peale. *Portrait of Benjamin Latrobe (1764–1820)*, c. 1816. Oil on canvas. Private collection

## THE BATTLE OF NEW ORLEANS

The natural enmity between the United States and Great Britain slowly began to escalate after the sale of the Louisiana Territory. Americans wanted to move westward over lands held by the Indian allies of the British in Canada, and boundary disputes erupted. Britain launched a campaign of harassment and seizure of American ships and of impressment of able-bodied American seamen into the Royal Navy. The Americans retaliated with trade embargos and seizure of British vessels. War was declared in June of 1812, and for a while the British held the upper hand both on land and at sea. They actually took Washington and burned the Capitol and the White House. But they were not on their own terrain and serious military reverses caused them to sue for peace. Negotiations were carried out at Ghent in the Belgian Netherlands and a treaty was signed on December 24, 1814, providing for a cessation of hostilities after ratifications were exchanged. The news of this event, however, did not reach the United States in time to prevent the last, and perhaps most memorable confrontation of the war, the Battle of New Orleans. In mid-December a British expeditionary fleet that had sailed from Halifax, Nova Scotia and other points arrived on the Louisiana coast with the aim of establishing a beachhead in New Orleans from which it could control traffic on the Mississippi. It soon won a naval victory in Lake Borgne. Then British foot soldiers under Major General Edward Pakenham disembarked along the lower Mississippi and advanced upstream.

On December 23, they encountered the Americans led by General Andrew Jackson at Chalmette Plantation, located just south of the city. When the dust cleared, both sides had suffered losses, but the British advance was halted long enough for Jackson's troops to regroup at Chalmette on the east bank of the river, throw up earthworks and bring in heavy artillery. The armies clashed on December 28 and Jackson's men were assisted by bombardments from a grounded warship, the *Louisiana*. Another confrontation took place on January 1, 1815, and despite intense fire from the large British guns, the Americans held their own. The major battle took place on January 8 (fig. 40). Pakenham's orderly brigades were reinforced by Seminole warriors and black troops from the British West Indies. The ragtag American forces were made up of regular United States army troops, Creole militia, Choctaws, free black soldiers and hundreds of pirates from the swampy regions of Barataria, among them Jean and Pierre Lafitte. In the course of the assaults, some of the British senior officers, including Pakenham, were killed. In the end, more than seven hundred of the Prince Regent's troops lay dead on the battlefield, and almost two thousand were wounded or taken prisoner, whereas Jackson's men sustained only minimal losses. The British redeployed, boarded their ships and sailed away. Gunnery fire and withering volleys of grapeshot aimed at the compact divisions of redcoats had been a deadly combination and had resulted in a complete American victory.

## CREOLE LIFE IN EARLY NINETEENTH-CENTURY NEW ORLEANS

Schools in the city had religious, especially Catholic, affiliations and for the most part were reserved for the children of the elite.[103] The first school of higher learning was the Collège d'Orléans, which operated between 1811 and 1825 in the Faubourg Tremé. The wealthiest members of the Creole gentry, however, sent their sons to be educated in Europe. They had polished manners, were notoriously prideful and contemptuous of those they considered uncivilized interlopers, i.e. the majority of the Anglo community.

In 1811, Benjamin Latrobe (fig. 41), the British-born architect of the United States Capitol and the first White House, was commissioned to build a waterworks for the New Orleans City Council.[104] That year he sent his son Henry to begin the work, but he succumbed there on September 3, 1817, during one of the epidemics of yellow fever that frequently afflicted the city. His father, who in 1807 had provided plans for the New Orleans Custom House, traveled to Louisiana that December to complete the project and rented a room in the Hôtel Trémoulet, at the corner of St. Peter and Levee Streets (fig. 42). By a cruel twist of fate, he was struck down by the same disease that had killed his son exactly three years to the day.

Fig. 42. Benjamin Latrobe. *View of the New Orleans Wharf in the Faubourg Sainte-Marie from the Top Floor of the Hôtel Trémoulet*, 1819. Pencil, pen and ink and watercolor. Maryland Historical Society, Baltimore

During his year and a half stay in New Orleans, the elder Latrobe consigned his impressions of the booming town to his journal. Like so many of America's intellectuals at the time, he was something of a polymath, and his commentary on the city is on the whole very enlightening. Latrobe took notice of the cruelty with which some white Creoles, among them women, treated their slaves and household servants, and he identified some real life examples of such "termagants," including the wives of the *hôtelier* Trémoulet and the planter Bernard de Marigny.[105]

> At the ball on Washington's birthday…the idea of these things destroyed all the pleasure I should otherwise have felt in seeing the brilliant assemblage of as many beautiful faces and forms, as I ever saw collected in one room. All pale, languid, and mild. I fancied, that I saw a cowskin in every pretty hand, gracefully waved in the dance; and admired the comparative aukwardness [*sic*] of look and motion of my countrywomen, whose arms had never been rendered pliant, by the exercise of the whip upon the bound and screaming slave. Whatever therefore this community may lose in taste and elegance, and exterior suavity, and acquire of serious and aukward bluntness, and commercial stiffness, may the change be as rapid as possible, if at the same time active humanity is introduced into the deplorable system of slavery which I fear must long, perhaps forever, prevail in this state![106]

The British novelist Frances (Fanny) Trollope (1780–1863) landed in New Orleans in the winter of 1827. Even more an abolitionist than Latrobe, she was given an introduction to Creole society which profoundly shocked her:

> Our stay in New Orleans was not long enough to permit our entering into society, but I was told that it contained two distinct sets of people, both celebrated, in their way, for their social meetings and elegant entertainments. The first of these is composed of Creole families, who are chiefly planters and merchants, with their wives and daughters; these meet together, eat together, and are very grand and aristocratic; each of their balls is a little Almack's,[107] and every portly dame of the set is as exclusive in her principles as a lady patroness. The other set consists of the excluded but amiable Quadroons, and such of the gentlemen of the former class as can by any means escape from the high places, where pure Creole blood swells the veins at the bare mention of any being tainted in the remotest degree with the Negro stain.

Of all the prejudices I have ever witnessed, this appears to me the most violent, and the most inveterate. Quadroon girls,[108] the acknowledged daughters of wealthy American or Creole fathers, educated with all of style and accomplishments which money can procure at New Orleans, and with all the decorum that care and affection can give; exquisitely beautiful, graceful, gentle, and amiable, these are not admitted, nay, are not on any terms admissable, into the society of the Creole families of Louisiana. They cannot marry; that is to say, no ceremony can render an union with them legal or binding; yet such is the powerful effect of their very peculiar grace, beauty, and sweetness of manner, that unfortunately they perpetually become the objects of choice and affection. If the Creole ladies have privilege to exercise the awful power of repulsion, the gentle Quadroon has the sweet but dangerous vengeance of possessing that of attraction. The unions formed with this unfortunate race are said to be often lasting and happy, as far as any unions can be so, to which a certain degree of disgrace is attached.[109]

In late 1831, during a trip to the United States that would culminate in *Democracy in America*, Alexis de Tocqueville and his traveling companion Gustave de Beaumont spent several days in New Orleans. One evening they attended the old French theater,[110] and were appalled by the way the audience was segregated: in the lower row of boxes sat whites, in the middle tier were women of mixed race and the highest seats were reserved for blacks. He observed how attractive and well-groomed young women of mixed race were kept as mistresses by white French or Spanish Creoles. Playing the role of extra-legal life partners, they were referred to as *placées* in the local parlance.[111] The irregular situation of the Quadroon women—midway between marriage and prostitution—was considered to be normal in Creole circles, and American planters soon caught on and followed suit. For example, unbeknownst to his family, before his death the young Henry Latrobe had fathered four illegitimate children by a free woman of color.

Since 1805, Quadroon balls had been held on a regular basis in public gathering places such as the public dance hall,[112] hotels and theaters where the *placées* were on display as if they were merchandise. Tocqueville, who was opposed to slavery in all of its forms, was present at a Quadroon Ball,[113] about which he commented in some stenographic notes: "Strange sight: all the men white, all the women coloured, or at least of African blood. Single tie created by immorality between the two races. A sort of bazaar. The women vowed as it were by law to concubinage. Incredible laxity of morals. Mothers, young girls, children at the dance; still another harmful consequence of slavery."[114]

A conversation Tocqueville had with the resident French Consul, J.N. François Guillemin, summed up the evils of a social phenomenon he had witnessed firsthand:

The law destines, as it were, coloured women to debauchery. You've no doubt noticed, in the place reserved for mulattoes in the theatre and elsewhere, women as white as the most beautiful Europeans. *Eh bien!* For all that they belong to the proscribed race, because tradition makes it known that there is African blood in their veins. Yet these women, and many others who, without being as white, possess yet almost the tint and the graces of Europeans and have often received an excellent education, are forbidden by law to marry into the ruling and rich race of whites. If they wish to contract a legitimate union, they have to marry with the men of their caste, and partake their humiliation. For the men of colour don't even enjoy the shameful privilege accorded their women. Even did neither their colour nor education betray them, and that's often the case, they would not be the less condemned to perpetual indignities. Not a [illegible] white but

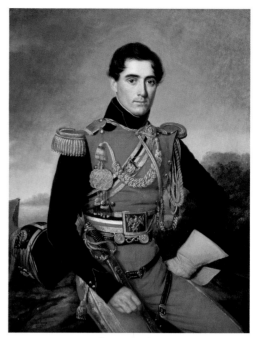

Fig. 43. Jean-Joseph Vaudechamp. *Portrait of Antoine-Jacques-Philippe de Marigny de Mandeville,* 1833. Oil on canvas. Collection of the Louisiana State Museum, Gift of the Friends of the Cabildo

has the right to maltreat the unhappy person in his way and to thrust him into the much crying: "Get out of the way, mulatto!" At the head of legal documents the law makes him write: *homme de couleur*. Free, they can hope for nothing. Yet among them I know men of virtue and of means. It's in isolating itself thus obstinately from all the rest that the aristocracy of the whites (like all aristocracies in general) exposes itself to danger on the American continent and to almost certain destruction in the Antilles. If, without giving the negro rights, it had at least taken in those of the coloured men whose birth and education most nearly approximated its own, the latter would infallibly have been attached to its cause, for they are in reality much closer to the whites than to the blacks. Only brute force would have remained for the negroes. By repelling the mulattoes, however, the white aristocracy gives the slaves, on the contrary, the only weapon they need to become free: intelligence and leadership.[115]

## THE EVOLUTION OF THE PICTORIAL ARTS IN FRENCH, SPANISH AND AMERICAN NEW ORLEANS

As for the art of painting, no practitioners of great merit are known to have worked in New Orleans in the French colonial phase of its history, but there were a number of portrait artists in the city while the Spanish were in power.[116] One such "limner," who was there between 1782 and his death in 1802, was José Francisco Xavier de Salazar y Mendoza, a native of Mérida on the Yucatan Peninsula. His style recalls that of Francisco Goya, but it is unclear when and where he could have acquired knowledge of the work of that great master or one of his pupils. Salazar is the author of the 1796 portrait of Almonester (fig. 29) in the Louisiana State Museum.

Most artists active in the city following the Louisiana Purchase were portraitists like their Spanish predecessors, and their sometimes primitive work did not adhere to the artistic standards enforced in academic schools, but their works often have a charm and poignancy lacking in the sophisticated productions of their European counterparts. Among the earliest painters of the Federal period were a miniaturist named Duval, a certain F. Godefroid and Jean François Vallée. John Wesley Jarvis (1780–1840), who was born in England, made a great deal of money in his portrait practice in the city between 1816 and 1834. Matthew Harris Jouett (1787–1827), a pupil of Gilbert Stuart, also painted portraits there, as did John Vanderlyn, Jr. (1805–1876). The ornithologist Jean-Jacques Audubon (1785–1851) worked in or near the Crescent City between 1821 and 1826, eking out a living as a portraitist and as a drawing master on a plantation.

The Louisiana State Museum in the Cabildo has strong holdings of works by a talented pupil of Anne Louis Girodet, Jean-Joseph Vaudechamp (1790–1886), who during the winter months between 1831 and 1840 traveled frequently to Louisiana, where he did a thriving business in his studio on Royal Street. One of his finest works is the dashing likeness of the young Antoine-Jacques-Philippe de Marigny de Mandeville (fig. 43) sporting the uniform of the Orleans Lancers of the Louisiana Militia.[117] Another artist was the nephew of the sculptor Antonio Canova, Domenico Canova, a muralist who decorated the dome of the St. Louis Hotel and walls of the residences of financial tycoons such as John Watt and James Robb. The itinerant Bostonian portrait painter George Peter Alexander Healy (1808–1894) resided in New Orleans in 1852 and 1861.

## THEATER AND MUSIC IN OLD NEW ORLEANS

Very little is known of cultural life in the early years of colonization in Louisiana. Excluding traditional songs and tunes played on rudimentary instruments, chants and other forms of church music may have been all that the first generations of New Orleanians were able

Fig. 44. J.W. Orr. *The St. Charles Theater,* 1873. Engraving from *Jewell's Crescent City Illustrated,* 1873. The Historic New Orleans Collection, New Orleans

to enjoy. A *Manuscrit des Ursulines de la Nouvelle-Orléans*[118] contains scores of well-known Baroque compositions.[119]

But by the early 1790s, the theater, music and dance were definitely important cultural attractions in the city.[120] Theaters served multiple purposes. They were mainly used for staging "high culture" entertainments, but they could easily be transformed into ball and supper rooms in which dances and carnival events were held, and these were the resort of the *demi-monde*. On the roster of the Théâtre Saint-Pierre, which was opened in 1792 by the brothers Louis Alexandre and Jean Marie Henry, could be tragedies, comedies, vaudevilles and grand, lyric and comic operas,[121] and ballets were performed by itinerant companies until the house closed around 1810. In 1808 appeared the Théâtre Saint-Philippe, whose traditional repertoire was expanded to include the most recent works by François André Boïeldieu, Nicolas Marie Dalayrac, Nicolò Isouard and Étienne Nicolas Méhul, as well as those of the Italian composers Luigi Cherubini and Giovanni Paisiello.

A French opera and playhouse, the Théâtre d'Orléans, was inaugurated in 1815 but was soon destroyed by fire. In 1819 a refugee from Saint-Domingue bearing the English name of John Davis presented a mostly French program at the rebuilt theater on Orleans Street, between Royal and Bourbon.[122] It continued to operate until the end of the 1850s, long after Davis died in 1839, and was succeeded by his son Pierre and another impresario, Charles Boudousquié.[123] Many European operas by such composers as Louis-Ferdinand-Joseph Hérold, Daniel-François Auber, Jacques Halévy, Adolphe-Charles Adam, Giacomo Meyerbeer, Gioacchino Rossini and Gaetano Donizetti were staged or had their American premières in his theater. Between 1827 and 1833, during the off-season Davis traveled with his Compagnie française de la Nouvelle-Orléans to New York and other East Coast cities, exporting French operas to other parts of the country.

An English-language theater was founded as early as 1817 at the old Théâtre Saint-Philippe by the actor Noah Ludlow. However, the French theater's main challenger was the American theater, which in 1824 took over the Saint-Philippe under the management of an enterprising English actor from Sheffield, James Caldwell.[124] In 1835, he built the St. Charles Theater (fig. 44), which could seat four thousand people. It was in its time the most monumental and resplendent playhouse in America. That year, Giacomo Meyerbeer's *Robert le Diable* was presented in the two rival theaters, and critics extolled the virtues of each performance according to a particular linguistic and cultural bias. Caldwell also had constructed in 1822 the New American Theater on Camp Street. Historically, New Orleans' theaters seem to have been plagued by fires, and both of Caldwell's houses burned to the ground in 1842, but were soon rebuilt, although in a less opulent style.[125]

The singer Jenny Lind, the dancer Fanny Elssler and the tragic actors Edwin and Junius Booth all performed on New Orleans stages.

### Early history of the press in New Orleans

French newspapers dominated for a time in New Orleans. Between 1785 and 1786 the *Courrier de la Nouvelle-Orléans* was published sporadically in the city. In 1794 Louis Duclot, a refugee from Saint-Domingue, launched the daily *Moniteur de la Louisiane*, the city's first real newspaper, which ran until 1814. Its editor was a French royalist émigré, Jean Baptiste Lesur-Fontaine. In the first two decades of the nineteenth-century, French newspapers in New Orleans sprouted like mushrooms and died like flies, just as they did in other francophone parts of the state. The long-running and ultimately bilingual *L'Abeille* first appeared in 1827 and did not disappear until 1925. Another political, commercial and literary journal read by French-speakers was *L'Orléanais*. Only in 1864, i.e. during the

Fig. 45. John William Hill and Benjamin Franklin Smith, Jr. *New Orleans from St. Patrick's Church,* 1852. Color engraving. The Historic New Orleans Collection, New Orleans

North's occupation of the city, would a newspaper addressing the concerns of the Creoles of color, *La Tribune de la Nouvelle-Orléans,* appear on the newsstands. It was founded by the Belgian astronomer Jean-Charles-Hippolyte-Joseph Houseau (1820–1888), who was a fierce advocate for the civil rights of former slaves.

The English-language *Louisiana Gazette* was distributed between 1804 and 1826, and the first issue of *The Picayune* was issued in January of 1837 by two printers, Francis Lumsden and George Kendall. (It survives to this day as *The Times Picayune.*) It competed with *The Louisiana Courier, The New Orleans Delta, The New Orleans Crescent, The Louisiana Advertiser, The True American* and *The Commercial Bulletin,* all of which have long been defunct.

### New Orleans as "Queen of the South"

By the 1840s, the port of New Orleans, with a fluctuating population of between one hundred thirty and one hundred forty thousand souls, emerged as an economic power in the United States. Steamboats,[126] packets, schooners and cargo and passenger sailing ships crowded into its harbor and foreign trade more than doubled (figs. 45 and 46). The rise of cotton, sugar products and rice as large export crops, the invention of the steam cotton press and the introduction of gas lighting all encouraged the outward thrust of the city. By that time great numbers of poor Irish and German immigrants (and some Italians) were disembarking and joining the work force. As the sociological makeup of the city changed, there was a frenzy of building activity, both in the public and the private sectors.[127]

Fig. 46. Hippolyte Sebron. *Giant Steamboats of New Orleans,* 1853. Oil on canvas. The Tulane University Collection, Tulane University, New Orleans. Gift of D.H. Holmes Co., New Orleans

To befit the newly thriving metropolis, the "Queen of the South," as it was by then called, superb dining establishments such as Antoine's, the oldest surviving restaurant in New Orleans,[128] were founded. In fact the city was gaining a reputation as America's gastronomic capital.[129] Luxury hotels catered to the needs of out-of-towners: the St. Louis (fig. 47) in the Vieux Carré, designed and built at the end of the 1830s by Jacques-Nicolas Bussière de Pouilly (1805–1875), attracted Creoles from Louisiana plantations and other francophones, while the St. Charles Hotel (fig. 48), built in 1835 by Charles Dakin and James Gallier for the theatrical manager James Caldwell, appealed to a mostly English-speaking clientele.

Business was actively carried out in New Orleans for the most part between the months of December and June and came to a virtual halt during the summer and early fall, when heat, mosquitoes and the threat of yellow fever made life very uncomfortable and drove those who could afford it out of the city.

### Further urban development and new means of transportation in the Crescent City

The financial panic of 1837 severely affected New Orleans, but in time it rebounded.

Fig. 47. *The St. Louis Hotel,* 1873. Engraving from *Jewell's Crescent City Illustrated,* 1873

Fig. 48. Jay Dearborn Edwards. *The St. Charles Hotel,* circa 1857-60. Print. The Historic New Orleans Collection, New Orleans

Indeed, by the mid-nineteenth century, with the exception of New York City, it eclipsed all American metropolises by its wealth and the size of its population. Tensions between the Creoles and Anglo-Americans were running high, however, and a buffer zone between the rival groups was created when the old Canal des Pêcheurs separating the French and American quarters in the Faubourg Sainte-Marie was being re-excavated to connect the Mississippi with Lake Ponchartrain via the Carondelet Canal and the Bayou St. John. The project was not brought to completion,[130] but the result was Canal Street, which became the city's widest and most commercially active thoroughfare.

Expansion continued apace, and this necessitated the creation of an interurban transportation network. Several types of public conveyance were devised to link the lakeside resort communities on the south shore of Ponchartrain[131] with the inner city. These included the second railway line built in the United States and a system of horse- or mule-drawn omnibuses. In 1835 the New Orleans and Carrollton Railroad Co. began operations, transporting passengers in primitive trains driven by steam locomotives along St. Charles Avenue into Jefferson Parish and to the then independent town of Carrollton, where a luxury hotel and pleasure garden attracted visitors. The oldest street railway in the world, it was the ancestor of the New Orleans electric streetcar lines.

### FREDERICK LAW OLMSTEAD'S VISIT TO THE CRESCENT CITY IN LATE 1853
One traveler who arrived in New Orleans through the back door as it were was the landscape architect, environmentalist and future designer of New York's Central Park, Frederick Law Olmstead (1822–1903). The account he wrote of his first impressions of the pre-Civil War metropolitan area—part of his great book on America's Deep South, *The Cotton Kingdom,* which he based on on-the-spot articles published in the *New-York Daily Times*—is so instructive that it deserves to be quoted at length:

> I was awakened, in the morning, by the loud ringing of a hand-bell….I found that the boat was made fast to a long wooden jetty, and the passengers were going ashore. A passage-ticket for New Orleans was handed me, as I crossed the gang-plank. There was a rail-track and a train of cars upon the wharf, but no locomotive, and I got my baggage checked, and walked on toward the shore.

> It was early daylight—a fog rested on the water, and only the nearest point could be discerned. There were many small buildings near the jetty, erected on piles over the water—bathing-houses, bowling-alleys, and billiard-rooms, with other indications of a place of holiday resort—and, on reaching the shore, I found a slumbering village. The first house from the wharf had a garden about it, with complex alleys, and tables, and arbours, and rustic seats, and cut shrubs, and shells, and statues, and vases, and a lamp was feebly burning in a large lantern over the entrance gate. I was thinking how like it was to a rural restaurant in France or Germany, when a locomotive backed, screaming hoarsely, down the jetty; and I returned to get my seat.

> Off we puffed, past the restaurant, into the village—the name of which I did not inquire, everybody near me seemed so cold and cross—through the little village of white houses—whatever it was—and away into a dense, gray cypress forest. For three or four rods, each side of the track, the trees had all been felled and removed, leaving a dreary strip of swamp, covered with stumps. This was bounded and intersected by broad ditches, or narrow and shallow canals, with a great number of very small punts in them. So it continued, for two or three miles; then the ground became dryer, there was an abrupt termination of the

gray wood; the fog was lifting and drifting off, in ragged, rosy clouds, disclosing a flat country, skirted still, and finally bounded, in the background, with the swamp-forest. A few low houses, one story high, all having verandahs before them, were scattered thinly over it.

At length, a broad road struck in by the side of the track; the houses became more frequent; soon forming a village street, with smoke ascending from breakfast fires; windows and doors opening, maids sweeping steps, bakers' wagons passing, and broad streets, little built upon, breaking off at right angles.

At the corners of these streets, were high poles, connected at the top by a rope, and furnished with blocks and halyards, by which great square lanterns were slung over the middle of the carriage-way. I thought again of France…and turning to one of my cold and cross companions—a man wrapped in a loose coat, with a cowl over his head—I asked the name of the village, for my geography was at fault. I had expected to be landed at New Orleans by the boat, and had not been informed of the railroad arrangement, and had no idea of what part of Louisiana we might be. "Note Anglische, sare," was the gruff reply.

There was a sign, *"Café du Faubourg,"* and, putting my head out of the window, I saw that we must have arrived at New Orleans. We reached the terminus, which was surrounded with *fiacres*, in the style of Paris. "To the Hotel St. Charles," I said to a driver, confused with the loud French and quiet English of the crowd about me. *"Oui,* yer 'onor," was the reply of my Irish-born fellow-citizen: another passenger was got, and away we rattled through narrow dirty streets, among grimy old stuccoed walls; high arched windows and doors, balconies and entresols, and French noises and French smells, French signs, ten to one of English, but with funny polyglotic arrangements, sometimes, from which less influential families were not excluded.

The other fare, to whom I had not ventured to speak, was set down at a *salle pour la vente des* somethings, and soon after the *fiacre* turned out upon a broad place, covered with bales of cotton, and casks of sugar, and weighing scales, and disclosing an astonishing number of steamboats, lying all close together in a line, the ends of which were lost in the mist, which still hung upon the river. Now the signs became English, and the new brick buildings American. We turned into a broad street, in which shutters were being taken from great glass store-fronts, and clerks were exercising their ingenuity in the display of muslin, and silks, and shawls. In the middle of the broad street there was an open space of waste ground, looking as if the corporation had not been able to pave the whole of it at once, and had left this interval to be attended to when the treasury was better filled. Crossing through a gap in this waste, we entered a narrow street of high buildings, French, Spanish, and English signs, the latter predominating; and at the second block, I was landed before the great Grecian portico of the stupendous, tasteless, ill-contrived, and inconvenient St. Charles Hotel.

After a bath and breakfast, I returned with great interest, to wander in the old French town, the characteristics of which I have sufficiently indicated. Among the houses, one occasionally sees a relic of ancient Spanish builders, while all the newer edifices have the characteristics of the dollar-pursuing Yankees.

I was delighted when I reached the old Place d'Armes, now a public garden, bright

Fig. 49. Anonymous artist (attributed to George Peter Alexander Healy). *Portrait of James Robb (1814-1881),* circa 1845. Oil on canvas. The Historic New Orleans Collection, New Orleans

with orange and lemon trees, and roses, and myrtles, and laurels, and jessamines of the south of France. Fronting upon it is the ancient Hotel de Ville, still the city court-house, a quaint old French structure, with scaly and vermiculated surface, and deep-worn door-sills, and smooth-rubbed corners; the most picturesque and historic-looking public building, except the highly preserved, little old court-house at Newport, that I can now think of in the United States.

Adjoining it is an old Spanish cathedral, damaged by paint, and late alterations and repairs, but still a fine thing in our desert of the reverend in architecture. Enough, that while it is not new, it is not shabby, and is not tricked out with much frippery, gingerbread and confectionary work. The door is open; coaches and crippled beggars are near it. A priest, with a face the expression of which first makes one think of an ape and then of an owl, is coming out. If he were not otherwise to be heartily welcomed to fresh air and sunlight, he should be

Fig. 50. *Baronne Delfau de Pontalba, née Micaela Leonarda Antonia Almonester y de la Ronde (1795-1874),* circa 1860. Photograph. Private collection

so, for the sake of the Sister of Charity who is following him, probably to some death-bed, with a corpse-like face herself, haggard but composed, pensive and absorbed, and with the eyes of a broken heart. I think that I may yet meet them looking down compassionately and soothingly, in some far distant prestilent or war-hospital. In lieu of holy-water, then, here is money for the poor-box, though the devil share it with good angels.

Dark shadows, and dusky light, and deep, subdued, low organ strains pervade the interior; and, on the bare floor, here are the kneeling women—"good" and "bad" women—and, ah! Yes, white and black women, bowed in equality before their common Father....

In the crowded market-place, there were not only the pure old Indian Americans, and the Spanish, French, English, Celtic, and African, but nearly all possible mixed varieties of these, and no doubt of some other breeds of mankind....

Some of the coloured women spoke French, Spanish, and English, as their customers demanded.

Three taverns, bearing the sign of "the Pig and Whistle," indicated the recent English, a cabaret to the Universal Republic, with a red flag, the French, and the Gasthaus zum Rheimplatz, the Teutonic contributions to the strength of our nation. A policeman, with the richest Irish brogue, directed me back to the St. Charles.[132]

The journal of Thomas Kelah Wharton (1814–1862),[133] the accomplished English-born architect who oversaw the construction of the United States Custom House on Canal Street, is another wonderfully informative source about life in antebellum New Orleans. Wharton comments on the climate, the fires that regularly swept through various districts of the city, the explosion of boats moored along the wharves, the rise and fall of the waters of the Mississippi, the breaching of levees and the frequent outbreaks of malignant diseases.

### Art collecting in mid nineteenth-century New Orleans

There existed no public art collection of any significance in America's Deep South. In New Orleans, a few desultory attempts had been made to create such an establishment.[134] In the 1840s a short-lived art society was founded on St. Charles Street in the "Garden District." One of its most prominent member was a native Pennsylvanian, James Robb (fig. 49), a high-rolling capitalist who had arrived almost penniless in New Orleans after the 1837 financial crash and took a job there as a cashier in a bank. He slowly amassed a fortune in banking and railroads and even played a role in state politics. He is reputed to have built the first gasworks in Havana in partnership with the widow of King Ferdinand VII of Spain, Maria-Cristina de Borbón. At the top of his game, he established eight banking and commercial houses with branches in several American cities and at Liverpool. President of the railroad convention that met in New Orleans in 1851, this tycoon financed the railway that linked the big city on the delta to the states up north.

In September of 1845, Robb had traveled to "Point Breeze" at Bordentown, New Jersey, where he attended the sale of the estate of the late Comte de Survilliers, i.e. Joseph Bonaparte (1768–1844), Napoleon I's older brother.[135] There he purchased a number of paintings, including Natoire's *Toilet of Psyche* (exhibited here as cat. no. 26) and works by, or attributed to, Salvator Rosa and Joseph Vernet. They were the plums of the collection that he kept in his houses in the Faubourg Sainte-Marie. The first was at 17 St. Charles Street and the other was a grandiose mansion taking up an entire city block[136] that he built between 1852 and 1853 on Washington Avenue, in the poshest area of the "Garden District."

In 1857, when speculation in American railway shares caused the market to collapse, Robb took a drubbing.[137] To keep his head above water, he was forced to sell off his works of the fine and decorative arts with which he had at one time hoped to create a permanent "national" museum. In the entry of his journal dated March 8 (Mardi Gras), 1859, Wharton critiqued the Robb collection that was then for sale:

At 11 Major Beauregard & I went up to see the collection of pictures &c. &c. now for sale at Mr. Robb's great mansion in the 4th. Dist. (Sic transit Gloria mundi!) The best pictures are those which graced Mr. Robb's gallery in the old house in St. Charles Street, chiefly purchased at the sale of Joseph Bonaparte at Bordentown. Joseph Vernet's great picture of mist, sunrise, ships, and sea shore

Fig. 51. J. Dürler, *View of Jackson Square Flanked by the Newly Constructed Pontalba Buildings,* circa 1855. Watercolor on paper. The Historic New Orleans Collection, New Orleans

figures. St. Denis'[138] "falls of Terni," and "Bay of Naples." Two other pictures by Vernet, "falls of Tivoli" and "falls of Terni," and a fine picture by Natoire "the toilet of Physche." To these add 2 very fine pictures by David Huntingdon, "the communion of the Sick" and "Imprisonment of early Christians at Rome." The "Cathedral at Burgos" by David Roberts of London is a charming picture, and the "Monastery in Madrid" (watercolour) by Louis Haghe of London, also very fine. The bronzes, vases, furniture, porcelain, &c. &c. Dresden, Sevres, & Bohemian were exceedingly elegant and tasteful. The Frescoes on walls, ceilings &c. wretched! Badly drawn, worse in color. Worst of all in contrast with the artistic gems which half conceal them. The house itself is an unwieldy mass of bad taste, and common, inelegant finish. The grounds, however, covering the entire square are fine, and the serpentine gravel walk quite English. There is but little statuary. The "angler" by Steinharner, is the best, and the 2 porphyry vases, in [the] basement are very beautiful. These, too, were purchased at the Bonaparte "Sale" and are said to have been the gift of Bernadotte to the Ex-king and executed in Sweden. These and the "St. Denis" "Vernet's" and "Huntingdons" I saw 10 years ago, when Mr. Robb was living in his old establishment in St. Charles Street, now the "Orleans Club House." His day dream of wealth and gilded splendour is now fading out, and this is the last closing scene of the gaudy drama.[139]

## CREOLES IN THE MINORITY IN ANTEBELLUM NEW ORLEANS

Although they long remained near the bottom of the social scale, the poorer European immigrants—mostly Irish, Germans and Italians—gradually melted into the Anglo-American community. The descendants of the French began to find themselves seriously outnumbered. Until the mid-1840s, the Creoles had kept the upper hand in the city's political arena.[140] French influence in the city receded into the background. After a visit he made in 1855 to New Orleans, the geographer Élisée Reclus (1830–1905)[141] detected a gradual americanization of the oldest part of the city, the Vieux Carré, and the slow disintegration of local customs and even of the French language:[142]

The oldest section of New Orleans, the one usually called the French Quarter, is

Fig. 52. Unidentified French artist. *Portrait of Madame Auguste De Gas, née Marie-Célestine Musson (1815-1847),* circa 1832-34. Gouache heightened with gold on ivory. New Orleans Museum of Art, New Orleans (gift of Joseph Baillio, 2006)

Fig. 53. Edgar Degas. *Self Portrait*, 1863. Oil on canvas. Museu Calouste Gulbenkian, Lisbon. Erich Lessing/Art Resource, NY

still the most elegant in the city, but the French constitute a very small minority there, and its houses have for the most part been purchased by American capitalists. It is there that the post office, major banks, stores selling Parisian goods, the cathedral and the Opera are to be found. The very name of the latter building is a proof of the gradual disappearance of the foreign or Creole elements. In days bygone, this theater only presented French plays, comedies or vaudevilles, but in order to continue filling the seats, it has had to change its repertory and its name. Now an American audience is patronizing it. It is obvious that the French language is slowly disappearing. As the population of New Orleans seasonally swells from 120,000 to 200,000 inhabitants, we can barely count six to ten thousand French, in other words a twentieth, and the same number of Creoles not yet completely americanized. Soon the Anglo-Saxon language will dominate without rival, and of the aboriginal Indians and French and Spanish colonists who had settled the country long before the immigrants of English descent, there will only remain street names: Tchoupitoulas, Perdido, Bienville, etc. The French Market that foreigners always visited in the past in order to hear a mixture of languages, resonates mostly with conversations in English. Germans, always ashamed of their homeland, try to show that they have become Yankees by their well articulated swear words and tavern humor. In their inexhaustible chatter, the negroes condescend to speak French only with a sort of pity for the person they are addressing, and the few Indian hunters, proud and sad like the imprisoned, respond to questions in monosyllabic English.[143]

Fig. 54. Odilon Redon. *Self Portrait,* 1867. Oil on panel. Musée d'Orsay, Paris. Erich Lessing/ Art Resource, NY

Both white and mixed-blood Creoles continued, however, to play a significant socio-economic role in the Crescent City. Micaela Almonester, the gutsy daughter of the old Spanish philanthropist Almonester y Roxas and best known to history as the Baronne de Pontalba (fig. 50),[144] left a considerable imprint on the city's history. In the mid-nineteenth century she devoted several years of her life and much money to the demolition of the buildings her father had constructed on either side of the Place d'Armes and their replacement by two symmetrical rows of elegant, three-storyed residential and commercial buildings designed by James Gallier and Henry Howard, the Upper and Lower Pontalba Buildings. She also made sure that the square was beautified and replanted. At her insistence it was renamed for Andrew Jackson, and a bronze cast of Clark Mill's equestrian statue of Jackson was placed in the middle of it. Architecturally, the Pontalba buildings are reminiscent of the brick and stone houses surrounding the Place des Vosges in Paris. They are today among New Orleans' most distinctive landmarks (fig. 51).

Another Creole of distinction was Marie-Célestine Musson (fig. 52), the wife of the Parisian banker Auguste De Gas and mother of the Impressionist painter Edgar Degas (fig. 53).[145] Her father Germain Musson (1787–1853)[146] was a planter and merchant originally from Saint-Domingue, and her mother, Marie-Céleste-Désirée Rillieux (1794–1819), was born and bred in New Orleans.[147] Marie-Célestine's cousin, Norbert Rillieux (1806–1894), was an engineer who invented the multiple-effect evaporator that revolutionized the industrial production of sugar. He was one of six children born to Marie-Céleste-Désirée's brother, Vincent Rillieux, and a free woman of color, Constance Vivant. The latter and her sister Eulalie had in their youth belonged to a wealthy New Orleans family, the Chevals. Norbert Soulié, Eulalie's son by a white Creole, was a successful architect.[148]

Fig. 55. *Ye Mystick Krewe of Comus Parade,* 1858. Engraving. The Historic New Orleans Collection, New Orleans

Other renowned New Orleans Creoles were the Confederate army general Pierre-Gustave Toutant de Beauregard (1818–1893); Marie "Odile" Guérin (1820–1909), the mother of the French Symbolist painter, draftsman and printmaker Odilon Redon (fig. 54), who was conceived in New Orleans and was born in Bordeaux; the concert pianist Louis

Fig. 56. *Panoramic View of New Orleans, with the National Fleet at Anchor in the River in Front, under Command of Flag Officer Farragut, April 25, 1862.* Published in *Frank Leslie's Illustrated Newspaper,* May 24, 1862. The Historic New Orleans Collection, New Orleans

Moreau Gottschalk (1829–1869), the first composer to combine Afro-American sounds with classical European musical forms;[149] the composer Ernest Guiraud (1837–1892), who taught Paul Dukas, Erik Satie and Claude Debussy at the Conservatoire national de Paris;[150] and the international chess champion Paul Charles Morphy (1837–1884), the son of a politician and his Creole wife, Louise-Thérèse-Félicité-Thelcide Le Carpentier. Two racially-mixed New Orleanians were outstanding musicians: the violinist Edmond Dédé (1827–1901) and the pianist Charles-Lucien Lambert (c. 1828–1896), a rival of Gottschalk. Both left Louisiana to study music in Paris, where they achieved considerable fame. And the notorious actress and dancer Adah Isaacs Menken (1835–1868)[151] was the daughter of a French Creole mother and a free black, Auguste Théodore.

### REVIVAL OF THE MARDI GRAS TRADITIONS OF THE CREOLES

The Mardi Gras masquerade parades and balls for which New Orleans has been known since the eighteenth century were the climax of the carnival season that began just after Christmas. For a long time they were dominated by the Creoles. By the mid-1850s streets revelries had become so uninhibited that they degenerated into mayhem.[152] There was talk in the French-language press of prohibiting them, notably in *L'Abeille.* They were given a new lease on life in 1857 when Ye Mystick Krewe of Comus was formed by an enterprising

Fig. 57. Edgar Degas. *Allegory of the Misfortunes of the Women of New Orleans during the Union's Occupation of the City (traditionally entitled "Scène de guerre au moyen-âge" or "Malheurs de la ville d'Orléans")*, 1865. *Peinture à l'essence* on canvas. Musée d'Orsay, Paris. Réunion des Musées Nationaux

group of Louisianians and Alabamans.[153] During the Mardi Gras that year, these young men financed a pageant on the theme of Milton's *Paradise Lost*, and this was the first time that floats were used. Thereafter, as "the greatest free show on earth," New Orleans' Mardi Gras festivities became an institution that has been perpetuated more or less in the form given it by the Krewe of Comus (fig. 55).[154]

### NEW ORLEANS DURING THE CIVIL WAR

Louisiana seceded from the Federal Union in January of 1861, at the very outset of the Civil War. The strategic location of New Orleans, its status as the largest city in the Confederacy, as well as its political and commercial importance, made it a prime target for the North. The Confederates failed to grasp the seriousness of the threat posed by the Western Gulf Blockading Squadron commanded by Captain David Farragut. He organized a squadron of heavy warships, gunboats and mortar schooners at the mouth of the Mississippi and attacked their positions at Forts Jackson and St. Philip on either side of the river in St. Bernard Parish, between which was stretched a cordon of heavy chains. The battle lasted seven days, but there were few if any casualties. The South's navy, although it included ironclads, was no match for the massive force confronting them. After heavy shelling, the Federal armada broke through the defences on April 24 and at noon the next day weighed anchor in the port of New Orleans (fig. 56), which was feebly defended by Confederate troops commanded by Major General Mansfield Lovell.

The occupation of the city was almost anticlimactic. In May, the Union army's expeditionary land force, commanded by General Benjamin Butler, entered the captured port and declared martial law. During his administration, New Orleans was kept supplied, clean and orderly, but from the outset of the occupation he acted with harshness towards the locals, who were still in the grip of war fever. His General Order no. 29, issued in the form of a broadside on May 15, 1861, decreed that if any woman were to insult a member of his staff or a soldier of the United States, she was to be treated as a prostitute plying her trade. This tactless move provoked protests throughout the divided country and even had repercussions abroad, particularly in England and France. It won him the nickname of "Beast Butler" and was chiefly responsible for his recall and replacement by General Nathaniel Banks in December of that year.

## New Orleans during Reconstruction

Throughout the Civil War, which officially ended in April of 1865 and the strife-torn Reconstruction era, New Orleans was the seat of government in the state of Louisiana. The constitutional conventions were held there, and it was the center of the struggle for control of the governorship and the legislature. Under Reconstruction (1865–1877), corruption was endemic in both the state and municipal governments. Radical Republicans like Henry Clay Warmouth and William Pitt Kellogg fought tooth and nail with southern Democrats. The latter were proponents of "home rule" and formed a segregationist movement spearheaded by the "White League." Civil disorder and even bloody street riots erupted in 1866 and 1874.

The postwar economy of Louisiana, like that of most of the South, was severely depressed. The war had caused an almost total disruption of commercial river traffic. The Confederates had destroyed almost all of the finest ships so that they would not fall into the hands of the enemy. The city of New Orleans' finances were so depleted that it defaulted on the interest of its bonded debt.

## The Creoles during the Civil War and Reconstruction

Some Creoles fled Louisiana in the aftermath of the Civil War, relocating to the Caribbean, South America and Europe, but most of them remained. Contrasting aspects of the world of the French Creole in post-Civil War New Orleans are exemplified in three much celebrated paintings.

As has been noted, the members of the painter Degas' family were New Orleans Creoles. Traumatized by the North's occupation of the city, several of the Musson women took flight. In June 1863, the matronly Odile Longer Musson, the wife of Degas' maternal uncle Michel, two of her daughters (the recently widowed Estelle-Angélina Musson Balfour[155] and the spinster Désirée) and her infant granddaughter Joséphine (Joe) Balfour sailed for France, where they were welcomed by their paternal uncles Eugène and Henri Musson and their De Gas relatives. They settled for a time in the little town of Bourg-en-Bresse, northeast of Lyon, where their kinsman Edgar visited them a number of times. He was so profoundly shocked by what he learned of the humiliations to which women in New Orleans had been subjected by General Butler's troops that in 1865 he executed a history painting (fig. 57) that he exhibited in May of that year at the Paris Salon. In the past that work has been incorrectly titled *The Misfortunes of the City of Orleans*. In his monograph on Degas, Henri Loyrette analyzed the true allegorical and contemporary subject of this picture that was first correctly identified by Hélène Adhémar:[156]

> During America's Civil War, the De Gas's...supported the armies of the South. It is very possible that the account of the atrocities perpetrated by the [northerners] as told to various members of the family by the three Louisiana ladies in exile—on May 1, 1862, after the taking of the city, the Northern soldiers exhibited a certain ferocity with respect to the women of New

Fig. 58. Edgar Degas. *Portraits in a Cotton Office,* 1873. Oil on canvas. Musée des Beaux-Arts, Pau. Réunion des Musées Nationaux/Art Resource, NY

Orleans—[is] the origin of *A Wartime Scene in the Middle Ages....*At the end of the Middle Ages, in an atonal landscape with leafless trees, burned houses, three horsemen pass among a group of nude women who have undoubtedly been raped, some dead or injured by incredible wounds. Firmly seated on their steeds, one of them is abducting a woman who is resisting; the other, flexing his bow, is preparing to shoot an arrow. The extreme cruelty of the subject is used as a pretext for an almost clinical observation of the female: the bodies are contorted, the hair falls, the sexual organs appear through rents in the clothing. Inanimate women in flight, crawling on the earth and riveted as if they were crucified on a tree. In this purposely enigmatic allegory, executed in the manner of many Renaissance compositions, Degas uses the frightful stories told by his aunt and two cousins in a middle-class sitting room in Bourg-en-Bresse to convey the tragic universality of a contemporary event in which he summarizes in a striking image what war has been from time immemorial: cruelty, rape, torture.[157]

Fig. 59. Detail of fig. 58

Fig. 60. John Singer Sargent. *Portrait of Madame X (Madame Pierre Gautreau, née Marie-Virginie-Amélie Avegno, 1859-1915),* 1883-84. Oil on canvas. The Metropolitan Museum of Art, New York

While in France, Estelle Musson Balfour met and fell in love with her first cousin René De Gas (1845–1921), who acted as traveling companion to his female relatives when they returned to New Orleans in 1865. This was the first of numerous transatlantic trips for him. After a brief stay in Louisiana, René went back to France but returned to Louisiana in 1866, accompanied by his somewhat older brother Achille (1838–1893). For a time, the two worked in their uncle's cotton firm, but in 1866 they set up their own import-export business, De Gas Brothers. With a dispensation from the Catholic church, René and Estelle, who had lost some of her sight, were wed on June 15, 1869, and between 1870 and 1876 the marriage produced five children.[158] During the Franco-Prussian War, René went to France to enlist in the French navy, but he soon returned to Louisiana. In June 1872, after Imperial Germany's defeat of the armies of Napoleon III, the fall of the Second Empire and the suppression of the Paris Commune, he once again traveled to Paris. His older brother Edgar had served in the artillery of the Garde nationale which was responsible for the defense of the capital, but his failing eyesight seriously handicapped him as a marksman. In mid-October René set sail for Louisiana with Edgar in tow. The latter lived and worked in New Orleans until late March of 1873. This is the only instance when a painter of the French Impressionist School visited the United States.[159] In New Orleans, the artist resided in the Musson house on Esplanade Avenue,[160] in a section of the city inhabited primarily by francophones.

Fig. 61. Robert Tebbs. *Parlange Plantation House, New Roads, Louisiana*, 1926. Photograph (gelatin silver print). Collection of the Louisiana State Museum (gift of Jeanne Tebbs)

During his stay, Degas painted one of the supreme masterpieces of nineteenth-century French art, *Portraits in a Cotton Office* (figs. 58 and 59).[161] The routine of the everyday lives of the merchant class is summed up in this multi-figured composition, which depicts the office of the cotton brokerage firm of Musson, Prestidge & Co., at the corner of Carondelet and Perdido Streets. In the left foreground sits the artist's uncle, the recently widowed cotton factor Michel Musson (1812–1885),[162] dressed in black and wearing a top hat, intently examining a piece of pure white fiber. In the background at the far left, Achille De Gas leans against a windowsill, and seated on a chair in the middle ground reading an issue of *The Daily Picayune* is René. To his right, William Bell (1836–1884), another of Musson's sons-in-law,[163] shows a cotton sample to a prospective buyer. Seated on a tall stool behind René is Michel Musson's American partner, James Prestidge, and to the far right the older man's other partner, John Livaudais, a member of a prominent French Creole family, examines the firm's ledger.

The subsequent life of Michel Musson is fraught with adversity, sorrow and even tragedy. He, his two De Gas nephews and William Bell had difficulty accepting the South's defeat, the period of Reconstruction and the resulting economic recession. As Confederate loyalists, they were active figures in the White League. Musson was forced to liquidate his business in February of 1873. Between 1877 and 1881 he had to mourn the loss of three of his De Gas grandchildren and his granddaughter, Joséphine (Joe) Balfour. His daughter Mathilde Bell died in September of 1878. Earlier that year, René De Gas had abandoned the now completely blind Estelle for América Durrive Olivier, the wife of a cotton merchant who was a neighbor and friend of the Musson-De Gas family. The two left New Orleans surreptitiously for the North with the Olivier children, were wed (bigamously) in Cleveland, began a new family while living in New York[164] and then relocated permanently in France.[165] Estelle obtained a divorce in 1879. René's two surviving children by her were adopted in 1883 by their grandfather, and their surname was legally changed to Musson.

Edgar Degas was too embarrassed to write to his uncle, but he finally sent him a letter in July of 1883 to announce the recent death in France of Henri Musson. In reply, Michel wrote: "But if I am losing a brother, I have found again a nephew. Prodigal son who comes back to me after having suffered so much, I open my arms to you and bless you! You are *that* Edgar that we still loved, the beloved child of my sister Célestine, my daughters' favorite. Like all four of them you are a *Creole* at heart; you are of course French by birth and intellectually; but you are not like *them* [René and Achille]…lazzaroni."[166] The painter was profoundly offended by the word "lazzaroni" (a snide reference to the Neapolitan side of the De Gas family) which had been used to insult his brothers, and thereafter he refused to communicate with his uncle. In 1885, the melancholy old man died, half crazed, riddled with debt and estranged from most of his De Gas and Bell relatives in France and in Louisiana.

High drama is also associated with a third painting with a Louisiana subject, John Singer Sargent's full-length portrait of *"Madame X"* (fig. 60). It records the appearance of a *belle Créole*, Madame Pierre Gautreau.[167] Her father, Anatole-Placide Avegno (1835–1862),[168] was a fairly prominent attorney, one of the young New Orleanians who in 1857 helped revive the old French tradition of the Mardi Gras street celebrations. The family of her mother, née Marie-Virginie Ternant (1837–1910), owned an indigo, sugar cane and cotton plantation (fig. 61) located on the False River in New Roads, Louisiana, which was easily accessible in the nineteenth century by Mississippi riverboat.[169] The Ternants, who had originally received their ten thousand acre land grant in the early 1750s, descended from early settlers who, like the de Marigny and Delfau de Pontalba families, had ties to France's hereditary nobility.[170] Amélie's mother even had some Acadian blood running through her veins.[171] Prior to the Civil War, members of this family divided their time between their townhouse on Toulouse Street in the French Quarter of New Orleans, the New Roads plantation and a Paris apartment on the rue de Luxembourg near the church of the Madeleine (today's rue Cambon). Avegno died from complications related to a leg amputation he sustained following the Battle of Shiloh,[172] and his widow and their two young daughters, Amélie and Valentine-Marie, settled permanently in Paris. At the age of nineteen, Amélie married a French banker, Pierre Gautreau, by whom she had a daughter but from whom she later became estranged.

In the last two decades of the nineteenth century, Amélie Gautreau frequented the chicest circles of Paris' intellectual society. Sargent, a fellow American expatriate living in Paris, probably met her in 1882 and was so struck by her good looks and the graceful manner in which she carried herself,[173] that he asked her to pose for him. The finished portrait, which required many sittings, changes of pose and preparatory studies, is the quintessential image of the sophisticated *femme fatale*. She is depicted wearing a black dress, with her head raised and turned in sharp profile. Adorning her hair is a small crescent moon that she often wore, a piece of jewelry that would normally designate her as the Greco-Roman goddess of the hunt Diana. In this case, however, the accessory is possibly meant to refer to the Crescent City in which she was born. Found particularly offensive were her provocatively low décolletage,[174] the ghostly pallor of her complexion and her air of triumphant *hauteur*, which must have come naturally to her in light of her ancestry,[175] wealth and social ambitions.

Sargent's portrait of Madame Gautreau offended the general public and a number of critics who viewed it at the Paris Salon of 1884.[176] The bad notices affected her decision not to acquire it, something she undoubtedly came to regret. Sargent considered it to be his masterpiece, and he only parted with it the year following Madame Gautreau's death, when it was bought by The Metropolitan Museum of Art. Amélie Gautreau later commissioned more flattering portraits of herself from other fashionable painters—Gustave Courtois (1891, Musée d'Orsay, Paris), Antonio de la Gandara (1897, private collection), Édouard Sain and Pierre Carrier-Belleuse—but none of them had the glamor and sex appeal of *Madame*

Fig. 62. Mahalia Jackson (1911-1972), circa 1957-58. Frank Driggs Collection, New York

Fig. 63. Louis Armstrong (1901-1971), circa 1931. Collection of the Louisiana State Museum, Gift of the New Orleans Jazz Club

*X.*[177] When her beauty faded, and she was no longer in the public eye, she withdrew from society and became a recluse.

Despite the difference in social class between the bourgeois Michel Musson and the aristocratic Amélie Avegno Gautreau, at least two common threads run through their personal histories. They each derived part of their income from the plantation system that had operated in Louisiana since its foundation as a French colony, and each of their lives came to a sad and bitter end.

### THE END OF RECONSTRUCTION AND A GRADUAL RETURN TO PROSPERITY IN NEW ORLEANS

In 1877, when the Democrat Francis Nicholls ousted Stephen Packard as Louisiana's governor, and President Rutherford B. Hayes ordered the withdrawal of Federal troops from New Orleans, a modicum of prosperity returned. By the mid-1880s, trade was again booming, and more than thirty steamboats could dock at one time along the waterfront to take on loads of cotton, sugar and various other commodities for export to different parts of the country or overseas. Banking, railroad and shipping magnates also made huge fortunes.

Newly enriched Anglo-Americans built more sumptuous villas in the Garden Districts of the old Faubourg Sainte-Marie, where many streets, avenues and boulevards were lined by sycamores and live oaks dripping with Spanish moss. They had their gardens landscaped with cedars, palm, citrus and banana trees, dogwoods, waxen-leaved magnolias, multi-colored caladiums, azaleas, camelias, hibiscus, bougainvilliers, lilies, oleanders, crepe myrtle, wisteria, sweet-smelling jasmines, gardenias, honeysuckle, aloes, ferns and all sorts of rare decorative and flowering plants.

In 1882, Mark Twain returned to New Orleans, which he had not seen in more than twenty years. He met with writer George Washington Cable, with whom he would later make lecture tours and in whose company he visited the city and its environs. He noted that the Civil War was the chief topic of conversation, that locals were in a sort of stasis. In his memoir *Life on the Mississippi*, which was published the following year, he compared the charms and beauties peculiar to the American and French areas of the city on either side of Canal Street.

> All the dwellings are of wood—in the American part of town, I mean—and all have a comfortable look. Those in the wealthy quarter are spacious; painted snow-white usually, and generally have wide verandas, or double-verandas, supported by ornamental columns. These mansions stand in the centre of large grounds, and rise, garlanded with roses, out of the midst of swelling masses of shining green foliage and many-colored blossoms. No houses could well be in better harmony with their surroundings, or more pleasing to the eye, or more home-like and comfortable-looking….

> The old French part of New Orleans—anciently the Spanish part—bears no resemblance to the American end of the city…which lies beyond the intervening brick business-centre. The houses are massed in blocks; are austerely plain and dignified; uniform of pattern, with here and there a departure from it with pleasant effect; all are plastered on the outside, and nearly all have long, iron-railed verandas running along the several stories. Their chief beauty is the deep, warm, varicoloured stain with which time and the weather have enriched the plaster. It harmonizes with all the surroundings, and has as natural a look of

belonging there as has the flush upon sunset clouds. This charming decoration cannot be successfully imitated; neither is it to be found elsewhere in America. The iron railings are a specialty also. The pattern is often exceedingly light and dainty, and airy and graceful—with a large cipher or monogram in the centre, a delicate cobweb of baffling, intricate forms, wrought in steel. The ancient railings are hand-made, and are now comparatively rare and proportionately valuable.[178]

Higher education became a priority in New Orleans. The University of Louisiana had been founded in 1847, when it merged with the Medical College of Louisiana which had opened its doors in New Orleans in 1834. Located on Common Street near Canal, this institution was on the verge of collapse in 1884, when it received a large donation of money and land from a former businessman of New Orleans, Paul Tulane (1801–1887), who was born near Princeton, New Jersey, the son of a French immigrant. In his honor it was renamed Tulane University of Louisiana. In 1886, the wealthy Josephine Louise Le Monnier Newcomb (1816–1901) provided the funds for the creation of a sister college for women (the first in the United States to be incorporated into a major university) in memory of her deceased daughter, Sophie Newcomb. As she had for Tulane, she also provided the school with a considerable endowment, which at her death was increased by more than two and a half million dollars. By 1895, the two schools were being relocated to the area of Carrollton now known as the University District in uptown New Orleans.

Each year the Mardi Gras parades became more elaborate and costly. They were organized around themes inspired by the world's religions, mythology, holidays, European literature, geographic locations and European and American (especially Louisiana) history. They were a great attraction for tourists who came in great numbers to see the colorful spectacles.[179] Originally, masks and costumes were imported from France, but after 1873 they and the parade floats were made locally. Over time, as the festivities became more elaborate, many other clubs or "krewes" such as the Twelfth Night Revelers, the Knights of Proteus, the Knights of Electra and the High Priests of Mithras sprang up. The first Rex Parade was held in 1872, during a visit to the city of a Russian Grand Duke. Mardi Gras became a legal holiday in the city in 1875.

### The birth of Jazz

The post-Civil War era witnessed the birth and development of New Orleans' greatest contribution to the performing arts, Jazz.[180] Music and dance had long played a significant role in the life of that large segment of the city's population that was of African descent. This was true from the time the first slaves were brought to the Louisiana colony. Church music made a substantial impact on the formation of Jazz.

Most members of the black and mixed-race communities were practicing Christians, and many of the momentous events of their lives were associated with their churches. Funerals of black New Orleanians were events in which music expressed both sorrow for the loss of a loved-one and joy at the thought of the deliverance of his or her soul.[181] Negro spirituals and traditional hymns gave hope and comfort to those who enjoyed emancipation in name only in the post-Civil War era. (It is not an insignificant fact that the greatest gospel singer of all time, Mahalia Jackson (fig. 62), the daughter of a Baptist preacher, was born and grew up in the "Black Pearl" section of Carrollton.) When the "Jim Crow laws" were instituted, they once again found themselves segregated and effectively disenfranchised. This was a great blow to those whose ancestors were manumitted people of color and who were used to certain privileges denied their brethren who lived and worked as slaves.

Fig. 64. *The French Opera House,* circa 1900. The Historic New Orleans Collection, New Orleans

Jazz was a product of the "gumbo" of ethnicities that made up the city's demography, and the exchange that resulted from the combination of Afro-American and European musical cultures in its various neighborhoods. The African and Caribbean sounds heard on Congo Square had been kept alive once gatherings in that location were prohibited before the Civil War. The jigs and marches of all-black brass bands, the Mardi Gras celebrations in which young men dressed as "Indians" confronted each other in groups with demonstrations of drum-beating and call-and-response singing, lively Cajun music and even the denigrating buffooneries of the minstrel shows, all were part of the mix. Also important were the soulful melodies of "Blues" singers and the syncopated rhythms of "Ragtime" played in the clubs and brothels of the tenderloin district beyond North Rampart Street (Storyville) or tamer areas of the city such as the amusement parks and resorts on Lake Ponchartrain.

As harsher segregation laws were passed, black and mixed-blood musicians in New Orleans united, and as they did they blended the "uptown" improvisational style with the more disciplined "downtown Creole"[182] approach. The result was the music of the first Jazz "greats:" John Robichaux (1866–1939),[183] Oscar Célestin (1884–1954), Joe "King" Oliver (1885–1934), Emile "Stalebread" Lacoume (1885–1946), Edward "Kid" Ory (1886–1973), Freddie Keppard (1890–1933), Ferdinand Joseph La Menthe (better known as "Jelly Roll Morton," 1890–1941) and Sidney Béchet (1897–1959). And it is not pure happenstance that the foremost jazzman of all, Louis Armstrong (fig. 63), came out of these late nineteenth-century New Orleans traditions. In the "City that Care Forgot," Jazz ended the nineteenth century and ushered in the twentieth.

### OTHER PERFORMING ARTS IN NEW ORLEANS

The old Théâtre d'Orléans was forced to close in the late 1850s, when it was put up for auction as part of the estate of its last owner, John McDonough.[184] In 1859, the impresario of the old Théâtre d'Orléans, Charles Boudousquié, had commissioned the architects James Gallier, Jr., and Richard Easterbrook to build the grand French Opera House (fig. 64) at the corner of Bourbon and Toulouse Streets. In addition to the regular repertory, works of Hector Berlioz, Charles Gounod, Georges Bizet, Charles Lalo, Jules Massenet and even Giuseppe Verdi, Pietro Mascagni and Richard Wagner were introduced there to the New Orleans public. It was the site of many gala events until it burned in 1919.[185] In the last quarter of the century, the city's theaters, opera, symphony and concert halls attracted the foremost entertainers of the day. Actors and singers from abroad such as Sarah Bernhardt, Emma Calvé, Léonce Escalaïs, John McCormack, Nellie Melba and Adelina Patti played to packed houses. New Orleans always welcomed innovation, and in 1896, Vitascope Hall, the world's first movie theater, was built on Canal Street.

This was the cultural environment of New Orleans at the end of the first decade of the twentieth century, when the city could boast of a population in excess of three hundred thousand inhabitants.

Fig. 65. *Isaac Delgado (1839-1912) in His Wheelchair,* circa 1900. Photograph courtesy of the New Orleans Museum of Art

## The New Orleans Museum of Art, Past and Present

Following the Civil War, the visual arts had benefited little from the economic development stemming from the South's booming commercial and manufacturing sectors. An Artists' Association was created in 1885, and in 1901 the Exhibition Club was founded. The two organizations merged in 1904 to form the Art Association of New Orleans, the goal of which was to foster the advancement of the pictorial and plastic arts by a program of juried contests and exhibitions.

Finally, in 1910, the elderly Isaac Delgado (fig. 65), an unmarried Jewish banker and business tycoon who was born in Jamaica and had migrated to New Orleans in 1853, provided the funding for the contruction of an art museum. One of the founders of the Louisiana Sugar Exchange, he was a generous philanthropist who made contributions to various causes. Although he never collected art, Delgado was persuaded by a friend of the aunt with whom he lived to donate $150,000 to his adopted city so that such an institution could be constructed.[186]

The site chosen was a circular plot of land at the entrance to the fifteen-hundred acre City Park, near the Bayou St. John, the Bayou Tchoupitoulas and Lake Ponchartrain. This recreational space was located at the end of Esplanade Avenue, on the site of the old sugar plantation and dairy farm of Jean Louis Allard, who had received it from his wife's father, Jacques Loreins. On it stood the famous Dueling Oaks, where in the early nineteenth century feisty New Orleanians settled their scores with rapiers or pistols.[187] The donor stipulated that it was to be called the Isaac Delgado Museum of Art and was to be governed by a Board of Administrators,[188] the Board of Commissioners of City Park and the Art Association of New Orleans. Unfortunately, he did not have the prescience to provide an endowment to finance the day-to-day operations (utilities, maintenance of the physical plant and a curator's salary) and acquisitions, which meant that the establishment was financially dependent on small appropriations from the City Council of New Orleans and local patronage. The original goals of the Delgado were the education and moral improvement of the general public. [189]

The museum's architect was selected in a competition won by Samuel A. Marx (1885–1964), of the Chicago firm of Lebenbaum & Marx, and the contractor was Julius Koch of New Orleans. The building was conceived as a neo-Greek temple (fig. 66) adapted to a semi-tropical climate. The cornerstone was laid on March 22, 1911, in the presence of Delgado. The portico was constructed in Bedford ashlar. Around its cornice ran a frieze bearing the names of celebrated painters, sculptors and architects. On the first floor was a spacious hall intended to house plaster casts of famous statuary, four exhibition rooms, a curatorial office and a meeting room for the board of administrators. On the balconied second floor were six exhibition rooms for the annual contests sponsored by the Art Association. Access to the museum was through an entrance gate built with monies given by a Sicilian immigrant, Antonio Monteleone, who had made a fortune after acquiring and expanding a hotel in the heart of the Vieux Carré, and an avenue then lined with palm trees. The formal opening of the museum on December 16, 1911 was not attended by the gravely ill Isaac Delgado, who died less than a month later.

During its first decades, the loan exhibitions were organized by the dictatorial Ellsworth Woodward (1861–1939), who taught art at Sophie Newcomb College for Women, was a member of the Delgado's Board of Administrators and founded the Southern States Art League. He served as Chairman of the museum's Art Committee, its acting Director, and President of the Board of Trustees. His agenda was uniquely involved with the promotion

Fig. 66. The Isaac Delgado Museum of Art soon after its construction. Photograph courtesy of the New Orleans Museum of Art

of southern regionalism, and he devoted little effort to creating a permanent collection or to making the arts of other countries and other centuries better known to museum visitors. As a result, the public cared very little for what was going on at the Delgado, and in the first decades following its creation, attendance was low. The only acquisitions of any significance made by the Delgado during his time came in the form of donations from the Durand-Ruel Gallery and the Fine Arts Club of New Orleans,[190] and bequests from wealthy benefactors such as Morgan Whitney,[191] Chapman H. Hyams and his wife,[192] Mrs. Benjamin M. Harrod,[193] Mrs. Emory Clapp,[194] Eugène Lacosst,[195] Alvin P. Howard[196] and I.M. Cline.[197] Woodward's policies also had a stifling effect on the formation of important collections of Old Master and modern art in New Orleans. In fact, his aversion for art of the modern European schools was so blatant that he alienated Hunt Henderson, whose important collection was lost to the Delgado.[198] In such circumstances, it was obvious that there was no need for a full-time director or even a professional curator of an institution whose permanent holdings were so meager.

Despite Woodward's influence, some good exhibitions of modern art managed to slip through the cracks and were held at the Delgado in the 1930s. In 1930, the museum hosted a commercial show of *Post Modern French Painting* that had originated on the West Coast.[199] Another exhibition of contemporary art took place in 1938, sponsored by the College Art Association. The paintings on display were from the dealer Paul Rosenberg, and the show had the support of local architect Arthur Feitel, who had joined the board in 1933 and was destined to serve as its director. In 1937 he arranged for works by six sculptors from the collections of the Museum of Modern Art in New York[200] to be shown. The following year, the Katherine Kuh Gallery in Chicago lent works by Léger, Picasso, Archipenko, Noguchi and Raymond Johnson.

The Delgado's holdings of Old Master European art was undistinguished until January of 1931, when the chain store magnate and philanthropist Samuel H. Kress (fig. 67) gave it a boost by donating the *Madonna del latte* by the fourteenth-century Florentine painter, Giovanni del Biondo. This was a milestone in the museum's history, because it led to a far more significant donation. It was the first of thirty-two pictures that Samuel Kress and his foundation eventually presented to the Delgado. In February and March of 1933, the philanthropist lent to the museum fifty-two paintings from his private collection and crowds flocked to see them.

Woodward's death in 1939 marked the end of an era of stagnation for the Delgado. The Board of Trustees appointed Arthur Feitel as acting Director. He implemented a number of improvements such as the reinstallation of certain galleries, the removal of mediocre works from public view, the modernization of the ventilating system and the storage spaces, the renewal of the exhibition program[201] and initiating a program of lectures, art films and art classes for children. Feitel was assisted in his task by members of the Bultman family, who had a remarkable appreciation and understanding of modern art. In March 1941 the painter Fritz Bultman (1919–1985) and his sister Muriel B. Francis (d. 1986) lent works from their eclectic collections of contemporary German, French, Spanish, Italian and Russian art and helped organize a monographic show of the works of Hans Hofmann.[202]

While most of the museum's shows continued to be regionalist in concept, Arthur Feitel brought two traveling exhibitions of modern art to the Delgado. The Museum of Modern Art in New York sent to New Orleans a revolutionary exhibition entitled *The Bauhaus, How It Worked* and a show entitled *The Evolution of the Skyscraper*. In May of 1940 the museum hosted a show of *Hitler Banned Art*, in which the works of avant-garde German Expressionist artists were richly represented.[203] In December of that year a major Picasso retrospective organized by The Museum of Modern Art in New York was sent to the Delgado, *Picasso: Forty Years of His Art*; and it included at least three blockbusters: *Les Demoiselles d'Avignon*,[204] *The Race*[205] and *Guernica*.[206] In late November of 1943 the Delgado presented to the New Orleans public an exhibition of modern works of French art that had just been presented in San Francisco and was being returned via the Panama Canal when the French army surrendered to Hitler's forces in June of 1940. Rerouted to New Orleans, they were placed in temporary storage in a warehouse. It took three years to obtain the loan from the French Committee of National Liberation. The show emphasized America's sympathy for the plight of the occupied French nation and its solidarity with the Free French forces. *Refugee French Art Treasures* featured paintings by Matisse, Picasso, Bonnard, Bourdelle, Degas, Dufy, Kisling, Rodin, Rouault, Vlaminck and Vuillard.

Feitel was elected president of the board in 1946, and he set about recruiting a full-time professional director for the institution. Alonzo Lansford, a former director of the Telfair Academy in Savannah, Georgia, and then an associate editor of the *Art Digest*, was hired two years later. Although short-staffed, the engaging and energetic Lansford[207] was full of initiative and promptly organized an important loan exhibition of French paintings belonging to important dealers, among them Durand-Ruel, Pierre Matisse, Paul Rosenberg, Rosenberg & Stiebel and Wildenstein. He was also instrumental in making the vetting practices of the Art Association exhibitions more inclusive and actively pursued the acquisition of works of art by Louisiana artists of the nineteenth century, which he displayed in a separate gallery, the Louisiana Room. He solicited donations of contemporary art from such collectors as the writer William E. Campbell, Muriel Bultman Francis and William H. Alexander.

Fig. 67. Samuel H. Kress (1863-1955), circa 1910

However, Lansford's greatest feat was persuading Samuel Kress to loan and then donate[208] to the Delgado thirty additional Italian paintings from the collection that he had assembled and that were earmarked as gifts to the newly founded National Gallery of Art and to a series of regional museums throughout the country. This "gift to the nation" remains the most important example of artistic philanthropy in the history of the United States. The Kress donation was officially dedicated in the museum in April of 1953. To accommodate the collection, a large gallery was divided into three, and new lighting and air-conditioning systems were installed. Lansford also laid the groundwork for an expansion of the Delgado's building by the addition of three wings, but his plans were thwarted by a decrepit and largely apathetic board.

In 1953, with the assistance of Georges Wildenstein (fig. 68), the Delgado organized an exhibition of masterpieces of French painting from public and private sources (including Nicolas Poussin's *Rebecca and Eliezer at the Well*, François Boucher's *Aurora and Cephalus*, Jean Baptiste Greuze's *Milkmaid* and Eugène Delacroix's *Greece Dying on the Ruins of Missolonghi*, all from the Louvre) in honor of the one hundred fiftieth anniversary of the Louisiana Purchase. President Dwight D. Eisenhower and the ambassadors of France and Spain were present at the opening. *Time* magazine trumpeted the event as a coup of major proportion:

Fig. 68. Cecil Beaton. *Portrait of Georges Wildenstein (1892-1963)*, 1937. Photograph

> When the city of New Orleans began making plans to celebrate this year's sesquicentennial of the Louisiana Purchase, the Delgado Museum put in its bid for a part in the show. It agreed to stage an exhibition of French painting, showing the cultural heritage that France bequeathed to its descendants overseas. Last week the results were on display in the museum's galleries: 82 borrowed French paintings, ranging from the 15th to the 20th centuries. American collections supplied 60 of the paintings; the remaining 22…came from the Louvre and six other French museums—the finest art loan ever made by the French government outside Europe. Even the Delgado's go-getting director, red-topped Alonzo Lansford, 43, was overwhelmed by the generosity of the lenders. "This exhibition is bigger and better than we deserve," he confessed. "It has set an extremely high standard." The chief organizer of the show was multimillionaire Art Dealer Georges Wildenstein, who has galleries in Manhattan, Paris, London and Buenos Aires. He rounded up the American contributions and helped persuade the French government to cooperate in celebrating a bargain that Frenchmen can only regard as a bad one. In a preface to the exhibition catalogue, Wildenstein boldly generalized the whole history of French painting and arrived at a conclusion which was probably as true as such sweeping statements about any subject can ever be. Throughout the show, he maintained, "we find a common approach to life conceived of charm and optimism. Without evasions and without false sentimentality, the French painter expresses his love, his mystic respect of nature and of man."[209]

Alonzo Lansford's next big undertaking was a Van Gogh exhibition that took place in 1955, the year during which he successfully negotiated the donation to the Delgado of the three-thousand piece glass collection of the shipping tycoon Melvin P. Billups, whose late wife had been born in New Orleans. Unfortunately, the board of administrators took umbrage at Lansford's high-profile performances, and he was summarily dismissed in March of 1957. A long, contentious and highly publicized battle took place, with Feitel as the archenemy of the dismissed director. The fallout of the fierce polemical debate in the press and in an open forum almost scuttled the Kress donation. Despite the bad press the museum received, Lansford was not rehired. The board, however, was given a new

Fig. 69. Mr. and Mrs. Frederick M. Stafford and Mrs. J. Frederick Muller at the first Odyssey Ball, New Orleans, November 13, 1967

look when old members resigned and more forward-thinking New Orleanians took their places.

Lansford's position was filled in June of the following year by Sue Thurman, the former director of the Junior Art Gallery in Louisville, but without much fanfare. She then took on full-time curators of the collection and the newly developing education department. In 1959 the Delgado's board was reorganized and enlarged, and it merged with the Art Association. The fiftieth anniversary of the museum's foundation was commemorated by a block-buster exhibition of modern European and American art, *The World of Art in 1910*. In June of 1961, following a rift between her and some of the board members, Sue Thurman resigned. The following February, the directorship was assumed by James B. Byrnes, a follower and protégé of the legendary German art historian William R. Valentiner, who had served successively as the director of the Detroit Institute of Arts, the Los Angeles County Museum of Art, the J. Paul Getty Museum and the North Carolina Museum of Art (where Byrnes had taken the post of director after Valentiner's death in 1958). Byrnes' first major exhibition was entitled *Fête de la palette*, which was a celebration of food in art from the Renaissance until the mid-twentieth century, an appropriate theme for New Orleans if ever there was one.

1964 was a banner year for the Delgado. Donations from Mr. and Mrs. Aage Qvistgaard-Petersen, Muriel Bultman Francis, Edith Rosenwald Stern (an heiress of the Sears, Roebuck and Co. fortune), Mr. and Mrs. S. J. Levin and Mr. and Mrs. Frederick M. Stafford enriched the permanent collection with a number of superb works of modern art: two drawings by Degas, Rodin's life-size *Age of Bronze* (cat. no. 52), Kees Van Dongen's *Woman in a Green Hat* (cat. no. 61), Wassily Kandinsky's *Sketch for "Several Circles"* (cat. no. 72) and Naum Gabo's *Construction in Space: Suspended* (cat. no. 86).

That year Byrnes also conceived the idea of a Degas exhibition. The artist was considered a "native son" of New Orleans because of his family affiliations in the city. At the same time, one of the works he painted during his stay in Louisiana in the early 1870s, a portrait of Estelle Musson De Gas arranging flowers (cat. no. 50), then in a private British collection, was brought to Byrnes' attention by the New York dealer Eugene Victor Thaw.[210] Certainly, the director felt that the opportunity was ripe for the Delgado to purchase a major New Orleans picture by the artist. A "Bring Estelle Home" campaign was launched. It raised the nearly $200,000 purchase price, reaching the goal in January of 1965. Estelle came home, and she was the focus of *Edgar Degas: His Family and Friends in New Orleans*, the exhibition that Byrnes had been dreaming of. To assist him in the preparation of the show and the drafting of the catalogue, he enlisted the help of the two world-recognized authorities on Degas' work at the time, John Rewald and Jean Sutherland Boggs.

In 1967, the Staffords lent the Delgado their wide-ranging art collection. The show was titled *Odyssey of an Art Collector*, and it was inaugurated with a fund event called the Odyssey Ball (fig. 69), an event that has since then taken place annually in the museum under the aegis of the Women's Volunteer Committee. The following year, the Staffords presented a cash gift to the Delgado, as well as Bonnard's magnificent *Study for the Poster "La Revue Blanche"* (cat. no. 57), and that year they were made lifetime members of the museum's board.

Alonzo Lansford's project for expanding the physical plant of the Delgado finally came to fruition in 1970 under James Byrnes' leadership. Three new wings (fig. 70) added more than eighteen thousand square feet of exhibition space to the museum, which in October of 1971 was officially renamed the New Orleans Museum of Art (NOMA). To mark the occasion, an exhibition entitled *New Orleans Collects* was held, and it included more than four hundred works of art of various national origins and many periods. The goal was to show the scope and range of collections in the city and to encourage more participation by locals in the growth of the museum's holdings. The newly enlarged museum was re-dedicated during the Odyssey Ball that fall in the presence of Count Basie and his orchestra.

Having accomplished so much, James Byrnes judged that the time was propitious for his departure, and he resigned in May of 1972. His replacement was the museum's fourth and present director, E. John Bullard, who had previously held curatorial positions at the J. Paul Getty Museum and the National Gallery of Art. He took up the post in April of 1973 and hit the ground running by assessing NOMA's strengths and weaknesses. In 1974, NOMA received several gifts, the most important of which was the large bequest of Victor Kermit Kiam (1896–1974; fig. 71). Although a native of Texas and a resident of New York, he had studied law at Tulane and began his career as an attorney in New Orleans. Among the treasures of his eclectic collection were a group of thirteen paintings

Fig. 70. Architect's aerial rendering of the New Orleans Museum of Art with its three building additions, circa 1970

Fig. 71. Victor K. Kiam

and four sculptures by twentieth-century artists of the caliber of Georges Braque, Pablo Picasso, Alberto Giacometti, Joan Miró, Jean Dubuffet and Jackson Pollock, all of which are included in the present exhibition. Other gifts came from the Latter-Schlesinger family (portrait miniatures) and Edith Rosenwald Stern (Central Andean Colonial Art).

John Bullard saw photography as a field in which NOMA could make its mark, and in the early 1980s he made major acquisitions in this area. In 1982, the museum received a generous gift of master prints from the photographer Clarence John Laughlin (1905–1985), known for his photographs of Louisiana plantations, some of which he published in 1948 in *Ghosts Along the Mississippi*. A specialist of American art, John Bullard also championed the acquisition of several superb works by artists as varied as John Singleton Copley, John Singer Sargent, Mary Cassatt, Georgia O'Keefe, Joseph Cornell, Richard Diebenkorn and Louise Bourgeois, all of which are included in Wildenstein's exhibition.

Collecting Old Master French art had never been a priority for the museum. This is all the more astonishing given New Orleans' historical ties to France, which founded and colonized it. The museum owned a portrait of Louis XIV (cat. no. 15), a gift from New York's Hirschl & Adler Gallery, and a major Natoire (cat. no. 26), but its holdings in this domain were otherwise insignificant. Realizing that this was a field in which one could acquire major paintings at reasonable prices, the new director saw this as a challenge and an opportunity and forged ahead. French art of the Ancien Régime became a priority. Since he has been at the helm, Bullard has added stellar works by major painters of the seventeenth and eighteenth centuries: Claude Lorrain, François Boucher, Carle Vanloo, Joseph Marie Vien, Jean Baptiste Greuze, Hubert Robert and Élisabeth Louise Vigée Le Brun.

Perhaps John Bullard's major success as director of the New Orleans Museum of Art has been the installation of the museum's sculpture garden. It, of course, could not have been created without two of the most generous benefactors that the mueum has ever had, Sydney and Walda Besthoff,[211] for whom it has been named. NOMA's five-acre Sydney and Walda Besthoff Sculpture Garden opened in November of 2003. Forty-one of the fifty sculptures decorating the grounds were donated by the Besthoffs, and among them are pieces by Louise Bourgeois, Sandro Chia, Barbara Hepworth, Jacques Lipchitz, Henry Moore, George Segal, Joel Shapiro and Ossip Zadkine. The Besthoff Sculpture Garden was formally dedicated at a gala in their honor on Saturday, October 30, 2004, at the New Orleans Museum of Art. Sadly, this was the part of NOMA's collections that sustained the most damage from Hurricane Katrina and the ensuing flood.

cat. no. 1 (detail)

## Highlights of the Present Exhibition

The New Orleans Museum of Art and a number of New Orleans private collectors can boast of strong concentrations of art and artifacts from Asia, Africa, Oceania, as well as objects created by the indigenous peoples of North, South and Meso America before and after the arrival of Europeans in the New World. NOMA has a considerable number of works by artists of America's Deep South, especially those of Louisiana. It is also a showcase for important pieces of American and European furniture, silverware, portrait miniatures, ceramics and other decorative arts. Its collection of ancient and modern glassware is so important that it can hold its own with those of the Toledo Museum of Art and the Corning Museum of Glass. The present exhibition, however, focuses on the pictorial, graphic and sculptural arts of Western Europe and the United States, and the time span covered is extensive.

The earliest paintings on display in the Wildenstein galleries date from circa 1360, and the show closes with a work produced in the last decade of the twentieth. When compiling the entries at the end of the catalogue, our goal was to provide the reader with the complete provenances, bibliographic references and exhibition histories of the exhibited works. Several stand out as particularly significant and warrant discussion.

### Italian painting of the late Middle Ages

As has been previously mentioned, a number of Italian pictures were donated to the museum at various times by the Samuel H. Kress Foundation. Among them are two panels of saints (cat. no. 2) by the greatest Sienese painter of the late fourteenth century, Taddeo di Bartolo. Gail E. Solberg has suggested that these panels were elements of one of Taddeo's last commissions, which was probably painted for the church of San Domenico at Gubbio. The central panel was a *Madonna and Child*, signed and dated 1418, now in the Fogg Art Museum at Cambridge, Mass., and two additional flanking panels depicting SS. James the Major and John the Baptist (also Kress donations) are in the Memphis Brooks Museum of Art. Other elements of this altarpiece have been traced.[212]

The Venetian master Bartolomeo Vivarini's brightly colored and monumental *Coronation of the Virgin* (cat. no. 3), which may have been painted for a Dominican church in Ferrara, was originally flanked by depictions of St. James the Great and St. Francis of Assisi, today in the John G. Johnson Collection, Philadelphia Museum of Art. In 1835, the painting was recorded in the prestigious Costabili collection in Ferrara, where it was attributed to Marco Zoppo. From a prominent family of painters, Vivarini is generally considered to be one of the first exponents of the new Renaissance style in northeastern Italian painting.

### The age of the Renaissance and the Baroque in Europe

In Garofalo's *Meditation of Saint Jerome* (cat. no. 5) of circa 1520–25, the old anchorite and Latin Church Father is shown as a penitent in a complex landscape, an iconographic innovation introduced in the Veneto about 1470. The artist was the leading Ferrarese master of his day. The composition is remarkable for the beautiful still life composed of a small Madonna and Child devotional painting in a tabernacle frame, an hourglass, writing instruments and an open book. The torsion of the figure recalls the pose of the Seated Prophets in Michelangelo's Sistine ceiling. Bernardino Luini's *Adoration of the Christ Child* (cat. no. 6), noteworthy for the nocturnal lighting effects in both the foreground and the background scenes, is the largest interpretation of a theme treated several times by this exceptionally gifted and still under-appreciated follower of Leonardo da Vinci. It comes from the notable collection of Renaissance paintings acquired *en bloc* by Joseph Duveen from Robert and Evelyn (Holford) Benson in 1927. Lorenzo Lotto's *Portrait of a Bearded*

*Man* (cat. no. 8) is in many respects the finest picture given to the museum by the Kress Foundation. The subject's elegant, static pose and authoritative air are unusual in the Venetian artist's portraiture; his figures are usually set at a diagonal and include numbers of narrative accessories. The work dates from the end of Lotto's first Venetian period and betrays the influence of Giovanni Girolamo Savoldo, as well as perhaps that of such Florentine masters as Bronzino.

Maerten van Heemskerk's *Apollo and the Muses* (cat. no. 9) is a celebration of the power of music on the human mind, and it constitutes a veritable conspectus of mid sixteenth-century musical instruments. The humanist theme was subsequently treated several times by the Dutch painter, but never as whimsically. The quirky, Mannerist figural style derives from a study of the sculpture of antiquity and Italian High Renaissance painting. (We know that van Heemskerk was indeed in Italy between 1532 and late 1536 or early 1537.) For instance, the flutist at the right is an almost direct quotation of a figure in Michelangelo's *Last Judgment*.

The seventeenth century is particularly well represented on NOMA's walls. An outstanding example of the work of Abraham Bloemaert depicts *Saint John the Baptist Preaching in the Wilderness* (cat. no. 10). The artist was a seminal figure in the history of Dutch art and the first real landscapist of that school. The subject of outdoor preaching was popular at that time and interpreted more than once by Bloemaert. Emphasizing large, secondary figures used as repoussoirs while the main protagonists of a scene (here the Baptist) are relegated to the middle ground is a typical Mannerist device. *Death Comes to the Banquet Table* (cat. no. 11) is a major work with a *momento mori* theme[213] by a relatively obscure Florentine Caravaggesque painter, Giovanni Martinelli. He has depicted the frightening apparition of a skeleton to a gathering of young men (*bravi*), a woman (possibly a prostitute) and servants. At various times, the painting has been attributed to a number of other European artists.[214] A fairly recent discovery, Simon Vouet's *Erato* (cat. no. 12) belongs to a series of nine *Muses*, only one of which, *Melpomene, the Muse of Tragedy*, remains to be discovered. Other panels in the set are *Clio* in the Staatliche Kunsthalle, Karlsruhe and the large *Urania and Calliope* in the National Gallery of Art, Washington, D.C. (Samuel H. Kress Collection).[215] A sublime *Madonna and Child with a Goldfinch* by Simone Cantarini (cat. no. 13), called Il Pesarese after his birthplace of Pesaro, was painted after 1637, when the painter quarreled with his master Guido Reni, in whose studio he had worked for four years in Bologna. In fact, NOMA's painting, which remains essentially unpublished, was attributed to Reni until Stephen Pepper correctly reassigned it in 1991 to Cantarini. What is possibly a related sheet of studies is in The Art Institute of Chicago.[216]

*The Vision of Saint Louis of Toulouse* (cat. no. 16) is a *modello* for an altarpiece commissioned from Carlo Dolci in 1675 by Canon Francesco Bocchineri for his chapel in the church of San Francesco at Prato, a picture that remained unfinished at the time of the painter's death, when it was acquired by the leading connoisseur and art patron in Tuscany, the *Gran Principe* Ferdinando de' Medici, who then had it finished by Dolci's pupil, Onorio Marinari. That work is today in the Palazzo Pitti, Florence. An autograph inscription on the back of NOMA's canvas records four payments to the artist in 1676, 1678, 1679 and 1681.[217] It is probably the "*modellino*" sold by Dolci's son Andrea to the Medici prince in 1690. Luca Giordano's large and impressive *Baptism of Christ* (cat. no. 17) is an undocumented work that undoubtedly functioned as an altarpiece. The loose facture and the dramatic use of light bring to mind the work of Tintoretto and the rich colorism harks back to Veronese. It was executed at a time when Luca was receiving a number of major commissions in Florence. The only French painting reflecting the influence of Nicolas Poussin in NOMA's collection is Nicolas Colombel's *Adoration of the Magi* (cat. no. 19),

cat. no. 8 (detail)

which was in all likelihood commissioned by the arms merchant Maximilien Titon, in whose postmortem inventory of 1711 it is mentioned. This may be the *Adoration* by Colombel that was sent to the Salon of 1704.

A portrait of the "Sun King," Louis XIV (cat. no. 15), for whom Louisiana was named, is the work of a major, but today little known portraitist, Claude Lefebvre. In the past it has been attributed to Pierre Mignard and Nicolas de Largillierre, under which name it was presented to the Delgado by the New York art firm of Hirschl & Adler in 1956. In all likelihood, it is the original portrait from which prints by Nicolas Pitau the Elder and Pierre Louis van Schuppen were executed in 1670.

## The eighteenth century

Eighteenth-century Italy is represented by two Venetian pictures, both gifts to NOMA from the Samuel H. Kress Collection. The first is one of Sebastiano and Marco Ricci's melancholic *capricci* (cat. no. 21). The architectural components, among them the partially ruined Pyramid of Caius Cestius and the Temple of Dolabella, were painted by Marco Ricci, whereas the figures are the work of his uncle Sebastiano. The atmospheric rendering of light and shadow and the sheer monumentality of the ruins that dwarf the picturesque staffage recall the imaginary tomb monuments of British worthies commissioned between 1723 and 1730 from the Riccis and other Italian artists working in tandem by the Irish theatrical manager and art agent, Owen McSwiny. The likely model for Giambattista Tiepolo's most sensitive and tender easel painting of a youth, his *Boy Holding a Book* (cat. no. 27), was the artist's youngest son, Lorenzo Baldissera Tiepolo (1736–1776), who later became one of eighteenth-century Europe's preeminent pastellists. Confirming the identification is Giambattista's chalk drawing of his son today in the Frits Lugt Collection, Fondation Custodia in Paris, in which the boy's widow's peak and pointed ears are very similar. Pulsating with life, this fanciful portrait ultimately derives from the head studies of Tiepolo's master Giovanni Battista Piazzetta. It is the type of picture that would have inspired Fragonard's so-called *Figures de fantaisie.* The painting must have enjoyed great popularity, for it was copied a number of times. Before it was sold in 1932 to Samuel H. Kress by his favorite dealer, Alessandro Contini Bonacossi, it was in the collection of the Milanese Visconti di Modrone family.

As New Orleans was founded by the French in the early eighteenth century, it is fitting that French art of that period constitutes one of this exhibition's strong suits. Nattier's newly rediscovered drawing of Peter Paul Rubens (cat. no. 20), which he apparently made after Paulus Pontius's oval engraving of Rubens' self portrait of 1623,[218] was produced in 1707 to serve as the model for Jean Audran's frontispiece for *La Gallerie du Palais du Luxembourg,* an in-folio book of engravings of the paintings in Rubens' *Life of Marie de Médicis* today in the Musée du Louvre but then in the Palais du Luxembourg.[219] The individual prints were executed by various engravers after red chalk drawings made by Jean Marc Nattier and his older brother Jean Baptiste.[220] NOMA's sensitively rendered drawing, which may once have been in the prestigious Gambier Parry collection, was auctioned in New Orleans in 2000, when it was acquired by George Roland, who made a gift of it the following year to NOMA.

The subject of Jean Restout II's dramatic history painting, *Hector Taking Leave of Andromache* (cat. no. 23), today in a prestigious New Orleans collection, is taken from Book VI of the *Iliad.* In the course of the war between the Trojans and the Greeks, the fighting was fierce and bloody, but the Greeks won the upper hand. Hector—one of the sons of King Priam and Queen Hecuba of Troy and the brother of Paris who had caused the war by abducting the daughter of King Agamemnon—prepares to go into battle. His wife Andromache pleads with him not to leave. Before returning to the fray, where he will be killed by his nemesis Achilles, Hector turns to his son Astyanax, but the child is frightened by the plumes on his helmet. Hector removes it and reaches for the infant. This is one of two versions of Restout's composition.[221] Among its previous owners was Louis XVI's controversial minister of finance, Charles Alexandre de Calonne (1734-1802), who had in his collection some spectacular masterpieces of European painting, including Nicolas Poussin's *Blind Orion Searching for the Rising Sun* of 1658, today in The Metropolitan Museum of Art, New York.

*The Toilet of Psyche* (cat. no. 26), a work dating from around 1735 by Charles Joseph Natoire, illustrates an episode from the ancient Greek fable of the maiden Psyche, beloved of the god Cupid and the personification of the human soul, of which the butterfly hovering above her head is the symbol. Solely in terms of its provenance, it is perhaps the most interesting painting in the New Orleans Museum of Art. As has been noted, this exceptionally well-documented picture arrived in the Crescent City in 1845, just after it was purchased at the estate sale of the former king of Spain, Joseph Bonaparte, Napoleon's older brother. Originally commissioned as one of a set of four mythologies meant to decorate a room of the Château de La Chevrette in the Vallée de Montmorency, which belonged to the financier La Live de Bellegarde, it subsequently entered the possession of the great collector of contemporary French art, Joseph de Paule de Rigaud, Comte de Vaudreuil (1740-1817). The nephew of one of the first French governors of Louisiana, the Marquis de Vaudreuil de Cavagnal (1704–1778), he was the owner of the plantations in Saint-Domingue where he was born and from which he derived a sizeable portion of his income prior to the French Revolution. Two of the painting's three companions—*Venus Showing Psyche to Cupid* and *Psyche Obtaining the Elixir of Beauty from Proserpine*—have been traced. The first is in a private collection in New York and the second was recently acquired by the Los Angeles County Museum of Art.

*The Surprise* (cat. no. 24) by the foremost painter of the Rococo, François Boucher, is a playfully erotic example of the latter's early genre paintings. The rendering of flesh, fabrics and fur is wonderfully assured and the high-toned palette is perfectly in keeping with the libertine subject. The composition was popular, and two other potentially autograph examples are known.[222] A pair of mid eighteenth-century *Russeries*[223] by Boucher's pupil, Jean Baptiste Le Prince (cat. no. 33), which were sent by the artist to the Salon of the Académie Royale de Peinture et de Sculpture in 1769, have been lent by a private collector. Their exotic subjects were no doubt inspired by scenes the artist witnessed during his treks through Imperial Russia in the late 1750s. Their collection history includes the name of Comte Jean Du Barry,[224] who introduced his mistress, Jeanne Bécu, into the bed of Louis XV once he had married her off to his own brother in order to facilitate her official reception at Court. When the pair of Le Princes were included in the sale of part of his art collection in 1774, Gabriel de Saint-Aubin made thumbnail sketches of them in the margins of his copy of the auction catalogue. Du Barry was guillotined in 1793 in his native Toulouse. Other owners were the Swiss-born banker Jean Frédéric Perregaux, whom Napoléon Bonaparte appointed in 1800 as one of the founders of the Banque de France, and his daughter Marie-Hortense, the wife of Louis de Marmont, Maréchal Duc de Raguse, famous for his betrayal of the Emperor. His wife would never forgive this act, and the two lived apart for a good period of their married life.

Two outstanding examples of French portraiture of the second half of the eighteenth century are in NOMA's collections. Greuze's *Madame Gougenot de Croissy* (cat. no. 29) is a likeness of a middle-class woman dressed in all of her winter finery and holding a shuttle with which she makes tiny knots to be used in embroidery or as trim for linens. This

cat. no. 19 (detail)

cat. no. 24 (detail)

activity related to lace-making occupied women of the wealthier classes, and there exist numbers of it.[225] The companion portrait of the sitter's husband, Georges Gougenot, a *conseiller-secrétaire* to Louis XV, is in the Musées royaux des Beaux-Arts, Brussels. In 1985, the acquisition by NOMA of Vigée Le Brun's large, full-length state portrait of Marie Antoinette (cat. no. 39) made headlines. This work, of which Versailles owns the signed and dated version that preceded it, is remarkable for the sumptuousness of the costume, accessories, furniture and décor. The two pictures differ in ways that distinguish each of them as a work of art in its own right: the pouf of blue satin and the aigrette are higher and more voluminous in the present example of the portrait, whereas the Baroque pearl eardrops are smaller and the Queen is not shown wearing a necklace. The composition and the painting from which it derives, Madame Le Brun's dynastic *Marie Antoinette and Her Children* (Salon of 1787, also in the Musée national des Châteaux de Versailles et de Trianon), are the most regal images of the Louis XVI's Austrian-born consort, who was sent to her death on the guillotine a little more than five years after they were completed. The New Orleans painting, which has retained its frame bearing the armorials of the ruling houses of Austria and France, was made for the subject's brother-in-law, the Comte d'Artois, the last of the kings of the senior branch of the house of Bourbon who reigned between 1824 and 1830 as Charles X. It should be noted that the engravings after the portrait, both bust- and half-length, were made from this autograph replica and not from the Versailles picture.

Because it includes a great jet of water rising from a fountain, the place represented in an elegant painting by Hubert Robert (cat. no. 31) has for many years been mistakenly said to be the Château de Saint-Cloud, the country residence of the Ducs d'Orléans located in the hills above the Seine between Paris and Versailles. Moreover, the date of the picture has been misread as 1768, which reinforced the mistake. In fact this work, formerly in the collections of the *couturier* Jacques Doucet and the Dukes of Roxburghe, was produced in 1760 when Robert was living in Rome and studying at the Académie de France in the Palazzo Mancini.[226] If the villa represented actually existed—in which case the picture would not be a *capriccio* but rather a *veduta*—it has not yet been identified. The staffage animating the outside stairway is particularly picturesque.

A small terracotta statuette of a nymph leaning on an urn (cat. no. 41), a personification of water, was acquired by NOMA at an auction held in New Orleans in 1997. Until it was conserved recently by Shinichi Doi, it was covered with a thick coat of paint that left its attribution to Joseph Charles Marin in doubt. When this disfiguring addition was removed, it was clear that this was indeed the work of Clodion's best follower. Another version of the small sculpture, which is distinguished by several variant details (the head of the duck is raised and the young woman's waist is wreathed with leaves) is signed and dated 1791.[227] It may be identical with a work entitled *"…une Bacchante, une porteuse de vase"* that was shown at the Salon of 1791.[228] A sumptuous late eighteenth-century bouquet of mixed flowers (cat. no. 42) from an anonymous collection is the work of the Franco-Flemish botanical painter, draftsman, watercolorist and engraver, Pierre Joseph Redouté. His mastery was such that in his lifetime he was made official painter to the two wives of Napoléon, Empresses Joséphine and Marie Louise, Queen Hortense, the Duchesse de Berry and Queen Marie-Amélie. The picture is remarkable on several accounts: the artist's breathtaking technical skill in rendering a large variety of plant life, his sense of color and compositional balance and his understanding of light and shadow.

The likeness of a wealthy merchant from Plymouth, Massachusetts, Colonel George Watson (1718–1800; cat. no. 32), was executed by the American painter John Singleton Copley in 1768, at a time when the thirteen American colonies were seething with revolutionary anger over the British Parliament's passage of the Townsend Acts, which levied taxes on imported goods. Artist and subject had family ties: Elizabeth Oliver Watson, the daughter of a judge, was the cousin of Copley's mother, Mary Singleton Copley. The painter's portrayal of Mrs. Watson in the Smithsonian American Art Museum in Washington, D.C., which he executed three years earlier, is generally considered as the pendant to NOMA's painting. The two works provide a sharp contrast in their color schemes and in the costumes: Elizabeth Watson wears a cherry red silk gown and her dark hair is unpowdered, while her husband is dressed far more soberly in a suit of dark brown velvet trimmed with gold braid and buttons and on his head sits a heavy white periwig. Their poses are characterized by a certain stiffness and formality, and their facial expressions are almost stern. The two images reflect the social standing of the sitters, their wealth and the austere, Congregationalist ethic that governed their lives. Watson is standing at his desk, attending to his correspondence. A Tory sympathizer and member of the British Royal Council in the American colonies, he was outspoken in his opposition to the growing rebellion. His unpopularity among local patriots helped persuade Copley to leave Boston with his family and migrate to England.

### NINETEENTH-CENTURY PAINTING AND SCULPTURE

An exquisitely poetic Hudson River School landscape owes its presence in New Orleans to James Robb, the collector who also brought to the city Natoire's *Toilet of Psyche* (cat. no. 26). Asher B. Durand's *Forenoon* (cat. no. 45) and its pendant *Afternoon* (now in the Mead Art Museum, Amherst College, Amherst, Mass.) originally hung in the entrance hall of Robb's mansion on Washington Avenue. He took great pride in the two works and lent them to prominent institutions in New York, Philadelphia and Boston. The golden tonalities of *Forenoon* recall Durand's slightly earlier *The Beeches* (1845, The Metropolitan Museum of Art, New York), and it harks back to certain seventeenth-century Dutch landscapes.

Jean-Léon Gérôme's scene of Turkish mercenaries engaged in a game of chess (cat. no. 49) is an outstanding example of nineteenth-century Orientalist genre painting. The colorful costumes and air of quiet absorption belie the true nature of the Bashi Bazouk,[229] irregular soldiers of the Ottoman army who were particularly ferocious in battle. A poetic landscape by Corot, *Woodland Scene* (cat. no. 51), offers a beautifully modulated play of light on the foreground shrubbery and the distant field. It was probably executed sometime in 1872–73, when the old artist traveled through northwestern and central France, producing a succession of landscapes remarkable for the freshness of their inspiration.

Most of NOMA's French Impressionist paintings, among them some important works by Camille Pissarro, Claude Monet and Alfred Sisley, could not be shown here due to a commitment to lend them to an exhibition at the The Louisiana Art & Science Museum in Baton Rouge,[230] which provided many resources to NOMA's staff during the critical months following Hurricane Katrina. However, we are able to present a splendid pen and India ink study of leafy branches by Pierre-Auguste Renoir (cat. no. 55). It represents the artist's classical period of the mid-1880s, when he abandoned the style of his more spontaneous and exuberant earlier work and moved toward the more disciplined, restrained "classicism" exemplified by the *Great Bathers* in the Philadelphia Museum of Art. Indeed, it has even been suggested that the New Orleans sheet served as a study for that masterpiece. The making of such drawings was an integral part of the academic training Renoir had received in the studio of his master, Charles Gleyre. A similar pen and ink drawing of trees from this precise moment of Renoir's career is in the National Gallery of Art, Washington, D.C., and another appeared recently at auction.[231]

cat. no. 26 (detail)

cat. no. 23 (detail)

Because of its Creole subject, the most emblematic of the New Orleans Museum of Art's paintings is undoubtedly Edgar Degas' soulful *Portrait of Estelle Musson De Gas* (cat. no. 50) of 1872. As has already been noted, the subject was the painter's first cousin and sister-in-law and was a native New Orleanian. Her tragic blindness is made more poignant by the sonorous chromatic harmonies and the superb floral still life that conceals the fact that she is several months pregnant. On the opposite end of the emotional scale is Mary Cassatt's *Mother and Child in the Conservatory* (cat. no. 65). Here the baby girl is alert, assured and faintly inquisitive as she encounters the viewer's gaze. The mother firmly supports her, expressing the quiet solicitousness that characterizes certain of Raphael's Madonnas. Sunlight, falling from the left with a dappled effect, bathes both figures. They are posed against a rapidly executed landscape that reappears in the composition as a reflection in the window pane at the right. A closely related picture, which includes a likeness of the model who posed for the figure of the mother,[232] was sold by Wildenstein to The White House in 1966.[233]

The formal portrait of Flora Wertheimer, née Joseph (d. 1922), is the work of the ultra-fashionable portraitist of Edwardian society, John Singer Sargent (cat. no. 58), whose earlier likeness of the New Orleans Creole Amélie Gautreau has been discussed at length. This and a companion portrait of her husband Asher B. Wertheimer (1844–1918), a successful London art dealer, were originally commissioned to mark the couple's silver wedding anniversary. Sargent painted a second likeness of Mrs. Wertheimer, as well as portraits of all ten of her children. These portraits—including that of her husband but excluding the one shown here, which descended to its last private owner through one of the subject's daughters—were bequeathed by Asher Wertheimer to the British nation and are now preserved in the Tate Britain, London. A memorable traveling exhibition in 1999–2000 reunited all of the Wertheimer portraits. The accompanying catalogue stressed the ties of affection that linked the normally reserved Sargent to the Wertheimers, who were barred from London's high society because they were Jewish. The artist clearly enjoyed the unusually warm relationship with the family, which he jocularly termed "a state of Chronic Wertheimerism."[234]

A bronze cast of Rodin's *Age of Bronze* (cat. no. 52), which was made in the artist's lifetime, is one of the museum's finest sculptures. It is the first of Rodin's full-length figures to have survived. The initial plaster was exhibited at the Cercle Artistique in Brussels in 1877 and was acquired by the French state three years later. The circumstances of its creation are well known—it made the young Rodin's reputation—and yet its meaning is still a subject of debate. Its initial title of *"Le Vaincu"* ("The Vanquished") suggests an allegory of France recently humbled by its defeat at the hands of Imperial Germany. Its traditional title, referring to mankind at the dawn of history—"physically perfect, but in the infancy of comprehension, and beginning to awake to the world's meaning," as one writer put it[235]—originated at the time of its showing at the Paris Salon of 1877. Paul Paulin's expressive, naturalistic bust of Degas (cat. no. 66), executed when the subject was seventy-two, is one of two portraits that the artist sculpted of the illustrious Impressionist. Trained as a dentist, Paulin worked for a time painting landscapes with Albert Lebourg. His first works as a sculptor date from 1881, and two years later, he came to Degas' attention. The New Orleans bust is one of an edition of nine dated January 1907. Another cast decorated the mantlepiece of Degas' dining room. A third bronze was acquired by the French state in 1909 and is today preserved at the Musée d'Orsay, Paris.[236]

Pierre Bonnard's preparatory watercolor and gouache study for the lithographed poster he made in 1894 as an advertisement for the influential Parisian literary journal *La Revue Blanche* (cat. no. 57) was presented to the museum in 1966 by Mr. and Mrs. Frederick

cat. no. 31 (detail)

M. Stafford. This Nabi masterpiece undoubtedly depicts Misia Godebska (1872–1950), the Polish wife and egeria of one of the periodical's founders, Thadée Natanson. Part of the important Muriel Bultman Francis bequest to NOMA are five works by Odilon Redon, most of supreme quality, which is very appropriate given the artist's connection to Louisiana. His father had traveled from France to New Orleans to seek his fortune, and there married a Creole woman. In 1840, the couple moved to Bordeaux, and soon thereafter Odilon, who as was noted earlier was conceived in the Crescent City, was born. Three works by the artist are exhibited here, including one of his so-called Noirs, *Shadow and Light* (cat. no. 59), which originally belonged to Redon's early champion, the dealer and collector Ambroise Vollard. A *tour de force* of graphic design in varying shades of black, it depicts a head, the left half of which is in dark shadow. The closed eyes and mouth suggest deep, ascetic meditation, one of this Symbolist artist's favorite themes.

### THE TWENTIETH CENTURY

Georges Braque's Fauve *Landscape at L'Estaque* (cat. no. 64) is one of the jewels of the Victor K. Kiam bequest to NOMA of early modern art. In October 1906, the painter journeyed to L'Estaque on the Côte d'Azur, a locale made famous by Cézanne, who died at the end of that month. Braque executed this scene when the older master's influence was making its strongest impact on French art and shortly before it inspired the revolutionary Cubist experiments initiated by him and Picasso. Yet little is known of the Fauve landscapes that Braque produced at L'Estaque. He actually bought back several such pictures, some of which he may have destroyed, after finding them unresolved. But in March-April 1907, six of them were presented at the Salon des Indépendants, where they were very well received. Five were promptly acquired by the German critic Wilhelm Uhde, among them *Le Vallon*, which remains unidentified. It could be the New Orleans picture, in which case Braque would have repurchased it. The hypothesis is worth considering since the earliest provenance for *Landscape at L'Estaque* is the artist's collection as of 1959.

Robert Henri's monumental *Blue Kimono* (cat. no. 67) was finished in August of 1909, and it won the Philadelphia Art Club's Gold Medal the following October. It was part of the large inaugural exhibition of the Isaac Delgado Museum of Art in 1911, but it was acquired by NOMA only sixty years later. In February 1908, Henri had been instrumental in establishing "The Eight," a group of realist painters who championed artistic freedom and the "painterly" art of masters such as Diego Velázquez, Frans Hals and Édouard Manet. NOMA's loosely executed *Blue Kimono* is very much in that mode. It depicts a young Japanese-American woman, Waki Kaji, who posed that same year for two other full-length portraits by Henri, one in which she is attired in a riding costume (Carnegie Museum of Art, Pittsburgh) and another in which she wears a pale blue dress and a large straw bonnet (collection of Mr. and Mrs. James W. McGlothlin, Austin, Texas).[237] The artist's interest in a distinctly Asian subject was part of a movement that James McNeil Whistler had helped launch, Japonisme. It reflected an idealist faith in the family of man, what Henri referred to as "my people." That year, Henri was introduced to the color theories of Hardesty Maratta, according to which a graded scale of bright tonal values should systematize the palette.

The Futurist sculpture *par excellence* is surely Umberto Boccioni's *Unique Forms of Continuity in Space* (cat. no. 68). This splendid polished bronze cast, which was modeled in 1913, has been lent by the Sydney and Walda Besthoff Foundation Collection in New Orleans. In keeping with Boccioni's aesthetic and that of Futurism in general, this large sculpture is a study of the human figure in motion and therefore takes into account the dimensions of volume, space and time. It was intended to be viewed principally from the side, and its dynamism is due to the emphatic diagonals within its geometry. The overall

cat. no. 36 (detail)

effect is that of a muscular figure striding though an imaginary wind tunnel. None of Boccioni's sculptures was cast in his short lifetime. The original plaster was exhibited in 1913 in Paris at the Galerie La Boétie, but it was ultimately shattered. The pieces were reassembled after the sculptor's death by two of his Futurist colleagues, one of whom, Filippo Tommaso Marinetti (1876–1944), took possession of the reconsituted sculpture and had it cast in bronze in an edition of two in 1931.[238] The Besthoff Foundation's cast was issued in an edition of eight in the prestigious foundry of Francesco Bruni in Rome for the Galleria La Medusa.

Wassily Kandinsky's *Sketch for "Several Circles"* (cat. no. 72) was executed in January 1926 as a study for the final work now in the Solomon R. Guggenheim Museum, New York.[239] By then the fifty-nine year old artist, under the influence of Russian Suprematism, had abandoned the organic forms of his abstract paintings for purely geometric ones, a development reinforced by his participation in the Bauhaus community at Weimar (between 1922 and 1925) and Dessau (after 1925). The circle held an increasing fascination for Kandinsky. Later in life he stated that this geometric form was as central to his aesthetic as the horse motif had been in earlier years. Circles of different sizes and colors and sometimes with radiant perimeters (as in the NOMA and Guggenheim composition) were aligned in diagonals to create dynamic compositions. In Kandinsky's art, the circular form had a mystical dimension and was inspired by the teachings of Theosophy. As one writer noted, "…the theosophist concept of a universal harmony underlying the apparent chaos of the natural world held great appeal for artists who were beginning to move towards abstraction…It seems to provide a way of finding eternal qualities and meaning in non-representational shapes."[240] The painting was donated to the museum in 1964 by Edith Rosenwald Stern, who considered it the favorite of all the paintings in her considerable collection.[241]

Constantin Brancusi claimed that his portraits were not abstract, and that in them he sought instead to capture through simplification of form the spirit or essence of his sitters' personalities. In *Sophisticated Young Lady* (cat. no. 74)—a rare masterpiece graciously lent by a private New Orleans collector who acquired it from the artist himself in 1954—the austere, featureless head is relieved by the whimsical addition of a chignon set at an angle. The beautifully polished bronze, the only rendering of the composition in this medium, has retained its original base. Brancusi's subject was the Anglo-American Nancy Clare Cunard (1896–1965), the daughter of Sir Bache Cunard, heir to the Cunard shipping fortune, and the renowned London hostess, the American-born Maud Alice ("Emerald") Burke. Renowned for her eccentric behavior, Nancy Cunard often dressed in male clothing and had lovers of both sexes, one of whom was Aldous Huxley.[242] An author in her own right, she was also a dedicated patroness of avant-garde art and literature.[243] She moved to Paris in 1920 and met Brancusi there through a mutual friend, the Romanian poet and co-founder of the Dada Movement, Tristan Tzara. Another member of her circle was Man Ray, who taught Brancusi the fine points of photography and shot a portrait of the ultra-thin and ultra-rich Cunard in 1926. Nancy Cunard had affairs with the French poet Louis Aragon and the African-American jazz pianist, Henry Crowder. In 1931 she published a polemical pamphlet entitled *Black Man and White Ladyship*, and three years later she edited a selection of African literature and art, *Negro: An Anthology*. The nature of Cunard's relationship with Brancusi is unknown, and there is no evidence that she commissioned, or even owned, a version of *Sophisticated Young Lady*. Indeed, she seems to have been unaware of the piece until around 1956, when she wrote to Marcel Duchamp, that its "…head resembles, at first sight, somewhat, a torso, a graceful curve, and then one sees the intention of that dear Brancusi, it is really the profile of a head extended in a lengthwise curve, with a tuft of hair, if you please, at the crown!"[244] Between 1925 and

1927, Brancusi had carved in walnut a first version of *Sophisticated Young Lady*,[245] a work that he later presented to Alexina (Teeny) Duchamp, whose husband Marcel Duchamp was a tireless promoter of the Romanian sculptor's work in America. In 1933, Duchamp organized a Brancusi exhibition at the Brummer Gallery in New York[246] in which the version in wood and the present bronze were shown. It was acquired in 1999 by the Nelson-Atkins Museum of Art in Kansas City.[247]

Although generally considered a member of the Surrealist movement based in Paris between the two World Wars, Joan Miró is one of the giants of twentieth-century art and defies categorization. A consummate draughtsman, a colorist inspired by the art of his native Catalonia, he was amazingly prolific. Moreover, he was endowed with an almost limitless imagination, and the organic forms and linear configurations prevalent in his best work, which often have a playful dimension, are difficult to interpret rationally. Exception must be made, however, for the series that Miró labeled his "*tableaux sauvages,*" which he executed between October 1935 and May 1936. Of these, NOMA's *Persons in the Presence of a Metamorphosis* (cat. no. 75) is the largest.[248] The term "*sauvage*" refers to an imagery in which individual forms confront each other in particularly detached, foolish and/or angry ways. To maximize their readability, Miró staged the confrontations in deep, wide settings against areas of sky. He assigned these pictures descriptive titles, an unusual practice for him. In the case of the present painting, two figures at the right observe the metamorphosis of (presumably) one of their own kind. The dark message of a depraved and brutish humanity is Miró's response to events that led up to the Spanish Civil War, which obliged him to take refuge in Paris where he remained until 1940. The present picture is one of several works by the master bequeathed to the museum by Victor Kiam, a longtime friend of the artist.

Miró's influence on postwar American painting was considerable. This is the case for the German expatriate, Hans Hofmann, who emigrated to the United States in 1932. Indeed, NOMA's *Abstraction of Chair and Miró* (cat. no. 77) makes reference to a picture by the Spanish artist which is said to have been in Hofmann's collection.[249] The complex composition of this canvas, unlike those of his later, better known, abstractions, is an almost realistic celebration of an artist's studio. Simply in terms of color, it is indebted to Miró. It is worth noting here that Hofmann's first one-man exhibition in an American museum took place at the Isaac Delgado Museum of Art in March of 1941. Its organizers were the painter's pupil Fritz Bultman (the brother of Muriel Bultman Francis, who bequeathed much of her collection to the museum), his father, A. Fred Bultman, Jr., and Hofmann's wife (Maria Wolfegg), who stayed with the Bultmans at their Louisiana Avenue home.[250]

Soon after the end of World War II, Jean Dubuffet devoted himself to portraiture. Certainly, to a creative spirit so dedicated to *Art brut* (which translates "raw art" or "outsider art")—the anti-academic movement launched by Dubuffet in 1948 in which art was to be shorn of all literary references and verisimilitude—the concept of commemorative likenesses would appear foreign. In the NOMA's *Paul Léautaud in a Caned Chair* (cat. no. 79), the thick, rough and deeply incised paint surface produces an image of primitive, almost childlike intensity in which individual attributes are reduced to crude shapes symbolizing rather than describing the subject. Paul Léautaud (1872–1956) was a writer and editor of the literary journal, the *Mercure de France*, and was one of a group of French writers who were part of Dubuffet's circle. During a gathering of such literary figures at one of the Thursday luncheons given by the American-born patroness of the arts, Florence Gould (1895–1983), the hostess suggested that he do a series of portraits honoring France's intellectual elite.[251] The result was a series of seventy-two works, thirty-seven oil paintings and thirty-five gouaches and drawings. Many of them, such as NOMA's picture, were

cat. no. 42 (detail)

cat. no. 45 (detail)

featured in an exhibition entitled *Les Gens sont bien plus beaux qu'ils croient—vive leur vraie figure* (People are better looking than they think—long live their real face),[252] which was held in October 1947 at the Paris gallery of René Drouin, who was himself the subject of a portrait by Dubuffet.

Jackson Pollock's *Composition (White, Black, Blue and Red on White)* (cat. no. 80) is one of the artist's drip paintings that were executed on paper rather than canvas between 1948 and 1949. Pollock produced about twenty-five such works, all of them of relatively modest scale, which may explain why they sold comparatively well during his lifetime. Nothing in their compositions differs in any substantial way from what one finds in his large paintings on canvas produced during the same period, with their interweaving, lyrical play of line, paint splatters and tiny fields of pigment. It was this innovative, indeed revolutionary technique that in 1949 elicited the question: "Is He the Greatest Living Painter in the United States?"[253]

In a letter dated October 26, 1950, to his New York-based dealer Alexandre Iolas, the Belgian Surrealist painter René Magritte spoke of a group of paintings that he was undertaking entitled "The Art of Conversation."[254] NOMA's picture of this title (cat. no. 82) is the first in the series. Seen from below are a series of gigantic stone letters spelling the word *REVE* ("Dream") set against the sky in which hovers a string of clouds. This is a direct reference to the subconscious. Typical of the painter's quirky sense of irony, the letters signifying an ephemeral dream state are rendered in a most permanent form, i.e. stone, which was one of his favorite motifs at the time. Another in the series includes the same word, but two minuscule spectators are depicted in the foreground, inviting a comparison with early Hollywood movie posters. Typically, Magritte's meaning here is open to interpretation. But in all likelihood, as was suggested by Michel Butor,[255] the image springs from a literary source like Charles Baudelaire's poem "La Beauté," in *Spleen et idéal*, the largest section of *Les Fleurs du mal*.

> Je suis belle, ô mortels! comme un rêve de pierre,
> Et mon sein, où chacun s'est meurtri tour à tour,
> Est fait pour inspirer au poète un amour
> Éternel et muet ainsi que la matière.
>
> Je trône dans l'azur comme un sphinx incompris;
> J'unis un cœur de neige à la blancheur des cygnes;
> Je hais le mouvement qui déplace les lignes,
> Et jamais je ne pleure et jamais je ne ris.
>
> Les poètes, devant mes grandes attitudes,
> Que j'ai l'air d'emprunter aux plus fiers monuments,
> Consumeront leurs jours en d'austères études;
>
> Car j'ai, pour fasciner ces dociles amants,
> De purs miroirs qui font toutes choses plus belles:
> Mes yeux, mes larges yeux aux clartés éternelles![256]

A series of incongruous, idiosyncratic images set in shadowbox frames aptly characterizes much of the art of Joseph Cornell, a member of the Surrealist school in New York. His intriguing *Radar Astronomy* (cat. no. 83), which was bequeathed to NOMA by Muriel Bultman Francis, aims at conveying the mechanisms of the cosmos, specifically the orbits of the solar system. Against a celestial backdrop he placed a pair of metal rods on which rests a cork ball symbolizing the sun. The two rings suspended from the rods are meant to suggest the paths of the planets, and below, a representation of the sun's rays is seen through a wine glass containing a green marble, another planet-like form. This is the second of two Cornell boxes[257] in the collection of Muriel Francis, who was in her time a rather high-profile figure in the New York theater and classical music scenes.

By the early 1920s, once he had discarded both the Cubist and Futurist approaches to abstract sculpture, the Russian-born Naum Gabo had laid the groundwork for his theories on the subject. He made use of the latest technology in choosing his materials, and in his work space and movement were determinant features. NOMA's *Construction in Space: Suspended* (cat. no. 86) was conceived around 1957, and in terms of chronology it follows the artist's "spheric theme" sculptures, which date from the late 1930s. With the purity of a mathematical equation, hundreds of strands of perspex (a plastic invented in 1937 and adopted soon after by Gabo) define the overall forms, imply kinetic movement, and catch light from a multitude of directions. The actual execution of *Construction in Space: Suspended* was due to Charles Wilson, a New Orleanian and former member of the Yale University studio art faculty, whom the sculptor hired to teach him metal welding. Wilson became Gabo's assistant around 1962 and eventually the sculptor treated him as something of a surrogate son. Under Gabo's direction, he produced some twenty examples of the work shown here.[258]

*Woman on Porch* (cat. no. 87) is one of the largest of the California artist Richard Diebenkorn's figural pictures and dates from three years after his decade-long foray into representational painting began in 1955. The thickly painted, flat, horizontal bands of bright pigment are reminiscent of the art of Matisse and Bonnard. The silhouette of tiny trees against the sky at the top is the sole indicator of an actual landscape, and the "porch" of the title is suggested by a simple, thin green line (defining space in a way pioneered by Matisse) and by the play of light on the seated figure. This addition to the composition recalls some of Diebenkorn's bold, highly schematized figural drawings, in which the static forms of isolated sitting or standing models are depicted indoors. It also invites comparison with the art of Edward Hopper, one of the artist's early idols. It was that painter's "use of light and shade and the atmosphere…kind of drenched, saturated with mood, and its kind of austerity"[259] that profoundly influenced NOMA's picture. While in the collection of Mr. and Mrs. David Lloyd Kreeger, *Woman on Porch* was shown in the West Wing of the White House.

Picasso painted his half-length *Woman in an Armchair* (cat. no. 90) on April 1, 1960, at his villa "La Californie," located in the hills overlooking the bay at Cannes. The model was his lover at the time, Jacqueline Roque (1926–1986), whom he had met in 1954 at the Madoura pottery works at Vallauris. She was the last in a succession of women who played a major role in Picasso's life, providing him with companionship and a source of stimulation for his prodigious creative energies. His attachment to Jacqueline was so strong that he married her in March of 1961, and they remained together until his death in 1973. He produced at least seventy portraits of her, far more than he painted of any of the other women in his life (Fernande Olivier, Marcelle Humbert, his first wife Olga Khokhlova, Marie-Thérèse Walter, Dora Maar and Françoise Gilot). Her image occurs repeatedly in his erotic series *The Painter and His Model*, and she is the main subject of his magnificent improvisations on Eugène Delacroix's *Women of Algiers*. In NOMA's painting, Picasso looked back to the fragmented forms and distortions of his revolutionary Cubist phase, showing her head both frontally and in profile. To emphasize her strong classical features and her abundance of dark hair, he severely restricted his palette to tones of black, white, gray, ocher and olive green, colors that are also reminiscent of his Cubist work.

cat. no. 46 (detail)

One of the most moving works in the exhibition is entitled *Bird's Nest* (cat. no. 94). It is the work of New Orleans artist Henry Casselli, a watercolorist of considerable stature to whom NOMA devoted a retrospective in 2000. He was born near the French Quarter in the Ninth Ward, in the easternmost, downriver portion of New Orleans. This racially mixed neighborhood, which was particularly hard hit in the aftermath of Hurricanes Katrina and Rita, had a lasting impact on Casselli, many of whose subjects are African-American people among whom he grew up. In the artist's words, "I don't feel that I selected black subject matter. I feel it selected me. I'm of the South and these are the people I live among." The model depicted here with such empathy and understanding is a young girl named Crow. She posed for him periodically during a relatively short period of time, but the memory of her continues to haunt him and remains a major inspiration for his art.[260] The subject is placed off center in front of a wooden brace in which a bird has built its nest. The watercolor is characterized by the contrasts between light and shadow and positive and negative space, all of which convey an aura of mystery to the composition.

## The Future of the New Orleans Museum of Art

Although NOMA was hit hard by Katrina, John Bullard and his staff are prepared to meet head on the enormous challenge facing them. Their ambition is to set the museum back on a firm economic footing, to bring its employees back to their pre-hurricane numbers, to reinvigorate its educational programs, to encourage more local, national and international support, to revive its exhibition and acquisition programs and to pursue the beautification of the grounds of Sydney and Walda Besthoff Sculpture Garden, which also entails the restoration of the damaged statuary. We at Wildenstein are hopeful that this exhibition and the present catalogue will bring these goals to the attention of the widest possible audience. The historic metropolis on the Mississippi Delta and its premier fine arts museum are national treasures, and none of us can afford to neglect them.

cat. no. 49 (detail)

cat. no. 59 (detail)

# NOTES

1. Primarily among them were George Washington Cable, Kate Chopin, Lafcadio Hearn and Grace King. Twentieth-century authors whose fiction was strongly influenced by a more or less protracted contact with the city of New Orleans were O. Henry, Sherwood Anderson, William Faulkner, Tennessee Williams, Lillian Hellman, Frances Parkinson Keyes and Truman Capote.

2. The classic, but somewhat bowdlerized account of events that filled the first one hundred thirty years of Louisiana's existence as a colony of France and Spain and as an American territorial possession and state is the *History of Louisiana* by the New Orleanian Creole, Charles-Étienne-Arthur Gayarré (1805–1895). The first three volumes were originally published in 1854 (devoted to the years of French and Spanish control) and the fourth in 1866 (treating the period of American domination). A superb general reference work is L.V. Huber's *New Orleans: A Pictorial History*, Gretna, La., 1971 and 1991. Anyone interested in the history of the city in all of its aspects should visit The Historic New Orleans Collection and The Williams Research Center located in New Orleans at 533 Royal Street and 410 Chartres Street in the city's French Quarter, the "Vieux Carré." Issues of *The Historic New Orleans Collection Quarterly* contain a wealth of iconographic and documentary information; some can be consulted on-line at www.hnoc.org. Much useful information on the history of New Orleans can be obtained from the website of the Louisiana Timeline, www.enlou.com/time/timelineindex.htm.

3. When de Soto was making his voyage, Spain was ruled by King Carlos I, otherwise known to history as the Holy Roman Emperor Charles V.

4. The name of the "Father of Waters," as the Mississippi is often called, comes from Algonquin or Ojibwe words meaning "great river."

5. The first two ships arrived in 1719.

6. The Compagnie des Indes Occidentales Françaises had been created in 1664 by Jean Baptiste Colbert in order to regulate commerce between France and territories in the Americas.

7. France's neglect of Louisiana was due principally to its costly involvement in the War of the Spanish Succession, which broke out after Louis XIV placed his grandson, the Duc d'Anjou (Filipo V), on the throne of Spain that until then had been held by the Habsburgs.

8. Mobile was made the capital of *"la Louisianne"* in 1704.

9. Many of the tribes encountered by the French at this time in the lower Mississippi Valley belonged to the western Muskogean family of Amerindians, and they represented for the most part the Choctaw and Chickasaw nations, and related peoples such as the Acolapissa, the Attakapaw, the Bayogoula, the Biloxi, the Chitimacha, the Houma, the Moctobi, the Natchez, the Pascagoula, the Quinipissalive and the Tangipahoa.

10. In terms of age, New Orleans was a relative newcomer among American settlements in comparison to St. Augustine (founded by the Spanish in 1565), Roanoake Island (settled by the English in 1586 but later abandoned) and Santa Fe (established and colonized by the Spanish in 1607).

11. Hence the name of the Crescent City by which New Orleans is still known.

12. The word *bayou* comes from the Choctaw *bayouk*, designating a minor stream or creek. *Tchoupic* was a word meaning muddy. The village of Tchoupitoulas was located about twelve miles above New Orleans.

13. Both belonged to the Choctaw nation.

14. Pénicaut, a ship's carpenter and interpreter who spent twenty-two years in Louisiana between 1699 and 1721, was present. His eyewitness account of events is contained in his unpublished manuscript entitled *"Relation, ou annale véritable de ce qui s'est passé dans le païs de la Louisiane pendant vingt-deux années consecutives...,"* which is preserved in the Bibliothèque nationale de France (Département des manuscrits, inv. no. Fr. 14613).

15. In French, *borgne* means one-eyed, and the name implies that this body of water was not a completely enclosed lake, but rather an inlet of the Gulf.

16. Both were titled concurrently or in turn Comte de Ponchartrain and Comte de Maurepas.

17. By two waterways, the Rigolets and Chef Menteur Pass.

18. It was only in 1900 that a U.S. Army physician discovered that mosquitoes transmitted this often deadly disease. In New Orleans, yellow fever epidemics were not eradicated before 1906.

19. Presumably Governor Le Moyne de Bienville.

20. The islands of the West Indies (Antilles) in the Caribbean.

21. F.-X. de Charlevoix, *Journal d'un voyage fait par ordre du roi dans l'Amérique septentrionale* (ed. by P. Berthiaume), Montréal, 1994, II, pp. 817–819. *"Me voici enfin arrivé dans cette fameuse Ville, qu'on a nommé la Nouvelle Orléans. (…) Cette Ville est la premiere, qu'un des plus grands Fleuves du Monde ait vû s'élever sur ses bords. Si les huit cent [sic] belles Maisons, & les cinq Paroisses, que lui donnoit le Mercure il y a deux ans, se réduisent encore aujourd'hui à une centaine de Barraques, placées sans beaucoup d'ordre; à un grand magazin, bâti de bois; à deux ou trois Maisons, qui ne pareroient pas un Village de France; & à la moitié d'un méchant magazin, qu'on a bien voulu prêter au Seigneur, & dont il avoit à peine pris possession, qu'on voulut l'en faire sortir, pour le loger sous une tente; quel plaisir d'un autre côté de voir croître insensiblement cette future Capitale d'un beau & vaste Pays, & de pouvoir dire, non pas en soupirant, comme le Héros de Virgile en parlant de sa chere Patrie consummée par les flammes:* & les Champs, où fut la Ville de Troye: *mais rempli de l'espérance la mieux fondée; ce lieu sauvage & désert, que les Cannes & les Arbres couvrent encore presque tout entier, sera un jour, & peut-être ce jour n'est-il pas éloigné, une Ville opulente, & la Métropole d'une grande & riche Colonie. / Vous me demanderez, Madame, sur quoi je fonde cette espérance? Je la fonde sur la situation de cette Ville à trente-trois lieuës de la Mer, & au bord d'un Fleuve navigable, qu'on peut remonter jusques-là en vin[g]t-quatre heures: sur la fertilité de son terroir; sur la douceur & la bonté de son climat, par les trente dégrez de latitude-Nord; sur l'industrie de ses Habitans; sur le voisinage du Méxique [sic], où l'on peut aller en quinze jours par Mer; sur celui de la Havane, qui est encore plus proche, des plus belles Isles de l'Amérique & des Colonies Angloises. En faut-il davantage pour rendre une Ville florissante? Rome & Paris n'ont pas eu des commencemens si considérables, n'on pas été bâtis sous de si heureux auspices, & leurs Fondateurs n'ont pas rencontré sur la Seine & sur le Tybre les avantages que nous avons trouvés sur le Micissipi [sic], auprès duquel ces deux Rivieres ne sont que des ruisseaux.."*

22. For the Duc de Bourbon.

23. For the Duc de Chartres, the oldest son of the Duc d'Orléans.

24. For the Prince de Conti.

25. For the Duc du Maine, one of the legitimized sons of Louis XIV and his mistress, Madame de Montespan.

26. For the French royal family.

27. For another of Louis XIV's legitimized sons, the Comte de Toulouse, Grand Admiral of France.

28. Because of flooding, some houses built in the old Colonial French style were erected on piles, and most were relatively simple in their architecture. As years went by and fortunes grew, private houses became larger, more elaborate and more elegant.

29. Originally under de Pauger's orders, they had major disputes with him and his successor Ignace François Broutin. Jean Pierre de Lassus was recalled in 1727 for insubordination. He did not go immediately to France, preferring to stay for a time on the island of Saint-Domingue, where in 1732 he married the daughter of a wealthy planter. After the death of his wife, he returned to France in 1740, served as a Capitoul in Toulouse, went back to Saint-Domingue to oversee his plantation (1751–1753), married the governess of his children and ended his life in a house in Paris on the rue de Vaugirard.

30. It is thus designated on the *Plan de la Ville / La Nouvelle Orléans / Capitale de la Province de la Louisiane* in the Historic New Orleans Collection (acc. no. 1939.8). For a color illustration of a detail of this print, which was made by a certain Thiery and shows the layout of the city as it appeared in 1755, see "In Search of Yesterday's Gardens: Landscapes of 19th-Century New Orleans," *The Historic New Orleans Collection Quarterly*, XIX, spring 2001, p. 2.

31. They were in charge of filling the street lamps with fish oil or bear and pelican grease.

32. Under the French, architects in New Orleans made extensive use of timber combined with brick or *bousillage* (mud mixed with animal hair and Spanish moss). The grander houses often had hipped, shingled roofs, thin columns or posts, verandas (*galeries*), multiple windows, and some of the doors were fitted with glass panes. Many dwellings were elevated on brick pillars, and if they had more than one story, the ground floor behind them was used for storage, substructures such as basements being unsuitable for the water-impregnated terrain. Living quarters where valuables were kept were found on the upper floors. Very few of the early French houses or cottages have survived, due to the climate, termites and the degradable nature of the materials used to build them.

33. Those of 1788 and 1794 were particularly devastating.

34. The inscription and legend on Thierry's map (fig. 21) reads as follows: *"PLAN DE LA VILLE / LA NOUVELLE / ORLEANS CAPITALE / DE LA PROVINCE / DE LA LOÜISIANE / fut découverte en 1680. par Mᵉ Cavalier / de rouen et par le pere hennepin Récolle / ayant remonté le fleuve S. laurent / au travers de tous les lac qu'il traver / sé il arrivenen par, La riviere des ili / nois*

cat. no. 64 (detail)

*jusqu'au fleuve Missisipi, il ny / avoit que quelque petit fort, ce fue / an 1720. que Mr le duc D'Orleans Ré / gent y fit rantporter vne colonie / fit Bâtire une ville dit la nouvelle / Orleans du Règne de sa Maj.té Louis xv. / Cette ville a 600 T. de long et 335 T. de / large les principales maisons sont Bâ / ties de Brique et Couvertes de tuille, les / autres maisons son Bâ / ties de Brique et Couvertes de tuille, les autres maisons sont Bâties de bois cou- / vertes de tuile, les autres maisons sont Bâties de bois cou. / vertes de méme Cette province est trés fertille / TABLE / les jesuites / A. les Capucin B. la prison C. le corps / de Garde D. maison du procur'ure / General E. les cazernes F. pavillion / des officies G. les arsenauxs H. / les magazin du Roi I. maison du Garde magazin K. maison du doien / des conseillers L. maison du major / M. maison de l'aide major N. mai / son de Brosse un de plus riche O. jar / din des plantes du Roy p. vielle mai / son des Religieuse Q. hopital R. nouvel / le maison des Religieuse S. maison de / pensionnaires T. ancien Gouverne= / ment….. Echelle de 100. Toises / Dessiné mis au net par le sieur Thierry / Geographe, Ancien dessinateur au Bu= / reau des fortifications et Bâtiment du Roy / 1755."*

35. The much harassed Le Moyne de Bienville's only predecessor was François Marie Sauvolle de Valantry. In all, d'Iberville served four terms in this post (1701–1713, 1716–1717, 1718–1724 and 1733–1743). When he finally relinquished the office, he moved to Paris and remained there until his death. Other French governors of the Louisiana territory were Antoine Laumet, called La Mothe Cadillac (1713–1716); Jean Michel de Lépinay (1717–1718); Pierre Dugé de Boisbriant (1724–1726); Étienne Périer (1726–1733); the Marquis de Vaudreuil Cavagnal (1743–1753); Louis Billouart de Kerlerec (1753–1763); Jean Jacques Blaise d'Abbadie (1763–1765); and the interim commandant, Charles Philippe Aubry (1765–1766).

36. The Natchez Revolt began in 1729, and the natives were joined by nearly three hundred black slaves owned by the Compagnie des Indes.

37. The governor at the time was Antoine Laumet de La Mothe de Cadillac (1658–1730). Prévost's Manon may have been inspired by a real-life deportee, Marianne Lescau.

38. *Hôpitaux.*

39. *Filles perdues* or *filles publiques.*

40. Le Havre, Rochefort, La Rochelle, Bordeaux, etc.

41. Louis de Rouvroy, Duc de Saint-Simon, *Mémoires complets et authentiques*, Paris, 1905, XI, pp. 284–285: *"A force de tourner et retourner ce Mississipi de tout sens, pour ne pas dire à force de jouer des gobelets sous ce nom, on eut envie, à l'exemple des Anglois, de faire dans ces vastes pays des établissements effectifs. Ce fut pour le peupler qu'on fit à Paris et dans tout le royaume des enlèvements de gens sans aveu et des mendiants valides, hommes et femmes, et de quantité de créatures publiques. Si cela eût été exécuté avec sagesse, discernement, les mesures et les précautions nécessaires, cela auroit rempli l'objet qu'on se proposoit, et soulagé Paris et les provinces d'un lourd fardeau inutile et souvent dangereux; mais on s'y prit à Paris et partout ailleurs avec tant de violence et tant de friponnerie encore pour enlever qui on vouloit, que cela excita de grands murmures. On n'avoit pas eu le moindre soin de pourvoir à la subsistance de tant de malheureux sur les chemins, ni même dans les lieux destinés à leur embarquement; on les enfermoit les nuits dans des granges sans leur donner à manger, et dans les fossés des lieux où il s'en trouvoit, d'où ils ne pussent sortir. Ils faisoient des cris qui excitoient la pitié et l'indignation; mais les aumônes n'y pouvant suffire, moins encore le peu que les conducteurs leur donnoient: [cela] en fit mourir partout un nombre effroyable. Cette inhumanité, jointe à la barbarie des conducteurs, à une violence d'espèce jusqu'alors inconnue et à la friponnerie d'enlèvement de gens qui n'étoient point de la qualité prescrite, mais dont on se vouloit défaire, en disant le mot à l'oreille et mettant de l'argent dans la main des préposés aux enlèvements, [de sorte] que les bruits s'élevèrent avec tant de fracas, et avec des termes et des tons si imposants qu'on trouva que la chose ne se pouvoit plus soutenir. Il s'en étoit embarqué quelques troupes, qui ne furent guère mieux traitées dans la traversée. Ce qui ne l'étoit pas encore fut lâché et devint ce qu'il put, et on cessa d'enlever personne. Law, regardé comme l'auteur de ces enlèvements, devint fort odieux, et M. le duc d'Orléans eut à se repentir de s'y être laissé entraîner."*

42. Slaves imported into French Louisiana usually came from Senegal and the Gambian region of West Africa (many belonged to the Bambara, Foulah, Mandigo and Wolof groups), as well as from Guinea, the Gold Coast and Angola. They were sent to the colony by the Compagnie Royale du Sénégal, either directly from the African coast (via the islands of the Cape Verde archipelago) or by way of islands in the Caribbean. Some were part of the Benin, Ewe, Fon, Kabye, Yoruba and Kongo tribes.

43. Coming from the Rhineland and parts of Switzerland, they were sent to Louisiana by the Compagnie des Indes and were originally settled in an area along the Mississippi that came to be known as *La Côte des Allemands* (the German Coast, now in St. John the Baptist, St. James and St. Charles Parishes).

44. The conditions in which they lived and their treatment led some of them to flee into the nearby forests and bayou lands where they established Maroon Camps, and some were helped by local natives. The first such escapes were recorded in 1725.

45. Foremost among them were the Jesuits and the Capuchins, who were constantly at odds with each other on matters of precedence and territory.

46. It became the seat of a diocese itself in 1795, upon the arrival of Bishop Luís Ignacio Maria Peñalver y Cárdenas.

47. The first four familes arrived in Louisiana in 1764.

48. Nova Scotia, Newfoundland and Prince Edward Island.

49. The entire region of southern Louisiana which these hardy people occupied is today called Acadiana, and their descendants number almost half a million.

50. Antonio de Ulloa (1765–1768), Alejandro O'Reilly (1769–1770), Luís Unzaga y Amezage (1770–1776), Bernardo de Gálvez (1776–1785), Esteban Rodrigues Miró (1785–1791), the Flemish Baron François Louis de Carondelet et Hoyelles (1791–1797), Manuel Luís Gayoso de Lemos (1797–1801), Nicolás María Vidal and Sebastián Basa Calvo (1799–1801) and Manuel Juan de Salcedo (1801–1803).

51. The acts and deliberations of the governing body of the Cabildo over the entire period of the Spanish domination of colonial Louisiana (1769–1803) were examined in the 1930s by scholars of the Work Projects Administration. By August 1939 they had produced a typewritten Digest of these archives, which is available in chronological and thematic form on line at http://www.nutrias.org/~nopl/inv/digest/digest.htm.

52. The New Orleanians actually petitioned Louis XV to reassert his control over the colony, but to no avail.

53. The classification system for people of mixed ancestry in mid nineteenth-century Louisiana is found in F.L. Olmstead, *The Cotton Kingdom: A Traveller's Observations on Cotton and Slavery in the American Slave States* (ed. by A.M. Schlesinger), New York, 1962, pp. 228–229.

54. Later Spanish administrations periodically attempted to close the river to American traffic.

55. The large number of canals and other drainage systems that have been laid out in New Orleans over time have become progressively more sophisticated. However, they have never really protected the city from the drenching, monsoon-like rains that often afflict it or the floods resulting from the breaching of the levees. The destruction following Hurricane Katrina was only the most recent episode in a long succession of devastating catastrophes.

56. By the 1850s, cast iron.

57. On Rillieux, see notes 58, 95, 147, 159 and 162.

58. After Rillieux's death, his widow donated the property to her son-in-law, Jacques Fréret. On June 2, 1801, the latter sold it to Joseph Faurie, who resided there and used it as his place of business. On January 26, 1805, it was acquired by Julien Poydras (see note 60), who made it the headquarters for the newly organized Banque de la Louisiane, of which he was president. The bank was the first financial institution that operated in all of the Louisiana Territory. Extensive renovations of the building at that time included the addition of a wrought iron balcony railing bearing the bank's monogram. The institution outlived its charter, and in 1820, the liquidators sold the property to Martin Gordon, a socially prominent Virginian who was clerk of the United States District Court and under President Andrew Jackson served as Collector of the Port of New Orleans. In 1841 the Gordon family lost the building to the Citizens' Bank, which sold it at auction to Judge Alonzo Morphy, a former state attorney general and a member of Louisiana's Supreme Court. His son, the chess champion Paul Charles Morphy (see note 95), died in in 1884 in the house, which passed to his brothers and sisters. One of the property's subsequent owners was William Ratcliffe Irby, who in 1920 donated it to Tulane University. It was leased to a number of tenants, among them Owen Edward Brennan, who converted it into the restaurant that still occupies it. It was seriously damaged by fire but was restored to its original elegance. In 1984, the Brennan family, the pre-eminent *restaurateurs* in New Orleans, purchased the building.

59. Almonester was born in Mayrena del Alcor, near Seville.

60. Another of the city's outstanding early philanthropists was the Frenchman Julien Poydras de Lalande (1746–1824), who in his youth joined the French royal navy, was captured by the British, escaped to Saint-Domingue and eventually made his way to Spanish New Orleans. There he began to build a fortune as a traveling merchant, a banker and a planter. He even made a reputation for himself as a man of letters. (His publications include *L'Épître à Don Bernard de Galvez,... intandant [sic] général de la province de la Louisianne: le Dieu et les nayades du fleuve St Louis*, New Orleans, 1777; and *La Prise du morne du Bâton-Rouge par Monseigneur de Galvez*, New Orleans, 1779.) The father of Louisiana's educational system, Poydras played an active role in politics after the Louisiana Purchase and in the early days of statehood. He died on his estate at Pointe Coupée, after endowing several orphanages and the Charity Hospital and having tried in vain to free his slaves.

61. Almonester's Iglesia de San Luís, which had two hexagonal domed bell towers with a spire between them, was re-dedicated as a Cathedral in 1795, when New Orleans became an official diocese separate from that of Havana. In 1819, a central bell tower was added to it by Benjamin Latrobe, and in 1850 J.N.B. de Pouilly remodeled the cathedral inside and out. The Presbytère was completed only in 1813, and its ground-level spaces were rented out to shopkeepers. The architect in charge of Almonester's project was Gilbert Guillemard. Both the Cabildo and the

Presbytère are part of the Louisiana State Museum.

62. To isolate the patients and avoid contamination, the San Lázaro leprosarium was built far outside the city limits near the Bayou Gentilly and Lake Ponchartrain.

63. The largely honorific post of royal standard-bearer for public ceremonies which could be given to a ranking member of the Cabildo, second in importance only to the governor and the *alcaldes ordinarios.*

64. It remained so until the middle of the nineteenth century. In 1819, Benjamin Latrobe described it as "neglected, the fences ragged, and in many places open. Part of it is let for a depot of firewood, paving stones are heaped up in it, and along the whole of the side next the river is a row of mean booths in which dry goods are sold...." (E.C. Carter II et al., eds., *The Journals of Benjamin Henry Latrobe 1799–1820, from Philadelphia to New Orleans*, III, New Haven and London, 1980, p. 173).

65. The lower story and entresol of this building were later rented out to shopkeepers, and the upper floor served as the Hôtel Trémoulet.

66. Her second husband was the French consul to Spanish New Orleans, Jean Baptiste Castillon.

67. In October 1795, George Washington's envoy to Spain, Thomas Pinckney, negotiated the Treaty of San Lorenzo with the Spanish minister Manuel Godoy giving Americans full navigation rights on the Mississippi and a right to deposit their goods at New Orleans so they could be transferred to ocean-going craft.

68. Although it contains a rather negative view of New Orleans, François Marie Perrin du Lac's *Voyage dans les deux Louisianes et chez les nations sauvages du Missouri, par les Etats-Unis, l'Ohio et les provinces qui le bordent en 1801, 1802 et 1803* (Paris, 1805) is a good source of information on the city during the last years of Spanish rule. The author, a French émigré from Saint-Domingue, described it as filthy, foul-smelling and unhealthy, the officials corrupt, the clergy debauched and the Creoles arrogant and hedonistic.

69. Quoted in *"A Great and Growing City": New Orleans in the Era of the Louisiana Purchase*, accessible on the website for an exhibition held in 2003 at the City Archives and Special Collections department of the New Orleans Public Library: http://nutrias.org/exhibits/purchase/lapintro.htm.

70. Her brother, Jean Noël d'Estréhan, was the owner of a sugar cane plantation. Now the property of the Historical Society of the River Road, it is featured in scenes of the 1994 movie *Interview with the Vampire*, which is based on a novel by New Orleans writer Anne Rice.

71. Another planter, Valcour Aimé, constructed the first sugar refinery in Louisiana on his plantation in St. James Parish.

72. See note 2.

73. In 1805, former Vice President Aaron Burr formed a cabal of politicians, army officers and planters whose objective was to set up an independent nation in the central and western parts of the North American continent, including Spanish Texas, and New Orleans was to be their capital. The plot was revealed to Thomas Jefferson; Burr was arrested and tried for treason in Richmond, Virginia, but was ultimately acquitted for lack of evidence.

74. When as many as five hundred field hands took up cane knives, axes and firearms in St. John the Baptist and St. Charles Parishes after one of their number killed the son of a planter and they felt themselves in jeopardy, they burned and pillaged a number of nearby plantations. They began to move on New Orleans, where a number of whites in the area had fled for protection. Units of Federal troops, militiamen and a group of vigilantes put down the rebellion. A number of slaves were executed, and their heads were displayed along the River Road to discourage future revolts.

75. It remained so until the seat of state government was transferred to Baton Rouge in 1849.

76. In French, a *faubourg* was an inhabited area that was *"fors le bourg,"* i.e. beyond the walls or gates of a city.

77. They and their peripheral offshoots remained quasi-independent until they were annexed and incorporated into greater New Orleans in the 1850s.

78. His great-grandfather, Jean François Philippe de Marigny (1685–1728), arrived in New Orleans just after it was founded by Bienville, and his grandfather, Antoine Enguerrand Philippe de Marigny (1722–1779), was an officer in the Spanish infantry. His father, Pierre Enguerrand Philippe, played host for a month to refugee members of the French royal family (Louis-Philippe d'Orléans, the future King of the French, and his brothers).

79. It has been claimed that Bernard de Marigny introduced "craps" into the gambling parlors of New Orleans and into the American vocabulary. This game of chance was given its name because of the position of the players, whose bodies' amphibian-like positions resembled splayed toads (*crapauds*). On de Marigny, see E. Larocque Tinker, *Creole City, Its Past and Its People*, New York, London and Toronto, 1953, pp. 3–69, and idem, *The Palingenesis of Craps*, New York, 1933.

80. The Ponchartrain Railroad, the second oldest rail line in the United States, was completed there in 1831.

81. One of the most remarkable of them was a free woman of color, Rosette Rochon (1767–1863), the daughter of a French shipbuilder and a freed slave. She arrived in New Orleans from Saint-Domingue around 1796, and became the *placée* of the tailor Joseph Forstall. She acquired considerable wealth and invested in real estate, both in the old French Quarter and in the Faubourg Marigny. Her house on Pauger Street is today a museum.

82. The old rue des Remparts.

83. It has long been the major center of African-American life in New Orleans.

84. Created around 1730 as the Place des Nègres, and later called the Place du Cirque and the Place Beauregard, Congo Square is today part of the much larger Louis Armstrong Park. The musical significance of the square was written about early in the nineteenth century by Benjamin Latrobe, who described in detail what he witnessed there in February of 1819 but failed to comprehend its significance. He found the music of the blacks as "villainous" as the chants he heard in St. Louis Cathedral: "...approaching the common I heard a most extraordinary noise, which I supposed to proceed from some horse Mill, the horses trampling on a wooden floor. I found however on emerging from the houses, onto the common, that it proceeded from a croud [sic] of 5 or 600 persons assembled in an open space or public square. I went to the spot and crouded near enough to see the performance. All those who were engaged in the business seemed to be *blacks*....they were formed into circular groups in the midst of four of which, which I examined (but there were more of them) was a ring, the largest not 10 feet in diameter. In the first were two women dancing. They held each a coarse handkerchief extended by the corners in their hands, and *set* to each other in a miserably dull and slow figure, hardly moving their feet or bodies. The music consisted of two drums and a stringed instrument. An old man sat astride of a Cylindrical drum about a foot in diameter, and beat it with incredible quickness with the edge of his hand and fingers. The other drum was an open staved thing held between the knees and beaten in the same manner. They made an incredible noise. The most curious instrument [the ancestor of the banjo] however was a stringed instrument which no doubt was imported from Africa. On the top of the finger board was the rude figure of a Man in a sitting posture, and two pegs behind him to which the strings were fastened. The body was a Calabash. It was played upon by a very little old man, apparently 80 or 90 Years old. The women squalled out a burthen to the playing, at intervals, consisting of two notes, as the Negroes working in our cities respond to the Song of their leader. Most of the circles contained the same sort of dancers. One was larger, in which a ring of a dozen women walked, by way of dancing, round the music in the Center. But the instruments were of different construction. One, which from the color of the wood seemed new, consisted of a block cut into something of the form of a cricket but with a long and deep mortice down the Center. This thing made a considerable noise, being beaten lustily on the side by a short stick. In the same Orchestra was a square drum looking like a stool, which made an abominable loud noise: also a Calabash with a round hole in it, the hole studded with brass nails which was beaten by a woman with two short sticks. A man sung an uncouth song to the dancing which I suppose was in some African language, for it was not French, and the Women screamed a detestable burthen on one single note. The allowed amusements of Sunday, have, it seems, perpetuated here, those of Africa among its inhabitants. I have never seen any thing more brutally savage, and at the same time dull and stupid than this whole exhibition. Continuing my walk about a mile along the Canal [see note 130], and returning after Sunset near the same spot, the noise was still heard. There was not the least disorder among the croud, nor do I learn, on enquiry, that these weekly meetings of the negroes have ever produced any mischief." (E.C. Carter II et al., 1980, op.cit., pp. 203–204).

85. G. King, *New Orleans, the Place and the People*, New York, 1922, p. 340.

86. In the Fon and Ewe languages, a word meaning "spirit." Vodou was banned after the arrival of the Creole exiles from the Caribbean, because its leaders were accused of inciting sedition among slaves.

87. The life of this legendary woman who made her living as a hairdresser in the French Quarter is shrouded in mystery. It has been claimed that she was the daughter of a planter from Saint-Domingue, Charles Leveaux, and a mixed black and Amerindian woman, Marguerite Darcantel. But she may well have been the daughter of a free man of color, Charles Laveau, who worked as a carpenter for the New Orleans Conseil de Ville in the early 1800s. Historian Ina Fandrich recently proposed that her mother was a free mulatto woman named Marguerite who gave birth to her in New Orleans in 1801 and that her grandmother was from the Congo. Since her death, her fame has grown, and she remains a cult personality to this day.

88. Plans were laid out by the architect and surveyor Barthélémy Lafon, who subdivided large portions of what is today the central business district and the Lower Garden District. His successor in these endeavors was Benjamin Buisson.

89. The Faubourgs Delord, Saulet, de La Course, de l'Annonciation, des Religieuses (named for the Ursulines who originally owned the plantation), Lafayette, Delassize, Plaisance, Delachaise, Saint-Joseph, Avart and Bouligny. Other portions of the Faubourg Sainte-Marie—Hurstville, Bloomingdale, Burtheville, Greenville and Frieburg—were located on terrain that had once been part of

cat. no. 87 (detail)

the plantation of Étienne de Boré (see notes 95 and 140). Audubon Park, Tulane University and Loyola University sit on land once part of the plantation of de Boré's son-in-law, Pierre Foucher.

90. They had been acquired between 1726 and 1743. When the order was expelled from the colony in 1763, the plantation was separated into six lots, which were sold to various private individuals.

91. This part of uptown New Orleans occupied the site of the old plantation of Louis Césaire Le Breton, which later belonged to Louis-Barthélémy de Macarty, the son of the sixth mayor of New Orleans. In 1833 it was divided into lots and sold to a consortium of owners; it was later named Carrollton for General William Carroll, who had fought with Andrew Jackson at the Battle of New Orleans.

92. The issue of the ownership of the Batture Sainte-Marie, a shoal formed by silt from the river, was hotly debated when New Orleans became part of the United States. When it was not covered with water, it was used as free anchorage by boats and rafts and therefore had enormous commercial potential. It also supplied sand and dirt for local inhabitants. It was thus important that it be considered by the legal courts as public property.

93. The food market near the levee to the left of the Place d'Armes as one faces the river was originally a place where Amerindians came to sell produce and game to French colonists. Butcher stands were built there under the Spanish regime. In 1811 arose an elegant structure created by Arsène Lacarrière Latour, but it was destroyed by a hurricane the following year. In 1813 it was replaced by an arcaded and columned market designed by the city surveyor Jacques Tanesse. For many years the locals called it the "Halles des boucheries," and in 1822 it was enlarged by Joseph Pilié and Jean-Félix Pinson to include vegetable, fruit and fish stands. Later in the nineteenth century facilities for a dry goods emporium were added. It still exists on Decatur Street (the former rue de la Levée), but in a much abridged form. It came to be known as the French Market. It is still the home of the famed Café du Monde, where locals and tourists alike flock to eat *beignets* and drink strong coffee flavored with chicory.

94. More duels were fought in New Orleans than in any other American metropolis. Creole honor, which was exquisitely sensitive to any perceived slight, could be injured by a trivial word, a side glance or a gesture, and a challenge might easily ensue. The Dueling Oaks in what is now City Park, at the top of Esplanade Avenue where the New Orleans Museum of Art sits, was a favorite site at which *affaires d'honneur* could be settled with firearms (pistols and even shotguns), bowie knives, sabers, rapiers or *colichemardes* (long swords with broad blades tapering into a slender, lozenge-shaped tip). Duels were sometimes provoked so that a so-called aggrieved party could display his fighting skills. Among the most frequent duelists were a United States Congressman Émile La Sère; Bernard de Marigny (reputed to have fought nineteen duels beneath The Oaks, seven of them the result of challenges he received when he escorted his second wife to a ball); and the finest New Orleans swordsman and marksman, the Spaniard José (Pepe) Llulla. Among the fatalities were the French *émigré* Marcel Dauphin (said to have been killed by a friend of Robespierre, a fencing master named Bonneval); Micajah Green Lewis, secretary to Governor Claiborne (1804); and George Augustus Waggaman (1782–1843), Louisiana's Secretary of State between 1830 and 1832 and a United States Senator from Louisiana between 1831 and 1835. Only in the 1850s did the laws prohibiting dueling begin to be enforced in the city.

95. The first Cimetière Saint-Louis, in which all the tombs are above ground, is the oldest and most interesting of the surviving "Cities of the Dead" in New Orleans. Located beyond the Ramparts on the northern border of the Vieux Carré, it was laid out on orders of the Cabildo after the epidemic and fire of 1788, replacing the much older and largely disaffected Cimetière Saint-Pierre at the corner of the rues Saint-Pierre and de Bourgogne, in which burials were underground. In it are buried two of the wives of Governor Claiborne, New Orleans' first mayor Étienne de Boré, the architect Benjamin Latrobe, the wealthy Creole planter Bernard de Marigny de Mandeville, (possibly) the *Vodou* priestess Marie Laveau (in the de Glapion family crypt; on Laveau, see above, note 87), members of the Musson family (including Edgar Degas' Rillieux great-grandparents, his maternal uncle Michel Musson and his first cousin and sister-in-law, Estelle Musson Balfour De Gas), the chess champion Paul Morphy and Homer Plessy (1862–1925), the plaintiff in the landmark 1896 Supreme Court case, Plessy vs. Ferguson, which declared separate as being equal.

96. The evocative novels, short stories and guidebooks of George Washington Cable and Lafcadio Hearn allow us to imagine today what this all but extinct tongue sounded like in old New Orleans. See especially L. Hearn, *Gombo zhèbes, Little Dictionary of Creole Proverbs* (Selected from six Creole dialects. Translated into French and into English, with notes, complete index to subjects and some brief remarks upon the Creole idioms of Louisiana), New York, n.d. [c. 1885] and E. Larocque Tinker, *Gombo, the Creole Dialect of Louisiana, together with a Bibliography*, Worcester, Mass., 1936.

97. Colonel J.R. Creecy, *Scenes in the South, and Other Miscellaneous Pieces*, Washington, D.C., 1860; quoted in U.B. Phillips, *Life and Labor in the Old South*, Boston, 1929, p. 150.

98. Louisiana *andouille* has absolutely nothing to do with the French sausage of the same name, which is made of pigs' entrails and is very strongly flavored but not at all spicy.

99. The word made its first appearance in print in Louisiana in 1872. Its etymology is controversial. For some, it is a combination of the French word for ham, *jambon*, and a West African word for rice, *yaya*, two of the main ingredients of the dish. However, the word does exist in the Occitan language of southern France. The Provençal poet Félix Peise uses it in a fable after La Fontaine published at Draguignan in 1873, "La Testo et la coua de la serp" (The Head and the Tail of the Serpent): "*…Aqueou jambalaia me remette en memori / Ce qu'arribet à un vieilho ser, / Quand sa coua vouguet ave l'er / De passar per davant….*"

100. *Filé* powder is made of dried and ground sassafras leaves; it was widely used by the native American peoples of Louisiana like the Choctaw. Traditionally, it was a flavor enhancer and thickener of gumbos in seasons during which okra was unavailable, and for traditionalists of Louisiana cooking, it is a cardinal sin to mix the two. Creations passed off as Creole or Cajun—blackened fish and meat, the hodgepodges of spice mixtures with additions of garlic and onion powder and that hybrid beast called the "turducken"—are of recent vintage and have nothing historically authentic about them. But no cooking was meant to stagnate, that of Louisiana perhaps least of all.

101. In Bantu languages, the word *ngombo* means okra, a vegetable that is often a key component of this hearty soup which has only the vaguest kinship with the French fish stew, bouillabaisse. By the third quarter of the nineteenth century, the dish was known in Paris. In the October 18, 1874 issue of the magazine he edited, *La Dernière Mode, Gazette du Monde et de la Famille*, the Symbolist poet Stéphane Mallarmé published a recipe for a "Gombo févis (Biscus excellentus)…" sent to him by "Une Dame Créole." (S. Mallarmé, *Oeuvres complètes*, Paris, Bibliothèque de la Pléiade, 1965, p. 770).

102. A primary reference work for the history of Creole cooking is J. Folse et al., *The Encyclopedia of Cajun & Creole Cuisine*, Gonzales, La., 2004.

103. A tax-supported public school system was created only in 1841.

104. He designed a pump station near the French Market and a system of wooden pipes providing water throughout the city. Until they were completed in 1823, untreated river water had to be delivered to individual households in the traditional way, i.e. in hogsheads transported on horse-drawn wagons.

105. See E.C. Carter II et al., 1980, op. cit., pp. 206–208. For another account of life at this time in New Orleans, see Arnaud Berquin-Duvallon, *Vue de la colonie espagnole du Mississippi, ou des provinces de Louisiane et Floride occidentale, en l'année 1802, par un observateur résident sur les lieux*, Paris, 1803.

106. Ibid., p. 209. During Latrobe's visit, he would have encountered the second Madame de Marigny, née Anna Matilda Morales (d. 1866), the daughter of the Spanish Intendant of West Florida and former *alcalde* of New Orleans.

107. Almack's Assembly Rooms was a London club in King Street which welcomed both men and women.

108. Quadroons were usually one-quarter African and three-quarters white.

109. Frances Trollope, *Domestic Manners of the Americans*, London, 1997, p. 16.

110. Presumably the Théâtre d'Orléans.

111. The *plaçage* system apparently operated in New Orleans until the Civil War.

112. In 1792, with the permission of the Cabildo, Philibert Farge constructed a dance hall for whites, the Salle Condé, on the site of a market at the corner of "Las Calles Du Maine y Condé." It had boxes for chaperones and girls too young to dance, as well as an adjoining game room. On Saturday nights free blacks and people of color were allowed to use the hall. Jacques Bernard Coquet and Joseph Antoine Boniquet, a pair of entrepreneurial refugees from Saint-Domingue, were granted the concession for these dances which became known as the *Bals tricolores*. They were in effect precursors for the Quadroon Balls and were publicly advertised.

113. The Quadroon Balls were organized for and sometimes by a group of free matriarchs of color, the *Société du Cordon bleu* (hence the alternate name for these events, the *Bals du Cordon bleu*). There they could present their daughters as if they were debutantes to prospective white lovers who would take them as mistresses for a price and set them up in style. Admission fees were high to keep out the riff-raff.

114. Translated and cited in G.W. Pierson, *Tocqueville in America*, Baltimore and London, 1996, pp. 628–629.

115. Ibid., p. 631.

116. On the development of the pictorial arts in New Orleans, see Chapter XLI of J.S. Kendall, *History of New Orleans*, Chicago, 1920, 3 vols.

117. Other portraits by him in the same collection record the features of other Louisiana Creoles.

118. The original manuscript, bound in six volumes, was published in Paris in 1737 by Philippe Nicolas Lottin (d. 1751) under the title *Nouvelles poésies spirituelles et morales sur les plus beaux airs de la musique française et italienne*. It contains the *Fables* of Jean de La Fontaine. The only known copy of the publication is preserved in the Bibliothèque de l'Arsenal in Paris. In 1998, the Ursulines of New Orleans transferred many of their archives to the Historic New Orleans Collection. Among them was an incomplete manuscript of *Nouvelles poésies* in four volumes that was drafted in Paris during the lenten season of the year 1736 by a certain "C.D." It contains two hundred ninety-four religious scores written by more than thirty French and Italian Baroque composers. In 1754, this manuscript was presented to the Ursulines in New Orleans by a "Monsieur Nicolet." (This information was kindly supplied by Mary Lee B. Harris, Director of Development, Ursuline Academy, New Orleans. See A.E. Lemmon, "Ursuline Collection Yields Rare Music Manuscript," *The Historic New Orleans Collection Quarterly*, XVIII, fall 2000, p. 10.)

119. In it were works by André Campra, Louis Nicolas Clérambault, François Couperin, Henry Desmarets, Jean Baptiste Lully, Louis Marchand, Marin Marais and Michel Pignolet de Monteclair.

120. See J.S. Kendall, *The Golden Age of the New Orleans Theater*, Baton Rouge, 1952.

121. Such as *Sylvain* by André Ernest Modeste Grétry and Jean François Marmontel, which premiered in the city on May 22, 1796.

122. The building survived until 1868, when it was consumed in a fire.

123. Mary Elizabeth Lyell, the wife of the Scottish geologist Charles Lyell (1797–1875) with whom she visited the United States, commented on an evening they spent at the French opera in February of 1846: "It is a very pretty little theatre & I hardly ever saw so many handsome faces. The Creoles are considered remarkably handsome & it is quite true. The original race came from Normandy, but they have improved here, it is so fine a style of face. They dress with true Parisian taste, but their manner of dressing the hair is *exquisite*, a great variety, each fit for a Grecian statue. Very, very long hair they must have, with such bright coloured ribbon, or a single flower, or pins stuck in. They are not so thin as American women are in general. We had a little French Vaudeville, some medium dancing & an act of the Freischutz. That was all we staid for. The theatre is very pretty, a gallery for the Negroes pretty well filled & another gallery & boxes for the quadroons." (Quoted in L.G. Wilson, *Lyell in America: Transatlantic Geology, 1841–1853*, Baltimore, 1998, p. 224.)

124. Caldwell was also a formidable businessman who did much to develop the Anglo-American Faubourg Sainte-Marie to the detriment of the Vieux Carré and the Faubourg Marigny. He and his partner Samuel J. Peters brought gas lighting to New Orleans. For a time, he served as a member of the City Council and the state legislature.

125. The second St. Charles Theater was again destroyed by fire, in 1899.

126. Mrs. Trollope described the excellent accommodations she and her traveling companions were witness to on board a river paddle steamer: "The innumerable steam boats, which are the stage coaches and fly waggons of this land of lakes and rivers, are totally unlike any I had seen in Europe, and greatly superior to them. The fabrics which I think they most resemble in appearance, are the floating baths (les bains Vigier) at Paris.…The room to which the double line of windows belongs, is a very handsome apartment; before each window a neat little cot is arranged in such a manner as to give its drapery the air of a window curtain. This room is called the gentlemen's cabin, and their exclusive right to it is somewhat uncourteously insisted upon. The breakfast, dinner, and supper are laid in this apartment, and the lady passengers are permitted to take their meals there."

127. In May 1857, when the twenty-one year old cub riverboat pilot Samuel Clemens (Mark Twain) arrived in New Orleans aboard the riverboat *Crescent City*, his senses went "reeling with delight. The market was as much a display of people as of products, their multi-toned voices, their variety of skin tones, their diversity of languages: 'groups of Italians, French, Dutch, Irish, Spaniards, Indians, Chinese, Americans, English, and the Lord knows how many more different kinds of people.' To him, the variety was an asset, the differences desirable, the community both tactilely sensual and raucously harmonious, his first experience with the American marketplace as a polyglot, multi-ethnic epitome of the national culture. His sheer pleasure in New Orleans was a step toward his gradual transcendence of Missouri slave culture provincialism and his increasing discomfort with xenophobia." (F. Kaplan, *The Singular Mark Twain: A Biography*, New York, 2005, pp. 65–66).

128. The twenty-seven year old French *restaurateur* Antoine Alciatoire worked two years in New York before settling in New Orleans. He was a chef in the kitchens of the St. Charles Hotel before opening a boarding house on St. Louis Street, the Pension Alciatoire. He married, founded a family and opened his restaurant on the same street in 1840. He moved to the restaurant's present location in 1868. In 1874, he returned to France where he died. His wife assumed direction of the restaurant and after an apprenticeship in France, their son Jules, the creator of Oysters Rockefeller, later took charge of the business. Antoine's is still owned by Alciatoire's descendants. The second oldest restaurant in the city is Tujague's on Decatur Street. It was opened in 1856 by two natives of Bordeaux, the French Market butcher Guillaume Tujague (d. 1912) and his wife Marie Abadie. Originally they served breakfast and lunch to dock workers, market laborers and seamen. At the turn of the twentieth century Tujague's was acquired by Philibert Guichet, who was born in Lafourche Parish. In 1914, he joined forces with Jean-Dominique Castet, and the two bought another famous New Orleans eatery, Bégué's, which had been established nearby in 1863 by Hippolyte Bégué and his well-known German wife, Elizabeth Kettenring (d. 1906). For many years it was operated by Castet's widow, Clémence Castet. Her heirs sold it in 1982. Another famous restaurant, Galatoire's, was a relative newcomer to the New Orleans gastronomic scene, having been founded on Bourbon Street in 1905 by a native of the village of Pardies in Aquitaine. Other highly reputed dining establishments were in the largest of New Orleans' hotels, such as the St. Louis and the St. Charles.

129. On this subject, see *Historical Sketch Book and Guide to New Orleans and Environs*, New York, 1885, pp. 84–91. In his introduction to this major travel resource, the publisher, Will H. Coleman, acknowledged his indebtedness to "many brilliant and interesting sketches, stories and descriptions, written at different times during the last thirty years for the press of New Orleans, by such eminent historians, littérateurs and journalists as the following: Hon. Charles Gayarré, Judge Alexander Walker, Charles E. Whitney, Mrs. Field ("Catherine Cole"), John and Charles Dimetry, Lafcadio Hearn [the guidebook's principal contributor], Marion A. Baker, Norman Walker, and a number of others long since under the sod."

130. This dream was only realized in 1921, when the Industrial Canal was completed.

131. Milneburg, West End and Spanish Fort (or Fort St. John). A photograph of the train taken in 1867 for Emperor Napoléon III by Theodore Lilienthal is in the Napoleonmuseum, Schloss Arenenberg, Salenstein, Switzerland.

132. F.L. Olmstead, 1962, op. cit., pp. 225–229.

133. S. Wilson, Jr., et al., eds., *Queen of the South—New Orleans, 1853–1862: The Journal of Thomas K. Wharton*, New Orleans, 1999.

134. A society for the exhibition of fine art was founded in the early 1840s on lower St. Charles Street and was grandiloquently called the National Gallery of Paintings. A sale of "Old Master" paintings, many of doubtful attribution, that had been put together by a trio of so-called Italian *cognoscenti* as the nucleus of an American national gallery of art, took place in the ballroom of the St. Louis Hotel in 1847.

135. After the collapse of the First Empire, Joseph Bonaparte (1768–1844), former King of Naples and Spain, retired to the United States and lived more or less incognito for a period of more than fifteen years in rural New Jersey as the Comte de Survilliers. He returned to Europe, died in Rome, and his American holdings were auctioned at Bordentown during the first weeks of September 1845.

136. A period photograph of the house is reproduced in S. Wilson, Jr., et al., 1999, op. cit., p. 79, as is T. K. Wharton's pen and ink sketch of it (p. 98).

137. Undaunted, he remade his fortune, and between 1866 and 1869 he was president of the Louisiana National Bank of which he was a founder.

138. The artist refered to by Wharton is certainly the Flemish landscape painter Simon Joseph Alexandre Clément Denis (1755–1813), who spent much of his career in southern Italy.

139. S. Wilson, Jr., et al., 1999, op. cit., p. 196.

140. All but two of the first fifteen elected mayors were Creoles: Étienne de Boré, James Pitot, John Watkins, James J. Mather, Charles Trudeau, Nicolas Girod (two terms), Le Breton Dorgenois, Augustin-François Macarty, Joseph Roffignac, Denis Prieur (two terms), Paul Bertus, Charles Génois, William Fréret (two terms), Paul Bertus and Joseph Montegut.

141. Reclus' anti-Bonapartist activities caused him to live in exile in Louisiana for a period of two and a half years. He was engaged as a tutor to the children of Septime Fortier at the Plantation Félicité on the west bank of the Mississippi in St. James Parish. A strict abolitionist, he was repulsed by what he saw of plantation life, and between 1860 and 1863 he published a series of anti-slavery articles in the *Revue des Deux-Mondes*.

142. Alarmed by the prospect of the total eradication of their culture, a group of New Orleans Creoles founded *L'Athénée louisianais* in 1876.

143. "*Le plus ancien quartier de la Nouvelle-Orléans, celui qu'on appelle par habitude le quartier français, est encore le plus élégant de la ville; mais les Français y sont en bien petite minorité, et ses maisons ont été pour la plupart achetées par des capitalistes américains: c'est là que se trouvent l'hôtel des postes, les principales banques, les magasins d'articles de Paris, la cathédrale et l'Opéra. Le nom même de ce dernier édifice est une preuve de la disparition graduelle de l'élément étranger ou créole. Autrefois, ce théâtre ne jouait que des pièces françaises, comédies ou vaudevilles; mais, pour continuer à faire des recettes, il a été obligé de changer ses affiches et son nom; maintenant, c'est le public américain qui lui accorde son patronage. Il est certain que la langue française disparaît de plus en plus. Sur la population de la Nouvelle-Orléans, qui s'élève, selon les saisons, de cent vingt mille à deux cent mille habitants, on ne compte guère que six à dix mille Français, c'est-à-dire un vingtième, et le même nombre de créoles non encore complètement américanisés. Bientôt l'idiome anglo-saxon dominera sans rival, et des Indiens aborigènes, des colons français et espagnols, qui s'étaient fixés dans le*

*pays bien avant les émigrants d'origine anglaise, il ne restera que des noms de rues: Tchoupitoulas, Perdido, Bienville, etc. Le marché français (french market) que les étrangers ne manquaient pas de visiter autrefois pour y entendre la confusion des langues, ne résonne plus guère que de conversations anglaises. Les Allemands, toujours honteux de leur patrie, cherchent à se prouver qu'ils sont devenus Yankees par des jurons bien articulés et des plaisanteries de taverne; les nègres, à l'intarissable babil, ne condescendent à parler français qu'avec une sorte de commisération pour leur interlocuteur, et les rares chasseurs indiens, fiers et tristes comme des prisonniers, répondent aux questions par des monosyllabes anglais."* (Élisée Reclus, "Fragment d'un voyage à la Nouvelle-Orléans [1855]," in *Le Tour du Monde*, 1st semester, 1860, p. 189).

144. At the age of sixteen, the girl married her French Creole third cousin, Célestin Delfau de Pontalba, and moved to a château near Senlis, north of Paris. The union produced three sons who grew to adulthood, but Micaela fought valiantly in the courts to protect her mother and father's inheritance of which Delfau's father and son tried to deprive her. This enraged her father-in-law to such a degree that in 1834 he shot and wounded her gravely and then turned one of his pistols on himself and committed suicide. The details of this lurid drama are recounted in Christina Vella's *Intimate Enemies: The Two Worlds of the Baroness de Pontalba* (Baton Rouge and London, 1997). The Baronne de Pontalba finally succeeded in having her dowry and her income-producing real estate in France and New Orleans restored to her. In 1836 she acquired in Paris the Hôtel d'Aguesseau on the rue du Faubourg Saint-Honoré and engaged the architect Louis Visconti to build for her in that location the Hôtel Pontalba, which today serves as the residence of the United States' Ambassador to France. In 1848, she returned to New Orleans, and it was then that she commissioned James Gallier, Henry Howard and Samuel Stewart to design and raise the beautiful Pontalba Buildings.

145. The artist contracted his surname of *De Gas* into the less "aristocratic" *Degas*.

146. Jean Baptiste Étienne Germain Musson was living in Mexico managing his silver mines when he was killed in a coach accident.

147. She was the daughter of Vincent Rillieux and Marie Antoinette Tronquet. In the entry dated August 14, 1820 of his journal, Benjamin Latrobe spoke of Madame Musson's demise: "I have…been present at a Mass said for the Soul of a Mrs. Musson [she had died the previous year, probably soon after the birth of her last son, Henry Germain Musson, on May 10, 1819], in which all the apparatus of a pompous funeral was exhibited, but without a coffin. The Church was filled with her friends, each of whom carried a lighted taper, and the service was *long* and *loud*." (E.C. Carter, II et al., 1980, op. cit., p. 337).

148. Another hugely successful free man of color was François Lacroix (d. 1876), a real estate tycoon and philanthropist who had been taken by his parents to New Orleans from his native Cuba and founded the Hospice de la Sainte Famille to help the poor and to whom the New Orleans Public Library devoted an exhibition in 2002. Consult website: http://nutrias.org/%7Enopl/exhibits/lacroix/lacroix.htm.

149. His best known compositions were inspired by his memories of the Place Congo: *Bamboula, danse des nègres* (1844–1845) and *Le Bananier, chanson nègre* (1845).

150. A pupil of Jacques-Fromental Halévy, Guiraud completed the orchestration of Jacques Offenbach's *Contes d'Hoffmann*.

151. During her short life, this provocative stage personality played the minstrel character "Mister Bones," impersonated the actor Edwin Booth and performed wearing only tights and strapped bare back on a horse, as she played "Mazeppa" on both American and European stages. In Paris, where she died and was buried, she had an affair with the old Alexandre Dumas *père*, himself the son of a racially mixed couple.

152. According to Mary Lyell, who witnessed the last day of the Mardi Gras festivities in 1846: "All the French population were dressed in masks, on horseback or in carriages, dressed up & in large wagons, in the most grotesque dresses flinging flour over one another & the passerby…It was so perfectly unlike anything I ever saw in this old World where there is so much work & so little play." (Quoted in L.G. Wilson, 1998, op. cit., p. 222).

153. Mardi Gras parades had been held in the formerly French town of Mobile since the early 1790s, and in 1835 its Cowbellion de Rakin society had paraded through the streets of the Crescent City.

154. Mark Twain came to New Orleans just in time to view the carnival parades of the Mardi Gras in March of 1859. "When he saw hundreds of men, women and children dressed 'in fine, fancy, splendid, ugly, coarse, ridiculous, grotesque, laughable costumes,' it suddenly dawned on him: 'This is Mardi-Gras!' Women in scant, alluring dress aroused him, though he put it in polite terms to his sister—'their costumes and actions were very trying to modest eyes.' He was fascinated by the erotic atmosphere, the variety of shapes and colorful appearances of human beings 'representing giants, Indians, nigger minstrels, monks, priests, clowns—birds, beasts—everything…that one could imagine.' Its freedom appealed to his senses, arousing a pleasure nerve that Victorian bleakness sometimes dulled but never destroyed. Strolling up St. Charles Street one evening, he joined a crowd waiting for 'the grand torchlight procession of the "mystic Krewe of Comus"' and managed to squeeze into an advantageous viewing position. After a number of false alarms, the parade began to appear in the distance. 'Five thousand people near me were tip-toeing and bobbing and peeping….Ever so far away down the street we could see a flare of light spreading away from a line of dancing colored spots. They approached faster…and here was the procession at last'—multicolored torches, an 'endless line of hearts and clubs…led by a mounted Knight Crusader in blazing gilt armor…then the Queen of the Fairies…then the King and Queen of the Genii.' To Clemens, this sensually exotic licentiousness seemed as much a part of the American experience as the genteel East Coast and the presbyterian West. 'I think that I may say that an American has not seen the United States until he has seen the Mardi-Gras in New Orleans.' " (F. Kaplan, 2005, op. cit., pp. 78–79).

155. Estelle is the subject of the portrait in the New Orleans Museum of Art exhibited here as cat. no. 50. Her husband, a Confederate officer Joseph Davis Balfour, had been killed on October 5, 1862 at the Battle of Davis Bridge near Corinth, Mississippi. A member of a family of planters from Madison County in the Yazoo part of that state, he was apparently related by blood to the president of the Confederacy, Jefferson Davis, a fellow Mississippian.

156. H. Adhémar, "Edgar Degas et la *Scène de guerre au Moyen Âge*," *Gazette des Beaux-Arts*, 6e pér., LXX, November 1967, pp. 295–298.

157. *"Les De Gas…prirent parti, lors de la guerre civile américaine, pour les armées sudistes; il est très probable que le récit des atrocités perpétrées par les [nordistes], rapporté aux divers membres de la famille par les trois Louisianaises en exil—le 1er mai 1862, après la prise de la ville, les soldats du Nord firent preuve à l'égard des femmes de la Nouvelle-Orléans d'une très certaine férocité—[est]…à l'origine de* Scène de guerre au Moyen Âge…: *à la fin du Moyen Âge, dans un paysage d'hiver atone, arbres défeuillés, maisons incendiées, trois cavaliers passent au milieu d'un groupe de femmes nues, violées sans doute, certaines mortes ou blessées d'incompréhensibles blessures; solidement campés sur leur montures, l'un d'eux enlève une femme qui se débat, l'autre, bandant son arc, s'apprête à décocher une flèche. L'aberrante cruauté du sujet sert de prétexte à une observation quasi clinique de la femme: les corps se tordent, les chevelures tombent, les sexes apparaissent dans la déchirure des vêtements; femmes inanimées, prenant la fuite, rampant à même le sol ou rivées comme crucifiées à un arbre. Dans cette allégorie, volontairement énigmatique à la manière de maintes compositions de la Renaissance, Degas, prenant sans doute prétexte des récits affolés que lui firent sa tante et ses deux cousines dans un salon bourgeois de Bourg-en-Bresse, traduit la tragique universalité d'un événement contemporain, résumant, en une image frappante, ce qui, de tout temps, fait la guerre: cruautés, viols, tortures."* (H. Loyrette, *Degas*, Paris, 1991, p. 181). See also the lengthier discussion by Henri Loyrette in exh. cat., Paris, Galeries nationales du Grand Palais, and elsewhere, *Degas*, 1988–1989, no. 45.

158. Michel-Auguste-Pierre, Odile-Geneviève, Jeanne-Georgine-Antoinette-Claire-Julie (born in 1872 during the visit to the city of her uncle Edgar, who was her godfather), Edgar-Achille-Gaston and René-Henri. Only two of them reached adulthood.

159. The New Orleans Museum of Art has devoted two major exhibitions to Degas' visit to New Orleans, the catalogues of which shed much light on the complex relationship between the De Gas family and their Musson and Rillieux kinsmen: *Edgar Degas, His Family and Friends in New Orleans* (with contributions by J. Rewald, J.B. Byrnes and J.S. Boggs), 1965 and *Degas and New Orleans: A French Impressionist in America* (G. Feigenbaum and J.S. Boggs, with essays by C. Benfey, M.R. Brown, J.B. Byrnes, V.E. Cooke and C. Vella), 1999. The majority of the paintings and drawings that Degas produced during his half-year stay in Louisiana were exhibited and/or discussed in the catalogue of these shows. See also exh. cat., Paris, Galeries nationales du Grand Palais, 1988–1989, op. cit., nos. 111–120. On the subject of Degas' New Orleans connections and Creole society, see also C. Benfey, *Degas in New Orleans: Encounters in the Creole World of Kate Chopin and George Washington Cable*, New York, 1998.

160. In the early 1850s, developers purchased old plantations in the area of the city known as Esplanade Ridge and turned them into neighborhoods for well-to-do French Creoles. The house occupied by the Musson-De Gas family was built in 1852 by the architect Benjamin Rodriguez as his own residence. With the garden, it occupied almost an entire block. The original house was divided into two sections during the 1920s, and one of them was moved twenty feet to the side creating in effect two houses. In Degas' time the Musson address was 125 Esplanade. Now no. 2306, it houses a bed-and-breakfast inn.

161. The finished painting was Degas' major contribution to the Second Impressionist Exhibition in 1876, and it was the first of his paintings to enter a public institution, in this case the Musée des Beaux-Arts in the city of Pau in early 1878.

162. He was the oldest of the six children born to Germain Musson and Marie Céleste Désirée Rillieux and the brother of Célestine Musson De Gas, Edgar Degas's mother. A former Postmaster of New Orleans and partner in the cotton firm of John Watt & Co., he was married to Geneviève-Odile Longer, by whom he had eight children. His wife had died in 1871.

163. Bell was married to Musson's oldest daughter Mathilde-Amélie.

164. The couple had four children, and from them descends the Nepveu-De Gas family, heirs to the estate of their uncle Edgar.

165. Edgar and René were for a long period of time alienated, but they finally reconciled, and in 1917 René inherited half of his oldest brother's estate. It was he who organized the four Degas Atelier sales.

166. *"Mais si je perds un frère, je retrouve un neveu—Enfant prodigue qui me revient après avoir beaucoup souffert, je t'ouvre mes bras et te bénis! Tu es bien* cet *Edgar que nous aimions toujours, le fils chéri de ma sœur Célestine, le préféré de mes filles. Comme elles quatre tu es* créole *par le cœur; de naissance et d'esprit tu es bien français; mais tu n'es pas comme* eux …*lazzaroni."* (Letter quoted in H. Loyrette, 1991, op. cit., p. 329).

167. The most important studies devoted to this famous painting are R. Ormond and E. Kilmurray, *John Singer Sargent: Complete Paintings*, I, *The Early Portraits*, New Haven and London, 1998, pp. 112–115, no. 114 (and related works, pp. 115–118) and D. Davis, *Strapless: John Singer Sargent and the Fall of Madame X*, New York, 2003.

168. His father, Filippo Giuseppe Maria Avegno (1785–1861), was born in Camogli, Italy and settled in New Orleans, where he accumulated a good deal of real estate. In 1821 Filippo (Philippe) Avegno married a French Creole, Catherine Génois (1801–1854), by whom he had eleven children, the eighth of whom was Anatole-Placide.

169. The plantation was about one hundred miles from New Orleans. During the Civil War, Union General Nathaniel Banks and Confederate General Dick Taylor used it as their headquarters. It remains a major tourist attraction in the area north of Baton Rouge. For a description of the house, its furnishings and garden, see H. de Bachellé Seebold, *Old Louisiana Plantation Homes and family trees*, Gretna, La., 1941, I, pp. 301–311.

170. The plantation's original owner, Claude Vincent Ternant, was a native of the village of Damvillers in Lorraine (now department of the Meuse). Amélie's maternal grandfather was Claude-Vincent Ternant II (c. 1786–1842), who in 1835 married his young ward, Marie-Virginie Trahan. The couple had four children: Marie-Virginie Ternant (1837–1910), who married Anatole-Placide Avegno; Marius-Claude-Vincent Ternant (1836–1861), who died without issue; Julie-Euriphile Ternant, who may have ended her life a suicide or institutionalized in a mental asylum; and a son, Henri who died by drowning on the plantation during his youth. In 1846, the widowed Madame Ternant, who actually ran the estate, married a French naval officer, Charles Parlange, in whose honor the property was renamed. After Marie-Virginie's death, it was inherited by her son Charles Parlange, a State Senator, United States District Attorney, Lieutenant Governor of Louisiana, Federal judge, and finally Justice of the Louisiana Supreme Court. It is today the property of Walter Parlange. (I would like to thank Angèle Parlange for providing me with information concerning her family.)

171. Marie-Virginie Trahan (b. 1818), was born in or near the village of Saint-Martin (today St. Martinville). The daughter of Joseph Lufroy Trahan, she was a descendant of a family whom the English had exiled from Acadia to Liverpool. They then lived for a time in Belle-Isle-en-Mer off the coast of Brittany and settled in Louisiana in 1785.

172. He was twenty-seven at his death. At Shiloh, he commanded the battalion of the 13th Louisiana Infantry that he and his brother Jean-Bernard had formed, the Avegno Zouaves.

173. She reportedly walked as if she were gliding on air. A photograph of her in the Bibliothèque nationale de France (illus. in D. Davis, 2003, op. cit., p. 206) shows how really stunning she was in her heyday.

174. In its original state, before Sargent reworked the picture, the strap on the left was off the shoulder.

175. A character trait of many of the Creole upper-class women featured in George W. Cable's short stories and novels, such as *The Grandissimes*, is their remarkable haughtiness.

176. The old Madame Avegno complained in tears to the artist that her daughter would die of shame and that her son-in-law would have to do battle with those who maligned her in the press.

177. Illus. in D. Davis, 2003, op. cit., color pls. between pp. 152 and 153 and pp. 206 and 208.

178. Mark Twain, *Life on the Mississippi*, in *Mississippi Writings* (The Library of America), New York, 1982, pp. 475–476, 485.

179. See *Historical Sketch Book and Guide to New Orleans*, 1885, op. cit., pp. 210–222.

180. The word "Jazz," which appears to have been coined in the late nineteenth-century brothels of New Orleans, has long since lost its original sexual connotation.

181. The tradition was old. Benjamin Latrobe had commented on such a burial that he witnessed in the late 1810s.

182. Many Creole musicians received at least some formal training and were adept at reading sheet music.

183. He was born in the small town of Thibodaux in Lafourche Parish and moved to New Orleans in 1891.

184. It was bought by a member of the Parlange family.

185. It was not replaced, but remained one of the primary centers of cultural life in New Orleans until its destruction. In 1878 Georges Bizet's *Carmen* was performed there for the first time in the United States.

186. The bulk of his fortune was used to found a manual trades school for boys, an institution that has grown into the Delgado Community College.

187. See note 94.

188. The original board members were business associates of Delgado or educators: Pierre Antoine Lelong, Joseph Bernard, Paul Capdevielle, Judge Charles Claiborne, Felix Dreyfous, Major Benjamin Harrod, E.W. Smith, Gustave Westfeldt, Ellsworth Woodward and Charles Wellington Boyle.

189. The most authoritative history of the New Orleans Museum of Art, from its founding until 1990, is P.N. Dunbar, *The New Orleans Museum of Art: The First Seventy-Five Years*, Baton Rouge and London, 1990. Much of the information contained in this brief survey of NOMA's past was gleaned from this book, one of only a handful of in-depth studies of the history of an American regional museum.

190. Asher B. Durand's *Forenoon*, cat. no. 45.

191. A collection of Oriental jades.

192. A group of nineteenth-century Salon paintings, including works by Gérôme and Corot, cat. nos. 49 and 51.

193. Decorative arts objects and silverware.

194. Medals.

195. Bronzes, marble sculpture and porcelain.

196. A major collection of ancient glass.

197. Chinese bronzes.

198. Henderson owned paintings by Delacroix, Daumier, Pissarro, Degas, Manet, Monet, Renoir, Cézanne, Gauguin, Toulouse-Lautrec, Picasso, Braque, Derain, Vlaminck, Rouault, Dufy, Laurencin, John Marin and Hartley; prints by the Japanese school, William Blake, Whistler and Mary Cassatt; and sculptures by Maillol and Paul Manship.

199. It included pictures by Derain, Dufy, André Lhote and Picasso.

200. Ernst Barlach, Charles Despiau, Jacob Epstein, George Kolbe, Gaston Lachaise and Aristide Maillol.

201. Despite the continued opposition of the Art Association's recalcitrant membership.

202. The Bultmans' father, A. Fred Bultman, Jr., was elected to the Board of Trustees in 1943. Muriel Francis served as a trustee and in 1968 was elected the first woman President of the Board.

203. Beckmann, Corinth, Feininger, Grosz, Klee, Kokoschka, Lembruch, Liebermann, Marc, Modersohn-Becker, Nolde and Pechstein.

204. 1907, Museum of Modern Art, New York.

205. 1922, Musée Picasso, Paris.

206. 1937, Museo Reina Sofia, Madrid.

207. According to P.N. Dunbar (1990, op. cit., p. 118), "he acted as the equivalent of a full staff at any other major museum."

208. Albeit with strings attached, for the donation only became permanent in 1961.

209. *Time*, November 16, 1953.

210. That the availability of Degas' *Portrait of Estelle Musson De Gas* was first signalled to Byrnes by Thaw himself was recently attested to by the latter (his e-mail of September 12, 2006, to the present author), The same source identifies the portrait's then owner as P. M. Samuel (see cat. no. 50).

211. The Besthoff drugstore chain was sold in 1997 to the Rite Aid Corporation. But since the 1970s, this couple managed to assemble a magnificent collection of modern and contemporary monumental sculpture in the offices of their foundation at the K & B Plaza on Lee Circle in New Orleans' Warehouse District.

212. Ex-Serristori collection, Florence and the Collegio Teutonico, Rome.

213. Latin phrase meaning "remember you must die." This genre was intended to remind the viewer of his or her mortality and of the brevity and fragility of life.

214. Bartolomeo Manfredi, Pietro Paolini, Louis Finson and Jean Leclerc, among others.

215. For an extensive discussion of Vouet's *Muses*, see exh. cat., New York, Wildenstein, *The Arts of France from Napoléon Iᵉʳ to François Iᵉʳ: A Centennial Celebration of Wildenstein's Presence in New York,* 2005–2006, pp. 109–110, no. 14.

216. H. Joachim and S.F. McCullagh, *Italian Drawings in The Art Institute of Chicago,* Chicago and London, 1979, pp. 60–61, no. 77, illus. p. 145, pl. 89.

217. In Dolci's oeuvre, there exist other examples of this kind of annotation.

218. Two autograph examples exist, one painted for King Charles I and now in the British royal collection at Windsor Castle and the other painted for Nicolas Claude Fabri de Peiresc now in the Australian National Gallery, Canberra.

219. The book was published in Paris by Gaspard Duchange in 1710.

220. Bibliothèque de l'Arsenal, Paris.

221. The earlier of the two was featured in 1990 in a sale in Paris (Hôtel Drouot, December 5, 1990, lot 73).

222. They recently appeared at auction: New York, Sotheby's, January 1, 1998, lot 168 and London, Christie's, July 6, 2005, lot 47.

223. Inquisitive European minds during the Enlightenment that produced the *Encyclopédie* were interested in cultures considered as exotic. Artists like Le Prince and Jean Étienne Liotard traveled to faraway places and recorded the customs and costumes of the people they encountered. The *Russerie* is akin to the *Chinoiserie* and the *Turquerie,* being a sub-category of Orientalism that enjoyed a tremendous vogue in the age of Louis XV in literature and the fine and decorative arts.

224. On the subject of the libertine Jean Du Barry, see A. Fauchier-Magnan, *Les Dubarry, Histoire d'une famille au XVIIIe siècle,* Paris, 1935 and Y. Bruand, "Les rapports Paris-Province: l'hôtel du comte Jean Dubarry à Toulouse," in *Le Progrès des arts réunis, 1763–1815: mythe culturel des origines de la Révolution à la fin de l'Empire* (Actes du colloque international d'histoire de l'art, Bordeaux-Toulouse, organized by D. Rabreau and B. Tollon), May 22–26, 1989, Bordeaux and Toulouse, 1992, pp. 281–289.

225. Among them are Louis Tocqué's *Madame Dangé* (Musée du Louvre), Joshua Reynolds' *Countess of Albermarle* (National Gallery, London), Jean Marc Nattier's *Marie Adélaïde de France* (Musée national des Châteaux de Versailles et de Trianon) and Jean Étienne Liotard's chalk drawing, *Archduchess Maria Antonia of Austria (the future Queen Marie Antoinette)* (Musées d'art et d'histoire, Geneva).

226. Two similar Roman *vedute* by Robert dating from the previous year, *A Colonnade and the Gardens of the Villa Medici* and *Figures in the Ruins of the Villa Giulia,* were sold at auction at Christie's in London on July 6, 2006 (lot 59) for the phenomenal sum of £3,368,000 ($6,237,037), a record price for works by the artist and for any eighteenth-century French landscape.

227. It was featured in a Paris sale (Drouot Richelieu, December 18 and 20, lot 157, illus. in color in cat. and on cover). In the Trécat d'Espagnac sale in Paris on May 22, 1973, lot 188 was identified as a *Naïade appuyée sur une urne* by Marin.

228. No. 493 of the handbook.

229. Translated literally from Turkish, "damaged head," meaning that they were leaderless and undisciplined.

230. *Impressionists and Modern Masters from the New Orleans Museum of Art,* September 16, 2006–January 7, 2007.

231. For those works, see exh. cat., Washington, D.C., National Gallery of Art, *Art for the Nation: Gifts in Honor of the 50ᵗʰ Anniversary of the National Gallery of Art,* March 17–June 16, 1991, p. 228, no number (entry by F.E. Coman), illus. p. 229 (color) and sale catalogue, Bern, Galerie Kornfeld, June 21, 1991, lot 889, illus. in cat., pl. 6.

232. She has been identified as Renée Chauvet, who lived in the hamlet of Le Mesnil-Théribus (Oise), near Mary Cassatt's country home.

233. See A.D. Breeskin, *Mary Cassatt: A Catalogue Raisonné of the Oils, Pastels, Watercolors, and Drawings,* Washington, D.C., 1970, p. 187, no. 501, illus.

234. J.S. Sargent to Lady Lewis, letter quoted (without date or source) in E. Charteris, *John Sargent,* New York, 1927, p. 164.

235. F. Lawton, *The Life and Work of Auguste Rodin,* London, 1904, pp. 44–45.

236. See A. Pingeot and L. de Margerie, *Musée d'Orsay: catalogue sommaire illustré des sculptures,* Paris, 1986, p. 207, no. RF 3868, illus. The same museum owns a plaster cast of the piece, dated January 1907, which was presented by the artist's widow and son in 1949 (for that work, see ibid., p. 206, no. RF 2649, illus.). The plaster formerly in Degas' collection was sold at Paris, Christie's, May 24, 2006, lot 22, illus. in cat. (color).

237. See exh. cat., Richmond, Virginia Museum of Fine Arts, *Capturing Beauty: American Impressionist and Realist Painting from the McGlothlin Collection* (cat. by D.P. Curry), May 19–September 18, 2005, p. 61, no number, illus. (color).

238. One of the two was acquired in 1948 by The Museum of Modern Art, New York.

239. H.K. Roethel and J.K. Benjamin, *Kandinsky: Catalogue Raisonné of the Oil-Paintings,* II, *1916–1944,* Ithaca, N.Y., 1984, p. 719, no. 767, illus. pp. 712 (color), 719. The painting was acquired in 1926 by the Staatliche Gemäldegalerie, Dresden, but was later banned as degenerate art by the German government in 1937 and sold. Solomon R Guggenheim then acquired the work two years later from Gutekunst and Klipstein, Bern (according to A.Z. Rudenstine, *The Guggenheim Museum Collection: Paintings, 1880–1945,* New York, 1976, I, p. 322).

240. A. Davis, "Theosophy," in *The Dictionary of Art,* London, 1996, XXX, p. 710.

241. G.W. Klein, *A Passion for Sharing: The Life of Edith Rosenwald Stern,* Chappaqua, N.Y., 1984, pp. 103–104.

242. Nancy Cunard was apparently the inspiration for one of the characters in Huxley's 1923 novel, *Antic Hay.*

243. In 1928, at her farmhouse retreat in Normandy, she founded the Hours Press, which published works by Ezra Pound and Samuel Beckett.

244. Letter dated April 12, 1956 (copy preserved in the Solomon R. Guggenheim Museum, New York), quoted in A.C. Chave, *Constantin Brancusi: Shifting the Bases of Art,* New Haven and London, 1993, p. 36.

245. See Paris, Musée national d'art moderne, Centre Georges Pompidou, *Constantin Brancusi, 1876–1957* (cat. by A. Temkin et al.), April 14–August 20, 1995, no. 89, illus. (color).

246. For a discussion of this exhibition and Duchamp's role in it, see ibid., pp. 64–66 (essay by A. Temkin, "Brancusi et ses collectionneurs américains").

247. Gift of the Hall Family Foundation, acquired from the Patsy and Raymond Nasher Collection, acc. no. F99–33/3. Brancusi's original plaster is in the Musée national d'art moderne, Centre Georges Pompidou, Paris (see Paris, Musée national d'art moderne, *La Collection: L'Atelier Brancusi* [ed. by M. Tabart], Paris, 1997, p. 108, illus.).

248. For the group of twelve paintings, see J. Dupin and L. Lelong-Mainaud, *Joan Miró: Catalogue raisonné. Paintings,* II, *1931–1941,* Paris, 2000, pp. 139–148, nos. 504–515.

249. No such painting with this composition or of this provenance is recorded in ibid.

250. P.N. Dunbar, 1990, op. cit., p. 82.

251. A. Franzke, *Dubuffet* (trans. from the German by R.E. Wolf), New York, 1981, pp. 41/44 and M. Thévoz, *Dubuffet,* Geneva, 1986, p. 53.

252. The sub-title was *PORTRAITS / à ressemblance extraite, / à ressemblance cuite et confite dans la mémoire, / à ressemblance éclatée dans la mémoire de / Mr. JEAN DUBUFFET / Peintre* (Translation: PORTRAITS with distilled likenesses, cooked and potted in the memory and fulminated in the memory of Mr. JEAN DUBUFFET, a Painter).

253. "Jackson Pollock: Is He the Greatest Living Painter in the United States?" *Life,* XXVII, August 8, 1949, pp. 42–43, 45.

254. D. Sylvester, ed., *René Magritte Catalogue Raisonné,* III, *Oil Paintings, Objects and Bronzes, 1949–1967* (by S. Whitfield and M. Raeburn), London, 1993, p. 169; for the complete series, see pp. 169–172, nos. 743–746.

255. See M. Butor, "Magritte et les mots," *Les Lettres françaises,* November 13, 1968, p. 8 (as cited in ibid., p. 171).

256. Translation:

> O mortals, I am beautiful like a dream in stone,
> And my breast, on which each in his turn has been bruised,
> Is made to inspire in the poet a love
> As eternal and mute as matter.
>
> I throne in the heavens like an unfathomable sphinx;
> I unite a heart of snow with the whiteness of swans;
> I despise motion which displaces lines,
> And never do I weep and never do I laugh.

cat. no. 94 (detail)

Poets faced with the great poses I strike,
Which I seem to take from the proudest monuments,
Will consume their days in austere study;

For to beguile these docile lovers, I have
Pure mirrors which render all things more beautiful:
My eyes, my large eyes with eternal sparks!

257. The earlier *History of Turkey* was actually given by Cornell to Muriel Bultman Francis. A red box holding shredded illustrations of Turkish scenes initially held candied violets. See exh. cat., New Orleans, New Orleans Museum of Art, *Profile of a Connoisseur: The Collection of Muriel Bultman Francis* (cat. by E.P. Caraco), November 10, 1985–January 12, 1986, no. 17, illus. p. 57.

258. M. Hammer and C. Lodder, *Constructing Modernity: The Art and Career of Naum Gabo*, New Haven and London, 2000, p. 438.

259. Richard Diebenkorn, interview with Susan Larsen, 1977, transcript (Archives of American Art, Smithsonian Institution, Washington, D.C.), pp. 15–16, as quoted in exh. cat., New York, Whitney Museum of American Art, and elsewhere, *The Art of Richard Diebenkorn*, 1997–1999, essay by J. Livingston, "The Art of Richard Diebenkorn," p. 21.

260. I wish to thank Henry Casselli and his wife for graciously allowing me to visit their home and the artist's studio earlier this year.

COLOR PLATES

1. Andrea di Vanni d'Andrea Salvani, *Adoration of the Magi*, c. 1360

2. Taddeo di Bartolo, *Saint Catherine of Alexandria* and *Bishop Saint*, 1418

3. Bartolomeo Vivarini, *The Coronation of the Virgin*, c. 1460–70

4. Bernardino Fungai, *The Martyrdom of Saint Lucy*, c. 1490

5. Benvenuto Tisi, called Il Garofalo, *Meditation of Saint Jerome*, c. 1520–25

6. Bernardino Luini, *Adoration of the Christ Child and the Annunciation to the Shepherds*, c. 1520–25

7. Adriaen Isenbrandt, *The Virgin Nursing the Christ Child*, c. 1525–30

8. Lorenzo Lotto, *Portrait of a Bearded Man*, c. 1530–35

9. Maerten van Heemskerck, *Apollo and the Muses*, c. 1555–60

10. Abraham Bloemaert, *Saint John the Baptist Preaching in the Wilderness*, c. 1625–30

11. Giovanni Martinelli, *Death Comes to the Banquet Table*, c. 1630

12. Simon Vouet, *Erato, The Muse of Love Poetry*, 1634–38

13. Simone Cantarini, called Il Pesarese, *Madonna and Child with a Goldfinch*, c. 1640

14. Claude Gellée, called Claude Lorrain, *Ideal View of Tivoli*, 1644

15. Claude Lefebvre, *Portrait of Louis XIV*, 1670

16. Carlo Dolci, *The Vision of Saint Louis of Toulouse*, c. 1675–76

17. Luca Giordano, *The Baptism of Christ*, c. 1684

18. Jean Baptiste Monnoyer, *Flowers in an Urn*, 1690

19. Nicolas Colombel, *Adoration of the Magi*, 1693–99

PIERRE PAVL RVBENS.

20. Jean Marc Nattier, *Portrait of Peter Paul Rubens*, 1707

21. Sebastiano Ricci and Marco Ricci, *Imaginary Scene with Ruins and Figures*, c. 1725

22. Christophe Huet, *Hound Guarding Hunt Trophies*, 1728

23. Jean Restout II, *Hector Taking Leave of Andromache* (from *The Iliad*, VI, 407–409), 1728
Lent by Mr. and Mrs. Joseph C. Canizaro, New Orleans

24. François Boucher, *The Surprise*, 1730–32

25. Carle Vanloo, *Noli me tangere*, 1735

26. Charles Joseph Natoire, *The Toilet of Psyche*, 1735–36

27. Giovanni Battista Tiepolo, *Boy Holding a Book (Portrait of Lorenzo Tiepolo)*, c. 1747-50

28. Joseph Marie Vien, *Saint Theresa of Avila*, 1754–55

29. Jean Baptiste Greuze, *Portrait of Madame Georges Gougenot de Croissy, née Marie Angélique Vérany de Varennes*, 1757

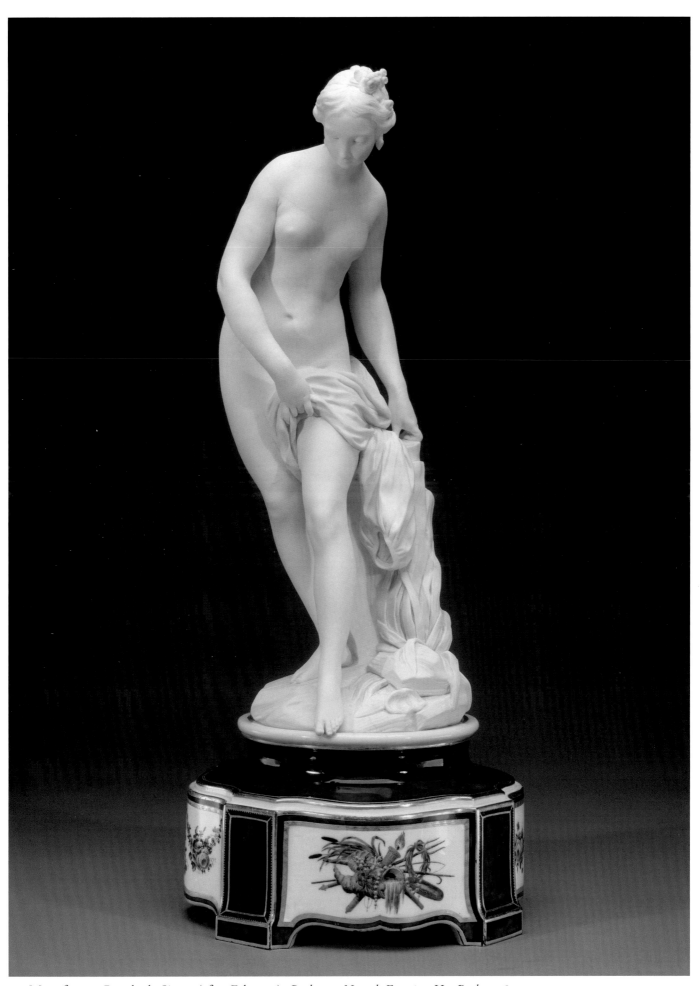

30. Manufacture Royale de Sèvres (after Falconet), *Bather or Nymph Entering Her Bath*, 1758

31. Hubert Robert, *A Stairway in the Park of an Italian Villa*, 1760

32. John Singleton Copley, *Portrait of Colonel George Watson*, 1768

33–1. Jean Baptiste Le Prince, *The Seesaw*, 1768
Loan from a private New Orleans collection

33–2. Jean Baptiste Le Prince, *The Russian Dance*, 1768
Loan from a private New Orleans collection

34. Étienne Aubry, *Woman in the Costume of a Sultana (The Dancer Rosalie Duthé?)*, 1779
Loan from a private New Orleans collection

35. Nicolas Marie Gatteaux,
*Profile Head of Marie Antoinette, Queen of France*, 1779

36. Claude Joseph Vernet, *The Morning, Port Scene*, 1780

37. Adélaïde Labille Guiard,
*Portrait of Madame Élisabeth de France*, c. 1787
Loan from a private New Orleans collection

38. Jean Germain Drouais, *Portrait of the Architect Auguste H. Cheval de Saint-Hubert*, c. 1787–88
Loan from a private New Orleans collection

39. Élisabeth Louise Vigée Le Brun, *Portrait of Marie Antoinette, Queen of France*, c. 1788

40. Jean Joseph Taillasson, *Coriolanus Beseeched by His Mother and Wife*, c. 1791

41. Joseph Charles Marin, *Water Nymph Leaning on an Urn (La Source)*, 1797

42. Pierre Joseph Redouté, *Still Life of Flowers in a Vase on a Marble Ledge*, c. 1800
Loan from a private New Orleans collection

43. Jean Baptiste Joseph Wicar, *Portrait of Colonel Antoine Jean Auguste Henri Durosnel*, 1805

44. Jean-Auguste-Dominique Ingres, *Compositional Study for "The Apotheosis of Homer,"* 1826

45. Asher B. Durand, *Forenoon*, 1847

46. Franz Xaver Winterhalter,
*Young Woman in a Ball Gown*, 1850

47. Albert-Ernest Carrier-Belleuse, *Woman in Reeds (Undine)*, c. 1865

48. Edgar Degas, *Study for a Portrait of a Woman*, 1867

49. Jean-Léon Gérôme, *Turkish Bashi Bazouk Mercenaries Playing Chess in a Market Place*, c. 1870–73

50. Edgar Degas, *Portrait of Estelle Musson De Gas*, 1872

51. Jean-Baptiste-Camille Corot, *Woodland Scene*, c. 1872–73

52. Auguste Rodin, *The Age of Bronze*, modeled 1875-76, cast during the artist's lifetime

53. James Tissot, *The Terrace at Trafalgar Tavern, Greenwich*, c. 1878

54. Edgar Degas, *Dancer Adjusting Her Stocking*, modeled c. 1880, cast 1919-21

55. Pierre-Auguste Renoir, *Study of a Tree*, c. 1884–86

56. Paul Gauguin, *Head of a Tahitian Woman*, c. 1891–93

57. Pierre Bonnard, *Study for the Poster, "La Revue Blanche,"* 1894

58. John Singer Sargent, *Portrait of Mrs. Asher B. Wertheimer*, c. 1898

59. Odilon Redon, *Shadow and Light*, c. 1900

60. Odilon Redon, *Beasts at the Bottom of the Sea*, c. 1900–05

61. Kees Van Dongen, *Woman in a Green Hat*, 1905

62. Maurice de Vlaminck, *Chatou, le pont*, 1905–06

63. Odilon Redon, *The Dream*, c. 1905

64. Georges Braque, *Landscape at L'Estaque*, 1906

65. Mary Cassatt, *Mother and Child in the Conservatory*, 1906

66. Paul Paulin, *Bust of Edgar Degas at the Age of Seventy-Two*, 1907

67. Robert Henri, *The Blue Kimono*, 1909

68. Umberto Boccioni, *Unique Forms of Continuity in Space*, modeled 1913, cast 1972
Lent by The Sydney and Walda Besthoff Foundation Collection, New Orleans

69. Jacques Lipchitz, *Bather III*, modeled 1916–17, cast 1941

70. Amedeo Modigliani, *Portrait of a Young Woman*, 1918

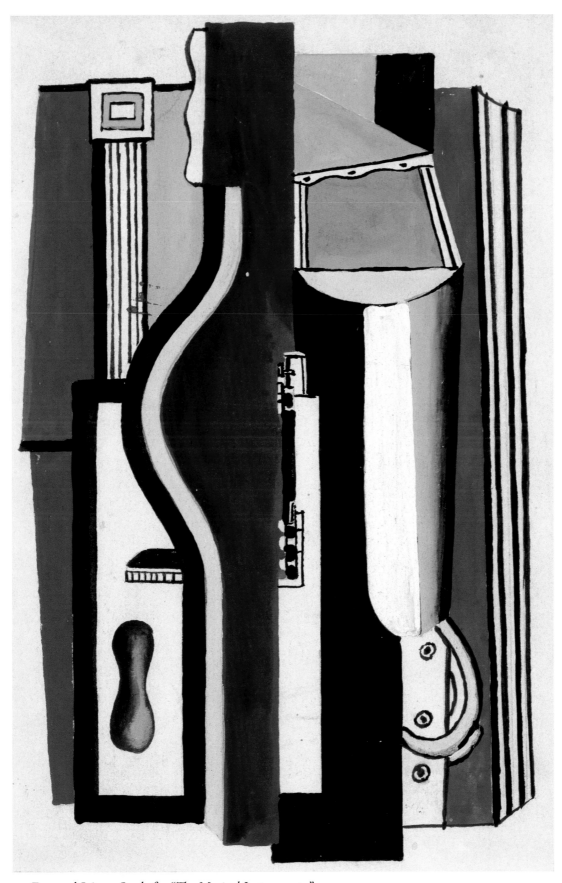

71. Fernand Léger, *Study for "The Musical Instruments,"* 1925

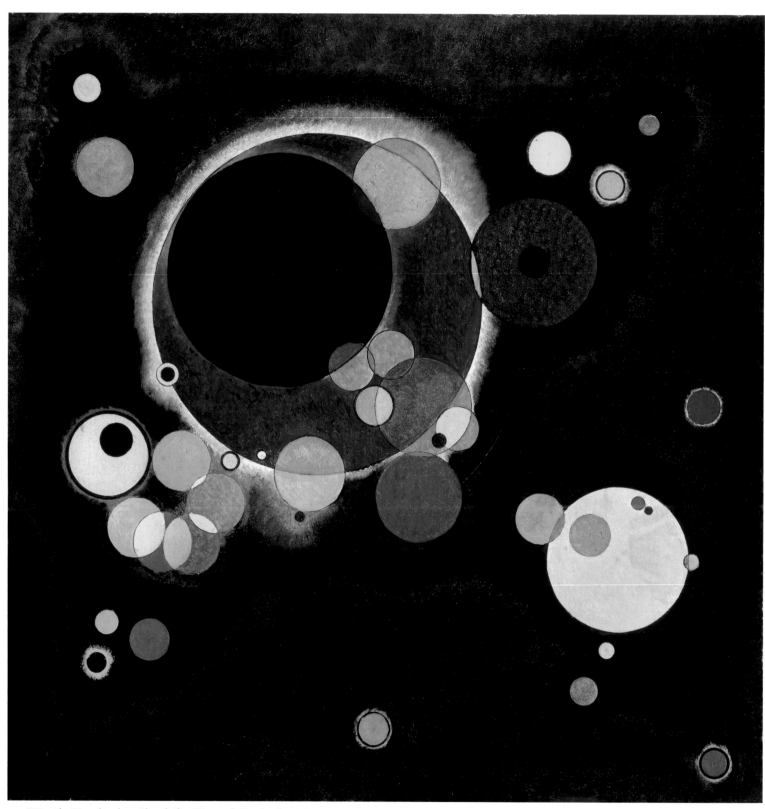

72. Wassily Kandinsky, *Sketch for "Several Circles,"* 1926

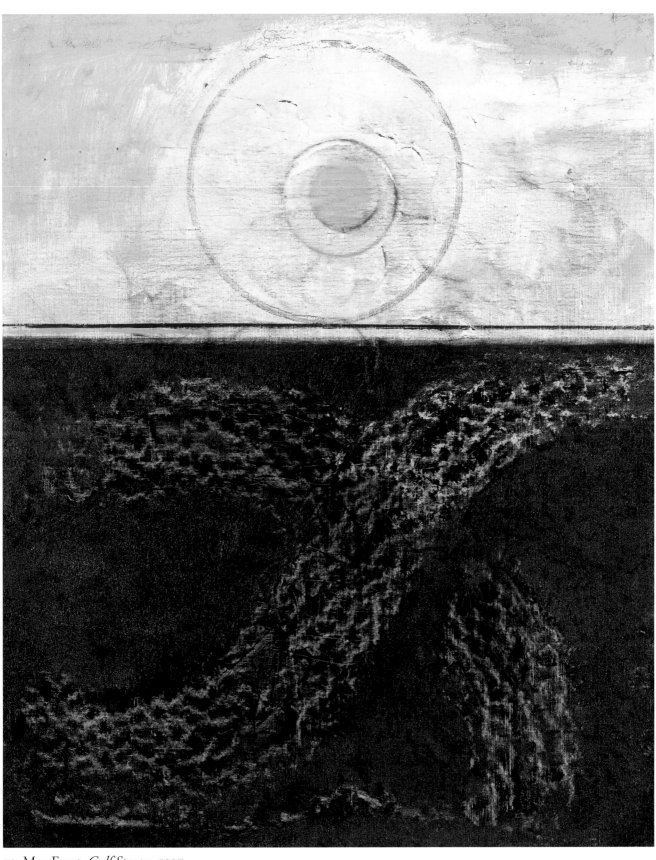

73. Max Ernst, *Gulf Stream*, 1927

74. Constantin Brancusi, *Sophisticated Young Lady (Nancy Cunard)*, modeled 1928, cast 1932
Loan from a private New Orleans collection

75. Joan Miró, *Persons in the Presence of a Metamorphosis*, 1936

76. Georgia O'Keeffe, *My Back Yard*, 1937

77. Hans Hofmann, *Abstraction of Chair and Miró*, 1943

78. Max Ernst, *Turtle*, modeled 1944, cast 1962

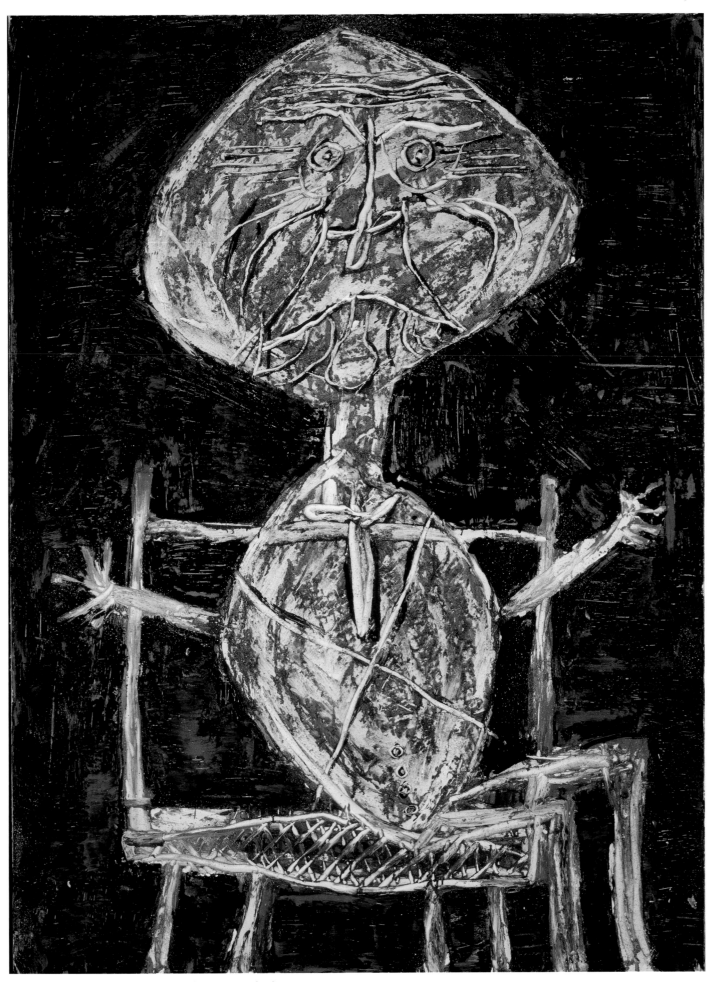

79. Jean Dubuffet, *Paul Léautaud in a Caned Chair*, 1946

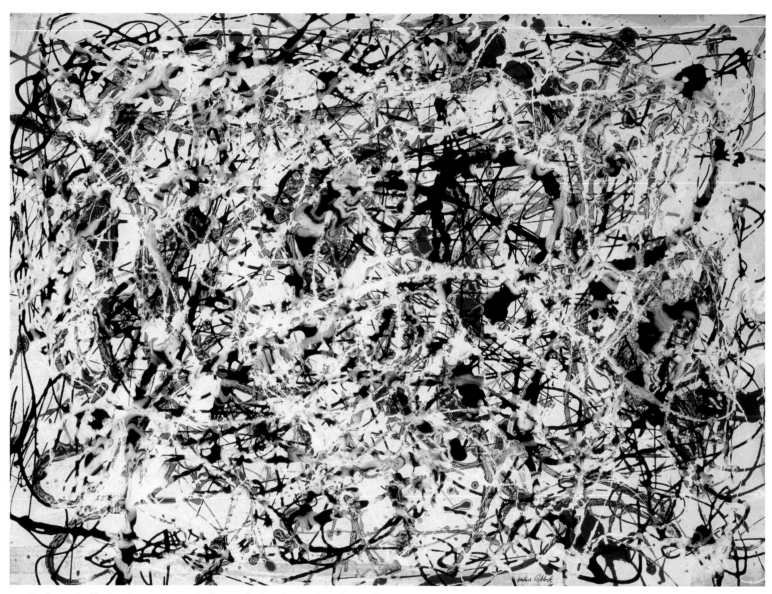

80. Jackson Pollock, *Composition (White, Black, Blue and Red on White)*, 1948

81. Pablo Picasso, *Mask of a Faun*, 1949–50

82. René Magritte, *The Art of Conversation*, 1950

83. Joseph Cornell, *Radar Astronomy*, 1952–56

84. Alberto Giacometti, *The Studio*, 1953

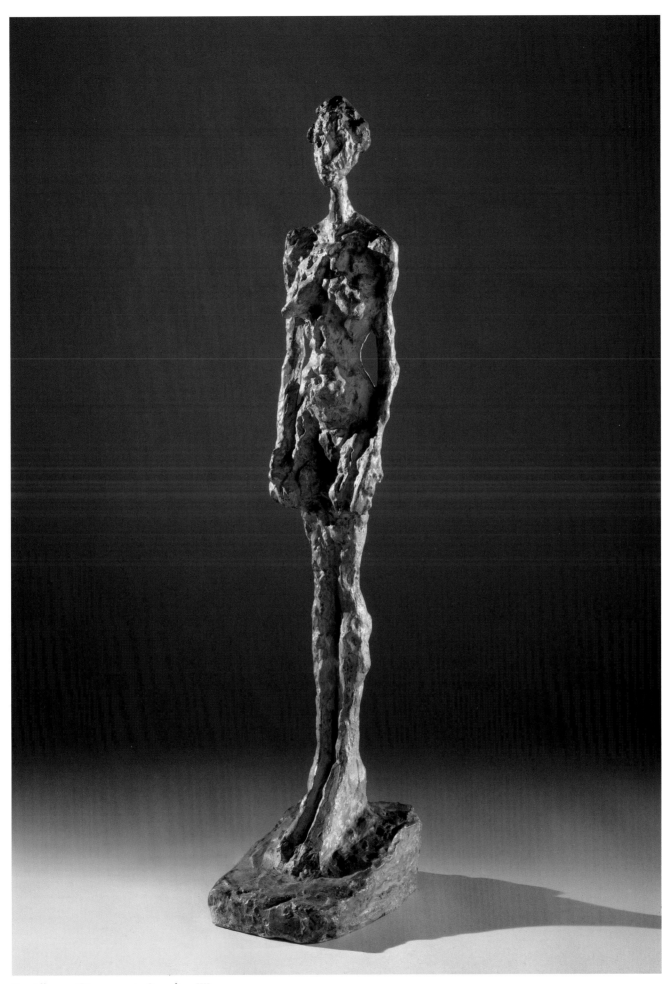

85. Alberto Giacometti, *Standing Woman*, c. 1953–55

86. Naum Gabo, *Construction in Space: Suspended*, conceived 1957, constructed c. 1963-64

87. Richard Diebenkorn, *Woman on Porch*, 1958

88. Sam Francis, *White Line I*, 1959

89. Joan Miró, *The Red Disk*, 1960

90. Pablo Picasso, *Woman in an Armchair (Jacqueline Roque Picasso)*, 1960

91. Louise Bourgeois, *Female Portrait*, 1962–82

92. Romare Bearden, *Jazz: Kansas City*, 1977

93. Louise Nevelson, *Cascades–Perpendicular XVIII*, 1980–82

94. Henry Casselli, *Bird's Nest*, 1987

95. Chuck Close, *Alex*, 1996

cat. no. 80 (detail)

CATALOGUE

*Unless otherwise indicated, all works of art are in the collection of the New Orleans Museum of Art*

1

Andrea di Vanni d'Andrea Salvani
(Sienese: c. 1330–1413)

*Adoration of the Magi,* circa 1360
Tempera and gold leaf on panel:
16 x 30 ½ inches (40.6 x 77.5 cm.)
The Samuel H. Kress Collection,
acc. no. 1961.61

PROVENANCE
(?) Thomas Blayds, Castle Hill, Englefield Green, Surrey; (?) his sale, London, Christie's, March 30–31, 1849, lot 187 (as "Giotto The Adoration of the Magi, with attendants and horses"); acquired there by the dealer Anthony; The Rev. John Fuller Russell (1813–1884), Eagle House, near Enfield, Middlesex, and (later) Greenhithe, Kent, as of 1854; his estate sale, London, Christie's, April 18, 1885, lot 103 (as Bartolo di Fredi); acquired there by Carrington; by descent to Hugh B. Carrington, Blacklands, Crowhurst, Sussex; his sale, London, Christie's, December 18, 1931, lot 87 (as Bartolo di Fredi); acquired there by Vitale Bloch (1900–1975), Berlin; Conte Alessandro Contini Bonacossi (1878–1955), Florence; acquired from him in 1932 by the Samuel H. Kress Collection; presented by them to the museum in 1961.

REFERENCES
G.F. Waagen, *Treasures of Art in Great Britain,* London, 1854, II, p. 462 (this and the following two references, as Bartolo di Fredi) // G.F. Waagen, *A Walk through the Art-Treasures Exhibition at Manchester: A Companion to the Official Catalogue,* London, 1857, p. 2, no. 35 // W. Bürger, *Trésors d'art en Angleterre* (3rd ed.), Paris, 1865, p. 25 // Roberto Longhi, written communication, 1932 (New Orleans Museum of Art collection files) (as Andrea Vanni and datable to c. 1360) // *National Gallery of Art: Preliminary Catalogue of Painting and Sculpture: Descriptive List with Notes,* Washington, D.C., 1941, p. 205, no. 222 (with incorrect early collection history) // W.E. Suida, *The Samuel H. Kress Collection in the Isaac Delgado Museum of Art,* New Orleans, 1953, p. 10, illus. p. 11 (with incorrect early collection history) [2nd ed., revised by P. Wescher, New Orleans, 1966, same pagination (with incorrect early collection history)] // F.R. Shapley, *Paintings*

*from the Samuel H. Kress Collection: Italian Schools,* I, *XIII-XV Century,* London, 1966, pp. 57–58, no. K233, illus. fig. 156 // B. Berenson, *Italian Pictures of the Renaissance: Central Italian and North Italian Schools,* London and New York, 1968, I, p. 441 // B.B. Fredericksen and F. Zeri, *Census of Pre-Nineteenth-Century Italian Paintings in North American Public Collections,* Cambridge, Mass., 1972, pp. 208, 272, 601 // C. de Benedictis, *La pittura senese, 1330–1370,* Florence, 1979, p. 97 // F. Russell, "A Means to Devotion: Italian Art and the Clerical Connoisseur," *Country Life,* CLXXVIII, December 5, 1985, p. 1751, illus. fig. 4 (color) // V.L. Wainwright, "Andrea di Vanni d'Andrea Salvani," in *Saur. Allgemeines Künstler-Lexikon. Die bildenden Künstler aller Zeiter und Völker,* III, Munich and Leipzig, 1992, p. 561 // F. Russell, "Russell, John Fuller," in *The Dictionary of Art,* London, 1996, XXVII, p. 359.

EXHIBITED
Manchester, *Art Treasures of the United Kingdom,* 1857, no. 35 (as Bartolo di Fredi) // London, Royal Academy of Arts, *Works by Old Masters,* winter 1878, no. 202 (as Bartolo di Fredi) // Washington, D.C., National Gallery of Art, 1941–1952, no. 222 // Athens, Georgia Museum of Art, *Sacred Treasures: Early Italian Paintings from Southern Collections* (cat. by P.L. Roberts), October 12, 2002–January 5, 2003, no. 13, also cited in essay by H.B.J. Maginnis, "The Sienese School," p. 25 and on p. 183, note 2, illus. p. 75 (color) (exhibition traveled to Birmingham, Alabama, Birmingham Museum of Art, January 26–April 13, 2003; and Sarasota, Florida, The John and Mable Ringling Museum of Art, May 31–August 10, 2003).

2

Taddeo di Bartolo
(Sienese: c. 1362–1422)

Pair of paintings, 1418

*Saint Catherine of Alexandria*
Tempera and gold leaf on panel:
59 ⅛ x 17 ½ inches (150.2 x 44.5 cm.)

*Bishop Saint (Martin, or Geminianus?)*
Tempera and gold leaf on panel:
58 ⅞ x 17 ⅛ inches (149.6 x 43.5 cm.)

The Samuel H. Kress Collection,
acc. nos. 1961.64 and 1961.63

PROVENANCE
(?) Frederick Mason Perkins (1874–1955), Assisi (as suggested by Solberg, 1991, cited below, pt. 1, p. 470); Dan Fellows Platt (1873–1937), Englewood, New Jersey, as of 1908; acquired from his estate in 1939 by the Samuel H. Kress Collection; presented by them to the museum in 1961.

REFERENCES
F.M. Perkins, "Ancora dei dipinti sconosciuti della scuola senese," *Rassegna d'arte senese,* IV, 1908, p. 8 // B. Berenson, *Central Italian Painters of the Renaissance,* London and New York, 1909, p. 256 // J.A. Crowe and G.B. Cavalcaselle, *A New History of Painting in Italy, from the II to the XVI Century* (ed. by E. Hutton), II, London and New York, 1909, p. 123, note 6 // F.M. Perkins, "Dipinti italiani nella raccolta Platt," *Rassegna d'arte,* XI, January 1911, p. 5 // R. Van Marle, *The Development of the Italian Schools of Painting,* II, The Hague, 1924, pp. 554/556, 559 [Italian ed., II, Florence and Rome, 1934, p. 611] // L. Dami, "Taddeo di Bartolo a Volterra," *Bollettino d'arte,* IV, August 1924, p. 70, illus. p. 72, fig. 2 (*Saint Catherine of Alexandria*) // B. Berenson, *Italian Pictures of the Renaissance,* Oxford, 1932, p. 551 // G.H. Edgell, *A History of Sienese Painting,* New York, 1932, p. 180, illus. fig. 238 // B. Berenson, *Pitture italiane del rinascimento* (trans. by E. Cecchi), Milan, 1936, p. 474 // F.M Perkins, "Taddeo di Bartolo," in *Allgemeines Lexikon der bildenden Künstler* (ed. by U. Thieme and F. Becker), XXXII, Leipzig, 1938, p. 397 // W.E. Suida, *The Samuel H. Kress Collection in the Isaac Delgado Museum of Art,* New Orleans, 1953, p. 14, illus. p. 15 [2nd ed., revised by P. Wescher, New Orleans, 1966, same pagination] // W.E. Suida, *The Samuel H. Kress Collection: Brooks Memorial Art Gallery,* Memphis, Tenn., 1958, p. 10 [2nd ed., revised by M. Milkovich, Memphis, Tenn., 1966, p. 14] // S. Symeonides, *Taddeo di Bartolo,* Siena, 1965, pp. 97–98, 212–213, illus. pl. XXXIV // F.R. Shapley, *Paintings from the Samuel H. Kress Collection: Italian Schools,* I, *XIII-XV Century,* London, 1966, p. 64, nos. K553 and K554, illus. figs. 167, 168 // B. Berenson, *Italian Pictures of the Renaissance: Central Italian and North Italian Schools,* London and New York, 1968, I, p. 420 // B.B. Fredericksen and F. Zeri, *Census of Pre-Nineteenth-Century Italian Paintings in North American Public Collections,* Cambridge, Mass., 1972, pp. 194, 272, 381, 400, 455, 601 // G.E. Solberg, "Taddeo di Bartolo: His Life and Work" (unpublished Ph.D. dissertation,

New York University), 1991, pt. 1, pp. 249, 365, 468, 470, 558–559, pt. 2, pp. 1203–1204, 1492, illus. pt. 2, p. 1589, figs. 246, 249 // G.E. Solberg, "Taddeo di Bartolo: A Polyptych to Reconstruct," *Brooks Museum Bulletin: Essays on the Collection*, I, 1994, n.p., illus. figs. 9 and 10 (color) // M.S. Frinta, *Punched Decoration on Late Medieval Panel and Miniature Painting*, pt. 1, *Catalogue Raisonné of All Punch Shapes*, Prague, 1998, pp. 229, 250, 518.

EXHIBITED

Memphis, Tenn., Memphis Brooks Museum of Art, "A Renaissance Reunion: Reconstructing Taddeo di Bartolo's Kress Altarpiece," February 26–May 22, 1994 (exhibition traveled to New Orleans, New Orleans Museum of Art, June 6–September 4, 1994: and Tulsa, Oklahoma, Philbrook Art Center, September 11–November 27, 1994) [for cat., see 1994 Reference, cited above].

3
Bartolomeo Vivarini
(Venetian: c. 1432–1491)

*The Coronation of the Virgin,*
circa 1460–70
Tempera and gold leaf on panel:
35 ⅛ x 23 ⅝ inches (89.2 x 60 cm.)
The Samuel H. Kress Collection,
acc. no. 1961.67

PROVENANCE

Conte Zini, Bologna; Conte (later Marchese) Giambattista Costabili Containi (1756–1841), Palazzo Costabili (formerly Palazzo Bevilacqua Aldobrandini), Ferrara; his collection inherited *en bloc* by his nephew, Giovanni Costabili (1815–1882), Ferrara; acquired 1884 by Angelo Genolini, Milan; sold (with a portion of the Costabili collection) at Milan, Teatro della Scala, foyer (auction organized by Galleria Sambon), April 27–29, 1885, lot 20 (as School of Murano, 15th Century); Conte Alessandro Contini Bonacossi (1878–1955), Florence; acquired from him in 1936 by the Samuel H. Kress Collection; presented by them to the museum in 1961.

REFERENCES

"Pitture della Raccolta del Co.te Gio Batta Costabili di Ferrara," 1835 (Bologna, Biblioteca dell'Archiginnasio, Ms. A1324), fol. 45, no. 575 (as Marco Zoppo) // C. Laderchi, *Descrizione della Quadreria Costabili*, IV, pt. 4, Ferrara, 1841, p. 50, no. 416 (as Zoppo) // [G. Giordani], *Catalogo de' quadri di varie scuole pittoriche nella Galleria Costabili in Ferrara*, Bologna, 1871–1872, no. 85 (as Zoppo) // J.A. Crowe and G.B. Cavalcaselle, *A History of Painting in North Italy…from the Fourteenth to the Sixteenth Century* (ed. by T. Borenius), New York, 1912, I, pp. 67, 68 and note 2 (as possibly a late work by Alvise Vivarini) // *National Gallery of Art: Preliminary Catalogue of Painting and Sculpture: Descriptive List with Notes*, Washington, D.C., 1941, p. 213, no. 343 // W.E. Suida, *The Samuel H. Kress Collection in the Isaac Delgado Museum of Art*, New Orleans, 1953, p. 20, illus. p. 21 [2nd ed., revised by P. Wescher, New Orleans, 1966, same pagination] // B. Berenson, *Italian Pictures of the Renaissance: Venetian School*, London, 1957, I, p. 202, illus. II, pl. 110 // R. Pallucchini, *I Vivarini (Antonio, Bartolomeo, Alvise)*, Venice, n.d. [1962], pp. 41–42, 118, no. 145, illus. fig. 145 // [B.B. Sweeny], *John G. Johnson Collection: Catalogue of Italian Paintings*, Philadelphia, 1966, p. 80 // F.R. Shapley, *Paintings from the Samuel H. Kress Collection: Italian Schools*, II, *XV-XVI Century*, London, 1968, p. 33, no. K423, illus. fig. 75 (as attributed to Bartolomeo Vivarini) // B.B. Fredericksen and F. Zeri, *Census of Pre-Nineteenth-Century Italian Paintings in North American Public Collections*, Cambridge, Mass., 1972, pp. 211, 309, 601 // Pfäffikon, Seedam-Kulturzentrum, and elsewhere, *Art vénitien en Suisse et au Liechtenstein* (ed. by M. Natale), 1978, p. 89, cited under no. 48 // J.G. Caldwell, *New Orleans Museum of Art—Handbook of the Collection* (ed. by B.N. McDermott), New Orleans, 1980, p. 27, illus. // C.T. Dowd, ed., "The Travel Diaries of Otto Mündler, 1855–1858," *The Walpole Society*, LI, 1985, p. 215 (records visit by Otto Mündler, then traveling agent for the National Gallery, London, to the Costabili collection, Ferrara, on March 28–29, 1858, at which point the painting is ascribed to Zoppo) // A. Ugolini, "Rividendo la collezione Costabili di Ferrara," *Paragone*, No. 489, November 1990, pp. 63–64 // *New Orleans Museum of Art—Handbook of the Collection*, New Orleans, 1995, p. 21 (entry by J.G. Caldwell), illus. (color) // M.S. Frinta, *Punched Decoration on Late Medieval Panel and Miniature Painting*, pt. 1, *Catalogue Raisonné of All Punch Shapes*, Prague, 1998, pp. 109, 125 // E. Mattaliano, *La Collezione Costabili* (ed. by G. Agostini), Venice, 1998, pp. 33–34, note, 125–126, no. 146, illus. p. 277 (color).

EXHIBITED

Washington, D.C., National Gallery of Art, 1941–1951, no. 343 // Little Rock, Arkansas, Arkansas Art Center, *Religion in Painting*, December 7, 1963–January 30, 1964, no. 16.

4
Bernardino Fungai
(Sienese: 1460–1516)

*The Martyrdom of Saint Lucy,* circa 1490
Tempera on panel: 16 x 23 ¾ inches
(40.6 x 60.3 cm.)
The Samuel H. Kress Collection,
acc. no. 1961.68

PROVENANCE

Sir Francis Ewan, London; Conte Alessandro Contini Bonacossi (1878–1955), Florence; acquired from him in 1933 by the Samuel H. Kress Collection; presented by them to the museum in 1961.

REFERENCES

*National Gallery of Art: Preliminary Catalogue of Painting and Sculpture: Descriptive List with Notes*, Washington, D.C., 1941, p. 68, no. 230 // W.E. Suida, *The Samuel H. Kress Collection in the Isaac Delgado Museum of Art*, New Orleans, 1953, p. 22, illus. p. 23 [2nd ed., revised by P. Wescher, New Orleans, 1966, same pagination] // B. Berenson, *Italian Pictures of the Renaissance: Central Italian and North Italian Schools*, London and New York, 1968, I, p. 151 // F.R. Shapley, *Paintings from the Samuel H. Kress Collection: Italian Schools*, II, *XV-XVI Century*, London, 1968, p. 109, no. K248, illus. fig. 271 // B.B. Fredericksen and F. Zeri, *Census of Pre-Nineteenth-Century Italian Paintings in North American Public Collections*, Cambridge, Mass., 1972, pp. 76, 426, 601 // Everett Fahy, verbally, May/June 2006 (as by the follower of Domenico Ghirlandaio known as the Pseudo-Granacci [also dubbed the Master of the Spiridon Story of Joseph], who is perhaps identifiable with Poggio Poggini, a *garzone* in Ghirlandaio's workshop in Pisa in 1493 and an assistant of Francesco Granacci as of 1495 [as suggested by E. Fahy, in Florence, Casa Buonarroti, *Il Giardino di San Marco: maestri e compagni del giovane Michelangelo* (ed. by P. Barocchi), 1992, pp. 51–52]).

EXHIBITED

Washington, D.C., National Gallery of Art, 1941–1951, no. 230.

## 5

Benvenuto Tisi, called Il Garofalo
(Ferrarese: c. 1476–1559)

*Meditation of Saint Jerome,* circa 1520–25
Tempera on panel: 20 ¼ x 23 ¾ inches
(51.4 x 60.3 cm.)
The Samuel H. Kress Collection,
acc. no. 1961.78

PROVENANCE
Conte Alessandro Contini Bonacossi (1878–1955), Florence; acquired from him in 1937 by the Samuel H. Kress Collection; presented by them to the museum in 1961.

REFERENCES
R. Longhi, "Ampliamenti nell'*Officina ferrarese*," *Critica d'arte*, IV, 1940, suppl., p. 29, illus. pl. XLI, fig. 77 [reprinted in R. Longhi, *Officina ferrarese, 1934…*, Florence, 1956, pp. 156–157, illus. fig. 374] // *National Gallery of Art: Preliminary Catalogue of Painting and Sculpture: Descriptive List with Notes*, Washington, D.C., 1941, p. 73, no. 473 // W.E. Suida, *The Samuel H. Kress Collection in the Isaac Delgado Museum of Art*, New Orleans, 1953, p. 42, illus. p. 43 [2nd ed., revised by P. Wescher, New Orleans, 1966, same pagination] // A. Neppi, *Il Garofalo, Benvenuto Tisi*, Milan, 1959, pp. 29, 55, illus. fig. 21 // G. Mazzariol, *Il Garofalo, Benvenuto Tisi*, Venice, 1960, pp. 23–24, illus. fig. 18 // B. Berenson, *Italian Pictures of the Renaissance: Central Italian and North Italian Schools*, London and New York, 1968, I, p. 156 // F.R. Shapley, *Paintings from the Samuel H. Kress Collection: Italian Schools*, II, *XV-XVI Century*, London, 1968, p. 79, no. K1111, illus. fig. 186 // B.B. Fredericksen and F. Zeri, *Census of Pre-Nineteenth-Century Italian Paintings in North American Public Collections*, Cambridge, Mass., 1972, pp. 78, 409, 602 // Ferrara, Palazzo dei Diamanti, *Affreschi ferraresi restaurati ed acquisizioni per la Pinacoteca Nazionale di Ferrara* (cat. by E. Riccomini), 1973–1974, p. 81 (as c. 1520) // A.M. Fioravanti Baraldi, "Benvenuto Tisi da Garofalo tra Rinascimento e Manierismo. Contributi alla catalogazione dell'artista dal 1512 al 1550," *Atti dell'Accademia delle Scienze di Ferrara*, LIV, 1976–1977, pp. 47, 121 // "Garofalo, Benvenuto Tisi," in *Dizionario enciclopedico dei pittori e degli incisori italiani: dall'XI al XX secolo*, V, Milan, 1981, p. 282 // A.M. Fioravanti Baraldi, *Il Garofalo, Benvenuto Tisi, pittore (c. 1476–1559): catalogo generale*, Rimini, 1993, pp. 151–152, no. 86, illus. p. 153 // S.A. Horsthemke, *Das Bild im Bild in der italienischen Malerei: Zur Darstellung religiöser Gemälde in der Renaissance*, Berlin, 1996, pp. 71, 227, illus. fig. 37.

EXHIBITED
Washington, D.C, National Gallery of Art, 1941–1951, no. 473 // Little Rock, Arkansas, Arkansas Art Center, *Religion in Painting*, December 7, 1963–January 30, 1964, no. 14.

## 6

Bernardino Luini
(Milanese: 1480/90–1532)

*Adoration of the Christ Child and the Annunciation to the Shepherds,* circa 1520–25
Oil on panel transferred to canvas:
69 ¾ x 47 inches (177.2 x 119.4 cm.)
The Samuel H. Kress Collection,
acc. no. 1961.77

PROVENANCE
Maestri family, Milan; Conte Giovanni Battista Lucini Passalaqua, Milan, and Villa Montrasio, Como; his estate sale, Milan, Teatro della Scala, foyer (auction organized by Galleria Sambon), April 14–18, 20–21, 1885, lot 1, illus. in cat., pl. 1; Charles Butler (1822–1910), Warren Wood, Shortgrove, Essex, and London, as of 1891; acquired from him that year by Robert Henry Benson (1850–1929) and Evelyn (Holford) Benson, London; acquired, with the Benson collection *en bloc*, in July 1927 by Duveen Brothers, New York and London; acquired from them by the Samuel H. Kress Collection in 1937; presented by them to the museum in 1961.

REFERENCES
*Catalogue de Tableaux, ecc. de M. le comte Lucini Passalacqua de Milan*, Milan, 1885, p. 5, illus. pl. 1 // C.J. Ffoulkes, "Le Esposizioni d'arte italiana a Londra, III: I Lombardi," *Archivio storico dell'arte*, VII, 1894, p. 258 // G. Frizzoni, "Exposition de maîtres de l'École Lombarde à Londres (deuxième et dernier article)," *Gazette des Beaux-Arts*, 3e pér., XX, November 1898, p. 399 // London, Burlington Fine Arts Club, *Illustrated Catalogue of Pictures by Masters of the Milanese and Allied Schools of Painting* (introd. by H.F. Cook), 1899, p. lxvii // G.C. Williamson, *Bernardino Luini*, London, 1900, p. 103 // L. Cust, "La Collection de M. R.H. Benson (Londres)," *Les Arts*, No. 70. 1907, p. 22, illus. p. 31 // B. Berenson, *North Italian Painters of the Renaissance*, New York and London, 1910, p. 247 // C.J. Ffoulkes, "Corrieri: Notizie d'Inghilterra. Esposizione di antichi maestri a Londra," *L'Arte*, XIII, 1910, p. 304 (as school of Luini) // L. Beltrami, *Luini, 1512–1532*, Milan, 1911, p. 339, illus. p. 341 // T. Borenius, *Catalogue of Italian Pictures at 16, South Street, Park Lane, London, and Buckhurst in Sussex, Collected by Robert and Evelyn Benson*, London, 1914, privately printed, p. 121, no. 62 // L. Venturi, *Italian Paintings in America*, New York and Milan, 1933, III, n.p., illus. pl. 489 // *Duveen Pictures in Public Collections of America*, New York, 1941, n.p., no. 141, illus. (as c. 1525) // *National Gallery of Art: Preliminary Catalogue of Painting and Sculpture: Descriptive List with Notes*, Washington, D.C., 1941, pp. 117–118, no. 455 // W.E. Suida, *The Samuel H. Kress Collection in the Isaac Delgado Museum of Art*, New Orleans, 1953, p. 40, illus. p. 41 [2nd ed., revised by P. Wescher, New Orleans, 1966, same pagination] // A. Ottino della Chiesa, *Bernardino Luini*, Novara, 1956, pp. 38, 122–123, no. 186, illus. fig. 129 // H. Haydon, *Great Art Treasures in America's Smaller Museums*, New York, 1967, p. 85 // B. Berenson, *Italian Pictures of the Renaissance: Central Italian and North Italian Schools*, London and New York, 1968, I, p. 233 // F.R. Shapley, *Paintings from the Samuel H. Kress Collection: Italian Schools*, II, *XV-XVI Century*, London, 1968, p. 143, no. K1087, illus., fig. 334 // B.B. Fredericksen and F. Zeri, *Census of Pre-Nineteenth-Century Italian Paintings in North American Public Collections*, Cambridge, Mass., 1972, pp. 114, 269, 271, 602 // C.T. Dowd, ed., "The Travel Diaries of Otto Mündler, 1855-1858," *The Walpole Society*, LI, 1985, p. 136 (records visit of October 10-11, 1856, by Otto Mündler, then traveling agent for the National Gallery, London, to the Lucini Passalacqua collection in Milan) // J. Shell, "Bernardino Luini's Lost Altarpiece for the Church of S. Vicenzo at Gravedona," *Arte lombarda*, N.S., Nos. 90–91, 1989, pp. 189–190, illus. p. 190, fig. 2 // *New Orleans Museum of Art—Handbook of the Collection*, New Orleans, 1995, p. 23 (entry by S.E. Stearns), illus. (color) // M. Secrest, *Duveen: A Life in Art*, New York, 2004, p. 459 (under "Paintings, Sculpture, and Objects Sold or Donated by Joseph Duveen, 1900–1939: A Partial List") // E.E. Gardner, *A Bibliographical Repertory of Italian Private Collections*, III, *Labia-Ovidi* (ed. by C. Ceschi, assisted by K. Baetjer), Venice, 2004, pp. 34-35.

EXHIBITED
London, Royal Academy of Arts, *Exhibition of*

Works by the Old Masters & by Deceased Masters of the British School, Including a Collection of Water Colour Drawings, winter 1891, no. 140 // London, The New Gallery, Exhibition of Early Italian Art, from 1300 to 1550, 1893–1894, no. 212 // London, Royal Academy of Arts, Exhibition of Works by the Old Masters & by Deceased Masters of the British School, winter 1910, no. 8 // Detroit, Detroit Institute of Arts, The Sixteenth Loan Exhibition of Old Masters: Italian Paintings of the XIV to XVI Century, March 8–30, 1933, no. 87, also cited in "Introduction" by W.R. Valentiner, n.p. // Washington, D.C, National Gallery of Art, 1941–1952, no. 455.

7
Adriaen Isenbrandt
(Early Netherlandish: c. 1490–1551)

*The Virgin Nursing the Christ Child,*
circa 1525–30
Oil on panel: 17 ¼ x 13 inches (43.8 x 33 cm.)
Gift of Mrs. Frederick M. Stafford,
acc. no. 1998.216

PROVENANCE
Galerie Van Diemen, Berlin; Friedrich Gutmann, Haarlem (as of 1934); N.V. Kunsthandel P. de Boer, Amsterdam; Otto Wertheimer, Paris, as of 1954; Mr. and Mrs. Frederick M. Stafford, New York and Paris; presented by Mrs. Stafford to the museum in 1998.

REFERENCES
M.J. Friedländer, *Die altniederländische Malerei,* XI, *Die antwerpener Manieristen, Adriaen Isenbrandt,* Leiden, 1934, p. 135, no. 174, illus. pl. LXVIII // M.J. Friedländer, *Early Netherlandish Painting* (ed. by H. Pauwels, assisted by A.-M. Hess, and trans. by H. Norden), XI, *The Antwerp Mannerists: Adriaen Ysenbrandt,* New York and Washington, D.C., 1974, p. 87, no. 174, illus. pl. 132, fig. 174 // M.J. Friedländer, *Early Netherlandish Painting: Supplements,* n.d. [c. 1976], p. 24 // J.C. Wilson, "Adriaen Isenbrant Reconsidered. The Making and Marketing of Art in Sixteenth-Century Bruges" (unpublished Ph. D. dissertation, The Johns Hopkins University), 1983, pp. 49–60, 208 // J.C. Wilson, "Connoisseurship and Copies: The Case of the Rouen Grouping," *Gazette des Beaux-Arts,* 6e pér., CXVII, May-June 1991, pp. 192–193, 196, 199, illus. p. 194, fig. 3 (as attributed to Adriaen Isenbrandt) //

J.C. Wilson, *Painting in Bruges at the Close of the Middle Ages: Studies in Society and Visual Culture,* University Park, Penna., 1998, pp. 91–92, 96, 100, 102, 108–109, 202, 219, note 13, illus. p. 93, fig. 33 (as attributed to Adriaen Isenbrandt).

EXHIBITED
Berlin, Kaiser Friedrich Museumsverein, Preussischen Akademie der Künste, 1929 // Paris, Musée des Arts Décoratifs, *Chefs-d'oeuvre de la curiosité du monde: 2e Exposition Internationale de la C.I.N.O.A.,* June 10–September 30, 1954, no. 58, illus. pl. 3 // New Orleans, The Isaac Delgado Museum of Art, *Odyssey of an Art Collector: Unity in Diversity—5,000 Years of Art,* November 11, 1966–January 8, 1967, no. 157, illus. (color).

8
Lorenzo Lotto
(Venetian: c. 1480–1556)

*Portrait of a Bearded Man,*
circa 1530–35
Oil on canvas: 38 ½ x 33 ½ inches (97.8 x 85.1 cm.)
The Samuel H. Kress Collection,
acc. no. 1961.79

PROVENANCE
Principe Giuseppe Giovanelli (died 1886), Casa Giovanelli, Venice; Conte Alessandro Contini Bonacossi (1878–1955), Florence; acquired from him in 1932 by the Samuel H. Kress Collection; presented by them to the museum in 1961.

REFERENCES
A.M. Frankfurter, "Fine Italian Paintings from Kress Exhibition," *Art News,* XXXII, March 3, 1934, p. 8, illus. p. 9 // H. Comstock, "The Connoisseur in America…Portraits of the Italian Renaissance," *Connoisseur,* CV, May 1940, p. 216 // *National Gallery of Art: Preliminary Catalogue of Painting and Sculpture: Descriptive List with Notes,* Washington, D.C., 1941, p. 114, no. 207 (as c. 1540) // R. Longhi, *Viatico per cinque secoli di pittura veneziana,* Florence, 1946, p. 62, illus. pl. 95 (as c. 1534) // A. Banti and A. Boschetto, *Lorenzo Lotto: regesti note e cataloghi,* Florence, n.d. [1953], p. 87, no. 105, illus. fig. 199 // L. Coletti, *Lotto* (2nd ed., revised by N. Zucchelli), Bergamo, 1953, p. 45, illus. pl. 119 // T. Pignatti, *Lorenzo Lotto,* Milan, 1953, p. 146, illus. fig. 129 (as c. 1540–45) // W.E.

Suida, *The Samuel H. Kress Collection in the Isaac Delgado Museum of Art,* New Orleans, 1953, p. 44, illus. p. 45 [2nd ed., revised by P. Wescher, New Orleans, 1966, same pagination and color pl. (frontispiece)] // G. Perocco, "Guida alla Mostra di Lorenzo Lotto," *Emporium,* CXVII, June 1953, p. 260 // B. Berenson, *Lorenzo Lotto: Complete Edition* (3rd, revised ed.), London, 1955, p. 119, illus. pl. 334 [Italian ed., trans. by L. Vertova, Milan, 1955, pp. 156–157, illus. pl. 334] // B. Berenson, *Italian Pictures of the Renaissance: Venetian School,* London, 1957, I, p. 104 // C. Seymour, Jr., *Art Treasures for America: An Anthology of Paintings & Sculpture in the Samuel H. Kress Collection,* London, 1961, pp. 101, 213, illus. p. 100, pl. 91 (color) (as c. 1525) // P. Bianconi, *All the Paintings of Lorenzo Lotto* (trans. by P. Colacicchi), New York, 1963, II, p. 85, illus. pl. 160 (as c. 1532–33) // M. Seidenberg, *Die Bildnisse des Lorenzo Lotto,* Lörrach, 1964, pp. 71, 96 (as c. 1539) // H. Haydon, *Great Art Treasures in America's Smaller Museums,* New York, 1967, p. 85 // F.R. Shapley, *Paintings from the Samuel H. Kress Collection: Italian Schools,* II, *XV-XVI Century,* London, 1968, p. 162, no. K208, illus. fig. 392 // M.S. Young, "Letter from U.S.A.: Spanish Moss and Old Mies," *Apollo,* LXXXVIII, September 1968, p. 223 // B.B. Fredericksen and F. Zeri, *Census of Pre-Nineteenth-Century Italian Paintings in North American Public Collections,* Cambridge, Mass., 1972, pp. 112, 526, 602 // R. Pallucchini and G. Mariani Canova, *L'Opera completa del Lotto,* Milan, 1974, p. 116, no. 222, illus. p. 114 (as c. 1535) // F. Caroli, *Lorenzo Lotto,* Florence, 1975, p. 296, illus. p. 297 (as 1534) // J.G. Caldwell, *New Orleans Museum of Art—Handbook of the Collection* (ed. by B.N. McDermott), New Orleans, 1980, p. 29, illus. pp. 13 (color), 29 // F. Caroli, *Lorenzo Lotto e la nascita della psicologia moderna,* Milan, 1980, p. 270, illus. p. 271 (as 1534) // *New Orleans Museum of Art—Handbook of the Collection,* New Orleans, 1995, p. 25 (entry by J.G. Caldwell), illus. (color) // E.E. Gardner, *A Bibliographical Repertory of Italian Private Collections,* II, *Dabalà – Kvitkta* (ed. by C. Ceschi, assisted by K. Baetjer), Venice, 2002, p. 177 // C. Pirovano, *Lotto,* Milan, 2002, p. 185, no. 128, illus. (as c. 1535) // N. Penny, *National Gallery Catalogues: The Sixteenth Century Italian Paintings,* I, *Paintings from Bergamo, Brescia and Cremona,* New Haven and London, 2004, p. 76 (as contemporary with Lotto's *Lucretia* in the National Gallery, London, which the author dates to the early 1520s).

EXHIBITED
Traveling exhibition, September 1933–June 1935, beginning at Seattle, Seattle Art Museum, *An Exhibition of Italian Paintings Lent by Mr. Samuel H. Kress of New York*, p. 46, no number, illus. (exhibition traveled to Portland, Oregon, Portland Art Museum; Sacramento, Calif., E.B. Crocker Art Gallery; San Francisco, California Palace of the Legion of Honor; Los Angeles, Los Angeles Museum of History, Science and Art; San Diego, Balboa Park, Fine Arts Gallery; San Antonio, Texas, Witte Memorial Museum; Nashville, Tenn., Parthenon; Montgomery, Alabama, Huntingdon College; Waco, Texas, Baylor University; Tampa, Florida, The Florida Fair Grounds; Winter Park, Florida, Rollins College, Morse Gallery of Art; Savannah, Georgia, Telfair Academy of Arts and Sciences; Charleston, South Carolina, Gibbes Art Gallery; and Charlotte, North Carolina, Mint Museum of Art) (as c. 1540) // San Francisco, California Palace of the Legion of Honor, *Exhibition of Venetian Painting, from the Fifteenth Century through the Eighteenth Century*, June 25–July 24, 1938, no. 39, illus. pl. 39 // Seattle, Seattle Art Museum, *Venetian Paintings from the Samuel H. Kress Collection*, August 1–25, 1938 (exhibition traveled to Portland, Oregon, Portland Art Museum, September 1–26, 1938; and Montgomery, Alabama, Montgomery Museum of Fine Arts, October 1–31, 1938) // New York, Knoedler & Co., *Italian Renaissance Portraits*, March 18–April 6, 1940, no. 15 // Washington, D.C., National Gallery of Art, 1941–1952 // Venice, Palazzo Ducale, *Mostra di Lorenzo Lotto* (cat. by P. Zampetti), June 14–October 18, 1953, no. 89, illus. p. 146 // Washington, D.C., National Gallery of Art, "Art Treasures for America," December 10, 1961–February 4, 1962, no. 55 [for cat., see Seymour, 1961, cited above].

9
Maerten van Heemskerck
(Dutch: 1498–1574)

*Apollo and the Muses,* circa 1555–60
Oil on panel: 38 ¼ x 54 ½ inches
(99.7 x 138.5 cm.)
Museum Purchase, General Acquisition Fund, acc. no. 1982.163

PROVENANCE
Possibly Ferdinand II (1578–1637), Holy Roman Emperor, Prague and Vienna (cf. entry in the 1621 inventory of his collection: "een poetische music vom Martin Heembskirche," as quoted in Harrison, Jr., 1987, cited below, II, p. 763; alternatively, Ferdinand II's painting may be identifiable with the 1565 picture of the same subject at The Chrysler Museum of Art, Norfolk, Virginia); Margaret, Lady Fortescue (born 1923), Castle Hill, Barnstaple, Devon (as by Marten de Vos); her sale, London, Christie's, June 28, 1974, lot 72 (as indistinctly signed), illus. in cat.; Colnaghi, London, as of 1982; acquired from them by the museum later that year.

REFERENCES
C. Limentani Virdis, "'Make Love Not War:' Nota in margine al tema tintorettesco di un dipinto di Martin de Vos," *Arte veneta*, XXIX, 1975, p. 183, illus. p. 185, fig. 4 // R. Grosshans, *Maerten van Heemskerck: Die Gemälde*, Berlin, 1980, pp. 44, 217–218, no. 86, illus. fig. 119 // P. Rubin, "Current and Forthcoming Exhibitions: London, Cinquecento at Colnaghi's," *Burlington Magazine*, CXXIV, October 1982, p. 645 // I.M. Veldman, "The *Concert of the Muses* in the Work of Maerten van Heemskerck," *Hoogsteder-Naumann Mercury*, I, 1985, pp. 35, 37, illus. p. 35, fig. 1 // J.C. Harrison, Jr., "The Detroit *Christ on Calvary* and the Cologne *Lamentation of Christ*: Two Early Haarlem Paintings by Maerten van Heemskerck," *Nederlands Kunsthistorisch Jaarboek*, XXXVII, 1986, pp. 184, 193, note 46, illus. p. 185, fig. 11 (as c. 1550–55) // J.C. Harrison, Jr., "The Paintings of Maerten van Heemskerck: A Catalogue Raisonné" (unpublished Ph. D. dissertation, University of Virginia), 1987, I, pp. 48–49, 67, 69, II, pp. 755–768, no. 82, 893, 896–897, illus. fig. 90 (as c. 1550–55) // *New Orleans Museum of Art—Handbook of the Collection*, New Orleans, 1995, p. 35 (entry by S.E. Stearns), illus. (color).

EXHIBITED
London, Colnaghi, *Discoveries from the Cinquecento* (cat. by C. Whitfield), June 17–August 7, 1982, no. 20, illus. // New York, Colnaghi, *Discoveries from the Cinquecento* (cat. by C. Whitfield), October 6–November 6, 1982, no. 16, illus. (color).

10
Abraham Bloemaert
(Dutch: 1566–1651)

*Saint John the Baptist Preaching in the Wilderness,* circa 1625–30
Oil on canvas: 35 ½ x 51 inches (90 x 130 cm.)
Museum Purchase and Gift, by exchange, of Mr. and Mrs. Frederick M. Stafford and Dr. and Mrs. Richard W. Levy, acc. no. 1987.108

PROVENANCE
Major Wallis, Drishane Castle, Millstreet Town, County Cork, Ireland; London, Christie's, April 15, 1983, lot 51, illus. in cat.; Richard L. Feigen & Co., New York; acquired from them by the museum in 1987.

REFERENCES
M.G. Roethlisberger, "Abraham Bloemaert, un grand maître hollandais encore trop méconnu," *L'Oeil*, No. 439, March 1992, p. 24, illus. fig. 5 (color) // M.G. Roethlisberger, *Abraham Bloemaert and His Sons: Paintings and Prints*, Doornspijk, 1993, I, pp. 37, 290, no. 446, illus. II, pl. XX (color) and fig. 619 // *New Orleans Museum of Art—Handbook of the Collection*, New Orleans, 1995, p. 36 (entry by S.E. Stearns), illus. (color).

EXHIBITED
St. Petersburg, Florida, The Museum of Fine Arts, *Abraham Bloemaert (1566–1651) and His Time*, January 28–April 8, 2001, no. 10, also cited in introduction by J. Hardin, p. 15, and in essay by M.G. Roethlisberger, "Positioning Abraham Bloemaert," p. 23, and on p. 56 (under "Paintings by Abraham Bloemaert in American Collections"), illus. p. 45 (color).

11

Giovanni Martinelli
(Florentine: 1600/04–1659)

*Death Comes to the Banquet Table,*
circa 1630
Oil on canvas: 47 ½ x 68 ½ inches
(120.6 x 174 cm.)
Gift of Mrs. William G. Helis, Sr., in memory
of her husband, acc. no. 1956.57

PROVENANCE
Joseph Brummer (1883–1947), New York;
acquired from him in 1920 by the Smith
College Museum of Art, Northampton, Mass.;
de-accessioned 1954 and acquired from them in
October 1954 (in partial exchange) by Hirschl &
Adler, New York; Lillye Menard; Mrs. William
G. Helis, Sr., New Orleans; presented by her to
the museum in 1956.

REFERENCES
*Handbook of the Art Collections of Smith College:
Paintings, Sculpture, Drawings, Prints, Ceramics,
Textiles,* Northampton, Mass., 1925, p. 25 (as
Bartolommeo Manfredi) // Charles Sterling,
verbally, c. 1950 (Smith College Museum of
Art curatorial files, as by Robert Tournier) //
A. Moir, "Memento Mori," *The Isaac Delgado
Museum of Art Bulletin,* September-October
1956, n.p., illus. (as attributed to Jean Leclerc)
// B. Nicolson, "Current and Forthcoming
Exhibitions:…'Figures at a Table' at Sarasota,"
*Burlington Magazine,* CII, May 1960, p. 226
(as by a Flemish artist, possibly in the circle
of Louis Finson) // D. Bodart, *Louis Finson
(Bruges, avant 1580; Amsterdam, 1617),* Brussels,
1970, p. 210, no. I // E. Borea, "Considerazioni
sulla mostra 'Caravaggio e i suoi seguaci'
a Cleveland," *Bollettino d'arte,* ser. 5, LVII,
July-December 1972, pp. 160–161, note 13,
illus. fig. 9 (as Florentine School, perhaps by
Giovanni Martinelli) // B.B. Fredericksen
and F. Zeri, *Census of Pre-Nineteenth-Century
Italian Paintings in North American Public
Collections,* Cambridge, Mass., 1972, pp. 157,
489, 601 (as attributed to Pietro Paolini) //
D.S. Pepper, "Caravaggio riveduto e corretto:
La mostra di Cleveland," *Arte illustrata,*
No. 48, March 1972, p. 171 (repeating a verbal
attribution of Carlo Volpe, as by a Tuscan
follower of Rutilio Manetti) // P. Rosenberg,
"Trois expositions italiennes, Cortone, Bologne,
Florence," *Revue de l'Art,* No. 15, 1972, p. 113,
illus. fig. 7 (as attributed to Jean Ducamps)
// R.E. Spear, "Unknown Pictures by the

Caravaggisti (with Notes on Caravaggio and
His Followers)," *Storia dell'arte,* No. 14, 1972,
p. 158 // C. Volpe, "Annotazioni sulla mostra
caravaggesca di Cleveland," *Paragone,* No. 263,
January 1972, pp. 64–65, illus. pl. 15 (records
attribution to Jean Ducamps, made verbally
by Roberto Longhi) // Rome, Académie de
France, Villa Medici, *I Caravaggeschi francesi*
(cat. by A. Brejon de Lavergnée and J.P. Cuzin),
1973–1974, p. 241 (tentatively attributed to Jean
Ducamps) [French ed. of cat., Paris, Grand
Palais, *Valentin et les caravagesques français,*
1974, pp. 248–249] // A. Brejon de Lavergnée
and J.P. Cuzin, "À propos de caravagesques
français," *La Revue du Louvre et des Musées de
France,* 1974, No. 1, p. 37 // F. Sricchia Santoro,
"'La Madonna di Pistoia' e l'attività romana
di Anastasio Fontebuoni," *Commentari,* N.S.,
XXV, January-June 1974, pp. 44, 46, note 31 //
R. Cantelli, "Proposte per Giovanni Martinelli,"
*Paradigma,* II, 1978, pp. 139–140, illus. fig. 28
// B. Nicolson, *The International Caravaggesque
Movement,* London, 1979, pp. 47, 67 (as by
Jean Ducamps) // J.G. Caldwell, *New Orleans
Museum of Art—Handbook of the Collection*
(ed. by B.N. McDermott), New Orleans, 1980,
p. 47, illus. (as Jean Ducamps) // C. Goldstein,
"Seventeenth-Century French Paintings,"
*Art Journal,* XLII, winter 1982, p. 330 //
A.F. Blunt and J.-P. Cuzin, "Current and
Forthcoming Exhibitions: New York: French
Seventeenth-century Paintings from American
Collections," *Burlington Magazine,* CXXIII,
August 1982, p. 529 (records the attributions
of Cuzin [see 1973–1974 Reference, above]
and Pierre Rosenberg [verbal] attribution to
the Florentine School, circle of Martinelli) //
R. Cantelli, *Repertorio della pittura fiorentina
del Seicento,* Fiesole, 1983, p. 108, illus. pl.
543 (as by Martinelli) // Florence, Palazzo
Strozzi, *Il Seicento fiorentino: Arte a Firenze da
Ferdinando I a Cosimo III: Pittura,* 1986–1987,
p. 327, cited under nos. 1.169 and 1.170 (entry
by C. D'Afflitto) // C. D'Afflitto, "Martinelli,
Giovanni" in M. Gregori and E. Schleier, eds.,
*La pittura in Italia: Il Seicento* (2nd, revised ed.),
Milan, 1989, II, p. 805 // P.N. Dunbar, *The
New Orleans Museum of Art: The First Seventy-
Five Years,* Baton Rouge and London, 1990,
p. 87 // B. Nicolson, *Caravaggism in Europe*
(2nd ed., revised by L. Vertova), Turin, 1990,
I, p. 104, no. 362, illus. II, fig. 362 // Tulsa,
Oklahoma, The Philbrook Museum of Art, and
elsewhere, *Botticelli to Tiepolo: Three Centuries of
Painting from Bob Jones University* (cat. by R.P.
Townsend), 1994–1995, cited in essay by E.M.

Zafran, "A History of Italian Baroque Painting
in America," p. 79 // *New Orleans Museum of
Art—Handbook of the Collection,* New Orleans,
1995, p. 27 (entry by S.E. Stearns), illus.
(color) // A. Barret, *Les Peintres du fantastique,*
Paris, 1996, p. 119, illus. p. 116 (color detail) //
C. D'Afflitto, "Martinelli, Giovanni," in *The
Dictionary of Art,* London, 1996, XX, p. 495.

EXHIBITED
Sarasota, Florida, John and Mable Ringling
Museum of Art, "Figures at a Table," February
7–March 6, 1960 (as by Cecco del Caravaggio)
[for cat., see C. Gilbert, *The Ringling Museum,
Sarasota, Florida. Bulletin,* I, February 1960,
n.p., no. 2, illus.] // New Orleans, The Isaac
Delgado Museum of Art, *Fêtes de la palette:
An Exhibition of European Paintings and
Decorative Arts from the Mid-Sixteenth through
the Mid-Eighteenth Century Dedicated to the
"Delights of the Bountiful Table,"* November
22, 1962–January 6, 1963, no. 25, also cited
in introductory essay by J.B. Byrnes, n.p.,
illus. pl. 61 (as attributed to Jean Leclerc) //
Jacksonville, Florida, Cummer Gallery of Art,
*The Age of Louis XIII,* October 29–December
7, 1969, no. 26, illus. (exhibition traveled
to St. Petersburg, Florida, The Museum
of Fine Arts, January 5–February 8, 1970)
// Cleveland, Cleveland Museum of Art,
*Caravaggio and His Followers* (cat. by R.E.
Spear), October 27, 1971–January 2, 1972,
no. 24, illus. [2nd, revised ed. of cat., New
York, 1975, same pagination] (as attributed
to Jean Ducamps and dating from c. 1625)
// Paris, Galeries nationales du Grand Palais,
*La Peinture française du XVIIe siècle dans les
collections américaines* (cat. by P. Rosenberg),
January 29–April 26, 1982, no. 124, illus.
pp. 64, 342 (as French School, 17th Century)
(exhibition traveled to New York, The
Metropolitan Museum of Art, as *France in
the Golden Age: Seventeenth-Century French
Paintings in American Collections,* May 26–
August 22, 1982; and Chicago, Art Institute of
Chicago, September 18–November 28, 1982)
(as French School, 17th century) [American ed.
of cat., no. 124, illus. pp. 64, 342] // Worcester,
Mass., Worcester Art Museum, *Hope and
Healing: Painting in Italy in a Time of Plague,
1500–1800* (ed. by G.A. Bailey et al.), April 3–
September 25, 2005, no. 4, also cited in essay
by F. Mormando, "Introduction: Response to
the Plague in Early Modern Italy: What the
Primary Sources, Printed and Painted, Reveal,"
p. 24, illus. in color, pp. 184, 185 (detail).

**12**
**Simon Vouet**
(French: 1590–1649)

*Erato, The Muse of Love Poetry,* 1634–38
Oil on oak panel: 32 x 25 ¼ inches
(81.3 x 64.1 cm.)
Museum Purchase, The Carrie Heiderich Fund,
acc. no. 1998.1

PROVENANCE
London, Sotheby's, April 11, 1990, lot 76 (as
Simon Vouet and studio), illus. in cat. (color)
(bought in); Colnaghi, London; Danny Katz,
London, as of 1995; New York, Sotheby's,
January 30, 1998, lot 57 (as "Property of a
Family Trust"), illus. in cat. (color); acquired
there by the museum.

REFERENCES
London and New York, Colnaghi, *A Collectors
Miscellany: European Paintings 1600–1800,* winter
1990–1991, pp. 19–20, illus. in color, p. 19
and pl. II // S. Loire, "Introduction: Simon
Vouet: nouvelles précisions et perspectives de
recherches," in *Simon Vouet: Actes du colloque
international, Galeries nationales du Grand Palais,
5–6–7 février 1991* (ed. by S. Loire), Paris, 1992,
p. 27, note 19, illus. p. 19, fig. 1 (as Vouet and
studio) // A. Brejon de Lavergnée, "Une série de
Muses de l'atelier de Simon Vouet," in *Ex Fumo
Lucem: Baroque Studies in Honour of Klára Garas,
Presented on Her Eightieth Birthday,* Budapest,
1999, I, pp. 168, 171–172, 175, 178, illus. p. 169,
fig. 7 (as workshop of Vouet, perhaps by Michel
Dorigny) // Oberlin, Ohio, The Allen Memorial
Art Museum, and elsewhere, *The Splendor of
Ruins in French Landscape Painting, 1630–1800,*
2005, pp. 169–170, and note 4 // New York,
Wildenstein, *The Arts of France from François
Ier to Napoléon Ier: A Centennial Celebration of
Wildenstein's Presence in New York,* 2005–2006,
p. 109, illus. fig. 14a.

**13**
**Simone Cantarini, called Il Pesarese**
(Bolognese: 1612–1648)

*Madonna and Child with a Goldfinch,* circa
1640
Oil on canvas, oval: 40 ⅝ x 30 ⅝ inches
(103.2 x 77.8 cm.)
Gift of the Azby Art Fund in memory of
Herbert J. Harvey, Jr., and Marion W. Harvey,
acc. no. 83.52

PROVENANCE
Hazlitt Gallery, London; J. Herbert Harvey, Jr.,
New Orleans; presented by the Azby Art Fund
to the museum in 1983.

REFERENCES
*New Orleans Museum of Art—Handbook of the
Collection,* New Orleans, 1995, p. 28 (entry by
S.E. Stearns), illus. in color, pp. 2 (detail: head
of Madonna), 28.

**14**
**Claude Gellée, called Claude Lorrain**
(French: 1600–1682)

*Ideal View of Tivoli,* 1644
Oil on canvas: 46 x 57 ⅞ inches
(116.8 x 147 cm.)
Museum Purchase, Art Acquisition Fund Drive,
acc. no. 1978.1

PROVENANCE
Private collection, Russia [unidentified seal on
back of frame]; acquired from there in 1919
by an unidentified art dealer, Berlin; acquired
soon after from that source by Ernst Cohen,
Göteborg, Sweden; his sale, London, Christie's,
June 25, 1971, lot 22, illus. in cat.; Marcel Joly,
Ceyrat (Puy-de-Dôme); Richard L. Feigen &
Co., New York, as of 1974; acquired from them
by the museum in 1978.

REFERENCES
M. Roethlisberger, "Quelques tableaux inédits
du XVIIe siècle français: Le Sueur, Claude
Lorrain, La Fosse," *Revue de l'Art,* No. 11, 1971,
pp. 80–82, illus. p. 79, figs. 13, 14 (detail), 15
(detail) // M. Roethlisberger, "Nuovi aspetti
di Claude Lorrain,» *Paragone,* No. 273,
November 1972, pp. 32–33, 36, note 39, illus.
pl. 26 // M. Röthlisberger and D. Cecchi,
*Tout l'oeuvre peint de Claude Lorrain,* Paris,
1977, pp. 103–104, no. 143, illus. fig. 143
(*Liber Veritatis* drawing) // M. Kitson, *Claude
Lorrain : Liber Veritatis,* London, 1978, pp.
103–104, cited under LV81 // M. Roethlisberger,
*Claude Lorrain, The Paintings* (2nd ed.), New
York, 1979, I, p. 231, cited under no. LV81 (as
lost) // J.G. Caldwell, *New Orleans Museum of
Art—Handbook of the Collection* (ed. by B.N.
McDermott), New Orleans, 1980, p. 48, illus.
pp. 15 (color), 48 // Paris, Galeries nationales
du Grand Palais, *La Peinture française du XVIIe
siècle dans les collections américaines* (cat. by
P. Rosenberg), 1982, p. 359, no. 9 (tentatively

attributes painting to Claude Lorrain),
illus. [American ed. of cat., New York, The
Metropolitan Museum of Art, and Chicago,
Art Institute of Chicago, *France in the Golden
Age: Seventeenth-Century French Paintings in
American Collections,* 1982, p. 359, illus. fig.
9] // P. Rosenberg and M.C. Stewart, *French
Paintings, 1500–1825: The Fine Arts Museums of
San Francisco,* San Francisco, 1987, pp. 57–58,
illus. p. 58, fig. 1 // P.N. Dunbar, *The New
Orleans Museum of Art: The First Seventy-Five
Years,* Baton Rouge and London, 1990, p. 290
// Raleigh, North Carolina Museum of Art,
and elsewhere, *A Gift to America: Masterpieces
of European Painting from the Samuel H. Kress
Collection,* 1994–1995, pp. 193, 194, note 4, cited
under no. 31 (entry by L.F. Orr), illus. p. 193,
fig. 1 // *New Orleans Museum of Art—Handbook
of the Collection,* New Orleans, 1995, p. 44
(entry by E.P. Caraco), illus. (color).

EXHIBITED
New York, The Metropolitan Museum of
Art, *Sixth Annual Exhibition Presented by
C.I.N.O.A.,* October 19, 1974–January 5, 1975,
no. 136, illus. // Munich, Haus der Kunst, *Im
Licht von Claude Lorrain: Landschaftsmalerei aus
drei Jahrhunderten* (cat. by M. Roethlisberger),
March 12–May 29, 1983, no. 13, illus. //
Orléans, Musée des Beaux-Arts, *Peintures
françaises du Museum of Art de la Nouvelle
Orléans,* May 9–September 15, 1984, no. 11
(entry by E.P. Caraco), illus. pp. 16 (color),
21 // San Francisco, Fine Arts Museums of
San Francisco, M.H. De Young Memorial
Museum, *Viewpoints XII—Claude Lorrain: A
Study in Connoisseurship* (brochure by S. Nash,
M.C. Stewart and J. Wright), May 5–June 24,
1990, no number, illus. p. 2, fig. 2 // Memphis,
Tenn., The Dixon Gallery and Gardens, *French
Paintings of Three Centuries from the New
Orleans Museum of Art,* January 5–March 1,
1992, no. 1 (entry by E.P. Caraco), also cited
in essay by M.R. Brown, "An Introduction
to French Paintings of Three Centuries," pp.
10, 12, illus. p. 17 (color) (exhibition traveled
to Miami, Center for the Fine Arts, March
15–May 3, 1992; Wilmington, Delaware Art
Museum, May 17–June 29, 1992; Grosse Point
Shores, Michigan, Edsel and Eleanor Ford
House, July 22–September 6, 1992; Oklahoma
City, Oklahoma City Art Museum, October
4–November 15, 1992; and Seattle, Seattle Art
Museum, December 17, 1992–February 14,
1993) // Koriyama, Koriyama City Museum of
Art, *French Art of Four Centuries from the New

*Orleans Museum of Art*, February 27–March 31, 1993, no. 1 (entry by E.P. Caraco), illus. pp. 31 (color) and 126 (exhibition traveled to Yokohama, Sogo Museum of Art, April 21–May 23, 1993; Nara, Nara Sogo Museum of Art, June 9–July 4, 1993; and Kitakyushu, Kitakyushu Municipal Museum of Art, July 10–August 22, 1993).

## 15
Claude Lefebvre
(French: 1632–1674)

*Portrait of Louis XIV,* 1670
Oil on canvas: 46 x 35 ¼ inches
(116.8 x 89.5 cm.)
Gift of Hirschl and Adler Gallery, New York, acc. no. 1956.67

PROVENANCE
London, Sotheby's, December 5, 1923, lot 102 (as Pierre Mignard); Hirschl and Adler Gallery, New York; presented by them to the museum (as by Nicolas de Largillierre) in 1956.

ENGRAVINGS
(1) Nicolas Pitau the Elder (1632–1671), 1670; (2) Pierre Louis van Schuppen (1627–1702), 1670 (in reverse, bust only); for these prints, see Wilhelm, 1994, cited below, pp. 24–25, 32, illus. p. 22, figs. 7 and 8.

REFERENCES
C. Maumené and L d'Harcourt, *Iconographie des rois de France*, pt. 2, *Louis XIV, Louis XV, Louis XVI*, Paris, 1931, p. 60 (cites portrait in the 1923 Sotheby's sale [see Provenance, above], describes it fully and attributes the painting to Lefebvre, as possibly that artist's original portrait of Louis XIV) // Paris, Galeries nationales du Grand Palais, *La Peinture française du XVIIe siècle dans les collections américaines* (cat. by P. Rosenberg), 1982, p. 355, no. 11, illus. [American ed. of cat.: New York, The Metropolitan Museum of Art, and Chicago, Art Institute of Chicago, as *France in the Golden Age: Seventeenth-Century French Paintings in American Collections*, 1982, p. 355, illus. fig. 11] // P.N. Dunbar, *The New Orleans Museum of Art: The First Seventy-Five Years*, Baton Rouge and London, 1990, p. 122 and note 35 // J. Wilhelm, "Quelques portraits peints par Claude Le Febvre (1632–1674)," *Revue du Louvre*, 1994, No. 2, pp. 24–25, 32, illus. p. 23, fig. 9 (color) // C. Constans, *Musée national du Château de Versailles: les peintures,*

Paris, 1995, II, p. 576 // T. Bajou, *La Peinture à Versailles: XVIIe siècle*, Paris, 1998, p. 128 // Jackson, Mississippi, Mississippi Arts Pavilion, *Splendors of Versailles* (ed. by C. Constans and X. Salmon), 1998, p. 59, cited under no. 2 (entry by C. Constans).

EXHIBITED
Orléans, Musée des Beaux-Arts, *Peintures françaises du Museum of Art de la Nouvelle Orléans*, May 9–September 15, 1984, no. 3 (entry by E.P. Caraco), illus. // Memphis, Tenn., The Dixon Gallery and Gardens, *French Paintings of Three Centuries from the New Orleans Museum of Art*, January 5–March 1, 1992, no. 2 (entry by E.P. Caraco), also cited in essay by M.R. Brown, "An Introduction to French Paintings of Three Centuries," p. 8, illus. p. 19 (color) (exhibition traveled to Miami, Center for the Fine Arts, March 15–May 3, 1992; Wilmington, Delaware Art Museum, May 17–June 29, 1992; Grosse Point Shores, Michigan, Edsel and Eleanor Ford House, July 22–September 6, 1992; Oklahoma City, Oklahoma City Art Museum, October 4–November 15, 1992; and Seattle, Seattle Art Museum, December 17, 1992–February 14, 1993)// // Koriyama, Koriyama City Museum of Art, *French Art of Four Centuries from the New Orleans Museum of Art*, February 27–March 31, 1993, no. 2 (entry by E.P. Caraco), also cited in essay by M.R. Brown, "An Introduction to French Art of Four Centuries," p. 23, illus. pp. 32 (color detail), 33 (color) and 127 (exhibition traveled to Yokohama, Sogo Museum of Art, April 21–May 23, 1993; Nara, Nara Sogo Museum of Art, June 9–July 4, 1993; and Kitakyushu, Kitakyushu Municipal Museum of Art, July 10–August 22, 1993) // Oklahoma City, Oklahoma City Art Museum, *The Age of Opulence: Arts of the Baroque*, December 10, 1998–March 14, 1999 (no catalogue) // New Orleans, The Historic New Orleans Collection, *A Fusion of Nations, A Fusion of Cultures: Spain, France, the United States and the Louisiana Purchase*, January 14–June 7, 2003, no. 4.

## 16
Carlo Dolci
(Florentine: 1616–1686)

*The Vision of Saint Louis of Toulouse,* circa 1675–76
Oil on panel: 21 ¾ x 14 ¼ inches
(55.3 x 36.2 cm.)
The Samuel H. Kress Collection, acc. no. 1961.84

PROVENANCE
Presumably identifiable with the "*Modellino effiogiatovi [sic] S. Lodovico di Tolosa in atto di far orazione..sc*[udi]. *20.-.—*" sold by Andrea Dolci, the artist's son and sole heir, on July 7, 1690, to Ferdinando de' Medici (1673–1713), *Gran Principe* of Tuscany, Florence (as suggested by Epe, 1990, cited below, p. 213, note 22; not recorded in subsequent inventories of his collection); private collection, New York (as attributed to Carlo Maratta); Sixtina, New York; acquired from them in 1949 by the Samuel H. Kress Collection; presented by them to the museum in 1961.

REFERENCES
W.E. Suida, *The Samuel H. Kress Collection in the Isaac Delgado Museum of Art*, New Orleans, 1953, p. 54, illus. p. 55 [2nd ed., revised by P. Wescher, New Orleans, 1966, p. 56, illus. p. 57] // C. Del Bravo, "Carlo Dolci, devoto del naturale," *Paragone*, No. 163, July 1963, p. 40, note 13 // B.B. Fredericksen and F. Zeri, *Census of Pre-Nineteenth-Century Italian Paintings in North American Public Collections*, Cambridge, Mass., 1972, pp. 65, 424, 602 // F.R. Shapley, *Paintings from the Samuel H. Kress Collection: Italian Schools*, III, *XVI-XVIII Century*, London, 1973, p. 87, no. K1637, illus. fig. 156 // *Gli Uffizi: catalogo generale*, Florence, 1979, p. 249, cited under no. P541 (entry by M. Gregori) // J.G. Caldwell, *New Orleans Museum of Art—Handbook of the Collection* (ed. by B.N. McDermott), New Orleans, 1980, p. 33, illus. // G. Cantelli, *Repertorio della pittura fiorentina del Seicento*, Fiesole, 1983, p. 74 // F. Baldassari, "Dolci, Carlo," in M. Gregori and E. Schleier, eds., *La pittura in Italia: Il Seicento* (2nd, revised ed.), Milan, 1989, II, p. 727 // E. Epe, *Die Gemäldesammlung des Ferdinando de' Medici, Erbprinz von Toskana (1663–1713)*, Marburg, 1990, pp. 85, 213, note 22 // O. Ferrari, *Bozzetti italiani dal Manierismo al Barocco*, Naples, 1990, p. 125, illus. p. 124 // M.B. Guerrieri Borsoi, "Dolci, Carlo," in *Dizionario biografico*

degli italiani, XL, Rome, 1991, p. 423 // *New Orleans Museum of Art—Handbook of the Collection*, New Orleans, 1995, p. 29 (entry by J.G. Caldwell), illus. (color) // F. Baldassari, *Carlo Dolci*, Turin, 1995, pp. 171, 173–174, no. 147, 175, illus. p. 175, fig. 147 // M. Chiarini and S. Padovani, eds., *La Galleria Palatina e gli Appartamenti Reali di Palazzo Pitti: Catalogo dei dipinti*, Florence, 2003, II, *Catalogo*, p. 151, cited under no. 235 (entry by M. Chiarini).

EXHIBITED
Hanover, New Hampshire, Dartmouth College, Hood Museum of Art, *The Age of the Marvelous* (ed by J. Kenseth), September 21–November 24, 1991, no. 217, also cited in essay by Z.Z. Filiczak, "'A Time Fertile in Miracles:' Miraculous Events in and through Art," p. 195, illus. p. 450 (exhibition traveled to Raleigh, North Carolina Museum of Art, January 25–March 22, 1992; Houston, The Museum of Fine Arts, May 24–August 25, 1992; and Atlanta, High Museum of Art, October 6, 1992–January 3, 1993).

17
Luca Giordano
(Neapolitan: 1632–1705)

*The Baptism of Christ,* circa 1684
Oil on canvas: 93 ½ x 76 inches
(237.5 x 193 cm.)
Museum Purchase, General Membership Funds and Women's Volunteer Committee, acc. no. 1974.43

PROVENANCE
Said to have come from a church in Buckinghamshire (unverified); Julius Weitzner, London, as of 1969; Herner Wengraf, London, as of 1971; Jacques Seligmann, New York, 1974; acquired from him by the museum later that year.

REFERENCES
T. Crombie, "London Galleries: The Dominant Dutch," *Apollo*, XCIII, April 1971, p. 325, illus. p. 326, fig. 5 // B. Nicolson, "Current and Forthcoming Exhibitions:…London," *Burlington Magazine*, CXIII, April 1971, p. 228, illus. p. 225, fig. 73 // J.G. Caldwell, *New Orleans Museum of Art—Handbook of the Collection* (ed. by B.N. McDermott), New Orleans, 1980, p. 34, illus. // O. Ferrari and G. Scavizzi, *Luca Giordano: l'Opera completa*

(2nd, revised ed.), Naples, 1992, I, p. 309, no. A344, illus. II, p. 649, fig. 448 // Tulsa, Oklahoma, The Philbrook Museum of Art, and elsewhere, *Botticelli to Tiepolo: Three Centuries of Painting from Bob Jones University* (cat. by R.P. Townsend), 1994–1995, cited in essay by E.M. Zafran, "A History of Italian Baroque Painting in America," p. 89 // *New Orleans Museum of Art—Handbook of the Collection*, New Orleans, 1995, p. 30 (entry by J.G. Caldwell), illus. (color) // O. Ferrari and G. Scavizzi, *Luca Giordano: nuove ricerche e inediti*, Naples, 2003, p. 63, no. A0150, also cited p. 113, under no. DO104.

EXHIBITED
London, Herner Wengraf/Old Master Galleries, *Quarterly Catalogue of Acquisitions: 17th & 18th Century Italian Paintings*, April-June 1971, no. 3, illus. // New Haven, Conn., Yale University Art Gallery, *A Taste for Angels: Neapolitan Painting in North America, 1650–1750*, September 9–November 29, 1987, no. 15 (entry by G. Hersey and S. O'Connell), also cited p. 120 (biographical essay by J. Colton: as painted between spring 1686 and May 1692), illus. p. 151 (color) (dates painting to early 1690s) (exhibition traveled to Sarasota, Florida, The John and Mable Ringling Museum of Art, January 13–March 13, 1988; and Kansas City, Missouri, The Nelson-Atkins Museum of Art, April 30–June 12, 1988) // Frankfurt, Schirn Kunsthalle, *Guido Reni und Europa: Ruhm und Nachruhm* (ed. by S. Ebert-Schifferer et al.), December 2, 1988–February 26, 1989, no. D58 (entry by W. Prohaska), illus. (color) (as c. 1692–94).

18
Jean Baptiste Monnoyer
(French: 1634–1699)

*Flowers in an Urn,* 1690
Oil on canvas: 38 ½ x 30 inches (98 x 76 cm.)
Signed and dated lower left: *J.B. Monnoyer 1690*
Gift of Sidney H. Lazard, Sr., in memory of his family, especially Rosemary Herold Lazard, June Gurvich Lazard and Sidney Herold Lazard, Jr., with gratitude to New Orleans for 160 years, acc. no. 2003.226

PROVENANCE
Sidney Herold Lazard, Jr., New Orleans; presented by him to the museum in 2003.

19
Nicolas Colombel
(French: 1644–1717)

*Adoration of the Magi,* 1693–99
Oil on canvas: 45 x 58 ½ inches (114.3 x 148.6 cm.)
Museum Purchase, Women's Volunteer Committee Fund, acc. no. 73.209

PROVENANCE
Maximilien Titon (1631–1711); his postmortem inventory, February 9, 1711, no. 204 (as quoted in Lavergne-Durey, 1989, cited below, p. 91, note 34); by inheritance to his son, Evrard Titon du Tillet (1677–1762), Paris; by inheritance to his elder son, Louis Maximilien Titon (died 1728); by inheritance to his son, Pierre Joseph Titon de Cogny (died 1758); by inheritance to his uncle, Titon du Tillet (died 1763); his postmortem inventory, January 15, 1763 (published in Lavergne-Durey, 1989, pp. 96, 98, no. 83); London, Christie's, December 13, 1968, lot 62; Jacques Seligmann & Co., New York; acquired from them by the museum in 1973.

REFERENCES
G. Brice, *Description de la ville de Paris et de tout ce qu'elle contient de plus remarquable*, Paris, 1725, II, p. 270 [1752 ed., II, p. 260] // E. Bonnaffé, *Dictionnaire des amateurs français au XVIIe siècle*, Paris, 1884, p. 306 // A.F. Blunt, "Nicolas Colombel," *Revue de l'Art*, No. 9, 1970, pp. 28/30, 39, illus. p. 33, fig. 16 // J.G. Caldwell, *New Orleans Museum of Art—Handbook of the Collection* (ed. by B.N. McDermott), New Orleans, 1980, p. 49, illus. // Paris, Galeries nationales du Grand Palais, *La Peinture française du XVIIe siècle dans les collections américaines* (cat. by P. Rosenberg), 1982, p. 350, no. 4, illus. [American ed. of cat.: New York, The Metropolitan Museum of Art; and Chicago, Art Institute of Chicago, as *France in the Golden Age: Seventeenth-Century French Paintings in American Collections*, 1982, p. 350, illus. fig. 4 (with caption in reverse)] // V. Lavergne-Durey, "Les Titon, mécènes et collectionneurs à Paris à la fin du XVIIe et au XVIIIe siècles," *Bulletin de la Société de l'Histoire de l'Art Français*, 1989, pp. 80, 85, 91, notes 33–35, 96, illus. p. 81, fig. 3 // P.N. Dunbar, *The New Orleans Museum of Art: The First Seventy-Five Years*, Baton Rouge and London, 1990, p. 271 // *New Orleans Museum of Art—Handbook of the Collection*, New Orleans, 1995, p. 45 (entry by E.P. Caraco),

illus. (color) // E. Stolpe, "Colombel, Nicolas," in *Saur. Allgemeines Künstler-Lexikon. Die bildenden Künstler aller Zeiten und Völker*, XX, Munich and Leipzig, 1998, p. 260 // P. Sanchez, *Dictionnaire des artistes exposant dans les Salons des XVII et XVIII^EME siècles à Paris et en province, 1673–1800*, Dijon, 2004, I, p. 389.

EXHIBITED

Paris, Salon, 1704, no number // Orléans, Musée des Beaux-Arts, *Peintures françaises du Museum of Art de la Nouvelle Orléans*, May 9–September 15, 1984, no. 4 (entry by E.P. Caraco), illus. // Rochester, N.Y., University of Rochester, Memorial Art Gallery, *La Grande Manière: Historical and Religious Painting in France, 1700–1800* (cat. by D.A. Rosenthal), May 2–July 26, 1987, no. 8, illus. (exhibition traveled to New Brunswick, N.J., Rutgers, The State University of New Jersey, Zimmerli Art Museum, September 6–November 8, 1987; and Atlanta, The High Museum of Art at Georgia-Pacific Center, December 7, 1987–January 22, 1988) // Memphis, Tenn., The Dixon Gallery and Gardens, *French Paintings of Three Centuries from the New Orleans Museum of Art*, January 5–March 1, 1992, no. 3 (entry by E.P. Caraco), also cited in essay by M.R. Brown, "An Introduction to French Paintings of Three Centuries," pp. 12, 14, illus. p. 21 (color) (exhibition traveled to Miami, Center for the Fine Arts, March 15–May 3, 1992; Wilmington, Delaware Art Museum, May 17–June 29, 1992; Grosse Point Shores, Michigan, Edsel and Eleanor Ford House, July 22–September 6, 1992; Oklahoma City, Oklahoma City Art Museum, October 4–November 15, 1992; and Seattle, Seattle Art Museum, December 17, 1992–February 14, 1993) // Koriyama, Koriyama City Museum of Art, *French Art of Four Centuries from the New Orleans Museum of Art*, February 27–March 31, 1993, no. 3 (entry by E.P. Caraco), illus. pp. 34 (color detail), 35 (color), 127 (exhibition traveled to Yokohama, Sogo Museum of Art, April 21–May 23, 1993; Nara, Nara Sogo Museum of Art, June 9–July 4, 1993; and Kitakyushu, Kitakyushu Municipal Museum of Art, July 10–August 22, 1993).

## 20

Jean Marc Nattier
(French: 1685–1766)

*Portrait of Peter Paul Rubens,* 1707
Black and white chalk on beige paper: 18 ¾ x 13 ¼ inches (476 x 337 mm.)

Signed, inscribed and dated lower left: *Nattier Le Jeune Del & inv*[e]*nit. 1707*
Inscribed below: *PIERRE PAVL RVBENS.*
Gift of George Roland, in honor of John Webster Keefe, acc. no. 2001.264

PROVENANCE

Gombier Perry, London (unverified; perhaps Thomas Gambier-Parry [1816–1888], Highnam Court, Highnam, Gloucestershire); sale, New Orleans, St. Charles Gallery, Inc., October 22, 2000, lot 1228, illus. in cat.; acquired there by George Roland, New Orleans; presented by him to the museum in 2001.

ENGRAVING

Jean Audran (1667–1756), 1710, with caption erroneously identifying the original portrait as by Anthony Van Dyck (see M. Roux, *Bibliothèque Nationale, Département des Estampes—Inventaire du Fonds Français, graveurs du dix-huitième siècle*, I, Paris, 1930, pp. 256–257, no. 25).

REFERENCES

D. Piersol, "A View to the Past: Old Master Prints and Drawings," *Arts Quarterly* [New Orleans Museum of Art], XXVI, October-December 2004, p. 9, illus. fig. 2.

## 21

Sebastiano Ricci (Venetian: 1659–1734) and Marco Ricci (Venetian: 1676–1730)

*Imaginary Scene with Ruins and Figures,* circa 1725
Oil on canvas: 53 ¾ x 69 inches (136.5 x 175.3 cm.)
The Samuel H. Kress Collection, acc. no. 1961.85
Inscribed on stone slab over the arch: *P*[ublio] *COR*[nelio] *P*[ublii]. *F*[ilio] *DOLABELLA CONS*[ule] / *IVNIVS C*[ivis]. *B*[onus]. *SILDINVS EL* [or *FL*]…/ *N*[umen] *ARTEMI EX S*[enatus]. *C*[onsulto]. *FACIENDUM / CURAVITN…A…M…QVE* [or *OVE*]… / *P…BA…RV* [Trans. (for which, see Shapley, 1973, cited below, p. 130): "In the consulship of Publius Cornelius, the son of Publius, Dolabella, Junius Sildinus (?), a good citizen, caused to be built, under the divine guidance of Artemis, and in accordance with a decree of the Senate"]

PROVENANCE

Private collection (? The Rev. Canon L.J. White-Thomson, Broomford Manor, Exmouth, Devon); London, Christie's, February 1, 1924, lot 88 (as Giovanni Paolo Panini); acquired there by "Field;" Antonio Grandi (dealer), Milan; Conte Alessandro Contini Bonacossi (1878–1955), Rome; acquired from him in 1930 by the Samuel H. Kress Collection; presented by them to the museum in 1961.

REFERENCES

H. Voss, "Studien zur venezianischen Vedutenmalerei des 18. Jahrhunderts," *Repertorium für Kunstwissenschaft*, XLVII, No. 1, 1926, pp. 13–14, note 1, illus. p. 14, fig. 3 // N. Pevsner, "Die Rokoko-Austellung in Venedig," *Zeitschrift für bildenden Kunst*, LXIII, No. 6, 1929, p. 75 // G. Fiocco, *La Pittura veneziana alla mostra del Settecento*, Venice, n.d. [1929?], p. 8 // G. Delogu, *Pittori veneti minori del Settecento*, Venice, 1930, p. 94, illus. pl. 23 // G. Fogolari, *Il Settecento italiano*, Milan, 1932, no. 108, illus. pl. 74 // W. Arslan, "Appunti su Magnasco, Sebastiano e Marco Ricci," *Bollettino d'arte*, ser. 3, XXVI, November 1932, pp. 217–218 // *National Gallery of Art: Preliminary Catalogue of Painting and Sculpture: Descriptive List with Notes*, Washington, D.C., 1941, p. 168, no. 166 // W.E. Suida, *The Samuel H. Kress Collection in the Isaac Delgado Museum of Art*, New Orleans, 1953, p. 56, illus. p. 57 [2^nd ed., revised by P. Wescher, New Orleans, 1966, p. 58, illus. p. 59 // R. Pallucchini, *La Pittura veneziana del Settecento*, Venice and Rome, 1960, p. 40, illus. fig. 103 // Bassano del Grappa, *Marco Ricci* (cat. by G.M. Pilo), 1963, p. 44 // G.M. Pilo, "Sebastiano and Marco Ricci in America," *Arte veneta*, XX, 1966, p. 305 // B.B. Fredericksen and F. Zeri, *Census of Pre-Nineteenth-Century Italian Paintings in North American Public Collections*, Cambridge, Mass., 1972, pp. 174, 504, 602 // F.R. Shapley, *Paintings from the Samuel H. Kress Collection: Italian Schools*, III, XVI-XVIII Century, London, 1973, pp. 130–131, no. K1026, illus. fig. 257 // J. Daniels, *L'Opera completa di Sebastiano Ricci*, Milan, 1976, p. 128, no. 430, illus. p. 129 // J. Daniels, *Sebastiano Ricci*, Hove, Sussex, 1976, p. 79, no. 260, also cited p. 103, illus. fig. 248 // J.G. Caldwell, *New Orleans Museum of Art—Handbook of the Collection* (ed. by B.N. McDermott), New Orleans, 1980, p. 35, illus. // A. Scarpa Sonino, *Marco Ricci*, Milan, 1991, p. 129, no. O-71, illus. p. 73, color pl. VI, and p. 226, fig. 94 // Tulsa, Oklahoma, The Philbrook

Museum of Art, and elsewhere, *Botticelli to Tiepolo: Three Centuries of Italian Painting from Bob Jones University* (cat. by R.P. Townsend), 1994–1995, cited in essay by E.M. Zafran, "A History of Italian Baroque Painting in America," pp. 56, 105, note 241 // *New Orleans Museum of Art—Handbook of the Collection*, New Orleans, 1995, p. 32 (entry by J.G. Caldwell), illus. (color) // R. Pallucchini, *La pittura nel Veneto: Il Settecento*, Milan 1995, I, p. 215, illus. p. 219, fig. 348 // E.E. Gardner, *A Bibliographical Repertory of Italian Private Collections* (ed. by C. Ceschi, assisted by K. Baetjer), II, *Dabalà-Kvitkta*, Vicenza, 2002, p. 193 // A. Scarpa, *Sebastiano Ricci*, Milan, 2006, p. 256, no. 322, illus. p. 622, fig. 563.

EXHIBITED

Venice, Biennale, Padiglione Italiano, *Il Settecento italiano: catalogo generale della mostra e delle sezione*, July 18–October 10, 1929, section 7, no. 25 // Traveling exhibition, October 23, 1932–June 2, 1935, beginning at Atlanta, Atlanta Art Association Galleries, *Italian Paintings Lent by Mr. Samuel H. Kress*, p. 53, no number (exhibition traveled to Memphis, Tenn., Brooks Memorial Art Gallery; Birmingham, Alabama, Birmingham Museum of Art; New Orleans, The Isaac Delgado Museum of Art; Houston, The Museum of Fine Arts; Dallas, Dallas Museum of Fine Arts; Denver, Denver Art Museum; Colorado Springs, Colorado Springs Fine Art Center; Salt Lake City, Utah Museum of Fine Arts; Seattle, Seattle Art Museum; Portland, Oregon, Portland Art Museum; Sacramento, Calif., E.B. Crocker Art Gallery; San Francisco, California Palace of the Legion of Honor; Los Angeles, Los Angeles Museum of History, Science and Art; San Diego, Balboa Park, Fine Arts Gallery; San Antonio, Texas, Witte Memorial Museum; Nashville, Tenn., Parthenon; Montgomery, Alabama, Huntingdon College; Waco, Texas, Baylor University; Tampa, Florida, The Florida Fair Grounds; Winter Park, Florida, Rollins College, Morse Gallery of Art; Savannah, Georgia, Telfair Academy of Arts and Sciences; Charleston, South Carolina, Gibbes Art Gallery; and Charlotte, North Carolina, Mint Museum of Art) // San Francisco, California Palace of the Legion of Honor, *Exhibition of Venetian Painting, from the Fifteenth Century through the Eighteenth Century*, June 25–July 24, 1938, no. 52, illus. fig. 52 // Seattle, Seattle Art Musem, *Venetian Paintings from the Samuel H. Kress Collection*, August 1–25, 1938 (exhibition

traveled to Portland, Oregon, Portland Art Museum, September 1–26, 1938; and Montgomery, Alabama, Montgomery Museum of Fine Arts, October 1–31, 1938) // Washington, D.C., National Gallery of Art, 1941–1952, no. 166 // Memphis, Tenn., Brooks Memorial Art Gallery, *Sebastiano and Marco Ricci in America* (cat. by M. Milkovich), December 19, 1965–January 23, 1966, no. 38, illus. p. 41 (exhibition traveled to Lexington, Kentucky, University of Kentucky Art Gallery, February 13–March 6, 1966).

## 22
## Christophe Huet
## (French: 1700–1759)

*Hound Guarding Hunt Trophies,* 1728
Oil on canvas: 37 x 49 ½ inches (94 x 125.7 cm.)
Signed and dated lower left: *C. Huet 1728*
Museum Purchase and Gift, by exchange, of Bert Piso, acc. no. 2002.193

PROVENANCE

Galerie Emmanuel Moatti, Paris; acquired from them by the museum in 2002.

REFERENCES

"New Acquisitions," *Arts Quarterly* [New Orleans Museum of Art], XXV, April-June 2003, illus. (color).

## 23
## Jean Restout II
## (French: 1692–1768)

*Hector Taking Leave of Andromache* (from *The Iliad*, VI, 407–409), 1728
Oil on canvas: 50 ½ x 76 ¼ inches (128.3 x 193.7 cm.)
Signed and dated on rock at lower right: *JRestout 1728*
Lent by Mr. and Mrs. Joseph C. Canizaro, New Orleans

PROVENANCE

Étienne Michel Bouret (1709–1777), tax farmer, Director of the royal postal service and secretary of the royal privy council (with pendant painting by Restout, *The Continence of Scipio*, now in the Gemäldegalerie, Berlin [Gouzi P.37]); Charles Alexandre Calonne (1734–1802), Contrôleur général des finances; his sale, Paris, April 21–30, 1788, lot 153; bought back by

Calonne through the intermediary of his dealer Jean Baptiste Pierre Le Brun, then exported to London when the former went into exile; Calonne sale, London, Skinner & Dyke, March 23–28, 1795, lot 43; Baroness Erwin Reitzes von Marienwert, née Pistener (died 1986), Palais Reitzes, Universitätstrasse, 5, Vienna, and New York; acquired from her by Ruth Blumka, New York; her estate sale, New York, Sotheby's, January 11, 1996, lot 73, illus. in cat. (color); acquired there by the present owner.

REFERENCES

L. Poinsinet de Sivry et al., *Le Nécrologe des hommes célèbres de France*, Paris, 1767–1782, IV, p. 59 // W. Buchanan, *Memoirs of Painting, with a Chronological History of the Importation of Pictures by the Great Masters into England since the French Revolution*, London, 1824, I, p. 230, no. 43 [reprint of 1795 Calonne collection sale catalogue] // P. Rosenberg, "Le Concours de peinture de 1727," *Revue de l'Art*, No. 37, 1977, p. 39, illus. figs. 14, 15 (detail: signature and date) // P. Rosenberg and A. Schnapper, "Paintings by Restout on Mythological and Historical Themes: Acquisition by the National Gallery of Canada of *Venus Presenting Arms to Aeneas*," *National Gallery of Canada Annual Bulletin*, VI, 1982–1983, pp. 50–51, 54, note 18 // Paris, Drouot Montaigne, *Importants tableaux anciens*, December 5, 1990, p. 88, cited under entry for lot 73 // New York, Christie's, *Important Old Master Paintings*, January 31, 1997, p. 96, cited under entry for lot 81 // C. Gouzi, *Jean Restout, 1692–1768, peintre d'histoire à Paris*, Paris, 2000, pp. 216–217, no. P.36, also cited pp. 41–42, 177, note 125, 192, 215, illus. pp. 24 (color), 216.

EXHIBITED

Paris, Galeries nationales du Grand Palais, *Les Amours des dieux: la peinture mythologique de Watteau à David* (cat. by C.B. Bailey), October 15, 1991–January 6, 1992, no. 34, illus. pp. 223 (color), 228, fig. 3 (detail: central figures) and 229, fig. 5 (detail: signature) (exhibition traveled, as *The Loves of the Gods: Mythological Painting from Watteau to David*, to Philadelphia, Philadelphia Museum of Art, February 23–April 26, 1992; and Fort Worth, Kimbell Art Museum, May 23–August 2, 1992).

**24**
**François Boucher**
(French: 1703–1770)

*The Surprise*, 1730–32
Oil on canvas: 32 x 25 ¾ inches (81.3 x 65.4 cm.)
Museum Purchase, Women's Volunteer
Committee Fund, acc. no. 1984.58

PROVENANCE
Possibly Paris, Hôtel d'Aligre, *Catalogue des Tableaux des Trois Ecoles…&c. du Cabinet de MM. \*\*\** [Sorbet?], April 1–3, 1776, lot 46; possibly collection of the architect Pierre Contant-d'Ivry (1698–1777); his estate sale, Paris, Hôtel Contant-d'Ivry, rue de Harlay, November 27, 1777 and days following, lot 6; acquired there by "Dulain" (according to annotated copy of sale catalogue in the Rijksbureau voor Kunsthistorische Documentatie, The Hague); possibly the Duc des Deux-Ponts (presumably Christian IV, Herzog von Zweibrücken); his estate sale, Paris, Hôtel d'Aligre, April 6, 1778, lot 71; acquired there by Noyer; perhaps sale of the collection of M. \*\*\*, Paris, Hôtel de Bullion, April 3, 1783 and days following, lot 9; Comte James-Alexandre de Pourtalès-Gorgier (1776–1855); his estate sale, Paris, February 6–March 21, 1865, lot 252 (as by Jean Baptiste Deshays); Prince Paul Demidoff (1839–1885), Paris; his sale, Paris, February 3, 1868, lot 21 (as by Deshays); possibly acquired there by Richard Seymour-Conway, 4th Marquess of Hertford (1800–1870), London (according to annotated copy of sale catalogue in the Cabinet des Estampes, Bibliothèque nationale de France, Paris; this ownership otherwise unverified); Samuel Joseph Bloomingdale (1873–1968), New York; his sale, New York, Parke-Bernet Galleries, October 30, 1942, lot 23, illus. in cat. (as by Deshays); Paul Drey, New York, as of 1951; Dr. Georg Schäfer (1896–1975), Schweinfurt; London, Christie's, July 14, 1978, lot 150, illus. in cat.; Galerie Cailleux, Paris; acquired from them by the museum in 1984.

REFERENCES
L. Soullié and C. Masson, "Catalogue raisonné de l'oeuvre peint et dessiné de François Boucher," in A. Michel, *François Boucher*, Paris, 1906, p. 65, no. 1170 // H. Voss, "François Boucher's Early Development," *Burlington Magazine*, XCV, March 1953, p. 90, illus. p. 92, fig. 67 // H. Voss, "Repliken im Oeuvre von François Boucher," in *Studies in the History of Art Dedicated to William E. Suida*, New York, 1959, pp. 353–354, illus. fig. 2 // A. Ananoff, *François Boucher*, Lausanne and Paris, 1976, I, pp. 212–213, no. 79, illus. fig. 348 // A. Ananoff, *L'Opera completa di Boucher*, Milan, 1980, p. 91, no. 78, illus. // London, Stair Sainty Matthiesen, and elsewhere, *The First Painters of the King: French Royal Taste from Louis XIV to the Revolution* (cat. by C.B. Bailey), 1985–1986, p. 131, no. 43 (A.P. Wintermute, "Inventory of Paintings by Ten 'First Painters to the King' in Public Collections in the United States"), also cited in essay by P. Conisbee, "Religious Painting in the Age of Reason," p. 20, illus. pp. 20, fig. 1, 131, fig. 43 // P. Rosenberg and M. Hilaire, *Boucher: 60 chefs-d'oeuvre*, Paris, 1986, illus. pl. 1 (color) // P.N. Dunbar, *The New Orleans Museum of Art: The First Seventy-Five Years*, Baton Rouge and London, 1990, p. 321 // New *Orleans Museum of Art—Handbook of the Collection*, New Orleans, 1995, p. 47 (entry by S.E. Stearns), illus. (color) // C.B. Bailey, "An Early Masterpiece by Boucher Rediscovered: *The Judgement of Susannah* in the National Gallery of Canada," *National Gallery of Canada Review* (Revue du Musée des Beaux-Arts du Canada), I, 2000, pp. 19, 31, note 22, illus. p. 18, fig. 10 [French text: pp. 104, 111, note 22].

EXHIBITED
Oberlin, Ohio, Oberlin College, Allen Memorial Art Museum, "Exhibition of Master Drawings of the 18th Century in France and Italy," winter 1951 (not in catalogue) (as by Jean François de Troy) // New York, The Metropolitan Museum of Art, *François Boucher, 1703–1770* (cat. by A. Laing), February 17–May 4, 1986, no. 2, illus. p. 93 (color) (exhibition traveled to Detroit, The Detroit Institute of Arts, May 27–August 17, 1986; and Paris, Grand Palais, September 19, 1986–January 5, 1987) [French ed. of cat.: no. 2, illus. p. 99 (color)] // Memphis, Tenn., The Dixon Gallery and Gardens, *French Paintings of Three Centuries from the New Orleans Museum of Art*, January 5–March 1, 1992, no. 5 (entry by S.E. Stearns), also cited in essay by M.R. Brown, "An Introduction to French Paintings of Three Centuries," pp. 9, 11–13, illus. p. 25 (color) (exhibition traveled to Miami, Center for the Fine Arts, March 15–May 3, 1992; Wilmington, Delaware Art Museum, May 17–June 29, 1992; Grosse Point Shores, Michigan, Edsel and Eleanor Ford House, July 22–September 6, 1992; Oklahoma City, Oklahoma City Art Museum, October 4–November 15, 1992; and Seattle, Seattle Art Museum, December 17, 1992–February 14, 1993) // Koriyama, Koriyama City Museum of Art, *French Art of Four Centuries from the New Orleans Museum of Art*, February 27–March 31, 1993, no. 5 (entry by S.E. Stearns), also cited in essay by M.R. Brown, "An Introduction to French Art of Four Centuries," pp. 23, 25–27 illus. pp. 37 (color) and 129 (exhibition traveled to Yokohama, Sogo Museum of Art, April 21–May 23, 1993; Nara, Nara Sogo Museum of Art, June 9–July 4, 1993; and Kitakyushu, Kitakyushu Municipal Museum of Art, July 10–August 22, 1993) // Hanover, New Hampshire, Dartmouth College, Hood Museum of Art, *Intimate Encounters: Love and Domesticity in Eighteenth-Century France* (cat. by R. Rand et al.), October 4, 1997–January 4, 1998, no. 11, illus. p. 111 (color) (exhibition traveled to Toledo, Ohio, The Toledo Museum of Art, February 15–May 10, 1998; and Houston, The Museum of Fine Arts, May 31–August 23, 1998).

**25**
**Charles André Van Loo,**
**called Carle Vanloo**
(French: 1705–1765)

*Noli me tangere*, 1735
Oil on canvas: 25 ½ x 19 ¼ inches
(64.8 x 48.8 cm.)
Museum Purchase, General Acquisition Fund, acc. no. 1983.2

PROVENANCE
Possibly the collection of the sculptor and frame-maker Philippe Cayeux (1688–1769); in which case, his estate sale, Paris, December 11–23, 1769, lot 41; acquired there by "Donjeu," i.e. the Paris dealer, Vincent Donjeux (died 1793) (according to annotated copy of sale catalogue in the Rijksbureau voor Kunsthistorische Documentatie, The Hague); possibly Jean Antoine Hubert Vassal de Saint-Hubert (1741–1782); in which case, his sale, Paris, January 17–21, 1774, lot 98; acquired there by the dealer Jean Baptiste Pierre Le Brun (1748–1813), Paris (according to annotated copy of sale catalogue in the Rijksbureau voor Kunsthistorische Documentatie, The Hague); possibly Dulac and Lachaise collection; in which case, their sale, Paris, November 30, 1778 and days following, lot 211; acquired there by Lenglier; possibly collection of the engraver Pierre Étienne Moitte (1722–1780); in which case, his estate sale, Paris, November 14, 1780

and days following, lot 135; Dr. and Mrs. Richard H. Rush, Greenwich, Conn., and Rye, New York, as of 1963; presented by them to the Finch College Museum of Art, New York; sold privately along with the collections of the Finch College Museum of Art, 1974; private collection, New York, 1974–1983; Stair Sainty Fine Art, New York; acquired from them by the museum in 1983.

ENGRAVING
M. Salvador Carmona, 1755.

REFERENCES
Possibly M.F. Dandré-Bardon, *Vie de Carle Van Loo*, Paris, 1765, p. 63 // L. Réau, "Carle Vanloo, 1705–1765," *Archives de l'Art Français*, N.S., XIX, 1938, p. 89 // Nice, Musée Chéret, and elsewhere, *Carle Vanloo, premier peintre du Roi* (cat. by M.-C. Sahut), 1977, p. 93, no. 203 (under "Lost Paintings"), illus. (Carmona engraving) // P.N. Dunbar, *The New Orleans Museum of Art: The First Seventy-Five Years*, Baton Rouge and London, 1990, p. 320 // *New Orleans Museum of Art—Handbook of the Collection*, New Orleans, 1995, p. 48 (entry by S.E. Stearns), illus. (color).

EXHIBITED
New York, Finch College Museum of Art, *French Masters of the Eighteenth Century*, February 27–April 7, 1963, no. 42 (addendum to catalogue) // Orléans, Musée des Beaux-Arts, *Peintures françaises du Museum of Art de la Nouvelle Orléans*, May 9–September 15, 1984, no. 6 (entry by E.P. Caraco), illus. // New York, Stair Sainty Matthiesen, *The First Painters of the King: French Royal Taste from Louis XIV to the Revolution* (cat. by C.B. Bailey), October 16–November 22, 1985, no. 13, also cited in essay by P. Conisbee, "Religious Painting in the Age of Reason," pp. 21, 27 and on p. 140 (A.P. Wintermute, "Inventory of Paintings by Ten 'First Painters to the King' in Public Collections in the United States"), illus. pp. 97 (color), 140 (exhibition traveled to New Orleans, New Orleans Museum of Art, December 10, 1985–January 19, 1986; and Columbus, Ohio, Columbus Museum of Art, February 8–March 26, 1986) // Memphis, Tenn., The Dixon Gallery and Gardens, *French Paintings of Three Centuries from the New Orleans Museum of Art*, January 5–March 1, 1992, no. 6 (entry by E.P. Caraco), illus. (color) (exhibition traveled to Miami, Center for the Fine Arts, March 15–May 3, 1992; Wilmington, Delaware Art

Museum, May 17–June 29, 1992; Grosse Point Shores, Michigan, Edsel and Eleanor Ford House, July 22–September 6, 1992; Oklahoma City, Oklahoma City Art Museum, October 4–November 15, 1992; and Seattle, Seattle Art Museum, December 17, 1992–February 14, 1993) // Koriyama, Koriyama City Museum of Art, *French Art of Four Centuries from the New Orleans Museum of Art*, February 27–March 31, 1993, no. 6 (entry by E.P. Caraco), illus. pp. 38 (color), 129 (exhibition traveled to Yokohama, Sogo Museum of Art, April 21–May 23, 1993; Nara, Nara Sogo Museum of Art, June 9–July 4, 1993; and Kitakyushu, Kitakyushu Municipal Museum of Art, July 10–August 22, 1993).

26
Charles Joseph Natoire
(French: 1700–1777)

*The Toilet of Psyche*, 1735–36
Oil on canvas: 78 x 66 ½ inches
(198.1 x 168.9 cm.)
Museum Purchase, through the bequest of Judge Charles F. Claiborne, acc. no. 1940.2

PROVENANCE
Commissioned by Louis Denis de La Live de Bellegarde (1679–1751), along with three other paintings by Natoire illustrating the story of Psyche, in 1734–35 for the *salon* of the Château de la Chevrette, near Saint-Denis; Joseph Hyacinthe François de Paule de Rigaud, Comte de Vaudreuil (1740–1817), Hôtel de Vaudreuil, Paris; his sale, Paris, November 26, 1787, lot 78 (sold with Natoire's *Vénus qui défend à l'Amour de voir Psyché*); acquired there by Jacques Firmin Beauvarlet (1731–1797); his estate sale, Paris, March 13, 1798, lot 26 (sold with *Vénus qui défend à l'Amour de voir cette divinité*); Joseph Bonaparte (1768–1844), "Point Breeze," near Bordentown, New Jersey; his estate sale, Bordentown, New Jersey, September 17–18, 1845, lot 17 (as *Toilet of Venus*); acquired there for $325 by James Robb (1814–1881), New Orleans; his sale, New Orleans, March 1, 1859, lot 78; acquired there by John Burnside (died 1881), New Orleans; acquired from his estate in 1897 by Randolph Newman, New Orleans; by descent to Hart D. Newman, New Orleans; acquired from him by the museum in 1940.

REFERENCES
L.V. Thiéry, *Guide des amateurs et des étrangers voyageurs à Paris, ou Description raisonnée de*

cette Ville, de sa Banlieue, & de tout ce qu'elle contiennent de remarquable, Paris, 1787, II, p. 543 // *The Broadway Journal*, August 30, 1845, p. 195 // A. Hawkins, *Creole Art Gallery Catalogue*, New Orleans, 1892, n.p., no. 13 // G. Bertin, *Joseph Bonaparte en Amérique*, Paris, 1893, pp. 87, 416, no. 52 ("Appendix B: Liste des tableaux de la Galerie de Joseph Bonaparte") // New Orleans, The Isaac Delgado Museum of Art, *Catalogue*, New Orleans, 1914, no. 103 // New Orleans, The Isaac Delgado Museum of Art, *Catalogue of Paintings, Sculpture, and Other Objects of Art in the Isaac Delgado Museum of Art*, New Orleans, 1932, p. 56, no. 2084 // F. Boyer, "Catalogue raisonné de l'oeuvre de Charles Natoire," *Archives de l'Art Français*, N.S., XXI, 1949, p. 48, no. 115 (as "Vénus à sa toilette") // A.W. Rutledge, *Cumulative Record of Exhibition Catalogues: The Pennsylvania Academy of Fine Arts 1807–1870; The Society of Artists, 1800–1814; The Artists' Fund Society, 1835–1845*, Philadelphia, 1955, p. 149 [2nd ed., revised by P.H. Falk, Madison, Conn., 1988, pp. 149, 352, 443] // M. Benisovich, "Sales of French Collections of Paintings in the United States During the First Half of the Nineteenth Century," *Art Quarterly*, XIX, autumn 1956, p. 298, illus. p. 293, fig. 5 // H. Haydon, *Great Art Treasures in America's Smaller Museums*, New York, 1967, p. 91, illus. // R.B. Toledano and W.J. Fulton, "Portrait Painting in Colonial and Ante-Bellum New Orleans," *Antiques Magazine*, CXIII, June 1968, p. 789 // K.B. Hiesinger, "The Sources of François Boucher's *Psyche* Tapestries," *Philadelphia Museum of Art Bulletin*, LXXII, November 1976, pp. 13/15, illus. p. 13, fig. 4 // J.G. Caldwell, *New Orleans Museum of Art—Handbook of the Collection* (ed. by B.N. McDermott), New Orleans, 1980, p. 50, illus. // W.J. Gavin and R.F. Perkins, Jr., *The Boston Athenaeum Art Exhibition Index, 1827–1874*, Boston, 1980, pp. 102, 218, 273 // N. Bryson, *Word and Image: French Painting of the Ancien Régime*, Cambridge, 1981, p. 92, illus. p. 93, fig. 35 // G.E. Jordan, "Robb and Clay: Politicians and Scholars," *The New Orleans Art Review*, III, January-February 1984, p. 7, illus. // Paris, Délégation à l'Action Artistique de la Ville de Paris, and Lunéville, Château-Musée de Lunéville, *Germain Boffrand, 1667–1754: l'aventure d'un architecte independent*, 1986, pp. 263, 267 // J.L. Yarnall and W.H. Gerdts, *The National Museum of American Art's Index to American Art Exhibition Catalogues from the Beginning through the 1876 Centennial Year*, Boston, 1986, IV, p. 2562, no. 65527 // C.B.

Bailey, "The Comte de Vaudreuil: Aristocratic Collecting on the Eve of the Révolution," *Apollo*, CXXX, July 1989, p. 25, illus. p. 26, fig. 9 // P.N. Dunbar, *The New Orleans Museum of Art: The First Seventy-Five Years*, Baton Rouge and London, 1990, pp. 4, 6, 24, 95, note 10, illus. front dust cover (color) // *New Orleans Museum of Art—Handbook of the Collection*, New Orleans, 1995, p. 49 (entry by E.P. Caraco), illus. (color) // K. Scott, *The Rococo Interior: Decoration and Social Spaces in Early Eighteenth-Century Paris*, New Haven and London, 1995, p. 25, illus. in color pp. vi (detail) and 26, fig. 29 // D. Jarrassé, *La Peinture française du XVIIIe siècle*, Paris, 1998, illus. p. 27 (color) // T.K. Wharton, *Queen of the South: New Orleans, 1853–1862: The Journal of Thomas K. Wharton* (ed. by S. Wilson, Jr., et al.), New Orleans and New York, 1999, p. 196 (entry of March 8, 1859) and note 13, illus. p. 197 // C.B. Bailey, *Patriotic Taste: Collecting Modern Art in Pre-Revolutionary Paris*, New Haven and London, 2002, pp. 38, 176, 255, note 17, 293, note 81, illus. p. 38, fig. 29 // P.T. Stroud, "Point Breeze: Joseph Bonaparte's American Retreat," *Antiques Magazine*, CLXII, October 2002, pp. 134, 139, note 9, illus. p. 134 (color) // Minneapolis, The Minneapolis Institute of Arts, *Currents of Change: Art and Life along the Mississippi River, 1850–1861* (cat. by J.T. Busch), 2004, cited in essay by J.T. Busch, "Handsomely Furnished in the Most Fashionable Style: Art and Decoration along the Mississippi River," pp. 116–117, illus. p. 120, fig. 27 (color) // P.T. Stroud, *The Man Who Had Been King: The American Exile of Napoleon's Brother Joseph*, Philadelphia, 2005, pp. 66, 233, note 26, illus. p. 68, fig. 14 // New York, The Metropolitan Museum of Art, and elsewhere, *French Drawings from the British Museum: Clouet to Seurat* (cat. by P. Stein), 2005–2006, p. 120, cited under no. 46, illus. fig. 1.

EXHIBITED

Boston, Armory Hall, *Paintings on Exhibition at Armory Hall*, 1845, no. 17 // Philadelphia, Pennsylvania Academy of Fine Arts, *Catalogue of the Twenty-Eighth Annual Exhibition*, spring 1851, no. 20 // Philadelphia, Pennsylvania Academy of Fine Arts, *Catalogue of the Twenty-Ninth Annual Exhibition*, spring 1852, no. 290 // Philadelphia, Pennsylvania Academy of Fine Arts, *Catalogue of the Thirtieth Annual Exhibition*, spring 1853, no. 335 // Boston, Athenaeum Gallery, *Catalogue of the Twenty-Seventh Exhibition of Paintings and Statuary*, 1854, no. 24 // Boston, Athenaeum Gallery, *Catalogue of the Twenty-Eighth Exhibition of Paintings and Statuary*, 1855, no. 19 // New Orleans, The Isaac Delgado Museum of Art, 1911–c. 1935, special loan // Toledo, Ohio, Toledo Museum of Art, *The Age of Louis XV: French Painting, 1710–1774* (cat. by P. Rosenberg), October 26–December 7, 1975, no. 72 (incorrectly dates painting to 1745), also cited p. ix, illus. pl. 68 (exhibition traveled to Chicago, Art Institute of Chicago, January 10–February 22, 1976; and Ottawa, National Gallery of Canada, March 21–May 2, 1976) // St. Petersburg, Florida, The Museum of Fine Arts, *Fragonard & His Friends: Changing Ideals in Eighteenth-Century Art* (cat. by M.L. Grayson), November 20, 1982–February 6, 1983, no. 48, illus. fig. 48 // Miami, Center for the Fine Arts, *In Quest of Excellence: Civic Pride, Patronage* (cat. by J. van der Marck), January 12–April 22, 1984, no. 87, also cited p. 160, illus. p. 107 (color) // Orléans, Musée des Beaux-Arts, *Peintures françaises du Museum of Art de la Nouvelle Orléans*, May 9–September 15, 1984, no. 7 (entry by E.P. Caraco), illus. (color) // Paris, Galeries nationales du Grand Palais, *Les Amours des dieux, la peinture mythologique de Watteau à David* (cat. by C.B. Bailey), October 15, 1991–January 6, 1992, no. 39, illus. in color, pp. 332 (detail: Psyche and attendant), 349 (exhibition traveled to Philadelphia, Philadelphia Museum of Art, and Fort Worth, Kimbell Art Museum, 1992; painting exhibited at Paris venue only) [American ed. of cat.: as *The Loves of the Gods: Mythological Painting from Watteau to David*: same pagination] // Memphis, Tenn., The Dixon Gallery and Gardens, *French Paintings of Three Centuries from the New Orleans Museum of Art*, January 5–March 1, 1992, no. 7 (entry by E.P. Caraco), also cited in essay by M.R. Brown, "An Introduction to French Paintings of Three Centuries," pp. 9, 12–14, illus. p. 29 (color) (exhibition traveled to Miami, Center for the Fine Arts, March 15–May 3, 1992; Wilmington, Delaware Art Museum, May 17–June 29, 1992; Grosse Point Shores, Michigan, Edsel and Eleanor Ford House, July 22–September 6, 1992; Oklahoma City, Oklahoma City Art Museum, October 4–November 15, 1992; and Seattle, Seattle Art Museum, December 17, 1992–February 14, 1993) // Koriyama, Koriyama City Museum of Art, *French Art of Four Centuries from the New Orleans Museum of Art*, February 27–March 31, 1993, no. 7 (entry by E.P. Caraco), also cited in essay by M.R. Brown, "An Introduction to French Art of Four Centuries," p. 27, illus. pp. 39 (color) and 130 (exhibition traveled to Yokohama, Sogo Museum of Art, April 21–May 23, 1993; Nara, Nara Sogo Museum of Art, June 9–July 4, 1993; and Kitakyushu, Kitakyushu Municipal Museum of Art, July 10–August 22, 1993).

27
Giovanni Battista Tiepolo
(Venetian: 1696–1770)

*Boy Holding a Book (Portrait of Lorenzo Tiepolo)*, circa 1747–50
Oil on canvas: 19 x 15 ⅜ inches (48.3 x 39.1 cm.)
The Samuel H. Kress Collection,
acc. no. 1961.87

PROVENANCE

Visconti di Modrone collection, Milan; Conte Alessandro Contini Bonacossi (1878–1955), Florence; acquired from him in 1932 by the Samuel H. Kress Collection; presented by them to the museum in 1961.

REFERENCES

*National Gallery of Art: Preliminary Catalogue of Painting and Sculpture: Descriptive List with Notes*, Washington, D.C., 1941, p. 193, no. 221 // W.E. Suida, *The Samuel H. Kress Collection in the Isaac Delgado Museum of Art*, New Orleans, 1953, p. 60, illus. p. 61 [2nd ed., revised by P. Wescher, New Orleans, 1966, p. 62, illus. p. 63] // A. Morassi, *A Complete Catalogue of the Paintings of G.B. Tiepolo*, London, 1962, p. 33 (as c. 1740–50) // H. Haydon, *Great Art Treasures in America's Smaller Museums*, New York, 1967, p. 85 // G. Piovene and A. Pallucchini, *L'Opera completa di Giambattista Tiepolo*, Milan, 1968, p. 111, no. 173, illus. (as c. 1745–46) // B.B. Fredericksen and F. Zeri, *Census of Pre-Nineteenth-Century Italian Paintings in North American Public Collections*, Cambridge, Mass., 1972, pp. 196, 528, 602 // F.R. Shapley, *Paintings from the Samuel H. Kress Collection: Italian Schools*, III, XVI-XVIII Century, London, 1973, pp. 142–143, no. K232, illus. fig. 279 (as c. 1725–30) // New York, Piero Corsini, Inc., *Important Old Master Paintings: Within the Image*, 1990, p. 96 // M. Gemin and F. Pedrocco, *Giambattista Tiepolo, I dipinti: Opera completa*, Venice, 1993, p. 344, no. 256, illus. (as c. 1743) // *New Orleans Museum of Art—Handbook of the Collection*, New Orleans, 1995, p. 31 (entry by S.E. Stearns), illus. (color) // Paris, Fondation Custodia, Institut Néerlandais, *Dessins vénitiens de la collection Frits Lugt: complétés par des lettres autographes* (cat. by H. Buijs and J. de Scheemaker), 1996, p. 55, under no. 85 // S. Loire, "Rezensionen…Massimo Gemin, Filippo Pedrocco, Giambattista Tiepolo. I dipinti…," *Kunstchronik*, L, 1997, p. 31.

EXHIBITED

Washington, D.C, National Gallery of Art, 1941–1952, no. 221 // Turin, Galleria Civica d'Arte Moderna, *Giacomo Ceruti e la ritrattistica del suo tempo nell'Italia settentrionale* (ed. by L. Mallè and G. Testori), February-March 1967, no. 97, illus. p. 76, pl. 8 // Raleigh, North Carolina Museum of Art, *A Gift to America: Masterpieces of European Painting from the Samuel H. Kress Collection*, February 5–April 24, 1994, no. 47 (entry by L.F. Orr), also cited in essay by M. Perry, "The Kress Collection," pp. 19, 21, illus. p. 246 (color) (exhibition traveled to Houston, The Museum of Fine Arts, May 22–August 14, 1994; Seattle, Seattle Art Museum, September 15–November 20, 1994; and San Francisco, Fine Arts Museums of San Francisco, December 17, 1994–March 4, 1995) // Venice, Museo del Settecento Veneziano, Ca' Rezzonico, *Giambattista Tiepolo, 1696–1770* (ed. by K. Christiansen), September 5–December 15, 1996 no. 44 (entry by D. De Grazia), also cited in essays by D. Posner, "Tiepolo and the Artistic Culture of Eighteenth-Century Europe," pp. 26–27, and by D. De Grazia, "Tiepolo and the 'Art' of Portraiture," p. 258, illus. p. 267 (color) (exhibition traveled to New York, The Metropolitan Museum of Art, January 24–April 27, 1997) // Paris, Musée du Petit Palais, *Giambattista Tiepolo, 1696–1770* (cat. by S. Loire and J. de Los Llanos), October 22, 1998–January 24, 1999, no. 32, illus. (color).

## 28
## Joseph Marie Vien
## (French: 1716–1809)

*Saint Theresa of Avila,* 1754–55
Oil on canvas: 43 ½ x 36 inches
(110.5 x 91.4 cm.)
Signed and dated on book cover: *Vien 175*[5?]
Museum Purchase, The Yomiuri Shimbun Fund, acc. no. 92.811

PROVENANCE

Stair Sainty Matthiesen, New York and London, as of 1985; acquired from them by the museum in 1992.

REFERENCES

F. Aubert, "Joseph-Marie Vien (quatrième article)," *Gazette des Beaux-Arts*, 1ère pér., XXIII, August 1867, p. 180 (author recounts imaginary reminiscence of the Comte de Caylus) // T.W. Gaehtgens and J. Lugand, *Joseph-Marie Vien, Peintre du Roi (1716–1809)*, Paris, 1988, p. 161, no. 137, also cited p. 396, illus. fig. 137.

EXHIBITED

New York, Stair Sainty Matthiesen, *The First Painters of the King: French Royal Taste from Louis XIV to the Revolution* (cat. by C.B. Bailey), October 16–November 22, 1985, no. 20, also cited in essay by P. Conisbee, "Religious Painting in the Age of Reason," pp. 27–28, illus. pp. 120 (detail: right hand and book), 121 (color) (exhibition traveled New Orleans, New Orleans Museum of Art, December 10, 1985–January 19, 1986; and Columbus, Ohio, Columbus Museum of Art, February 8–March 26, 1986) // Rochester, N.Y., University of Rochester, Memorial Art Gallery, *La Grande Manière: Historical and Religious Painting in France, 1700–1800* (cat. by D.A. Rosenthal), May 2–July 26, 1987, no. 58, illus. (exhibition traveled to New Brunswick, N.J., Rutgers, The State University of New Jersey, Zimmerli Art Museum, September 6–November 8, 1987; and Atlanta, The High Museum of Art at Georgia-Pacific Center, December 7, 1987–January 22, 1988) // New Orleans, New Orleans Museum of Art, *New Art for a New Building*, April 18–August 15, 1993, p. 6, no number, illus. (color).

## 29
## Jean Baptiste Greuze
## (French: 1725–1805)

*Portrait of Marie Angélique Vérany de Varennes, Mme Georges Gougenot de Croissy,* 1757
Oil on canvas: 31 ½ x 24 ¼ inches
(80 x 62.8 cm.)
Museum Purchase, Ella West Freeman Foundation Matching Fund, Women's Volunteer Committee Fund and an anonymous gift to 1976 Acquisitions Fund Drive, acc. no. 1976.268

PROVENANCE

Baron de Soucy, Paris, as of 1888; his sale, Paris, Galerie Jean Charpentier, December 14, 1937, lot B (as attributed to Greuze; bought in), illus. in cat.; by descent to Baron de Soucy's daughter, Comtesse Joachim de Dreux-Brézé, Paris, as of 1953; to her son, Comte Charles Evrard de Dreux-Brézé, Paris, as of 1958; Galerie Cailleux, Paris, as of 1968; private collection, New York; Dr. Klaus Virch, Kiel; acquired from him by the museum in 1976.

REFERENCES

A. de Champeaux, "Exposition de l'art français sous Louis XIV et sous Louis XV à l'Hôtel de Chimay," *Gazette des Beaux-Arts*, 2e pér., XXXVIII, July 1888, p. 35 // P. Bautier, "Le Portrait de Georges Gougenot de Croissy par Greuze au Musée de Bruxelles," *Musées Royaux des Beaux-Arts: Bulletin*, II, 1953, pp. 30–31, illus. p. 28, fig. 1 // R.A. d'Hulst, *Le Musée de Bruxelles, art ancien*, Paris, 1965, p. 144 // *Musées royaux des Beaux-Arts de Belgique à Bruxelles: art ancien*, Brussels, 1971, n.p., cited under no. 105 (entry by H.M. Bussers) // J.G. Caldwell, *New Orleans Museum of Art—Handbook of the Collection* (ed. by B.N. McDermott), New Orleans, 1980, p. 51, illus. pp. 16 (color), 51 // Brussels, Musées royaux des Beaux-Arts de Belgique, *Catalogue inventaire de la peinture ancienne*, Brussels, 1984, p. 126 // P.N. Dunbar, *The New Orleans Museum of Art: The First Seventy-Five Years*, Baton Rouge and London, 1990, p. 290 // J. Baillio, "Les Portraits du Dauphin et de la Dauphine par Greuze," *Gazette des Beaux-Arts*, 6e pér., CXXII, October 1993, p. 146, illus. p. 145, fig. 14 // *New Orleans Museum of Art—Handbook of the Collection*, New Orleans, 1995, p. 50 (entry by E.P. Caraco and S.E. Stearns), illus. (color) // H. Guicharnaud, "Un Collectionneur parisien, ami de Greuze et de Pigalle, l'abbé Louis Gougenot, 1724–1767," *Gazette des Beaux-Arts*, 6e pér., CXXXIV, July/August 1999, p. 4, illus. fig. 5 // New York, The Frick Collection, and elsewhere, *Greuze the Draughtsman* (cat. by E. Munhall), 2002, cited in essay by I. Novosselskaya, "The Collection of Drawings by Jean-Baptiste Greuze in St. Petersburg," p. 34, illus. p. 33, fig. 22 (detail : sitter's hands).

EXHIBITED

Paris, École des Beaux-Arts, Hôtel de Chimay, *Exposition de l'art français sous Louis XIV et sous Louis XV*, 1888, no. 12 *bis* // Hartford, Conn., Wadsworth Atheneum, *Jean-Baptiste Greuze, 1725–1805* (cat. by E. Munhall), December 1, 1976–January 23, 1977, no. 18, also cited in introduction, p. 16, and on p. 54, under no. 16, illus. p. 57 (exhibition traveled to San Francisco, California Palace of the Legion of Honor,

March 5–May 1, 1977; and Dijon, Musée des Beaux-Arts, June 4–July 31, 1977) [French ed. of cat.: same pagination] // Atlanta, High Museum of Art, *The Rococo Age: French Masterpieces of the Eighteenth Century* (cat. by E.M. Zafran), October 15–December 31, 1983, no. 32, also cited in essay by J.-L. Bordeaux, "The Rococo Age," p. 20, illus. p. 72 (color) // Orléans, Musée des Beaux-Arts, *Peintures françaises du Museum of Art de la Nouvelle Orléans*, May 9–September 15, 1984, no. 8 (entry by E.P. Caraco), illus. (color) // Memphis, Tenn., The Dixon Gallery and Gardens, *French Paintings of Three Centuries from the New Orleans Museum of Art*, January 5–March 1, 1992, no. 8 (entry by E.P. Caraco and S.E. Stearns), also cited in essay by M.R. Brown, "An Introduction to French Paintings of Three Centuries," pp. 9, 12, 14, illus. p. 31 (color) (exhibition traveled to Miami, Center for the Fine Arts, March 15–May 3, 1992; Wilmington, Delaware Art Museum, May 17–June 29, 1992; Grosse Point Shores, Michigan, Edsel and Eleanor Ford House, July 22–September 6, 1992; Oklahoma City, Oklahoma City Art Museum, October 4–November 15; and Seattle, Seattle Art Museum, December 17, 1992–February 14, 1993) // Koriyama, Koriyama City Museum of Art, *French Art of Four Centuries from the New Orleans Museum of Art*, February 27–March 31, 1993, no. 8 (entry by E.P. Caraco and S.E. Stearns), also cited in essay by M.R. Brown, "An Introduction to French Art of Four Centuries," p. 27, illus. pp. 40 (color) and 131 (exhibition traveled to Yokohama, Sogo Museum of Art, April 21–May 23, 1993; Nara, Nara Sogo Museum of Art, June 9–July 4, 1993; and Kitakyushu, Kitakyushu Municipal Museum of Art, July 10–August 22, 1993) // Mobile, Alabama, Mobile Museum of Art, *Picturing French Style: Three Hundred Years of Art and Fashion*, September 6, 2002–January 5, 2003, no. 6, illus. (color) (exhibition traveled to West Palm Beach, Florida, Norton Museum of Art, February 4–April 27, 2003).

## 30
Manufacture Royale de Sèvres, after a sculpture of 1757 by Étienne Maurice Falconet (1716–1791)

*Bather or Nymph Entering Her Bath,* 1758
Soft-paste porcelain, unglazed biscuit figure on a separate polychrome glazed base (one reserve with a trophy and three with flower garlands with blue ground and parcel gilt), overall height: 19 ¾ inches (50 cm.)
Museum Purchase, Carrie Heiderich Fund, acc. no. 2002.194

PROVENANCE
Galerie Jean-Gabriel Peyre, Paris; acquired from them by the museum in 2002.

## 31
Hubert Robert
(French: 1733–1808)

*A Stairway in the Park of an Italian Villa,* 1760
Oil on canvas: 31 x 39 ½ inches (78.7 x 100.3 cm.)
Signed and dated, lower right, on the lowest step of the staircase: *H. Roberti 1760*
Museum Purchase and Gift, by exchange, of Edith Rosenwald Stern, acc. no. 1995.312

PROVENANCE
Jacques Doucet (1853–1929), Paris; his sale, Paris, Galerie Georges Petit, June 6, 1912 (part II), lot 176, illus. in cat.; acquired there by Gabriel Cognacq (1880–1951), Paris ; (?) M. Stettiner; Duchess of Roxburghe, née Mary Goelet (died 1937), as of 1933; by descent to her son, George Victor Robert John Innes Ker, 9th Duke of Roxburghe (1913–1974); by descent to his son, Guy David Innes Ker, 10th Duke of Roxburghe, Floors Castle, north of Kelso, Borders, Scotland; acquired from him, via Simon Dickinson, Inc., New York, by the museum in 1995.

REFERENCES
R.E. D[ell]., "Art in France," *Burlington Magazine*, XXI, July 1912, p. 238 // I. Errera, *Répertoire des peintures datées*, I, Brussels, 1920, p. 422 // L. Gillet, "Masterpieces of French Art at the Paris Exhibition," *Connoisseur*, CI, January 1938, illus. p. 5 // D. Sutton, "Selected Prefaces: Boucher to Bonnard, Part II: VII. Frivolity and Reason," *Apollo*, CXXV, February

1987, illus. p. 90, fig. 13 // *New Orleans Museum of Art—Handbook of the Collection*, New Orleans, 1995, p. 51 (entry by S.E. Stearns), illus. (color) // S.E. Stearns, "New Acquisition: Hubert Robert's *The Park at Saint Cloud*," *Arts Quarterly* [New Orleans Museum of Art], XVIII, January-March 1996, p. 16, illus.

EXHIBITED
London, 25 Park Lane [residence of Sir Phillip Sassoon], *Three French Reigns (Louis XIV, XV and XVI)*, February 21–April 5, 1933, no. 28, illus. pl. 47 // Paris, Palais national des Arts (Musée d'Art Moderne), *Chefs-d'œuvre de l'art français*, June-December 1937, no. 214 // Manchester, City Art Gallery, *Art Treasures Centenary Exhibition of European Old Masters*, October 30–December 31, 1957, no. 182, illus. (in *Illustrated Souvenir*, p. 33) // London, Royal Academy of Arts, *France in the Eighteenth Century* (cat. by D. Sutton), January 6–March 3, 1968, no. 581, illus. fig. 256.

## 32
John Singleton Copley
(American: 1738–1815)

*Portrait of Colonel George Watson,* 1768
Oil on canvas: 50 x 40 inches (127 x 101.6 cm.)
Inscribed on the letter beneath the fingers of sitter's right hand: …..*1767*
Signed and dated on the letter in sitter's left hand: *JSC P 1768*
Museum Purchase and Gift, by exchange, of Isaac Cline, Herman E. Cooper, F. Julius Dreyfous, Durand-Ruel & Sons, and Lora Tortue, acc. no. 1977.37

PROVENANCE
George Watson Brimmer, Boston, as of 1830; by descent to his nephew (and the sitter's great-grandson), Martin Brimmer (1829–1896), Boston, as of 1879; by descent to the Inches family; Henderson Inches (died 1947), Boston and (later) Brookline, Mass., as of 1930; by descent to Henderson Inches, Jr., Chestnut Hill, Mass.; consigned to Steven Straw, New York, as of 1976; acquired from him by "a group of dentists seeking an investment" (see 1995 Reference, cited below, p. 285); sold via Peter Findlay, New York, to the museum in 1977.

REFERENCES
E. Strahan, ed., *The Art Treasures of America, Being the Choicest Works of Art in the Public*

and Private Collections of North America,
Philadelphia, 1879, III, pp. 83, 93 // "February
Meeting, 1896," Publications of the Colonial
Society of Massachusetts, III, Transactions, 1895–
1897, 1900, p. 199 // F.W. Bayley, Five Colonial
Artists of New England: Joseph Badger, Joseph
Blackburn, John Singleton Copley, Robert Feke,
John Smibert, Boston, 1929, privately printed,
illus. p. 281 // B.N. Parker and A.B. Wheeler,
John Singleton Copley: American Portraits in
Oil, Pastel, and Miniature, Boston, 1938, pp.
204–205, illus. pl. 86 // V. Barker, American
Painting: History and Interpretation, New York,
1950, p. 140 // J.D. Prown, John Singleton Copley
in America, 1738–1774, Cambridge, Mass., 1966,
pp. 61, 115, 233, illus. fig. 222 // J.G. Caldwell,
New Orleans Museum of Art—Handbook of
the Collection (ed. by B.N. McDermott), New
Orleans, 1980, p. 126, illus. pp. 23 (color), 126
// W.J. Gavin and R.F. Perkins, Jr., The Boston
Athenaeum Art Exhibition Index, 1827–1874,
Boston, 1980, pp. 40, 188, 274 // P.N. Dunbar,
The New Orleans Museum of Art: The First
Seventy-Five Years, Baton Rouge and London,
1990, pp. 285–290 // New Orleans Museum of
Art: Handbook of the Collection, New Orleans,
1995, p. 162 (entry by J.G. Caldwell), illus.
(color) // New York, The Metropolitan Mueum
of Art, and elsewhere, John Singleton Copley
in America (cat. by C. Rebora, P. Staiti et al.),
1995–1996, p. 208, cited under no. 20 (earlier
companion portrait of Mrs. George Watson,
née Elizabeth Oliver, now in the Smithsonian
American Art Museum, Washington, D.C.;
entry by C. Rebora), illus. p. 206, fig. 183.

EXHIBITED
Boston, Athenaeum Gallery, 1830, no. 179 //
Boston, Museum of Fine Arts, 1924, special
loan // Boston, Museum of Fine Arts, Loan
Exhibition of One Hundred Colonial Portraits,
June 19–September 21, 1930, p. 94, no number,
illus. // Boston, Museum of Fine Arts, Fifty-
Three Early American Portraits, July-September
1935, checklist // New York, The Metropolitan
Museum of Art, An Exhibition of Paintings by
John Singleton Copley in Commemoration of the
Two-Hundreth Anniversary of His Birth (cat.
by H.B. Wehle), December 22, 1936–February
14, 1937, no. 25, illus. // Miami, Center for the
Fine Arts, In Quest of Excellence: Civic Pride,
Patronage, Connoisseurship (cat. by J. van der
Marck), January 12–April 22, 1984, no. 70, also
cited p. 162, illus. p. 161.

33
Jean Baptiste Le Prince
(French: 1734–1781)

Pair of paintings, 1768

The Seesaw
Oil on canvas, oval: 16 ⅞ x 14 inches
(42.9 x 35.6 cm.)
Signed and dated at left: Le Prince 1768

The Russian Dance
Oil on canvas, oval: 16 ⅞ x 14 inches (42.9 x
35.6 cm.)

Loan from a private New Orleans collection

PROVENANCE
Comte Jean Du Barry (1723–1794), Paris
and Toulouse; his sale, Paris, Catalogue
de tableaux originaux des bons maîtres des
trois écoles…qui composent le Cabinet de
M.L.C. de D., November 21, 1774 and days
following, lot 99 ("Deux tableaux, suivant
le costume Russe, composés agréablement,
& peints en 1768 sur toile, de forme ovale…
"); the banker Jean Frédéric Perregaux
(1744–1808), Hôtel Perregaux (formerly the
Hôtel Guimard), rue de la Chaussée d'Antin,
Paris; his postmortem inventory, February
25, 1808 and days following (drawn up by
the Parisian notary Jean Baptiste Théodore
Sensier; Archives nationales de France,
Paris, Minutier Central, Étude X, liasse 882:
"Dans le Salon…Item, deux paysages avec
figures de scène Russe sur toile par Leprince
cadre de bois doré Prisés trois Cents francs,
Cy…300"); by inheritance to his daughter,
the Maréchale Duchesse de Raguse, née
Marie Hortense Perregaux (1779–1855),
Paris and Viry-Châtillon (Essonne); her
postmortem inventory, June 8, 1857 (drawn
up by the Parisian notary Arsène Aumont-
Théville; Archives nationales de France,
Paris, Minutier Central, Étude X, liasse 1255:
"Dans la chambre à coucher du Rez-de-
chaussée / [N°] 5433 Deux tableaux ovales de
Leprince contenant des Scènes champêtres
prisés trois cents francs…300."); her estate
sale, Paris, Hôtel des Commissaires-Priseurs,
December 14–15, 1857, lots 35 and 36;
Gustave Rothan (1822–1890); his estate sale,
Paris, Galerie Georges Petit, May 29–30,
1890, lots 168 and 169; private collection,
Paris; Galerie Heim, Paris; acquired from
them by the present owner in 1971.

REFERENCES
J. Hédou, Jean Le Prince et son œuvre, suivi de
nombreux documents inédits, Paris, 1879, pp. 46,
318 // É. Dacier, Catalogues de ventes et livrets
de Salons illustrés par Gabriel de Saint-Aubin,
I, I.—Catalogue de la Collection Crozat (1755),
II.—Livret du Salon de 1769, Paris, 1909, p. 78
and p. 16 of the Salon handbook (facsimile
reproduction of page with Saint-Aubin's
thumbnail sketches of both paintings); II,
III.—Catalogue de la Vente A. Du Barry (1774),
IV.—Livret du Salon de 1777, 1910, p. 27 and
note 2 and pp. 39–40 of Du Barry sale catalogue
(facsimile reproduction of page with Saint-
Aubin's thumbnail sketches) // Denis Diderot,
Salons (ed. by J. Seznec), IV, Salons of 1769,
1771, 1775 and 1781, London, 1967, pp. 32, 97
// K. Rorschach, "Jean-Baptiste Le Prince: An
Eighteenth-Century French Artist in Russia,"
The Smart Museum of Art Bulletin, V, 1993–1994,
pp. 5–6, illus. p. 6, fig. 3 // Denis Diderot,
Salons (ed. by E.M. Bukdahl, M. Delon,
D. Kahn and A. Lorenceau), IV, Salons of 1769,
1771, 1775 and 1781, Paris, 1995, p. 71 and note
179, illus. figs. 12, 13 // P. Sanchez, Dictionnaire
des artistes exposant dans les Salons des XVII et
XVIII^EME siècles à Paris et en province, 1673–1800,
Dijon, 2004, II, p. 1067.

EXHIBITED
Paris, Salon, 1769, nos. 77 (The Russian Dance)
and 78 (The Seesaw) // Atlanta, High Museum
of Art, The Rococo Age: French Masterpieces of
the Eighteenth Century (cat. by E.M. Zafran),
October 15–December 31, 1983, nos. 52a and
52b, illus. p. 106 (color) // Philadelphia, The
Rosenbach Museum and Library, Drawings
by Jean-Baptiste Le Prince for the "Voyage en
Sibérie" (cat. by K. Rorschach), October 16,
1986–January 4, 1987, nos. 37 and 38, also cited
p. 15, illus. (exhibition traveled to Pittsburgh,
Frick Art Museum, January 29–March 29, 1987;
and New York, The Frick Collection, April
21–June 14, 1987) // Milwaukee, Milwaukee Art
Museum, Escape to Eden: The Pastoral Vision in
Eighteenth-Century France, March 19–May 30,
1999, checklist, no number, illus.

34
Étienne Aubry
(French: 1745–1781)

*Woman in the Costume of a Sultana
(The Dancer Rosalie Duthé?),* 1779
Oil on canvas: 25 ½ x 32 ¼ inches
(64.8 x 81.9 cm.)
Signed and dated center right, above cushion:
*E. Aubry. 1779.*

Loan from a private New Orleans collection

PROVENANCE
Comte de Ribes, Paris; Heim Gallery, Paris,
as of 1964; acquired from them by the present
owner in 1971.

REFERENCES
*Bordeaux, Revue Municipale,* March 1964,
p. 19, illus. // A. Watt, "Trends & Fashions:
The Paris Market for Old Masters," *Apollo,*
LXXX, September 1964, illus. p. 245, fig. 3 //
A. Ribeiro, *Dress in Eighteenth-Century Europe,
1715–1789,* London, 1984, p. 176, illus. p. 177,
fig. 112 // N. Jeffares, *A Catalogue of the Works of
Jacques-Antoine-Marie Lemoine, Rouen 1751–
Paris, 1824,* London, 1996, privately printed,
p. 49 // P. Stein, "Exoticism as Metaphor:
*Turquerie* in Eighteenth-Century French Art"
(unpublished Ph.D. dissertation, New York
University), 1997, pp. 203–204, illus. pl. 109 //
A. Ribeiro, *Dress in Eighteenth-Century Europe,*
New Haven and London, 2002, p. 270, illus.
fig. 187 (color).

EXHIBITED
Bordeaux, Musée des Beaux-Arts, *La Femme et
l'artiste, de Bellini à Picasso* (cat. by G. Martin-
Méry), May 22–September 20, 1964, no. 74
// London, Heim Gallery, *French Paintings &
Sculptures of the 18th Century,* January 10–March
15, 1968, no. 30, illus. // New Orleans, New
Orleans Museum of Art, March-November 1978
and June-November 1981, special loan.

35
Nicolas Marie Gatteaux
(French: 1751–1832)

*Profile Head of Marie Antoinette,
Queen of France,* 1779
Plaster, modeled and carved, with blue-tinted
background, diameter: 11 ½ inches (29.4 cm.)
Signed and dated lower right: *Gatteaux | 1779*

Museum Purchase, George S. Frierson, Jr.,
Fund, acc. no. 2002.295

PROVENANCE
David and Constance Yates, New York;
acquired from them by the museum in 2002.

EXHIBITED
New Orleans, New Orleans Museum of
Art, *Jefferson's America & Napoleon's France:
An Exhibition for the Louisiana Purchase
Bicentennial* (cat. by G. Feigenbaum), April
12–August 31, 2003, no. 3, illus. p. 27 (color).

36
Claude Joseph Vernet
(French: 1714–1789)

*The Morning, Port Scene,* 1780
Oil on canvas: 34 ½ x 51 ½ inches
(87.6 x 130.8 cm.)
Signed and dated lower right on stone
outcropping: *J. Vernet f. 1780*
Museum Purchase and Gift, by exchange, of
Edith Rosenwald Stern and Muriel Bultman
Francis, acc. no. 1996.11

PROVENANCE
Commissioned with its pendant, a now-lost
*Seaport* (Ingersoll-Smouse 1044), by Jean
Girardot de Marigny (1733–1796) and paid in
four installments between October 7, 1779,
and June 28, 1780, for a total price of 6,000
*livres*; displayed at Girardot de Marigny's Paris
home, the Hôtel Colbert; recorded in Girardot's
postmortem inventory, April 12, 1796 (for which,
see Bailey, 2002, cited below, p. 241); M. Emler,
Paris; his sale, Paris, 5 rue Sentier, December
27 [originally scheduled for October 30],
1809, lot 34; private collection, United States;
presented by the latter to the Addison Gallery of
American Art, The Phillips Academy, Andover,
Mass.; their sale, New York, Christie's, May
31, 1990, lot 138, illus. in cat. (color) (together
with three other Vernet paintings originally in
Girardot de Marigny's collection: *A Moonlight
Scene* [Ingersoll-Smouse 1067], *Fishing Scene at
Sunrise* [Ingersoll-Smouse 1189] and *Riverscape
with Female Bathers* [Ingersoll-Smouse 1190]);
Stair Sainty Matthiesen, in association with
Newhouse Galleries and Verner Åmell Gallery,
New York and London; New York, Sotheby's,
January 15, 1993, lot 63 (bought in), illus. in cat.
(color); acquired from Stair Sainty Matthiesen,
New York, by the museum in 1996.

REFERENCES
L. Lagrange, *Joseph Vernet et la peinture du
XVIIIᵉ siècle,* Paris, 1864, pp. 267, 370–371,
467, 475 // F. Ingersoll-Smouse, *Joseph Vernet
(1714–1789), peintre de marine: Étude critique et
catalogue raisonné,* Paris, 1926, II, p. 32, no. 1045,
also cited I, pp. 31, 38 (under chronology),
illus. II, pl. CXVII, fig. 255 // Denis Diderot,
*Salons* (ed. by J. Seznec), IV, *Salons of 1769,
1771, 1775 and 1781,* London, 1967, pp. 318, 361
// Denis Diderot, *Salons* (E.M. Bukdahl, M.
Delon, D. Kahn and A. Lorenceau, eds.), IV,
*Salons of 1769, 1771, 1775 and 1781,* Paris, 1995,
p. 317 and note 61 // C.B. Bailey, *Patriotic Taste:
Collecting Modern Art in Pre-Revolutionary Paris,*
New Haven and London, 2002, pp. 158, 241,
288, note 149 // (?) P. Sanchez, *Dictionnaire
des artistes exposant dans les Salons des XVII et
XVIIIᵉᵐᵉ siècles à Paris et en province, 1673–1800,*
Dijon, 2004, III, p. 1684.

EXHIBITED
Presumably Paris, Salon, 1781, no. 54 (as one of
"*Quatre Tableaux de Marine. De 4 pieds 6 pouces
de large, sur 5 pieds de haut, appartenant à M.
Girardot de Marigny*") // New York, Newhouse
Galleries, *Old Master Paintings: An Exhibition of
European Paintings from the 16th Century to the
19th Century,* April 4–May 3, 1991, no. 23, illus.
(color) (exhibition traveled to London, Verner
Åmell Gallery, June 5–July 19, 1991).

37
Adélaïde Labille Guiard
(French: 1749–1803)

*Portrait of Madame Élisabeth de France,*
circa 1787
Pastel on seven sheets of paper, joined and
applied to an oval, stretched canvas:
29 ⅞ x 24 inches (75.9 x 61 cm.)
Cartouches on frame bearing the inscriptions:
*LABILLE GUIARD | MADAME ELISABETH*
and the inventory number 128

Loan from a private New Orleans collection

PROVENANCE
Estate of the artist; by inheritance to her
husband, François André Vincent (1746–1816),
Paris; his estate sale, Paris, 1 rue de Seine,
October 17–19, 1816, lot 56; acquired there
by the artist's pupil, Marie Gabrielle Capet
(1761–1818); recorded in Capet's postmortem
inventory, November 14, 1818 (for which,

239

see Passez, 1973, cited below, p. 313); Jacques Mayer, as of 1909; Madame Louis Paraf, née Élisabeth Wildenstein, Paris; Galerie Pardo, Paris; William H. Schab Gallery, New York, as of 1969; acquired from the latter by the present owner.

REFERENCES
R. Portalis, *Adélaïde Labille-Guiard*, Paris, 1902, p. 94 // G. Mourey, "Exposition rétrospective de portraits de femmes sous les trois Républiques," *Les Arts*, No. 91, July 1909, p. 28 // A.M. Passez, *Adélaïde Labille-Guiard, 1749–1803, biographie et catalogue raisonné de son œuvre*, Paris, 1973, p. 178, no. 76, also cited p. 172, under no. 72, and p. 313, illus. p. 179, pl. LXIII // N. Jeffares, *Dictionary of Pastellists before 1800*, London, 2006, p. 271, illus.

EXHIBITED
Paris, Palais du Domaine de Bagatelle, *Catalogue de portraits de femmes sous les trois républiques*, May 15–July 15, 1909, no. 128 // New York, William H. Schab Gallery, *Pastel and Gouache Drawings of the Eighteenth Century from French Collections: Thirtieth Anniversary Exhibition*, October 17–November 15, 1969, no. 22, illus.

## 38

## Jean Germain Drouais
## (French: 1763–1788)

*Portrait of the Architect Auguste H. Cheval de Saint-Hubert,* circa 1787–88
Oil on canvas: 31 ⅛ x 25 ⅝ inches (79.1 x 65.1 cm.)
Inscribed on back of stretcher: *portrait d'Augh…, peint à Rome par son ami Germain Drouais qui n'a pas été terminé à cause de la mort de ce …*

Loan from a private New Orleans collection

PROVENANCE
Madame François Hubert Drouais, née Anne Françoise Doré (1732–1809), the artist's mother; by inheritance to her sister, Marie Jeanne Doré; inherited or acquired by Achille Valois; the Valois family, until 1972; Galerie Heim, Paris; acquired from them by the present owner in 1976.

REFERENCES
Rennes, Musée des Beaux-Arts, *Jean-Germain Drouais, 1763–1788* (cat. by P. Ramade et al.),

1985, no. 22, also cited p. 63, illus. p. 61 // S. Lee, "Exhibition Reviews: Rennes, Drouais," *Burlington Magazine*, CXXVII, August 1985, pp. 565–566 // P. Ramade, "Jean-Germain Drouais: Recent Discoveries," *Burlington Magazine*, CXXX, May 1988, p. 365 // M. Ledbury, "Unpublished Letters to Jacques-Louis David from His Pupils in Italy," *Burlington Magazine*, CXLII, May 2000, p. 298.

## 39

## Élisabeth Louise Vigée Le Brun (French: 1755–1842)

*Portrait of Marie Antoinette, Queen of France,* circa 1788
Oil on canvas: 109 ½ x 75 ½ inches (278.1 x 192 cm.)
Museum Purchase, Women's Volunteer Committee and Carrie Heiderich Funds, acc. no. 1985.90

PROVENANCE
Charles Philippe, Comte d'Artois (1757–1836), the future King Charles X (reigned 1824–1830); to his son, Charles Ferdinand de Bourbon, Duc de Berry (1778–1820); presented by him to a member of his house guard, the Comte de Ginestous; to his daughter, Marie-Thérèse-Béatrice de Ginestous, wife of Adolphe-Charles-Louis de Saporta, Aix-en-Provence; possibly by inheritance to their son, Anne-Charles-Félix-Gaston de Saporta (1877–1963), Château de Fonscolombe, Aix-en-Provence; Duveen Brothers, London, as of 1906; (Alfred) Eugène Kraemer (1852–1912), Paris; his estate sale, Paris, Galerie Georges Petit, May 5–6, 1913, lot 49, illus. in cat.; Edwin Marriott Hodgkins, Paris; Samuel G. Archibald, Paris and Montreal; his estate sale, New York, Parke-Bernet Galleries, March 30–31, 1951, lot 250, illus. in cat.; Mr. and Mrs. John Bond Trevor, New York; by inheritance to their son, Bronson Trevor, Oyster Bay, New York; his sale, London, Sotheby Parke-Bernet, July 8, 1981, lot 114, illus. in cat. (color) (bought in); acquired from Bronson Trevor, via Richard L. Feigen & Co., New York, by the museum in 1985.

ENGRAVINGS
(1) Charles François Adrien Macret, 1789; (2) Charles François Gabriel Le Vachez (active 1760–1820), 1792; (3) Pierre Michel Alix (1762–1817), colored print made as a pendant to Sergent's engraving of portrait of Louis XVI (see

M. Roux, *Inventaire du Fonds Français: graveurs du dix-huitième siècle*, I, Paris, 1930, p. 78, no. 1); (4) Schinker; (5) Madame veuve Jacques Bonnefoix; and (6) Laurens.

REFERENCES
P. de Nolhac, *Madame Vigée-Le Brun, peintre de la reine Marie Antoinette*, Paris, 1908, p. 71 [2nd, revised ed., Paris, 1912, p. 123] // W.H. Helm, *Vigée-Lebrun: Her Life, Works and Friendships*, London, n.d. [1915], p. 210 // A. Blum, *Madame Vigée-Lebrun, peintre des grandes dames du XVIIIe siècle*, Paris, 1919, p. 105 // M. Jallut, "Les Peintres et les portraits de Marie-Antoinette" (Mémoire de recherche de 3ᵉ cycle, École du Louvre; copy preserved in the library of the École du Louvre), 1936, pp. 208–209 (author incorrectly gives chronological priority to this painting over the signed and dated painting in the Musée national du Château de Versailles) // M. Jallut, *Marie-Antoinette et ses peintres*, Paris, 1955, pp. 48–49 // J. Baillio, "Le Dossier d'une oeuvre d'actualité politique: *Marie-Antoinette et ses enfants* par Mme Vigée Le Brun (deuxième partie)," *L'Oeil*, No. 310, May 1981, p. 91, note 30 // E. Tufts, "Vigée-Le Brun," *Art Journal*, XLII, winter 1982, p. 336, illus. fig. 2 // E.P. Caraco, "75th Anniversary Purchase: Portrait of Marie Antoinette," *Arts Quarterly* [New Orleans Museum of Art], VIII, January-March 1986, pp. 3–6, illus. pp. 3, fig. 1 and 5 (detail: bouquet of flowers) // P.N. Dunbar, *The New Orleans Museum of Art : The First Seventy-Five Years*, Baton Rouge and London, 1990, pp. 321–322, 347 and 360, illus. between pp. 56 and 57 // New *Orleans Museum of Art—Handbook of the Collection*, New Orleans, 1995, p. 52 (entry by S.E. Stearns), illus. (color) // C. Constans, *Musée national du Château de Versailles: les peintures*, Paris, 1995, II, p. 931 // Jackson, Mississippi, Mississippi Arts Pavilion, *Splendors of Versailles* (ed. by C. Constans and X. Salmon), 1998, p. 79, cited under no. 17 (entry by C. Constans) // New Orleans, New Orleans Museum of Art, *Jefferson's America & Napoleon's France: An Exhibition for the Louisiana Purchase Bicentennial* (cat. by G. Feigenbaum), 2003, illus. in essay by S. Taylor-Leduc, "Thomas Jefferson's Paris Years: A Franco-American Affair," p. 5, fig. 5 (color) // X. Salmon, *Marie-Antoinette, images d'un destin*, Neuilly-sur-Seine, 2005, p. 114 // Bordeaux, Musée des Arts Décoratifs, *Marie-Antoinette à Versailles—le goût d'une reine*, 2005–2006, pp. 92/94, cited under no. 16 (entry by X. Salmon), illus. p. 79.

EXHIBITED
London, Duveen Brothers, *An Exhibition of Masterpieces of French Painters of the XVIII Century*, 1906, no. 1 // Berlin, Königliche Akademie der Künste, *Exposition d'oeuvres de l'art français au XVIIIe siècle*, January 26–March 6, 1910, no. 74, illus. // Fort Worth, Kimbell Art Museum, *Élisabeth Louise Vigée Le Brun 1755–1842* (cat. by J. Baillio), June 5–August 8, 1982, no. 27, illus. p. 79.

## 40
## Jean Joseph Taillasson
(French: 1745–1809)

*Coriolanus Beseeched by His Mother and Wife*, circa 1791
Oil on canvas: 45 x 57 inches (114.3 x 144.8 cm.)
Museum Purchase, George S. Frierson, Jr., Fund and Gift, by exchange, of Mrs. Charles Kohlmeyer, Dr. and Mrs. Richard W. Levy, Mrs. Charles F. Lynch and Mr. and Mrs. Moise S. Steeg, Jr., acc. no. 1994.7

PROVENANCE
Private collection, France; Richard L. Feigen & Co., New York, as of 1994; acquired from them by the museum in late 1994.

REFERENCES
*New Orleans Museum of Art—Handbook of the Collection*, New Orleans, 1995, p. 53 (entry by S.E. Stearns), illus. p. 53 (color) // S.E. Stearns, "Jean-Joseph Taillasson's *Coriolanus Beseeched by His Mother and Wife*," *Arts Quarterly* [New Orleans Museum of Art], XVII, July-September 1995, p. 15, illus.

EXHIBITED
New York, Richard L. Feigen & Co., *Neo-Classicism and Romanticism: French Painting, 1774–1826*, May 17–July 15, 1994, no. 56, illus.

## 41
## Joseph Charles Marin
(French: 1759–1834)

*Water Nymph Leaning on an Urn (La Source)*, 1797
Terracotta, height: 11 ¾ inches (29.8 cm.)
Signed and dated on rock at the rear:
*Marin 1797*
Museum Purchase, William McDonald Boles and Eva Carol Boles Fund, acc. no. 1997.636

PROVENANCE
Rosenberg & Stiebel, New York; Bernard Weinberger, New Orleans, as of c. 1982; Ken McBride, New Orleans; New Orleans Auction Galleries, November 19, 1997, lot 75; acquired there by the museum.

REFERENCES
J.W. Keefe, "Curator's Choice: *La Source* by Joseph-Charles Marin (French, 1759–1834)," *Arts Quarterly* [New Orleans Museum of Art], XXVII, July-September 2005, pp. 8–9, illus. p. 8.

## 42
## Pierre Joseph Redouté
(Franco-Flemish: 1759–1840)

*Still Life of Flowers in a Vase on a Marble Ledge*, circa 1800
Oil on canvas: 23 ⅝ x 19 ¼ inches (60 x 49 cm.)
Indistinctly signed with the artist's initials on ledge at lower left: …*R*
Loan from a private New Orleans collection

PROVENANCE
Robert Maury, Ermenonville (Oise); acquired through the intermediary of Le Cabinet d'amateur, Paris, by the present owner in 1971.

REFERENCES
M. and F. Faré, *La Vie silencieuse en France: la nature morte au XVIIIe siècle*, Fribourg, 1976, p. 317, illus. fig. 508.

EXHIBITED
Greenwich, Conn., Bruce Museum of Arts & Science, *The Floral Art of Pierre-Joseph Redouté* (cat. by M. Roland Michel, P.C. Sutton, C.R. Rebbert and C.A. Drayton), July 20–October 20, 2002, no. 5, illus. p. 45 (color) (exhibition traveled to Fort Worth, Kimbell Art Museum, November 17, 2002–March 2, 2003).

## 43
## Jean Baptiste Joseph Wicar
(French: 1762–1834)

*Portrait of Colonel Antoine Jean Auguste Henri Durosnel*, 1805
Oil on canvas: 29 x 24 inches (73.7 x 61 cm.)
Signed and dated lower right: *J.B. Wicar 1805*
Museum Purchase, Women's Volunteer Committee Fund, acc. no. 83.72

PROVENANCE
Duc de Costa d'Aragon; his sale, Monte Carlo, Sotheby's Monaco, February 14, 1983, lot 702, illus. in cat.; Stair Sainty Fine Art, Inc., New York; acquired from them by the museum in 1983.

REFERENCES
P.N. Dunbar, *The New Orleans Museum of Art: The First Seventy-Five Years*, Baton Rouge and London, 1990, p. 320.

EXHIBITED
Orléans, Musée des Beaux-Arts, *Peintures françaises du Museum of Art de la Nouvelle Orléans*, May 9–September 15, 1984, no. 11 (entry by E.P. Caraco), illus. // Memphis, Tenn., The Dixon Gallery and Gardens, *French Paintings of Three Centuries from the New Orleans Museum of Art*, January 5–March 1, 1992, no. 13 (entry by E.P. Caraco), also cited in essay by M.R. Brown, "An Introduction to French Paintings of Three Centuries," p. 12, illus. p. 41 (color) (exhibition traveled to Miami, Center for the Fine Arts, March 15–May 3, 1992; Wilmington, Delaware Art Museum, May 17–June 29, 1992; Grosse Point Shores, Michigan, Edsel and Eleanor Ford House, July 22–September 6, 1992; Oklahoma City, Oklahoma City Art Museum, October 4–November 15, 1992; and Seattle, Seattle Art Museum, December 17, 1992–February 14, 1993) // Koriyama, Koriyama City Museum of Art, *French Art of Four Centuries from the New Orleans Museum of Art*, February 27–March 31, 1993, no. 13 (entry by E.P. Caraco), also cited in essay by M.R. Brown, "An Introduction to French Art of Four Centuries," p. 26, illus. pp. 45 (color) and 135 (exhibition traveled to Yokohama, Sogo Museum of Art, April 21–May 23, 1993; Nara, Nara Sogo Museum of Art, June 9–July 4, 1993; and Kitakyushu, Kitakyushu Municipal Museum of Art, July 10–August 22, 1993).

**44**
Jean-Auguste-Dominique Ingres
(French: 1780–1867)

*Compositional Study for "The Apotheosis of Homer,"* 1826
Graphite and pen and ink on paper, squared for transfer: 9 ⅞ x 12 ¾ inches (251 x 324 mm.)
Signed and inscribed below center: *Ingres à son excellent ami M. Fritz Reiset*
Inscribed on the pediment from left to right: *les arts / l'iliade / l'odissé / les par… d'homère*
Inscribed on the left edge above the figural grouping: *horace*
The Muriel Bultman Francis Collection,
acc. no. 1986.225

PROVENANCE
Presented by the artist to his friend, Frédéric Reiset (1815–1890), Paris [see inscription, quoted above]; his estate sale, Paris, Hôtel Drouot, June 25, 1895, lot 55 (as one of "*Onze dessins: figures nues, draperies, etc. Études pour ses principaux tableaux.—Plusieurs de ces dessins sont mis au carreau. Ce numéro sera divisé.*"); M. Marcel; acquired from him by Edgar Degas (1834–1917), Paris; his estate sale, Paris, Galerie Georges Petit, March 26–27, 1918, lot 199; acquired there by Bellot; Norman Schlenoff, New York, until 1959; Muriel Bultman Francis (died 1986), New Orleans and (later) New York; bequeathed by her to the museum in 1986.

REFERENCES
H. Delaborde, *Ingres, sa vie, ses travaux, sa doctrine*, Paris, 1870, p. 269, no. 177 // N. Schlenoff, *Ingres, ses sources littéraires*, Paris, 1956, p. 193, illus. // A.M. Wagner, "Degas' Collection of Art, an Introductory Essay and Catalogue" (unpublished M.A. thesis, Brown University), 1974, p. 120 // *New Orleans Museum of Art—Handbook of the Collection*, New Orleans, 1995, p. 55 (entry by S.E. Stearns), illus. (color) // C.T. Ives et al., *The Private Collection of Edgar Degas: A Summary Catalogue*, New York, 1997, p. 74, no. 653 // New York, The Metropolitan Museum of Art, *The Private Collection of Edgar Degas* (ed. by A. Dumas et al.), 1997–1998, cited in essay by A. Dumas, "Degas and His Collection," pp. 33, 70, notes 145, 147.

EXHIBITED
New Orleans, New Orleans Museum of Art, *Profile of a Connoisseur: The Collection of Muriel Bultman Francis* (cat. by E.P. Caraco), November

10, 1985–January 12, 1986, no. 46, also cited p. 10, illus. p. 84 // New Orleans, New Orleans Museum of Art, *Fifty Master Drawings from the New Orleans Museum of Art* (cat. by V.L. Olsen), July 15–August 20, 1989, no. 23 (exhibition traveled to Monroe, Louisiana, Masur Museum of Art, September 9–October 1, 1989; Lake Charles, Imperial Calcasieu Museum, October 7–November 26, 1989; Shreveport, Meadows Museum of Art, January 27–March 11, 1990; Baton Rouge, Louisiana Arts and Science Center, March 17–May 13, 1990; Alexandria, Alexandria Museum of Art, May 19–June 30, 1990; and Lafayette, University Art Museum, September 1–November 16, 1990) // Koriyama, Koriyama City Museum of Art, *French Art of Four Centuries from the New Orleans Museum of Art*, February 27–March 31, 1993, no. 14 (entry by S.E. Stearns), illus. pp. 46 (color) and 135 (exhibition traveled to Yokohama, Sogo Museum of Art, April 21–May 23, 1993; Nara, Nara Sogo Museum of Art, June 9–July 4, 1993; and Kitakyushu, Kitakyushu Municipal Museum of Art, July 10–August 22, 1993).

**45**
Asher B. Durand
(American: 1796–1886)

*Forenoon,* 1847
Oil on canvas: 60 ¼ x 48 ¼ inches
(153 x 122.5 cm.)
Signed and dated lower center:
*A.B. Durand 18…*
Gift of the Fine Arts Club of New Orleans,
acc. no. 1916.4

PROVENANCE
Commissioned from the artist, with pendant painting "Afternoon," by James Robb (1814–1881), New Orleans; his sale, New Orleans, March 1, 1859, lot 29; Theodore Wilkinson; presented by the Fine Arts Club of New Orleans to the museum in 1916.

REFERENCES
[C. Lanman], "A Pair of Landscapes. By Durand," *Literary World*, I, February 6, 1847, pp. 15–16 // C. Lanman, "Our Landscape Painters," *Southern Literary Messenger*, XVI, May 1850, pp. 272–273 [for this and additional early exhibition reviews, see Lawall, 1978, cited below, pp. 60–61] // J. Durand, *The Life and Times of Asher Brown Durand*, New York, 1894, p. 173 // New Orleans, The Isaac

Delgado Museum of Art, *Catalogue of Paintings, Sculpture, and Other Objects of Art in the Isaac Delgado Museum of Art*, New Orleans, 1932, p. 18, no. 134 // *National Academy of Design Exhibition Record, 1826–1860*, New York, 1943, I, p. 138 // D.B. Lawall, *Asher Brown Durand: His Art and Art Theory in Relation to His Times*, New York, 1977, pp. 300, 338, 350, 472, illus. fig. 110 // D.B. Lawall, *Asher B. Durand: A Documentary Catalogue of the Narrative and Landscape Paintings*, New York, 1978, pp. 57–61, no. 110 // J.G. Caldwell, *New Orleans Museum of Art—Handbook of the Collection* (ed. by B.N. McDermott), New Orleans, 1980, p. 133, illus. // W.J. Gavin and R.F. Perkins, Jr., *The Boston Athenaeum Art Exhibition Index, 1827–1874*, Boston, 1980, pp. 52, 218, 254 // A.W. Rutledge, *The Annual Exhibition Record of the Pennsylvania Academy of the Fine Arts, 1807–1870* [2nd ed., revised by P.H. Falk, Madison, Conn., 1988, pp. 67, 352] // P.N. Dunbar, *The New Orleans Museum of Art: The First Seventy-Five Years*, Baton Rouge and London, 1990, pp. 29–30 // *New Orleans Museum of Art—Handbook of the Collection*, New Orleans, 1995, p. 117 (entry by J.G. Caldwell), illus. (color) // K. Maddox, "Durand, Asher Brown," in *Saur. Allgemeines Künstler-Lexikon. Die bildenden Künstler aller Zeiten und Völker*, XXXI, Munich and Leipzig, 2002, p. 135 // Minneapolis, The Minneapolis Institute of Arts, *Currents of Change: Art and Life along the Mississippi River, 1850–1861* (cat. by J.T. Busch), 2004, p. 118, no. 104, also cited in essay by J.T. Busch, "Handsomely Furnished in the Most Fashionable Style: Art and Decoration along the Mississippi River," p. 117, illus. p. 118 (color).

EXHIBITED
New York, National Academy of Design, *Catalogue of the Twenty-Second Annual Exhibition*, April-July 1847, no. 24 // Philadelphia, Pennsylvania Academy of Fine Arts, *Catalogue of the Twenty-Eighth Annual Exhibition*, spring 1851, no. 150 // Philadelphia, Pennsylvania Academy of Fine Arts, *Catalogue of the Twenty-Ninth Annual Exhibition*, spring 1852, no. 350 // Philadelphia, Pennsylvania Academy of Fine Arts, *Catalogue of the Thirtieth Annual Exhibition*, spring 1853, no. 387 // Boston, Athenaeum Gallery, *Catalogue of the Twenty-Seventh Exhibition of Paintings and Statuary*, 1854, no. 124 // Boston, Athenaeum Gallery, *Catalogue of the Twenty-Eighth Exhibition of Paintings and Statuary*, 1855, no. 80.

46
Franz Xaver Winterhalter
(German: 1806–1873)

*Young Woman in a Ball Gown,* 1850
Oil on canvas, oval: 51 ¼ x 38 inches
(130.2 x 96.5 cm.)
Signed, inscribed and dated lower right:
*F. Winterhalter | Paris 1850*
Museum Purchase, Carrie Heiderich Fund
and Gift, by exchange, of Mr. and Mrs. Harris
Masterson, acc. no. 1987.32

PROVENANCE
Private collection; Monaco, Sotheby's, June
21, 1986, lot 80, illus. in cat. (color); Bruno
Meissner, Zurich; Richard L. Feigen & Co.,
New York, as of June 1987; acquired from them
for the museum in late 1987.

REFERENCES
E.C. Pennington, "New Acquisition: Franz
Xaver Winterhalter's *A Young Lady in a Ball
Gown,*" *Arts Quarterly* [New Orleans Museum
of Art], X, April-June 1988, pp. 20–21, illus.
p. 20, fig. 1 // *New Orleans Museum of Art—
Handbook of the Collection,* New Orleans, 1995,
p. 59 (entry by S.E. Stearns), illus. (color).

EXHIBITED
Chicago, Richard L. Feigen and Co., *Portraits,
1500 to 1900,* June 19–August 20, 1987, checklist,
no number, illus. on cover // Memphis, Tenn.,
The Dixon Gallery and Gardens, *French Paintings
of Three Centuries from the New Orleans Museum
of Art,* January 5–March 1, 1992, no. 18 (entry by
S.E. Stearns), also cited in essay by M.R. Brown,
"An Introduction to French Paintings of Three
Centuries," p. 13, illus. p. 51 (color) (exhibition
traveled to Miami, Center for the Fine Arts,
March 15–May 3, 1992; Wilmington, Delaware
Art Museum, May 17–June 29, 1992; Grosse
Point Shores, Michigan, Edsel and Eleanor Ford
House, July 22–September 6, 1992; Oklahoma
City, Oklahoma City Art Museum, October
4–November 15, 1992; and Seattle, Seattle Art
Museum, December 17, 1992–February 14, 1993)
// Koriyama, Koriyama City Museum of Art,
*French Art of Four Centuries from the New Orleans
Museum of Art,* February 27–March 31, 1993, no.
39 (entry by S.E. Stearns), illus. pp. 73 (color),
154 (exhibition traveled to Yokohama, Sogo
Museum of Art, April 21–May 23, 1993; Nara,
Nara Sogo Museum of Art, June 9–July 4, 1993;
and Kitakyushu, Kitakyushu Municipal Museum
of Art, July 10–August 22, 1993).

47
Albert-Ernest Carrier-Belleuse
(French: 1824–1887)

*Woman in Reeds (Undine),* circa 1865
Bronze with green and gold patination,
height: 30 ½ inches (77.5 cm.)
Signed on front of base, at left: *A. CARRIER*
On the back of the base, the foundry mark of
E. Lohse, Paris
Gift of John G. Agar, in memory of his father,
William Agar, acc. no. 1915.51

PROVENANCE
John Giraud Agar (1856–1935), New Orleans;
presented by him to the museum in 1915.

REFERENCES
New Orleans, The Isaac Delgado Museum of
Art, *Catalogue of Paintings, Sculpture, and Other
Objects of Art in the Isaac Delgado Museum
of Art,* New Orleans, 1932, p. 10, no. 14 (as
"Woman in Forest"). <u>Comparative References</u>:
J.E. Hargrove, *The Life and Work of Albert
Carrier-Belleuse,* New York and London, 1977,
pp. 47–48, illus. pl. 10 (terracotta reduction,
dated 1865, in the collection of David Barclay,
London).

48
Edgar Degas
(French: 1834–1917)

*Study for a Portrait of a Woman,* 1867
Graphite and watercolor on paper:
11 ¼ x 8 ½ inches (286 x 216 mm.)
Signed and dated right center: *Degas 1867*
Lower left, stamp of the Atelier Degas sale
On reverse, at center:
oval stamp of the Atelier Degas sale
The Muriel Bultman Francis Collection,
acc. no. 1986.179

PROVENANCE
Estate of the artist; fourth Atelier Degas sale,
Paris, Galerie Georges Petit, July 2–4, 1919, lot
100d, illus. in cat., p. 95; Durand-Ruel, Paris;
Olivier Senn (1864–1959), Paris, as of 1931;
Paris, Galerie Charpentier, December 10, 1959,
lot 11, illus. in cat., pl. I; Jacques Seligmann
& Co., New York, as of 1960; acquired from
them by Muriel Bultman Francis (died 1986),
New Orleans and (later) New York, as of 1967;
bequeathed by her to the museum in 1986.

EXHIBITED
Paris, Musée de l'Orangerie, *Degas,* July
19–October 1, 1931, no. 115 // New York,
Jacques Seligmann & Co., *Master Drawings,*
November 7–28, 1960, no. 11 // St. Louis, City
Art Museum, *Drawings by Degas* (cat. by J.S.
Boggs), January 20–February 26, 1967, no. 51,
illus. p. 88 (exhibition traveled to Philadelphia,
Philadelphia Museum of Art, March 10–April 30,
1967; and Minneapolis, The Minneapolis Society
of Fine Arts, May 18–June 25, 1967) // New
Orleans, New Orleans Museum of Art, *Profile of
a Connoisseur: The Collection of Muriel Bultman
Francis* (cat. by E.P. Caraco), November 10,
1985–January 12, 1986, no. 23, illus. p. 63 // New
Orleans, New Orleans Museum of Art, *Fifty
Master Drawings from the New Orleans Museum
of Art* (cat. by V.L. Olsen), July 15–August 20,
1989, no. 9 (exhibition traveled to Monroe,
Louisiana, Masur Museum of Art, September
9–October 1, 1989; Lake Charles, Imperial
Calcasieu Museum, October 7–November 26,
1989; Shreveport, Meadows Museum of Art,
January 27–March 11, 1990; Baton Rouge,
Louisiana Arts and Science Center, March 17–
May 13, 1990; Alexandria, Alexandria Museum
of Art, May 19–June 30, 1990; and Lafayette,
University Art Museum, September 1–November
16, 1990) // Koriyama, Koriyama City Museum
of Art, *French Art of Four Centuries from the New
Orleans Museum of Art,* February 27–March 31,
1993, no. 35 (entry by S.E. Stearns), illus. pp. 70
(color), 151 (exhibition traveled to Yokohama,
Sogo Museum of Art, April 21–May 23, 1993;
Nara, Nara Sogo Museum of Art, June 9–July
4, 1993; and Kitakyushu, Kitakyushu Municipal
Museum of Art, July 10–August 22, 1993).

49
Jean-Léon Gérôme
(French: 1824–1904)

*Turkish Bashi Bazouk Mercenaries Playing
Chess in a Market Place,*
circa 1870–73
Oil on canvas: 25 ¼ x 21 ¼ inches (64 x 54 cm.)
Signed lower left, on stone: *J.L. GEROME*
Gift of Mr. and Mrs. Chapman H. Hyams,
acc. no. 1915.14

PROVENANCE
Knoedler & Co., New York; Mr. and Mrs.
Chapman H. Hyams, New Orleans; bequeathed
by Mrs. Hyams (née Sara Lavinia Todd) to the
museum in 1915.

REFERENCES

Bernard Prost, "Catalogue des dessins et des peintures de Gérôme" (Ms., Paris, Bibliothèque nationale de France), 1883, p. 43 // R.B. Mayfield, *The Art Collection of Mr. and Mrs. Chapman H. Hyams*, New Orleans, 1915, n.p., no. 13 [revised ed., New Orleans, 1964, n.p., no. 13, illus.] // New Orleans, The Isaac Delgado Museum of Art, *Catalogue of Paintings, Sculpture, and Other Objects of Art in the Isaac Delgado Museum of Art*, New Orleans, 1932, p. 35, no. H-13 // J.G. Caldwell, *New Orleans Museum of Art—Handbook of the Collection* (ed. by B.N. McDermott), New Orleans, 1980, p. 55, illus. // G.M. Ackerman, *La Vie et l'oeuvre de Jean-Léon Gérôme*, Paris, 1986, p. 228, no. 204, also cited p. 206, under no. 116, illus. p. 229 // J. Ingamells, *The Wallace Collection: Catalogue of Pictures*, II, *French Nineteenth Century*, London, 1986, p. 128, note 2 // P.N. Dunbar, *The New Orleans Museum of Art: The First Seventy-Five Years*, Baton Rouge and London, 1990, p. 35 // *New Orleans Museum of Art—Handbook of the Collection*, New Orleans, 1995, p. 60 (entry by J.G. Caldwell), illus. (color).

EXHIBITED

New Orleans, The Isaac Delgado Museum of Art, *The World of Art in 1910*, November 15–December 31, 1960, n.p., illus. // Memphis, Tenn., The Dixon Gallery and Gardens, *French Paintings of Three Centuries from the New Orleans Museum of Art*, January 5–March 1, 1992, no. 19 (entry by J.G. Caldwell), also cited in essay by M.R. Brown, "An Introduction to French Paintings of Three Centuries," p. 13, illus. p. 53 (color) (exhibition traveled to Miami, Center for the Fine Arts, March 15–May 3, 1992; Wilmington, Delaware Art Museum, May 17–June 29, 1992; Grosse Point Shores, Michigan, Edsel and Eleanor Ford House, July 22–September 6, 1992; Oklahoma City, Oklahoma City Art Museum, October 4–November 15, 1992; and Seattle, Seattle Art Museum, December 17, 1992–February 14, 1993) // Koriyama, Koriyama City Museum of Art, *French Art of Four Centuries from the New Orleans Museum of Art*, February 27–March 31, 1993, no. 40 (entry by J.G. Caldwell), also cited in essay by M.R. Brown, "Introduction to French Art of Four Centuries," p. 26, illus. pp. 74 (color) and 155 (exhibition traveled to Yokohama, Sogo Museum of Art, April 21–May 23, 1993; Nara, Nara Sogo Museum of Art, June 9–July 4, 1993; and Kitakyushu, Kitakyushu Municipal Museum of Art, July

10–August 22, 1993) // Laurel, Mississippi, Lauren Rogers Museum of Art, *The French Legacy: The American and Euopean Collections of the Lauren Rogers Museum of Art* (cat. by M.P. De Marsche), May 1–September 6, 1998, p. 22, no number.

50
Edgar Degas
(French: 1834–1917)

*Portrait of Estelle Musson De Gas,* 1872
Oil on canvas: 39 ⅜ x 54 inches (100 x 137 cm.)
Museum Purchase by Public Subscription,
acc. no. 1965.1

PROVENANCE

Estate of the artist; first Atelier Degas sale, Paris, Galerie Georges Petit, May 6–8, 1918, lot 12, illus. in cat.; acquired there by Jacques Seligmann (1858–1923), New York and Paris; his sale, New York, American Art Association, Hotel Plaza, January 27, 1921, lot 66, illus. in cat.; acquired there by Ambrose Vollard (1866–1939), Paris; acquired from him by Paul Eugene Cremetti (born 1889), London; Lucerne, Hôtel National, September 8, 1924, lot 41, illus. in cat. (bought in); Thannhauser collection, Zürich [presumably Justin K. Thannhauser (1892–1976)]; Dr. Kurt Oppenheim, Blonay-Vevey, Switzerland, as of 1937; private collection, Switzerland, as of 1952; possibly Marlborough Galleries, London, as of mid-1963; the Hon. Peter Montefiore Samuel, later 4th Viscount Bearsted of Maidstone (1911–1996), London, as of 1963; consigned by him to Eugene Victor Thaw, New York, as of 1964 (the identity of the consignor, hitherto unpublished, was kindly supplied by Mr. Thaw [his e-mail to Joseph Baillio, September 12, 2006]); acquired from him by the museum in 1965.

REFERENCES

J.B. Manson, *The Life and Work of Edgar Degas*, London, 1927, p. 18, illus. pl. 12 // J. Rewald, "Degas and His Family in New Orleans," *Gazette des Beaux-Arts*, 6e pér., XXX, August 1946, p. 118, illus. p. 121, fig. 15 [reprinted in idem, *Studies in Impressionism* (ed. by I. Gordon and F. Weitzenhoffer), New York and London, 1985, pp. 35, 37, illus. p. 30, fig. 16] // P.A. Lemoisne, *Degas et son oeuvre*, Paris, 1947, II, p. 154, no. 306, illus. p. 155 // J.S. Boggs, *Portraits by Degas*, Berkeley and Los Angeles, 1962, pp. 41, 126, illus. pl. 77 // "Degas's

American Cousins," *Life*, LIX, July 2, 1965, pp. 52–53, illus. (color) // J.B. Byrnes, "The Day the People Bought a Painting," *Museum News*, XLIII, May 1965, pp. 24–27, illus. pp. 25, 27 (detail: head of sitter) // J.B. Byrnes, "Edgar Degas' New Orleans Paintings," *Antiques Magazine*, LXXXVIII, November 1965, p. 665, illus. p. 664 (color) // H. Haydon, *Great Art Treasures in America's Smaller Museums*, New York, 1967, pp. 84, 86/91, illus. p. 84 // M.S. Young, "Letter from U.S.A.: Spanish Moss and Old Mies," *Apollo*, LXXXVIII, September 1968, p. 223, illus. fig. 3 // J.G. Caldwell, *New Orleans Museum of Art—Handbook of the Collection* (ed. by B.N. McDermott), New Orleans, 1980, p. 59, illus. pp. 18 (color), 59 // E. De Keyser, *Degas, réalité et métaphore*, Louvain, 1981, p. 53, illus. pl. 18 // P. Failling, "The Objects of Their Affection," *Art News*, LXXXI, November 1982, p. 130, illus. // D. Sutton, *Edgar Degas: Life and Work*, New York, 1986, p. 97 // J. Lassaigne and F. Minervino, *Tout l'oeuvre peint de Degas* (revised ed. by S. de Naurois), Paris, 1988, p. 102, no. 342, illus. // Montgomery, Alabama, Museum of Fine Arts, *The Grand Tour: The Tradition of Patronage in Southern Art Museums* (cat. by M.L. Ausfeld), 1988–1989, p. 64 // Paris, Galeries nationales du Grand Palais, and elsewhere, *Degas*, 1988–1989, pp. 181–182, cited under no. 112 [American ed. of cat., p. 182] // P.N. Dunbar, *The New Orleans Museum of Art: The First Seventy-Five Years*, Baton Rouge and London, 1990, pp. xii, 70, 226–232, 258 and 259, illus. pl. following p. 56 // *New Orleans Museum of Art—Handbook of the Collection*, New Orleans, 1995, p. 63 (entry by E.P. Caraco), illus. (color) // R. Delehanty, "Waiting for the Resurrection: New Orleans in the Aftermath," *Museum News*, LXXXV, May-June 2006, illus. p. 57 (color).

EXHIBITED

Paris, Orangerie des Tuileries, *Degas*, March-April 1937, no. 17, illus. pl. IX // Bern, Kunstmuseum, *Degas*, November 25, 1951–January 13, 1952, no. 18, illus. // London, Marlborough Fine Art, Ltd., *A Great Period of French Painting: An Exhibition Held in Memory of the Late Miss Clarica Davidson*, June-July 1963, no. 9, illus. (color) and on cover (color detail) // New Orleans, The Isaac Delgado Museum of Art, *Edgar Degas: His Family and Friends in New Orleans*, May 2–June 16, 1965, no number, also cited p. 24 (Rewald article) and in essays by J.B. Byrnes, "Edgar Degas: His Family and His Friends in New Orleans," pp. 33–42 *passim*, and by J.S. Boggs, "Degas, the Painter in New Orleans," pp. 85–89, illus. p. 27, fig. 15 (Rewald article), color pl. facing p. 32, p. 34, fig. 1 (painting with additions, as featured in 1918 sale) and on front cover (color detail) // Orléans, Musée des Beaux-Arts, *Peintures françaises du Museum of Art de la Nouvelle Orléans*, May 9–September 15, 1984, no. 20 (entry by E.P. Caraco), illus. in color, p. 57 and on front cover // Memphis, Tenn., The Dixon Gallery and Gardens, *French Paintings of Three Centuries from the New Orleans Museum of Art*, January 5–March 1, 1992, no. 23 (entry by E.P. Caraco), also cited in essay by M.R. Brown, "An Introduction to French Paintings of Three Centuries," pp. 12–13, 15, illus. p. 61 (color) (exhibition traveled to Miami, Center for the Fine Arts, March 15–May 3, 1992; Wilmington, Delaware Art Museum, May 17–June 29, 1992; Grosse Point Shores, Michigan, Edsel and Eleanor Ford House, July 22–September 6, 1992; Oklahoma City, Oklahoma City Art Museum, October 4–November 15; and Seattle, Seattle Art Museum, December 17, 1992–February 14, 1993) // Koriyama, Koriyama City Museum of Art, *French Art of Four Centuries from the New Orleans Museum of Art*, February 27–March 31, 1993, no. 36 (entry by E.P. Caraco), also cited in essay by M.R. Brown, "An Introduction to French Art of Four Centuries," p. 28, illus. pp. 72 (color), 152 (exhibition traveled to Yokohama, Sogo Museum of Art, April 21–May 23, 1993; Nara, Nara Sogo Museum of Art, June 9–July 4, 1993; and Kitakyushu, Kitakyushu Municipal Museum of Art, July 10–August 22, 1993) // New Orleans, New Orleans Museum of Art, *Degas and New Orleans: A French Impressionist in America* (cat. by J.S. Boggs), May 1–August 29, 1999, pp. 211 and 266, no. 28, also cited in essay by G. Feigenbaum, "Edgar Degas, Almost a Son of Louisiana," pp. 15–16, 19–20, and on pp. 210/212, 213, illus. pp. 15, 66 (color detail), 211 (color) (exhibition traveled to Copenhagen, Ordrupgaard, September 16–November 28, 1999) // Atlanta, High Museum of Art, *Degas and America: The Early Collectors*, March 3–May 27, 2001, no. 27 (entry by G. Vigtel), also cited in essays by A. Dumas, "Degas in America," p. 25, by D.A. Brenneman, "Degas and His American Critics," p. 55, and by P. Siebert, "Appendix: Selected Degas Exhibitions in America, 1878–1936," p. 249, illus. p. 136 (color) (exhibition traveled to Minneapolis, Minneapolis Institute of Arts, June 16–September 9, 2001) // New York, AXA Gallery,

*The Big Easy in the Big Apple: Two Centuries of Art in Louisiana from the Battle of New Orleans to Katrina. An Exhibition from the Collection of the New Orleans Museum of Art*, March 10–May 20, 2006 (no catalogue).

## 51
## Jean-Baptiste-Camille Corot
(French: 1796–1875)

*Woodland Scene,* circa 1872–73
Oil on canvas: 14 ½ x 23 ½ inches
(36.8 x 59.7 cm.)
Signed lower left: *COROT*
Gift of Mr. and Mrs. Chapman H. Hyams, acc. no. 1915.8

PROVENANCE
Presented by the artist to M. Estienne; M.M. Verdier and Tempelaere, Paris; Hattat collection, as of 1880; Mr. and Mrs. Chapman H. Hyams, New Orleans; bequeathed by Mrs. Hyams (née Sara Lavinia Todd) to the museum in 1915.

REFERENCES
A. Robaut, *L'Oeuvre de Corot: catalogue raisonné et illustré*, Paris, 1905, III, p. 278, no. 2100 (dates painting to 1865–71), illus. (drawing by Alfred Robaut) // R.B. Mayfield, *The Art Collection of Mr. and Mrs. Chapman H. Hyams*, New Orleans, 1915, no. 8 [revised ed., New Orleans, 1964, n.p., no. 8, illus.] // New Orleans, The Isaac Delgado Museum of Art, *Catalogue of Paintings, Sculpture, and Other Objects of Art in the Isaac Delgado Museum of Art*, New Orleans, 1932, p. 35, no. H-8 // J.G. Caldwell, *New Orleans Museum of Art—Handbook of the Collection* (ed. by B.N. McDermott), New Orleans, 1980, p. 53, illus. // P.N. Dunbar, *The New Orleans Museum of Art: The First Seventy-Five Years*, Baton Rouge and London, 1990, p. 35 // *New Orleans Museum of Art—Handbook of the Collection*, New Orleans, 1995, p. 57 (entry by G.P. Caldwell), illus. (color).

EXHIBITED
New Orleans, The Isaac Delgado Museum of Art, *The World of Art in 1910*, November 15–December 31, 1960, n.p., no number // Orléans, Musée des Beaux-Arts, *Peintures françaises du Museum of Art de la Nouvelle Orléans*, May 9–September 15, 1984, no. 12 (entry by E.P. Caraco), illus. // Montgomery, Alabama, Montgomery Museum of Fine Arts, *The Grand*

*Tour: The Tradition of Patronage in Southern Art Museums*, September 18, 1988–February 5, 1989, p. 66 // Tokyo, Odakyu Grand Gallery, *J.B. Camille Corot* (cat. by G.P. Weisberg et al.), September 13–October 1, 1989, no. 57 (entry by G.P. Weisberg), illus. pl. 57 (color) (exhibition traveled to Osaka, Navio Museum of Art, October 20–November 14, 1989; and Yokohama, Sogo Museum of Art, January 18–February 25, 1990) // Memphis, Tenn., The Dixon Gallery and Gardens, *French Paintings of Three Centuries from the New Orleans Museum of Art*, January 5–March 1, 1992, no. 15 (entry by E.P. Caraco), also cited in essay by M.R. Brown, "An Introduction to French Paintings of Three Centuries," pp. 10, 13, illus. p. 45 (color) (exhibition traveled to Miami, Center for the Fine Arts, March 15–May 3, 1992; Wilmington, Delaware Art Museum, May 17–June 29, 1992; Grosse Point Shores, Michigan, Edsel and Eleanor Ford House, July 22–September 6, 1992; Oklahoma City, Oklahoma City Art Museum, October 4–November 15, 1992; and Seattle, Seattle Art Museum, December 17, 1992–February 14, 1993) // Koriyama, Koriyama City Museum of Art, *French Art of Four Centuries from the New Orleans Museum of Art*, February 27–March 31, 1993, no. 17 (entry by E.P. Caraco), illus. pp. 48 (color detail), 49 (color) and 138 (exhibition traveled to Yokohama, Sogo Museum of Art, April 21–May 23, 1993; Nara, Nara Sogo Museum of Art, June 9–July 4, 1993; and Kitakyushu, Kitakyushu Municipal Museum of Art, July 10–August 22, 1993).

## 52
## Auguste Rodin
(French: 1840–1917)

*The Age of Bronze,* modeled 1875–76, cast during the artist's lifetime
Bronze, height: 72 inches (182.9 cm.)
Signed on top of base at right: *Rodin*
Foundry mark on back of base at left: *Alexis RUDIER. / Fondeur. PARIS.*
Gift of Mr. and Mrs. Aage Qvistgaard-Petersen, acc. no. 1964.21

PROVENANCE
Viggo Qvistgaard-Petersen (1888-1955), Monte Carlo; by descent to his brother, Aage Qvistgaard-Petersen (1886-1976) and his wife, née Adele Lange, New Orleans; presented by them to the museum in 1964.

REFERENCES
A.T. Spear, *A Supplement to "Rodin Sculpture in The Cleveland Museum of Art*," Cleveland, 1974, p. 126S, under cat. no. VII // J. Tancock, *The Sculpture of Auguste Rodin: The Collection of the Rodin Museum, Philadelphia*, Philadelphia, 1976, p. 355 // J.G. Caldwell, *New Orleans Museum of Art—Handbook of the Collection* (ed. by B.N. McDermott), New Orleans, 1980, p. 63, illus. // P.N. Dunbar, *The New Orleans Museum of Art: The First Seventy-Five Years*, Baton Rouge and London, 1990, p. 233 // *New Orleans Museum of Art—Handbook of the Collection*, New Orleans, 1995, p. 67 (entry by J.G. Caldwell), illus. (color). Comparative References: A.E. Elsen, *Rodin*, New York, The Museum of Modern Art, 1963, pp. 21–26, illus. p. 20 (Minneapolis Institute of Arts cast) // I. Jianou and C. Goldscheider, *Rodin*, Paris, 1967, p. 86, illus. pls. 6–7 (cast at Musée Rodin, Paris) // C. Goldscheider, *Auguste Rodin: Catalogue raisonné de l'oeuvre sculpté*, I, *1840–1886*, Paris, 1989, p. 116, no. 95b, illus. p. 117 (Cleveland Museum of Art cast).

EXHIBITED
Raleigh, North Carolina Museum of Art, *Rodin: Sculpture from the Iris and B. Gerald Cantor Collection and Additional Works*, April 16–August 13, 2000, brochure, no number, illus. n.p.

53
Joseph-Jacques Tissot,
called James Tissot
(French: 1836–1902)

*The Terrace at Trafalgar Tavern, Greenwich,*
circa 1878
Oil on panel: 10 ⅝ x 14 ⅛ inches (27 x 35.9 cm.)
Signed on top of balustrade at lower right with artist's monogram
Gift of Merryl Israel Aron, in memory of Sam Israel, acc. no. 1996.78

PROVENANCE
Sir Thomas Wilson, Bart.; his sale, London, Sotheby's Belgravia, May 20, 1970, lot 72, illus. in cat.; acquired there by Richard Green, London; private collection ("A Lady of Title"); her sale, London, Christie's, November 5, 1993, lot 160, illus. in cat. (color); Merryl Israel Aron; presented by her to the museum in 1996.

REFERENCES
G. Keen, "Tissot Terrace Scene Fetches £ 4,100," *The Times* [London], May 21, 1970, illus. // F. Davis, "Talking about Sale-Rooms," *Country Life*, CXLVIII, August 6, 1970, p. 346 // *Connaissance des Art*, No. 224, October 1970, p. 129, illus. // W.E. Misfeldt, *The Albums of James Tissot*, Bowling Green, Ohio, 1982, p. 59, no. III-16 // M. Wentworth, *James Tissot*, Oxford, 1984, p. 131, illus. pl. 121 // Nantes, Musée des Beaux-Arts, *James Tissot et ses maîtres* (cat. by C. Sciama), 2005–2006, cited in essay by A. Smith, "James Tissot et l'Angleterre," pp. 78, 149, under no. 27.

EXHIBITED
Roslyn Harbor, N.Y., Nassau County Museum of Art, *La Belle Époque*, June 11–September 24, 1995, p. 91, no number, illus. p. 45 (color).

54
Edgar Degas
(French: 1834–1917)

*Dancer Adjusting Her Stocking,*
modeled circa 1880, cast 1919–21
Bronze, height: 16 ¾ inches (42.5 cm.)
Stamped on base: *70 / HER.D*
Stamped with foundry mark:
*A.A.Hébrard, cire perdue*
Museum Purchase, Elle West Freeman Foundation Matching Fund, acc. no. 1972.21

PROVENANCE
Cast by the A.A. Hébrard foundry, Paris, for the artist's heirs; Paris, Hôtel Drouot, December 2, 1946, lot 118b, illus. on front cover of cat.; Galerie Marcel Bernheim, Paris; acquired there on October 10, 1963, by The Alex Hillman Family Foundation, New York; their sale, New York, Parke-Bernet Galleries, March 1, 1972, lot 21j; acquired by the museum later that year.

REFERENCES
J.G. Caldwell, *New Orleans Museum of Art—Handbook of the Collection* (ed. by B.N. McDermott), New Orleans, 1980, p. 61, illus. // E. Braun, *Manet to Matisse: The Hillman Family Collection*, New York, Seattle and London, 1994, cited in "Appendix: Works Formerly in The Hillman Family Collection," p. 194, no. 23, also cited in essay "The Hillman Family Collection," p. 27, illus. p. 194 // *New Orleans Museum of Art—Handbook of the Collection*, New Orleans, 1995, p. 66 (entry by J.G. Caldwell), illus. (color) // S. Campbell, "A Catalogue of Degas' Bronzes," *Apollo*, CXLII, August 1995, p. 45 // J.S. Czestochowski and A. Pingeot, *Degas Sculptures: Catalogue Raisonné of the Bronzes*, Memphis, 2002, p. 259, no. 70–HER.D, illus. p. 258 (Norton Simon Art Foundation cast). Comparative References: J. Rewald, *Degas. Works in Sculpture. A Complete Catalogue*, New York, 1944, p. 27, no. LVIII, illus. p. 123 (another cast) [reprint: San Francisco, 1990, p. 154, no. LVIII, illus. (another cast)] // J. Rewald, *The Complete Works of Degas: Sculpture*, New York, 1956, p. 154, no. LVIII, illus. pl. 73 (another cast) // F. Russoli, *L'Opera completa di Degas*, Milan, 1970, p. 140, no. S[13], illus. p. 141 (another cast) // C.W. Millard, *The Sculpture of Degas*, Princeton, 1976, p. 35, note 49 and p. 69, illus. fig. 104 (wax model) // J. Lassaigne and F. Minervino, *Tout l'oeuvre peint de Degas*, Paris, 1988, p. 141, S[13], illus. (another cast) // A. Pingeot, *Degas Sculptures*, Paris, 1991, p. 158, no. 13, illus. pp. 126, 127, 158 (Musée d'Orsay cast).

55
Pierre-Auguste Renoir
(French: 1841–1919)

*Study of a Tree,* circa 1884–86
Pen and India ink on canvas, mounted on board: 20 x 24 ½ inches (508 x 623 mm.)
Signed with initial, lower center: *R*
The Muriel Bultman Francis Collection, acc. no. 1986.285

PROVENANCE
Paul Pétridès, Paris; Hugo Gallery, New York, until 1951; Muriel Bultman Francis (died 1986), New Orleans and (later) New York; bequeathed by her to the museum in 1986.

REFERENCES
A. Vollard, *Tableaux, pastels et dessins de Pierre-Auguste Renoir*, Paris, 1918, I, illus. pl. XII // B.E. White, *Renoir: His Life, Art and Letters*, New York, 1984, p. 166, illus. p. 173 // S. Monneret, *Renoir* (trans. by E. Read), London, 1989, p. 108, illus. fig. 1 // P.N. Dunbar, *The New Orleans Museum of Art: The First Seventy-Five Years*, Baton Rouge and London, 1990, p. 348 // C. Riopelle, "Renoir: The Great Bathers," *Philadelphia Museum of Art Bulletin*, LXXXVI, autumn 1990, p. 24, illus. p. 25, fig. 26.

EXHIBITED
New Orleans, New Orleans Museum of Art, *Profile of a Connoisseur: The Collection of Muriel Bultman Francis* (cat. by E.P. Caraco), November 10, 1985–January 12, 1986, no. 83, illus. p. 121 // New Orleans, New Orleans Museum of Art, *Fifty Master Drawings from the New Orleans Museum of Art* (cat. by V.L. Olsen), July 15–August 20, 1989, no. 44 (exhibition traveled to Monroe, Louisiana, Masur Museum of Art, September 9–October 1, 1989; Lake Charles, Imperial Calcasieu Museum, October 7–November 26, 1989; Shreveport, Meadows Museum of Art, January 27–March 11, 1990; Baton Rouge, Louisiana Arts and Science Center, March 17–May 13, 1990; Alexandria, Alexandria Museum of Art, May 19–June 30, 1990; and Lafayette, University Art Museum, September 1–November 16, 1990) // Philadelphia, Philadelphia Museum of Art, "Renoir: The Great Bathers," September 9–November 25, 1990 [for cat., see 1990 Reference, cited above] // Koriyama, Koriyama City Museum of Art, *French Art of Four Centuries from the New Orleans Museum of Art*, February 27–March 31, 1993, no. 25 (entry by S.E. Stearns), illus. pp. 58 (color), 144 (exhibition traveled to Yokohama, Sogo Museum of Art, April 21–May 23, 1993; Nara, Nara Sogo Museum of Art, June 9–July 4, 1993; and Kitakyushu, Kitakyushu Municipal Museum of Art, July 10–August 22, 1993).

56
Paul Gauguin
(French: 1848–1903)

*Head of a Tahitian Woman,* circa 1891–93
Charcoal and brownish-red chalk on paper:
11 ¼ x 11 ½ inches (285 x 292 mm.)
Museum Purchase, City of New Orleans Miscellaneous Capital Fund, acc. no. 1966.12

PROVENANCE
Kurt Guprader, Paris; Mme Alfred Varnan, Paris; D. Malingue; Geneva, Nicolas Rauch s.a., June 13–15, 1960, lot 481, illus. in cat.; Knoedler & Co., New York; acquired from them by the museum in 1966.

REFERENCES
G. Diehl, *Gauguin*, n.d., p. 30 // G. Boudaille, *Gauguin*, Paris, 1963, p. 268, illus. p. 150 (as 1892).

EXHIBITED
New Orleans, New Orleans Museum of Art, *Fifty Master Drawings from the New Orleans Museum of Art* (cat. by V.L. Olsen), July 15–August 20, 1989, no. 15, illus. (exhibition traveled to Monroe, Louisiana, Masur Museum of Art, September 9–October 1, 1989; Lake Charles, Imperial Calcasieu Museum, October 7–November 26, 1989; Shreveport, Meadows Museum of Art, January 27–March 11, 1990; Baton Rouge, Louisiana Arts and Science Center, March 17–May 13, 1990; Alexandria, Alexandria Museum of Art, May 19–June 30, 1990; and Lafayette, University Art Museum, September 1–November 16, 1990) // Koriyama, Koriyama City Museum of Art, *French Art of Four Centuries from the New Orleans Museum of Art*, February 27–March 31, 1993, no. 34 (entry by S.E. Stearns), also cited in essay by M.R. Brown, "An Introduction to French Art of Four Centuries," p. 24, illus. pp. 67 (color), 150 (exhibition traveled to Yokohama, Sogo Museum of Art, April 21–May 23, 1993; Nara, Nara Sogo Museum of Art, June 9–July 4, 1993; and Kitakyushu, Kitakyushu Municipal Museum of Art, July 10–August 22, 1993).

57
Pierre Bonnard
(French: 1867–1947)

*Study for the Poster, "La Revue Blanche,"* 1894
Ink, charcoal, watercolor and chalk on paper:
31 ¼ x 23 ½ inches (794 x 597 mm.)
Signed lower right: *P. Bonnard*
Gift of Mr. and Mrs. Frederick M. Stafford, acc. no. 1976.421

PROVENANCE
Possibly Thadée Natanson (1868–1951), Paris; Mr. and Mrs. Frederick M. Stafford, Paris and New York; presented by them to the museum in 1976.

REFERENCES
A. Humbert, *Les Nabis et leur époque, 1888–1900*, Geneva, 1954, illus. pl. 6 [reference is to the poster, signed and dated 1894, in the Musée national d'art moderne, Paris, although the New Orleans Museum of Art's drawing is illustrated inadvertently] // J.G. Caldwell, *New Orleans Museum of Art—Handbook of the Collection* (ed. by B.N. McDermott), New Orleans, 1980, p. 68, illus. // L.S. Dietrich, *The*

*Subject Vision of French Impressionism*, Tampa, Florida, 1981, p. 51 // P.N. Dunbar, *The New Orleans Museum of Art: The First Seventy-Five Years*, Baton Rouge and London, 1990, p. 242 // New *Orleans Museum of Art—Handbook of the Collection*, New Orleans, 1995, p. 71 (entry by E.P. Caraco), illus. (color).

EXHIBITED
New Orleans, The Isaac Delgado Museum of Art, *Odyssey of an Art Collector: Unity in Diversity—5,000 Years of Art*, November 11, 1966–January 8, 1967, no. 191, illus. p. 121 // Tampa, Florida, Museum of Art, *The Subjective Vision of French Impressionism*, 1981, no. 3 // Rochester, N.Y., University of Rochester, Memorial Art Gallery, *The Artists of La Revue Blanche: Bonnard, Toulouse-Lautrec, Vallotton, Vuillard*, January 22–April 15, 1984, no. 2, also cited in essay by B. Waller, "Artists and the Revue Blanche," p. 18, illus. p. 11 // Orléans, Musée des Beaux-Arts, *Peintures françaises du Museum of Art de la Nouvelle Orléans*, May 9–September 15, 1984, no. 28 (entry by E.P. Caraco), illus. // New York, The Metropolitan Museum of Art, *Pierre Bonnard: The Graphic Art* (cat. by C.T. Ives et al.), December 2, 1989–February 4, 1990, no. 34 (with incorrect information re. inscription), also cited in essay by C.T. Ives, "City Life," pp. 109–110 and on p. 237 (chronology), illus. p. 109, fig. 152 (exhibition traveled to Houston, The Museum of Fine Arts, February 25–April 29, 1990; and Boston, Museum of Fine Arts, May 25–July 29, 1990) // Memphis, Tenn., The Dixon Gallery and Gardens, *French Paintings of Three Centuries from the New Orleans Museum of Art*, January 5–March 1, 1992, no. 35 (entry by E.P. Caraco), also cited in essay by M.R. Brown, "An Introduction to French Paintings of Three Centuries," p. 10, illus. p. 85 (color) (exhibition traveled to Miami, Center for the Fine Arts, March 15–May 3, 1992; Wilmington, Delaware Art Museum, May 17–June 29, 1992; Grosse Point Shores, Michigan, Edsel and Eleanor Ford House, July 22–September 6, 1992; Oklahoma City, Oklahoma City Art Museum, October 4–November 15, 1992; and Seattle, Seattle Art Museum, December 17, 1992–February 14, 1993) // Koriyama, Koriyama City Museum of Art, *French Art of Four Centuries from the New Orleans Museum of Art*, February 27–March 31, 1993, no. 48 (entry by E.P. Caraco), illus. pp. 84 (color), 160 (exhibition traveled to Yokohama, Sogo Museum of Art, April 21–May 23, 1993; Nara, Nara Sogo Museum of Art, June 9–July

4, 1993; and Kitakyushu, Kitakyushu Municipal Museum of Art, July 10–August 22, 1993) // Mobile, Alabama, Mobile Museum of Art, *Picturing French Style: Three Hundred Years of Art and Fashion*, September 6, 2002–January 5, 2003, no. 49, illus. (color) (exhibition traveled to West Palm Beach, Florida, Norton Museum of Art, February 4–April 27, 2003).

## 58
## John Singer Sargent
## (American: 1856–1925)

*Portrait of Mrs. Asher B. Wertheimer,* circa 1898
Oil on canvas: 58 x 37 ½ inches (147.3 x 95.2 cm.)
Signed upper left: *John Singer Sargent*
Museum Purchase, in memory of William H. Henderson, acc. no. 1978.3

PROVENANCE
Asher B. Wertheimer (1844–1918) and his wife (the subject of this portrait), née Flora Joseph (died 1922), London; by descent to their daughter, Mrs. H. Wilson-Young, née Hylda Wertheimer (1878–?1938); to her son, Ian Wilson-Young; to his widow, Mrs. Ian Wilson-Young; to their son, Conway Wilson-Young; Julius Weitzner (1895–1986), London; Knoedler & Co., New York, as of 1976; Hammer Galleries, New York, 1978; acquired from them by the museum in 1978.

REFERENCES
"Art. The Sky-Line at the Royal Academy," *Academy*, May 14, 1898, p. 530 // R. Ross, "The Wertheimer Sargents," *Art Journal*, LXXIII, 1911, pp. 8, 10, note // "Letters and Art: A Sargent Year…," *Literary Digest*, LIII, September 9, 1916, p. 609 // W.H. Downes, *John S. Sargent: His Life and Work*, Boston, 1925, p. 183 [London, 1926 ed.: same pagination] // E. Charteris, *John Sargent*, London, 1927, pp. 164, 267 // W.M. Mount, *John Singer Sargent: A Biography*, New York, 1955, pp. 225, 435, no. 982 [later eds., London, 1957, pp. 187, 344, no. 982; New York, 1969, pp. 225, 456, no. 982] // D. McKibbin, *Sargent's Boston: With an Essay & a Biographical Summary & a Complete Check List of Sargent's Portraits*, Boston, 1956, p. 130 // R. Ormond, *John Singer Sargent: Paintings, Drawings, Watercolours*, London, 1970, p. 248 // J.B. Caldwell, *New Orleans Museum of Art—Handbook of the*

*Collection* (ed. by B.N. McDermott), New Orleans, 1980, p. 139, illus. pp. 24 (color), 139 and on front cover (color detail) // New York, Coe Kerr Gallery, *John Singer Sargent, His Own Work*, 1980, checklist, n.p. // "The Eternal Masterpieces: Portrait of Mrs. Asher B. Wertheimer," *Franklin Mint Almanac*, XII, November-December 1981, p. 15 // Allentown, Penna., Allentown Art Museum, *A Delicate Art: Flemish Lace, 1700–1940* (cat. by M. Vincent), 1986, p. 15, illus. fig. 10 // P.N. Dunbar, *The New Orleans Museum of Art: The First Seventy-Five Years*, Baton Rouge and London, 1990, p. 290 // *New Orleans Museum of Art—Handbook of the Collection*, New Orleans, 1995, p. 122 (entry by J.G. Caldwell), illus. (color) // K. Adler, "John Singer Sargent's Portraits of the Wertheimer Family," in L. Nochlin and T. Garb, eds., *The Jew in the Text: Modernity and the Construction of Identity*, London, 1995, pp. 84, 313, note 1 // London, Tate Gallery, and elsewhere, *John Singer Sargent* (ed. by E. Kilmurray and R. Ormond), 1998–1999, p. 148, cited under no. 54 (entry by R. Ormond) // T.J. Fairbrother, *John Singer Sargent: The Sensualist*, New Haven and London, 2000, pp. 87/89, illus. p. 86, fig. 3.14 (color) // G. Feigenbaum, "John Singer Sargent's State of Chronic Wertheimerism," *Arts Quarterly* [New Orleans Museum of Art], XXII, January-March 2000, pp. 5–7 // R. Ormond and E. Kilmurray, *John Singer Sargent: Complete Paintings*, II, *Portraits of the 1890s*, New Haven and London, 2002, pp. 134 and 188, no. 348, also cited pp. xvi (under chronology), 80, 132, illus. p. 135 (color) (with previous references); III, *The Later Portraits*, 2003, p. 125.

EXHIBITED
London, Royal Academy of Arts, *The One Hundred and Thirtieth Exhibition*, May 2–August 1, 1898, no. 936 // Glasgow, The Royal Glasgow Institute of the Fine Arts, 1913, no. 340 (or, possibly, the 1904 likeness of Mrs. Wertheimer [Ormond/Kilmurray 468]) // New York, The Jewish Museum, *John Singer Sargent: Portraits of the Wertheimer Family* (ed. by N.L. Kleeblatt), October 17, 1999–February 6, 2000, no. 2, also cited in essay by K. Adler, "John Singer Sargent's Portraits of the Wertheimer Family," p. 22, illus. p. 67, pl. 12 (color) (exhibition traveled to New Orleans, New Orleans Museum of Art, March 4–May 21, 2000; Richmond, Virginia Museum of Fine Arts, July 11–October 29, 2000; and Seattle, Seattle Art Museum, December 14, 2000–March 18, 2001).

## 59
## Odilon Redon
## (French: 1840–1916)

*Shadow and Light,* circa 1900
Black chalk on paper: 19 ¾ x 14 ¾ inches (502 x 375 mm.)
Signed and dated lower right: *ODILON REDON*
The Muriel Bultman Francis Collection, acc. no. 1986.282

PROVENANCE
Ambroise Vollard (1866–1939), Paris; Abris Silberman (died 1968), New York; Jacques Seligmann & Co., New York, as of 1951; acquired from them on May 3, 1952, by Muriel Bultman Francis (died 1986), New Orleans and (later) New York; bequeathed by her to the museum in 1986.

REFERENCES
M. Breuning, "Odilon Redon's World of Symbolic Illusion," *The Art Digest*, XXVI, November 1, 1951, illus. p. 55 // (?) D.E. Gordon, *Modern Art Exhibitions, 1900–1916: Selected Catalogue Documentation*, Munich, 1974, II, p. 35 // P.N. Dunbar, *The New Orleans Museum of Art: The First Seventy-Five Years*, Baton Rouge and London, 1990, p. 348 // A. Wildenstein, *Odilon Redon: Catalogue raisonné de l'oeuvre peint et dessiné*, I, *Portraits et figures*, Lausanne and Paris, 1992, pp. 173, 183, no. 460, illus. p. 183; IV, 1998, p. 301.

EXHIBITED
(?) The Hague, *Eerste Internationale Tentoonsteling / Première exposition internationale de peinture*, May 9–June 12, 1901, no. 179 (cat. entry reprinted in Gordon, 1974, cited above) // New York, Jacques Seligmann & Co., *Odilon Redon, 1840–1916: Pastels and Drawings*, October 22–November 10, 1951, no. 30 (exhibition traveled to Cleveland, Cleveland Museum of Art, November 29, 1951–January 20, 1952; and Minneapolis, Walker Art Center, February 1–March 1, 1952) // New Orleans, New Orleans Museum of Art, *Profile of a Connoisseur: The Collection of Muriel Bultman Francis* (cat. by E.P. Caraco), November 10, 1985–January 12, 1986, no. 79, also cited p. 15, illus. p. 117 // Tokyo, The National Museum of Art, *Odilon Redon*, March 17–May 7, 1989, no. 87, illus. (color) (exhibition traveled to Kobe, The Hyogo Prefectural Museum of Modern Art, May 14–June 25, 1989; and Nagoya, Aichi

Prefectural Art Gallery, July 7–23, 1989) // New Orleans, New Orleans Museum of Art, *Fifty Master Drawings from the New Orleans Museum of Art* (cat. by V.L. Olsen), July 15–August 20, 1989, no. 42 (exhibition traveled to Monroe, Louisiana, Masur Museum of Art, September 9–October 1, 1989; Lake Charles, Imperial Calcasieu Museum, October 7–November 26, 1989; Shreveport, Meadows Museum of Art, January 27–March 11, 1990; Baton Rouge, Louisiana Arts and Science Center, March 17–May 13, 1990; Alexandria, Alexandria Museum of Art, May 19–June 30, 1990; and Lafayette, University Art Museum, September 1–November 16, 1990) // Gunma, Musée d'Art Moderne, *Odilon Redon, entre rêve et mystère*, February 24–March 25, 2001, no. 27, illus. p. 50 (color) (exhibition traveled to Yamagata, Musée des Beaux-Arts de Yamagata, April 5–May 6, 2001; Odakyu, Musée Odakyu, May 16–June 10, 2001; and Hiroshima, Musée des Beaux-Arts de Hiroshima, July 7–August 9, 2001).

## 60
## Odilon Redon
(French: 1840–1916)

*Beasts at the Bottom of the Sea,*
circa 1900–05
Pastel on paper: 24 x 19 ¾ inches (61 x 50.2 cm.)
Signed lower left: *ODILON REDON*
The Muriel Bultman Francis Collection,
acc. no. 1983.69

PROVENANCE
Galerie E. Druet, Paris, from March 26, 1918 to February 5, 1919, and from March 22, 1920 to July 28, 1926; Arthur F. Egner (1882–1943), South Orange, New Jersey; his estate sale, New York, Parke-Bernet Galleries, May 4, 1945, lot 93, illus. in cat.; E. and A. Silberman Galleries, New York, as of 1949; Muriel Bultman Francis (died 1986), New Orleans and (later) New York; presented by her to the museum in 1983.

REFERENCES
G. Henriot, "À Propos d'Odilon Redon," *Mobilier et Décoration*, March 1926, illus. p. 25 // C. Fegdal, *Odilon Redon*, Paris, 1929, p. 64, no. 60, illus. pl. LX (in reverse) // C. Roger-Marx, "À propos de l'exposition Blake. Les visionnaires," *Beaux-Arts*, No. 213, January 29, 1937, illus. p. 1 (in reverse) // P.N. Dunbar, *The New Orleans Museum of Art: The First Seventy-Five Years*, Baton Rouge and London,

1990, p. 348 // A. Wildenstein, *Odilon Redon: Catalogue raisonné de l'oeuvre peint et dessiné*, II, *Mythes et légendes*, Lausanne and Paris, 1994, p. 295, no. 1291, illus. // *New Orleans Museum of Art—Handbook of the Collection*, New Orleans, 1995, p. 73 (entry by S.E. Stearns), illus. (color) // M. Gibson, *Odilon Redon, Le prince des rêves*, Cologne, 1995, p. 81, illus. p. 80 (color).

EXHIBITED
Paris, Galerie E. Druet, *Exposition d'oeuvres de Odilon Redon*, June 11–30, 1923, no. 99 // Atlanta, High Museum of Art, *Painting and Sculpture. Gothic to Surrealism*, January 8–February 5, 1950, no. 19 // New Orleans, New Orleans Museum of Art, *Profile of a Connoisseur: The Collection of Muriel Bultman Francis* (cat. by E.P. Caraco), November 10, 1985–January 12, 1986, no. 78, also cited in essay by E.P. Caraco, "Redon," pp. 14–15, illus. p. 116 // Tokyo, The National Museum of Art, *Odilon Redon*, March 17–May 7, 1989, no. 82, illus. (color) (exhibition traveled to Kobe, The Hyogo Prefectural Museum of Modern Art, May 14–June 25, 1989; and Nagoya, Aichi Prefectural Art Gallery, July 7–23, 1989) // Memphis, Tenn., The Dixon Gallery and Gardens, *French Paintings of Three Centuries from the New Orleans Museum of Art*, January 5–March 1, 1992, no. 37 (entry by S.E. Stearns), illus. (color) (exhibition traveled to Miami, Center for the Fine Arts, March 15–May 3, 1992; Wilmington, Delaware Art Museum, May 17–June 29, 1992; Grosse Point Shores, Michigan, Edsel and Eleanor Ford House, July 22–September 6, 1992; Oklahoma City, Oklahoma City Art Museum, October 4–November 15, 1992; and Seattle, Seattle Art Museum, December 17, 1992–February 14, 1993) // Koriyama, Koriyama City Museum of Art, *French Art of Four Centuries from the New Orleans Museum of Art*, February 27–March 31, 1993, no. 44 (entry by S.E. Stearns), illus. pp. 80 (color), 157 (exhibition traveled to Yokohama, Sogo Museum of Art, April 21–May 23, 1993; Nara, Nara Sogo Museum of Art, June 9–July 4, 1993; and Kitakyushu, Kitakyushu Municipal Museum of Art, July 10–August 22, 1993).

## 61
## Kees Van Dongen
(French: 1877–1968)

*Woman in a Green Hat,* 1905
Oil on cardboard: 18 x 14 ⅜ inches
(45.7 x 36.5 cm.)
Signed lower right: *Van Dongen*
Gift of Mr. and Mrs. Samuel J. Levin,
acc. no. 1963.39

PROVENANCE
Mr. and Mrs. Samuel J. Levin, St. Louis, and Miami Beach; presented by them to the museum in 1963.

REFERENCES
J.G. Caldwell, *New Orleans Museum of Art—Handbook of the Collection* (ed. by B.N. McDermott), New Orleans, 1980, p. 69, illus. pp. 20 (color), 69 // P.C. Sutton, *A Guide to Dutch Art in America*, Grand Rapids, Michigan, and Kampen (The Netherlands), 1986, p. 169, illus. // P.N. Dunbar, *The New Orleans Museum of Art: The First Seventy-Five Years*, Baton Rouge and London, 1990, p. 233 // *New Orleans Museum of Art—Handbook of the Collection*, New Orleans, 1995, p. 75 (entry by S.E. Stearns), illus. (color).

EXHIBITED
Tucson, University of Arizona Museum of Art, *Cornelis Theodorus Marie Van Dongen, 1877–1968* (cat. by W.E. Steadman), February 4–March 14, 1971, no. 52, illus. p. 133 (color) (exhibition traveled to Kansas City, Missouri, The Nelson Gallery of Art-Atkins Museum of Fine Art, April 25–May 23, 1971) // Orléans, Musée des Beaux-Arts, *Peintures françaises du Museum of Art de la Nouvelle Orléans*, May 9–September 15, 1984, no. 31 (entry by E.P. Caraco), illus. // Koriyama, Koriyama City Museum of Art, *French Art of Four Centuries from the New Orleans Museum of Art*, February 27–March 31, 1993, no. 56 (entry by S.E. Stearns), also cited in essay by M.R. Brown, "Introduction to French Art of Four Centuries," p. 28, illus. pp. 94 (color), 165 (exhibition traveled to Yokohama, Sogo Museum of Art, April 21–May 23, 1993; Nara, Nara Sogo Museum of Art, June 9–July 4, 1993; and Kitakyushu, Kitakyushu Municipal Museum of Art, July 10–August 22, 1993).

62
Maurice de Vlaminck
(French: 1876–1958)

*Chatou, le pont*, 1905–06
Oil on canvas: 18 ½ x 22 inches (47 x 55.9 cm.)
Signed lower right: *Vlaminck*
Partial and Promised Gift of Mrs. John N. Weinstock in memory of Mr. and Mrs. B. Bernard Kreisler, acc. no. 1995.393

PROVENANCE
Ambroise Vollard (1866–1939), Paris (no. 4084); Galeria Denis, Caracas (Cauvin photograph no. 14372); Schoneman Galleries, New York; Mr. and Mrs. B. Bernard Kreisler, New York and Greenwich, Conn.; by inheritance to Mrs. Kreisler (died 1976), New York; by inheritance to her niece, Mrs. John N. Weinstock, New Orleans; New York, Christie's, November 4, 2003, lot 27, illus in cat. (color) (bought in); Mrs. John N. Weinstock, New Orleans (partial gift to the museum with a life interest).

REFERENCES
*New Orleans Museum of Art—Handbook of the Collection*, New Orleans, 1995, p. 76 (entry by E.P. Caraco), illus. (color).

EXHIBITED
Orléans, Musée des Beaux-Arts, *Peintures françaises du Museum of Art de la Nouvelle Orléans*, May 9–September 15, 1984, no. 30 (entry by E.P. Caraco), illus. // Koriyama, Koriyama City Museum of Art, *French Art of Four Centuries from the New Orleans Museum of Art*, February 27–March 31, 1993, no. 53 (entry by E.P. Caraco), illus. pp. 90 (color), 163 (exhibition traveled to Yokohama, Sogo Museum of Art, April 21–May 23, 1993; Nara, Nara Sogo Museum of Art, June 9–July 4, 1993; and Kitakyushu, Kitakyushu Municipal Museum of Art, July 10–August 22, 1993) // New Orleans, New Orleans Museum of Art, *New Art for a New Building*, April 18–August 15, 1993, p. 15, no number, illus. (color).

63
Odilon Redon
(French: 1840–1916)

*The Dream*, circa 1905
Pastel on paper: 26 ¼ x 22 ½ inches (66.6 x 57.2 cm.)
Signed lower left: *ODILON REDON*
The Muriel Bultman Francis Collection, acc. no. 1986.283

PROVENANCE
Jacques Dubourg (1897–1981), Paris; Jos Hessel (1894–1941), Paris; Ambroise Vollard (1866–1939), Paris; E. and A. Silberman Galleries, New York, until 1954; private collection, c. 1974; acquired in 1978 by Muriel Bultman Francis (died 1986), New Orleans and (later) New York; bequeathed by her to the museum in 1986.

REFERENCES
P.N. Dunbar, *The New Orleans Museum of Art: The First Seventy-Five Years*, Baton Rouge and London, 1990, p. 348 // A. Wildenstein, *Odilon Redon: Catalogue raisonné de l'oeuvre peint et dessiné*, I, *Portraits et figures*, Lausanne and Paris, 1992, pp. 140–141, no. 345, illus. // *New Orleans Museum of Art—Handbook of the Collection*, New Orleans, 1995, p. 74 (entry by S.E. Stearns), illus. (color).

EXHIBITED
(?) Moscow, 1913 [according to 1992 Reference, cited above; unverified] // New Orleans, New Orleans Museum of Art, *Profile of A Connoiseur: The Collection of Muriel Bultman Francis* (cat. by E.P. Caraco), November 10, 1985–January 12, 1986, no. 81, also cited in essay by E.P. Caraco, "Redon," p. 15, illus. p. 119 // Tokyo, The National Museum of Modern Art, *Odilon Redon*, March 17–May 7, 1989, no. 129, illus. (color) (exhibition traveled to Kobe, The Hyogo Prefectural Museum of Modern Art, May 14–June 25, 1989; and Nagoya, Aichi Prefectural Art Gallery, July 7–23, 1989) // Koriyama, Koriyama City Museum of Art, *French Art of Four Centuries from the New Orleans Museum of Art*, February 27–March 31, 1993, no. 45 (entry by S.E. Stearns), illus. pp. 81 (color), 158 (exhibition traveled to Yokohama, Sogo Museum of Art, April 21–May 23, 1993; Nara, Nara Sogo Museum of Art, June 9–July 4, 1993; and Kitakyushu, Kitakyushu Municipal Museum of Art, July 10–August 22, 1993).

64
Georges Braque
(French: 1882–1963)

*Landscape at L'Estaque*, 1906
Oil on canvas: 20 x 23 ¼ inches (50.8 x 59.1 cm.)
Signed and dated lower right: *G. Braque 06*
Bequest of Victor K. Kiam, acc. no. 1977.284

PROVENANCE
Collection of the artist, until 1959; Galerie Maeght, Paris; acquired from them by Victor Kermit Kiam (1896–1974), New York; bequeathed by him to the museum in 1977.

REFERENCES
*Hommage à Georges Braque*, Paris, Maeght ed., 1964, pp. 12–13, illus. // F. Ponge et al., *G. Braque* (trans. by R. Howard and L. Dunlop), New York, 1971, p. 89, illus. // A.R. Martin III, "George Braque, Stylistic Formation and Transition, 1900–1909" (unpublished Ph.D. dissertation, Harvard University), 1979, I, pp. 102–104, illus. II, p. 351, fig. 68 // J.G. Caldwell, *New Orleans Museum of Art—Handbook of the Collection* (ed. by B.N. McDermott), New Orleans, 1980, p. 70, illus. pp. 19 (color), 70 // P.N. Dunbar, *The New Orleans Museum of Art: The First Seventy-Five Years*, Baton Rouge and London, 1990, p. 276 // *New Orleans Museum of Art—Handbook of the Collection*, New Orleans, 1995, p. 77 (entry by E.P. Caraco), illus. (color).

EXHIBITED
New York, Saidenberg Gallery, *Georges Braque, 1882–1963: An American Tribute*, April 7–May 2, 1964, no. 3, illus. // Paris, Musée national d'art moderne, *Le Fauvisme français et les débuts de l'Expressionnisme allemand*, January 15–March 6, 1966, no. 6 (exhibition traveled to Munich, Haus der Kunst, March 26–May 15, 1966) // Orléans, Musée des Beaux-Arts, *Peintures françaises du Museum of Art de la Nouvelle Orléans*, May 9–September 15, 1984, no. 34 (entry by E.P. Caraco), illus. (color) // Los Angeles, Los Angeles County Museum of Art, *The Fauve Landscape* (cat. by J. Freeman), October 4–December 30, 1990, p. 270, no number, also cited in chronology, p. 101, illus. p. 98, pl. 112 (exhibition traveled to New York, The Metropolitan Museum of Art, February 19–May 5, 1991; and London, Royal Academy of Arts, June 10–September 1, 1991) // Koriyama, Koriyama City Museum of Art, *French Art of Four Centuries from*

the New Orleans Museum of Art, February 27–March 31, 1993, no. 58 (entry by E.P. Caraco), illus. pp. 96 (color detail), 97 (color), 167 (exhibition traveled to Yokohama, Sogo Museum of Art, April 21–May 23, 1993; Nara, Nara Sogo Museum of Art, June 9–July 4, 1993; and Kitakyushu, Kitakyushu Municipal Museum of Art, July 10–August 22, 1993) // Marseille, Musée Cantini, *L'Estaque: naissance du paysage moderne, 1870–1910*, June 25–September 25, 1994, no. 22, illus. (color) // San Antonio, Texas, San Antonio Museum of Art, *Five Hundred Years of French Art* (cat. by D.K.S. Hyland), April 8–August 20, 1995, p. 75, no number, also cited in essay by J. Hutton, "Impressionism: Revisions, Revolts, Schools and Schisms," p. 63, illus. p. 64, fig. 66 (color) // Portland, Maine, Portland Museum of Art, *Impressions of the Riviera: Monet, Renoir, Matisse and Their Contemporaries*, June 25–October 18, 1998, no. 10, also cited in essay by J. House, "That Magical Light: Impressionists and Post-Impressionists on the Riviera," p. 24, illus. fig. 15 (color) // Paris, Musée d'Art moderne de la Ville de Paris, *Le Fauvisme ou "l'épreuve du feu." Eruption de la modernité en Europe*, October 29, 1999–February 27, 2000, no. 90, illus. p. 218 (color).

## 65
## Mary Cassatt
(American: 1845–1927)

*Mother and Child in the Conservatory*, 1906
Oil on canvas: 36 ⅛ x 28 ¾ inches
(91.8 x 73 cm.)
Signed lower left: *Mary Cassatt*
Museum Purchase, with funds contributed by Mr. and Mrs. Harold Forgotston, acc. no. 1982.124

PROVENANCE
James A. Stillman (1850–1918), Paris and New York, as of 1913 (probably acquired directly from the artist); Mrs. Frank A. Vanderlip, née Narcissa Cox (died 1966), Scarborough-on-Hudson, New York; Charles Lock Galleries, New York, as of 1954; Mr. and Mrs. Allan Bronfman, Montreal; Hammer Gallery, New York, as of 1980; Knoedler & Co., New York, as of 1981; acquired from them by the museum in 1982.

REFERENCES
A. Segard, *Mary Cassatt, un peintre des enfants et des mères*, Paris, 1913, illus. following p. 144 (dates painting to 1907) // A.D. Breeskin, *Mary Cassatt: A Catalogue Raisonné of the Oils, Pastels, Watercolors, and Drawings*, Washington, D.C., 1970, p. 184, no. 487, illus. // E.J. Bullard, "New Acquisitions: Mary Cassatt," *Arts Quarterly* [New Orleans Museum of Art], V, March 1983, pp. 14–15, illus. p. 14 and color pl. following p. 14 // *New Orleans Museum of Art—Handbook of the Collection*, New Orleans, 1995, p. 123 (entry by S.E. Stearns), illus. (color) // Chicago, Art Institute of Chicago, and elsewhere, *Mary Cassatt: Modern Woman* (cat. by J.A. Barter), 1998–1999, cited in essay by K. Sharp, "How Mary Cassatt Became an American Artist," p. 175, note 66 // New York, Sotheby's, November 5, 2002, p. 55, cited under entry for lot 15, illus. fig. 4.

EXHIBITED
New York, Wildenstein, *A Loan Exhibition of Mary Cassatt* (cat. by A.D. Breeskin), October 29–December 6, 1947, no. 36, illus. p. 43 (erroneously dates painting to c. 1903) // New York, Hammer Galleries, *Collecting 19th & 20th Century European and American Paintings*, July 1–August 29, 1980, no number, illus. (color) // Tokyo, Isetan Museum of Art, *The Art of Mary Cassatt (1844–1926)* (cat. by A.D. Breeskin), June 11–July 7, 1981, no. 43, illus. p. 61 (color) (exhibition traveled to Nara, Nara Prefectural Museum of Art, July 18–August 23, 1981).

## 66
## Paul Paulin
(French: 1852–1937)

*Bust of Edgar Degas at the Age of Seventy-Two*, 1907
Bronze: 19 ¾ x 16 ⅛ x 11 ¾ inches
(50 x 41.5 x 30 cm.)
Dated at rear: *Janvier / 1907*
Inscribed at rear: *à Degas / P. Paulin*
Gift in memory of Bennett A. Molter, Jr., by his wife, Jetta Hansen Molter, acc. no. 1991.425

PROVENANCE
Mr. and Mrs. Bennett A. Molter, Jr., Lafayette, Louisiana; presented by her to the museum in 1991.

REFERENCES
"New Art for a New Building," *Arts Quarterly* [New Orleans Museum of Art], January-March 1992, illus. p. 17.

EXHIBITED
New Orleans, New Orleans Museum of Art, *New Art for a New Building*, April 18–August 15, 1993, p. 11, no number, illus. (color).

## 67
## Robert Henri
(American: 1865–1929)

*The Blue Kimono*, 1909
Oil on canvas: 77 x 37 inches (195.6 x 94 cm.)
Signed lower left: *ROBERT HENRI*
Museum Purchase, Ella West Freeman Foundation Matching Fund, acc. no. 1971.16

PROVENANCE
Estate of the artist, inventory no. 38F; Chapellier Galleries, New York; acquired from them by the museum in 1971.

REFERENCES
Robert Henri, "Diary," p. 233 (Ms. in the collection of the artist's niece by marriage, Janet Le Clair; entry dated August 21, 1909) // G. Pène Du Bois, "Robert Henri: Realist and Idealist [Living American Painters—Thirteenth Article]," *Arts & Decoration*, II, April 1912, illus. p. 215 // W.S. Howard, "Robert Henri," *Harper's Monthly Magazine*, CXXV, October 1912, illus. following p. 706 // J.G. Caldwell, *New Orleans Museum of Art—Handbook of the Collection* (ed. by B.N. McDermott), New Orleans, 1980, p. 141, illus. // Wilmington, Delaware Art Museum, *Robert Henri, Painter*, 1984, p. 169, cited under chronology // P.N. Dunbar, *The New Orleans Museum of Art: The First Seventy-Five Years*, Baton Rouge and London, 1990, pp. 24–25, 246 // B.B. Perlman, *Robert Henri: His Life and Art*, New York, 1991, pp. 92, 98, 151 (under "A Checklist of Paintings by Robert Henri in Public Collections"), 155 (chronology) // *New Orleans Museum of Art—Handbook of the Collection*, New Orleans, 1995, p. 125 (entry by J.G. Caldwell), illus. (color).

EXHIBITED
Philadelphia, Philadelphia Arts Club, *20th Annual Exhibition*, 1909 // New York, The Union League Club, *Art Exhibition: Paintings by American Artists*, April 13–15, 1911, no. 8 // New Orleans, The Isaac Delgado Museum of Art, *Catalogue of Inaugural Exhibit*, December 16, 1911, no. 274 // San Francisco, *Panama-Pacific Exposition: Catalogue De Luxe* (ed. by J.E.D. Trask and J.N. Laurvik), February

20–December 4, 1915, I, p. 197, no. 2498, II, p. 323, no. 2498 // New York, The Metropolitan Museum of Art, *Memorial Exhibition of the Work of Robert Henri,* March 9–April 19, 1931, no. 42, illus. // New York, Grand Central Galleries, *Robert Henri Today,* January 9–28, 1939, no. 7 // New York, Hirschl & Adler Galleries, *Full-Length Portraits and Paintings of Children by Robert Henri, 1865–1929,* January 5–30, 1960, no. 6 // New York, Chapellier Galleries, *Robert Henri 1865–1929* (cat. by D.F. Hoopes), October 15–November 27, 1976, no. 39, illus. (color) // Orlando, Florida, Orlando Museum of Art, *My People: The Portraits of Robert Henri* (cat. by V.A. Leeds), October 22, 1994–January 8, 1995, no. 24, also cited in essay by V.A. Leeds, "The Portraits of Robert Henri," pp. 28, 44, note 57, illus. (color) (exhibition traveled to Fort Lauderdale, Florida, Museum of Art, February 5–April 2, 1995; and Columbus, Georgia, The Columbus Museum, April 30–June 25, 1995) // Oklahoma City, Oklahoma City Museum of Art, *Americans in Paris, 1850–1910: The Academy, The Salon, The Studio, and the Artists' Colony,* September 4–November 30, 2003, no. 56, also cited in essay by G.P. Weisberg, "Reflections on American Genre Painting in a European Context," p. 58, illus. p. 59 (color).

68
Umberto Boccioni
(Italian: 1882–1916)

*Unique Forms of Continuity in Space,* modeled 1913, cast by the Francesco Bruni foundry, 1972
Polished bronze: 46 ¼ x 34 ½ x 14 ½ inches (117.5 x 87.6 x 36.8 cm.)
Stamped on back of base: *FUSIONE Eseguita per la Galleria LA MEDUSA, ROMA SETTEMBRE 1972 ⅝ FONDERIA Francesco B*[runi].

Lent by The Sydney and Walda Besthoff Foundation Collection, New Orleans

PROVENANCE
London, Christie's, December 2, 1975, lot 51, illus. in cat.; Sidney Janis Gallery, New York; acquired from them in 1981.

REFERENCES
*New Art in an Old City—The Virlane Foundation and K. & B. Corporation Collections,*

New Orleans, 1994, cited in essay by E. Lucie-Smith, n.p., illus. pl. 118 (color). Comparative References: A. Palazzeschi and G. Bruno, *L'Opera completa di Boccioni,* Milan, 1969, p. 111, no. 166, illus. color pl. XLIII-XLV and p. 111 (bronze, cast c. 1928, then in the Mattioli collection, Milan) // R. Allen, *Catalogue of the Tate Gallery's Collection of Modern Art Other Than Works by British Artists,* London, 1981, pp. 60–61, no. T.1589, illus. p. 60 (bronze, cast in 1972, at the Tate Modern, London) // M. Calvesi and E. Coen, *Boccioni,* Milan, 1983, pp. 466–467, illus. figs. 856 a-d (original plaster, reconstructed, now at the Museu de Arte Contemporânea da Universidade de São Paulo, São Paulo), 856e (bronze, cast in 1921, at the Civica Galleria d'Arte Moderna, Milan).

EXHIBITED
(?) New York, Sidney Janis Gallery, *Masters in 20th Century Art,* October 2–November 3, 1979 // La Jolla, Calif., La Jolla Museum of Contemporary Art, *Seven Decades of Twentieth-Century Art from the Sidney and Harriet Janis Collection of the Museum of Modern Art and the Sidney Janis Gallery Collection* (introd. by W. Rubin), March 29–May 11, 1980, p. 22, no number, illus. (exhibition traveled to Santa Barbara, Calif., The Santa Barbara Museum of Art, June 6–August 10, 1980).

69
Jacques Lipchitz
(French/American, born in Lithuania: 1891–1973)

*Bather III,* modeled 1916–17, cast by the Modern Art Foundry, Long Island City, 1941
Bronze with gold patina, height: 27 inches (68.6 cm.)
Numbered and signed at top of base, at rear: *1/7 | JLipchitz*
Anonymous Gift through The American Federation of Arts, acc. no. 1960.38

PROVENANCE
Fine Arts Associates, New York; private collection; presented by them to the museum in 1960.

REFERENCES
H. Haydon, *Great Art Treasures in America's Smaller Museums,* New York, 1967, p. 91, illus. p. 86 // J.G. Caldwell, *New Orleans Museum of Art—Handbook of the Collection* (ed. by B.N.

McDermott), New Orleans, 1980, p. 72, illus. // *New Orleans Museum of Art—Handbook of the Collection,* New Orleans, 1995, p. 82 (entry by J.G. Caldwell), illus. (color). Comparative References: A.M. Hammacher, *Jacques Lipchitz* (trans. by J. Brockway), New York, 1975, illus. pls. 73–75 (stone at the Barnes Foundation) // N. Barbier, *Collections du Musée national d'art moderne: Oeuvres de Jacques Lipchitz (1891–1973),* Paris, 1978, p. 37, no. 11, illus. (plaster at the Musée national d'art moderne, Paris, gift of the artist) // A.G. Wilkinson, *The Sculpture of Jacques Lipchitz: A Catalogue Raisonné,* I, *The Paris Years, 1910–1940,* London, 1996, p. 47, no. 62, illus. pp. 47, 147 (another cast).

70
Amedeo Modigliani
(Italian: 1884–1920)

*Portrait of a Young Woman,* 1918
Oil on canvas: 24 x 18 inches (61 x 45.7 cm.)
Signed upper right: *modigliani*
Gift of Marjorie Fry Davis and Walter Davis, Jr., through the Davis Family Fund, acc. no. 1992.68

PROVENANCE
Reid & Lefevre, London; César M. De Hauke (1900–1965), New York, as of 1929; R. Sturgis Ingersoll, Philadelphia; acquired in 1972 by Marjorie Fry Davis and Walter Davis, Jr., New Orleans; presented by them to the museum in 1992.

REFERENCES
A. Pfannstiel, *Modigliani,* Paris, 1929, p. 42 // U. Apollonio, "Amedeo Modigliani, 1884–1920," *Cahiers d'Arts,* No. 1, 1950, illus. p. 180 // A. Pfannstiel, *Modigliani et son oeuvre: étude critique et catalogue raisonné,* Paris, 1956, p. 141, no. 264 // J. Lanthemann, *Modigliani, 1884–1920: catalogue raisonné. Sa vie, son oeuvre complet, son art,* Barcelona, 1970, p. 125, no. 263, illus. p. 230, fig. 263 // *New Orleans Museum of Art—Handbook of the Collection,* New Orleans, 1995, p. 87 (entry by S.E. Stearns), illus. (color).

EXHIBITED
New York, César De Hauke, *Modigliani,* October 21–November 9, 1929, n.p., no number, illus. on front cover // New York, Aquavella Galleries, *Amedeo Modigliani,* October 14–November 13, 1971, no. 38, illus. pl. 38 (color) // Princeton, N.J., Princeton

University, University Art Museum, *European and American Art from Princeton Alumni Collections*, May 7–June 11, 1972, no. 92, illus. // Monroe, Louisiana, Masur Museum of Art, *Selections from the Walter Davis Collection*, 1973, no. 21, illus. // Orléans, Musée des Beaux-Arts, *Peintures françaises du Museum of Art de la Nouvelle Orléans*, May 9–September 15, 1984, no. 38 (entry by E.P. Caraco), illus. // New Orleans, New Orleans Museum of Art, *New Art for a New Building*, April 18–August 15, 1993, p. 17, no number, illus. (color) // Paris, Musée du Luxembourg, *Modigliani, l'ange du visage grave* (cat. by M. Restellini and M.-C. Decrooq), October 23, 2002–March 2, 2003, no. 88, illus. p. 355 (color) (exhibition traveled to Milan, Palazzo Reale, March 21–July 6, 2003 [Italian ed. of cat., as *Amedeo Modigliani, l'angelo dal volto severo*, no. 61, illus. p. 301 (color)] // Rome, Complesso del Vittoriano, *Modigliani* (ed. by R. Chiappini), February 23–June 18, 2006, no. 37, illus. in color, front cover (detail) and p. 201 (as dating from 1918–19).

71
Fernand Léger
(French: 1881–1955)

*Study for "The Musical Instruments,"* 1925
Gouache on paper: 8 ⅜ x 3 ⅝ inches
(213 x 92 mm.)
The Muriel Bultman Francis Collection,
acc. no. 1986.253

PROVENANCE

Yvonne and Christian Zervos, Paris; Alexandre Iolas (1908–1987), Paris; Bodley Gallery, New York, until 1971; Muriel Bultman Francis (died 1986), New Orleans and (later) New York; bequeathed by her to the museum in 1986.

EXHIBITED

New York, Bodley Gallery, *Modern Master Drawings*, February 16–March 6, 1971, no. 16, illus. (color) // New Orleans, The New Orleans Museum of Art, *New Orleans Collects: A Selection of Works of Art Owned by New Orleanians*, November 14, 1971–January 9, 1972, no. 102, illus. // Koriyama, Koriyama City Museum of Art, *French Art of Four Centuries from the New Orleans Museum of Art*, February 27–March 31, 1993, no. 66 (entry by S.E. Stearns), illus. pp. 106 (color), 172 (exhibition traveled to Yokohama, Sogo Museum of Art, April 21–May 23, 1993; Nara, Nara Sogo Museum of Art, June 9–July

4, 1993; and Kitakyushu, Kitakyushu Municipal Museum of Art, July 10–August 22, 1993).

72
Wassily Kandinsky
(Russian: 1866–1944)

*Sketch for "Several Circles,"* 1926
Oil on canvas: 27 ⅝ x 27 ⅝ inches
(70.2 x 70.2 cm.)
Gift of Mrs. Edgar B. Stern, acc. no. 1964.31

PROVENANCE

Collection of the artist; acquired from him in April 1944 by Madame Noelle Lecouture, Paris; Mme Anne Lewenstein; Heinz Berggruen, Paris; The New Gallery, New York; Galerie Chalette, New York; Mrs. Edgar B. Stern, née Edith Rosenwald (1895–1980), New Orleans; presented by her to the museum in 1964.

REFERENCES

W. Kandinsky, "Handlist II [list in the artist's hand of his paintings, from 1909 to 1926]," n.d. [c. 1926], no. 322 // W. Grohmann, *Wassily Kandinsky: Life and Work*, New York, 1958, p. 335 // A.Z. Rudenstine, *The Guggenheim Museum Collection: Paintings, 1880–1945*, New York, 1976, I, pp. 322–323, cited under no. 111 // J.G. Caldwell, *New Orleans Museum of Art—Handbook of the Collection* (ed. by B.N. McDermott), New Orleans, 1980, p. 89, illus. // V.E. Barnett, *Kandinsky at the Guggenheim*, New York, 1983, pp. 42–43, 184–185, illus. p. 185, fig. b // G.W. Klein, *A Passion for Sharing: The Life of Edith Rosenwald Stern*, Chappaqua, N.Y., 1984, pp. 103–104 // H.K. Roethel and J.K. Benjamin, *Kandinsky: Catalogue Raisonné of the Oil-Paintings*, II, *1916–1944*, Ithaca, N.Y., 1984, p. 718, no. 766, illus. // P.N. Dunbar, *The New Orleans Museum of Art: The First Seventy-Five Years*, Baton Rouge and London, 1990, pp. 219, 233 // *New Orleans Museum of Art—Handbook of the Collection*, New Orleans, 1995, p. 88 (entry by J.G. Caldwell), illus. (color).

EXHIBITED

Paris, Galerie L'Esquisse, "Peintures abstraites, composition de matières: Domela, Kandinsky, Magnelli, de Staël," April 1944 (no catalogue) // Tokyo, The National Museum of Modern Art, *Kandinsky Retrospective: Hidden Construction*, May 28–August 9, 1987, no. 61, illus. (color) (exhibition traveled to Kyoto, The National Museum of Modern Art, August 18–Ocotber 4, 1987).

73
Max Ernst
(German: 1891–1976)

*Gulf Stream,* 1927
Oil on canvas: 25 ¼ x 20 ½ inches
(64.1 x 52.1 cm.)
The Muriel Bultman Francis Collection,
acc. no. 1986.183

PROVENANCE

Galerie Jeanne Bucher, Paris; private collection, Sweden; Barry Miller, London; Bodley Gallery, New York, until 1968; Muriel Bultman Francis (died 1986), New Orleans and (later) New York; bequeathed by her to the museum in 1986.

REFERENCES

*New Orleans Museum of Art—Handbook of the Collection*, New Orleans, 1995, p. 95 (entry by S.E. Stearns), illus. (color).

EXHIBITED

New Orleans, New Orleans Museum of Art, *Profile of a Connoisseur: The Collection of Muriel Bultman Francis* (cat. by E.P. Caraco), November 10, 1985–January 12, 1986, no. 27, also cited in essay by E.P. Caraco, "Surrealism," pp. 17–18, illus. p. 67 (color) // Berkeley, University of California, University Art Museum, *Anxious Visions: Surrealist Art* (cat. by S. Stich), October 3–December 30, 1990, p. 285, no number, also cited in essay by S. Stich, "Anxious Visions," p. 100, illus. p. 101, pl. 127 (color) // Koriyama, Koriyama City Museum of Art, *French Art of Four Centuries from the New Orleans Museum of Art*, February 27–March 31, 1993, no. 74 (entry by S.E. Stearns), illus. pp. 115 (color), 178 (exhibition traveled to Yokohama, Sogo Museum of Art, April 21–May 23, 1993; Nara, Nara Sogo Museum of Art, June 9–July 4, 1993; and Kitakyushu, Kitakyushu Municipal Museum of Art, July 10–August 22, 1993).

74
Constantin Brancusi
(Rumanian: 1876–1957)

*Sophisticated Young Lady
(Nancy Cunard),* modeled 1928,
cast (presumably) in 1932
Polished bronze on a marble base, height
without base: 21 ¾ inches (55.2 cm.)
height with base: 31 ⅛ inches (79.1 cm.)
Inscribed on bottom of bronze: *C. Brancusi /
PAR C Brancusi 1932 / PARIS 1928*

Loan from a private New Orleans collection

PROVENANCE
Acquired from the artist by the present owner
in Paris in 1954.

REFERENCES
R. Huyghe, *Dialogue avec le visible*, Paris,
1955, p. 114 // Nancy Cunard to Marcel
Duchamp, letter dated April 12, 1956 (Ms.,
copy, Solomon R. Guggenheim Museum,
New York: "The head resembles, at first sight,
somewhat, a torso, a graceful curve, and then
one sees the intention of that dear Brancusi,
it is really the profile of a head extended
in a lengthwise curve, with a tuft of hair,
if you please, at the crown!" as quoted in
Chave, 1993, cited below, p. 36) // C. Zervos,
*Constantin Brancusi: Sculptures, peintures,
fresques, dessins*, Paris, 1957, illus. p. 78 //
C. Giedion-Welcker, *Constantin Brancusi*,
Basel, 1958, illus. p. 114, fig. 52 // C. Giedion-
Welcker, "Rolle und Pragung des Sockels
bei Brancusi," *Werk* [Winterthur], No. 46,
1959 // I. Jianou, *Brancusi*, New York, 1963,
p. 110, illus. pl. 59 // S. Geist, "Letters to the
Editor…," *Art Bulletin*, XLVIII, September-
December 1966, p. 463 // S. Geist, *Brancusi:
A Study of the Sculpture*, New York, 1968,
p. 229, no. 181, also cited pp. 93–94, 227,
illus. p. 110 [revised ed., New York, 1983,
p. 229, no. 181, also cited pp. 93–94, 227,
275, illus. p. 110] // S. Geist, "Brancusi, the
Meyers, and *Portrait of Mrs. Eugene Meyer,
Jr.*," *Studies in the History of Art*, VI, 1974,
pp. 199, 211, illus. p. 195, fig. 6 (photograph
of *Sophisticated Young Lady* as exhibited at
the Brummer Gallery, New York, 1933–34) //
S. Geist, *Brancusi: The Sculpture and Drawings*,
New York, 1975, p. 191, no. 205, also cited
pp. 22, 189, illus. p. 145 (color) // R. Cohen,
"Kindred Spirits," *Art News*, LXXXII, March
1983, p. 87, illus. p. 84 (color photograph

of the sculpture as exhibited at the Sidney
Janis Gallery, New York, 1982) // P. Hulten,
N. Dumistrescu and A. Istrati, *Brancusi*, Paris,
1986, p. 311, no. 194, also cited p. 254, illus.
pp. 204, 235 (photograph of Brancusi's studio,
c. 1943), 311 // R. Varia, *Brancusi* (trans. from
the French by M. Vaudoyer), New York, 1986,
pp. 186, 303, note 5, illus. p. 188 (color) //
W.A. Fagaly, "Brancusi's *Sophisticated Young
Lady* on Loan for the 75th Anniversary," *Arts
Quarterly* [New Orleans Museum of Art],
VIII, July-September 1986, p. 38, illus. // F.T.
Bach, *Constantin Brancusi: Metamorphosen
plastischer Form*, Cologne, 1987, p. 495, no.
255, illus. // E. Shanes, *Constantin Brancusi*,
New York, 1989, pp. 63–64 // A.C. Chave,
*Constantin Brancusi: Shifting the Bases of
Art*, New Haven and London, 1993, pp. 36,
41, 187/189, illus. pp. 37, fig. 1.16 and 188,
fig. 5.15 // S. Miller, *Constantin Brancusi:
A Survey of His Work*, Oxford, 1995, pp. 149/151
// L. Stéphane, "Formes et matières dans
las sculpture de Brancusi," *Les Cahiers du
Musée National d'Art Moderne*, No. 54, winter
1995, illus. p. 50 (photograph by the artist
of *Sophisticated Young Lady*, with an image
of Brancusi) // M.E. Vetrocq, "Re-reading
Brancusi: the Philadelphia Story…," *Art in
America*, LXXXIV, January 1996, p. 123, illus.
p. 63 (photograph of *Sophisticated Young Lady*
in the artist's studio, c. 1935) // Paris, Musée
d'Art Moderne, Centre Georges Pompidou,
*La Collection: L'Atelier Brancusi* (ed. by
M. Tabart), Paris, 1997, pp. 108, 154, cited
under no. 87, illus. pp. 108 (photograph by
the artist), 195 (photograph of *Sophisticated
Young Lady* as exhibited at the Brummer
Gallery, New York, 1933–34) // P. Cabanne,
*Constantin Brancusi*, Paris, 2002, illus. p. 147
(view of Brancusi's studio c. 1940–45 showing
*Sophisticated Young Lady*) // L. Cumming,
"Seine Stealers," *The* [London] *Observer*,
January 27, 2002.

EXHIBITED
New York, Brummer Gallery, *Brancusi*
(exh. organized by Marcel Duchamp),
November 17, 1933–January 13, 1934, no. 26
(for a photograph of the Brummer Gallery
installation showing *Sophisticated Young Lady*,
see exh. cat., Paris, 1995, cited below, p. 64,
fig. 17; for a sketch by Duchamp showing
the placement of the lent works of art, see
ibid., p. 64, fig. 16) // Amsterdam, Stedelijk
Museum, *Tentoonstelling Abstracte Kunst*,
April 2–24, 1938, no. 10 (as "Miss N.C.")

// New York, Solomon R. Guggenheim
Museum, *Constantin Brancusi*, October
25, 1955–January 8, 1956, no. 55 (exhibition
traveled to Philadelphia, Philadelphia
Museum of Art, February 1956) // New York,
World House Galleries, *The Struggle for New
Form*, January 22–February 23, 1957, no. 9
// New York, Staempfli Gallery, *Constantin
Brancusi, 1876–1957: Sculpture, Drawings,
Gouaches*, November 29–December 31, 1960,
no. 13, illus. // New Orleans, The Isaac
Delgado Museum of Art, *Odyssey of an Art
Collector: Unity in Diversity—5,000 Years of
Art*, November 11, 1966–February 19, 1967,
no. 219, illus., pl. 136 and on front cover //
Philadelphia, Philadelphia Museum of Art,
*Constantin Brancusi 1876–1957, A Retrospective
Exhibition* (cat. by S. Geist), September
23–November 2, 1969, p. 126, no number,
illus. p. 127, pl. 127 (exhibition traveled
to New York, Solomon R. Guggenheim
Museum, November 20, 1969–February 15,
1970; and Chicago, Art Institute of Chicago,
March 14–April 26, 1970 // New York,
Solomon R. Guggenheim Museum, as of
July 1970, special loan // New Orleans, New
Orleans Museum of Art, September 1, 1971–
September 1974, special loan // New York,
The Metropolitan Museum of Art, placed on
extended loan (with several interruptions),
beginning May 8, 1978 // San Antonio, Texas,
San Antonio Museum of Art, and elsewhere,
*Brancusi as Photographer*, January 31–April 4,
1982 (exhibited at San Antonio venue only)
// New York, Sidney Janis Gallery, *Brancusi
+ Mondrian*, December 2–31, 1982, no. 13,
illus. // New Orleans, New Orleans Museum
of Art, *Diamond Jubilee Celebration*, January
1986–March 1987 // Paris, Musée national
d'art moderne, Centre Georges Pompidou,
*Constantin Brancusi, 1876–1957* (cat. by F.T.
Bach, M. Rowell and A. Temkin), April
14–August 21, 1995, no. 90, illus. (black &
white and color) (exhibition traveled to
Philadelphia, Philadelphia Museum of Art,
October 8–December 31, 1995) [American ed.
of cat.: same pagination] // New York, The
Metropolitan Museum of Art, *The Florene
M. Schoenborn Bequest: 12 Artists of the School
of Paris*, February 11–May 4, 1997 (not in
catalogue) // London, Royal Academy of Arts,
*Paris: Capital of the Arts, 1900–1968* (cat. by S.
Wilson et al.), January 26–April 19, 2002, no.
75, illus. (color) (exhibition traveled to Bilbao,
Guggenheim Museum, May 21–September 3,
2002).

75
Joan Miró
(Spanish: 1893–1983)

*Persons in the Presence of a Metamorphosis,*
1936
Tempera on masonite: 19 ¾ x 22 ⅝ inches
(50.2 x 57.5 cm.)
Signed upper right: *Miró.*
Inscribed on the back: *Joan Miró | Figures
devant une métamorphose | 20/1–31/1/36*
Bequest of Victor K. Kiam, acc. no. 1977.295

PROVENANCE
Dorothy Rieber Joralemon (1893–1987),
Berkeley, California; Pierre Matisse Gallery,
New York; acquired from them by Victor
Kermit Kiam (1896–1974), New York;
bequeathed by him to the museum in 1977.

REFERENCES
M. Davidson, "Subconscious Pictography by
Joan Miró," *Art News,* XXXV, December 5,
1936, illus. p. 11 // A.E. Gallatin et al., *Museum
of Living Art: A.E. Gallatin Collection,* New
York, 1940, illus. n.p. (photograph of the artist
in his studio) // C. Greenberg, *Joan Miró,* New
York, 1948, illus. p. 79, pl. XLI (with incorrect
ownership) // J. Prévert and G. Ribemont-
Dessaignes, *Joan Miró,* Paris, 1956, illus. p. 136
// F. Porter, "Reviews and Previews: Miró,"
*Art News,* LVII, December 1958, p. 12 // M.D.
Schwartz, "News and Views from New York:
Miró at The Museum of Modern Art," *Apollo,*
LXIX, May 1959, p. 151 // J. Dupin, *Joan
Miró,* Paris, 1961, pp. 262–263, 517, no. 421,
illus. p. 517 [English trans., as *Joan Miró: Life
and Work,* New York, 1961, p. 287, no. 421,
illus. p. 553] // J. Lassaigne, *Miró,* Paris, 1963,
p. 76 // W. Rubin, *Miró in the Collection of the
Museum of Modern Art,* Greenwich, Conn.,
1973, illus. frontispiece (photograph of painting
on display at the Galerie Pierre, Paris, 1936)
// J.G. Caldwell, *New Orleans Museum of
Art—Handbook of the Collection* (ed. by B.N.
McDermott), New Orleans, 1980, p. 77, illus. //
Kodansha, Ltd., *25 Great Masterpieces of Modern
Art: Miro,* Tokyo, 1981, pp. 115–116, illus.
pl. 26 // M. Rowell et al., "Miró," *Philadelphia
Museum of Art Bulletin,* LXXXIII, autumn
1987, illus. p. 2 (photograph of the artist in his
studio, 1936) // W. Erben, *Joan Miró, 1893–1983:
The Man and His Work,* Cologne, 1988, p. 78,
illus. (color) // P.N. Dunbar, *The New Orleans
of Art: The First Seventy-Five Years,* Baton
Rouge and London, 1990, pp. 274, 276 //

C. Lichtenstern, *Metamorphose in der Kunst des
19. und 20. Jahrhunderts,* Weinheim, 1992, II,
*Metamorphose vom Mythos zum Prozeßdenken,*
pp. 183, 205, note 163, illus. p. 184, fig. 135 //
*New Orleans Museum of Art—Handbook of the
Collection,* New Orleans, 1995, p. 94 (entry
by J.G. Caldwell), illus. (color) // B. Fer, *On
Abstract Art,* New Haven and London, 1997,
pp. 102–103, illus. p. 104, pl. 50 // J. Dupin
and A. Lelong-Mainaud, *Joan Miró: Catalogue
raisonné. Paintings,* II, *1931–1941,* Paris, 2000,
p. 140, no. 506, illus. (color) // New York,
The Pierpont Morgan Library, *Pierre Matisse
and His Artists* (cat. by W.M. Griswold and
J. Tonkovich), 2002, p. 172, cited under
"Chronology" by A. Carnielli and M. Loudon.

EXHIBITED
New York, Pierre Matisse Gallery, *Joan Miró,*
November 13–December 26, 1936, no. 18 // New
York, Pierre Matisse Gallery, *Joan Miró,* March
16–April 10, 1948, no. 7 // New York, Pierre
Matisse Gallery, *Joan Miro, "peintures sauvages,"
1934 to 1953* (introd. by J. Fitzsimmons),
November 4–29, 1958, no. 7, illus. n.p. //
New York, Museum of Modern Art, *Joan
Miró* (cat. by J.T. Soby), March 18–May 10,
1959, no. 60, illus. p. 87 (exhibition traveled
to Los Angeles, Los Angeles County Museum
of Art, June 10–July 21, 1959) // London, Tate
Gallery, *Joan Miró,* August 27–October 11,
1964, no. 134 (exhibition traveled to Zurich,
Kunsthaus, October 31–December 6, 1964) //
Washington, D.C., Smithsonian Institution,
Hirshhorn Museum and Sculpture Garden,
*Miró: Selected Paintings* (cat. by C.W. Millard),
March 20–June 8, 1980, no. 23, also cited in
essay by C.W. Millard, "Miró," p. 26, illus. p. 72
(color) (exhibition traveled to Buffalo, N.Y.,
Albright-Knox Art Gallery, June 17–August
27, 1980) // Edinburgh, Scottish National
Gallery of Modern Art, *Miró's People: Joan
Miró—Paintings and Graphics of the Human
Figure,* August 12–October 3, 1982, no. 11, illus.
p. 20 (color) // Houston, The Museum of Fine
Arts, *Miró in America* (cat. by J. McCandless),
April 21–June 27, 1982, no number, illus.
p. 61, fig. 53 // Orléans, Musée des Beaux-
Arts, *Peintures françaises du Museum of Art
de la Nouvelle Orléans,* May 9–September 15,
1984, no. 42 (entry by E.P. Caraco), illus. //
Zurich, Kunsthaus, *Joan Miró,* November 21,
1986–February 1, 1987, no. 96, illus. (color)
(exhibition traveled to Düsseldorf, Städtische
Kunsthalle, February 14–April 20, 1987) //
New York, Solomon R. Guggenheim Museum,

*Joan Miró: A Retrospective,* May 15–August 23,
1987, no. 81, illus. p. 158 (color) // Barcelona,
Fundació Joan Miró, *Impactes. Joan Miró,
1929–1941,* November 24, 1988–January 15, 1989,
no. 43, illus. p. 76 (color) (exhibition traveled
to London, Whitechapel Art Gallery, February
3–April 23, 1989) // Saint-Paul-de-Vence,
Fondation Maeght, *Joan Miró: Rétrospective de
l'oeuvre peint* (cat. by J.-L. Prat), July 4–October
7, 1990, no. 45, illus. (color) // Koriyama,
Koriyama City Museum of Art, *French Art of
Four Centuries from the New Orleans Museum
of Art,* February 27–March 31, 1993, no. 77
(entry by E.P. Caraco), illus. pp. 119 (color),
180 (exhibition traveled to Yokohama, Sogo
Museum of Art, April 21–May 23, 1993; Nara,
Nara Sogo Museum of Art, June 9–July 4,
1993; and Kitakyushu, Kitakyushu Municipal
Museum of Art, July 10–August 22, 1993)
// New York, The Museum of Modern Art,
*Joan Miró* (cat. by C. Lanchner and L. Tone),
October 17, 1993–January 11, 1994, no. 134,
illus. pp. 212 (color), 332 (photograph of the
artist with painting, 1936), 408 // Paris, Musée
national d'art moderne, Centre Georges
Pompidou, *Face à l'histoire: l'artiste moderne
devant l'événement historique,* December 9,
1996–April 7, 1997, p. 608, no number, illus.
p. 181 (color) // St. Petersburg, Florida, Salvador
Dalí Museum, *Masterpieces of Surrealism* (cat.
by W. Jeffett), January 29–April 16, 2000, no.
48, illus. p. 160 (color) // Paris, Musée national
d'art moderne, Centre Georges Pompidou, *La
Révolution surréaliste* (ed. by W. Spies), May
6–June 24, 2002, p. 439, no number, illus.
p. 231 (color) (exhibition traveled to Düsseldorf,
Kunstsammlung Nordrhein-Westfalen, July-
November 2002).


76
Georgia O'Keeffe
(American: 1887–1986)

*My Back Yard,* 1937
Oil on canvas: 20 x 36 inches (50.8 x 91.4 cm.)
Museum Purchase, City of New Orleans
Capital Fund, acc. no. 1973.8

PROVENANCE
Acquired from the artist (through her
representative Doris Bry) by the museum in
1973.

REFERENCES
J.G. Caldwell, *New Orleans Museum of*

Art—Handbook of the Collection (ed. by B.N. McDermott), New Orleans, 1980, p. 144, illus. // P.J. Broder, *The American West: The Modern Vision*, Boston, 1984, p. 172, illus. // R. Robinson, *Georgia O'Keeffe: A Life*, New York, 1989, p. 415 // P.N. Dunbar, *The New Orleans Museum of Art: The First Seventy-Five Years*, Baton Rouge and London, 1990, p. 271 // *New Orleans Museum of Art—Handbook of the Collection*, New Orleans, 1995, p. 129 (entry by J.G. Caldwell), illus. (color) // B.B. Lynes, *Georgia O'Keeffe: Catalogue Raisonné*, New Haven and London, 1999, I, p. 581, no. 932, illus. I, p. 580 (color) and II, p. 1128, fig. 68 (Stieglitz installation photograph of New York, 1937–38 exhibition) // J. Hobbs et al., *The Visual Experience*, Worcester, Mass., 2004, pp. 28, 134.

EXHIBITED
New York, An American Place, *Georgia O'Keeffe: Catalogue of the 14th Annual Exhibition of Paintings, with Some Recent O'Keeffe Letters*, December 27, 1937–February 11, 1938, no. 21 // Albany, Georgia, Albany Museum of Art, *Stieglitz: Photographs / Georgia O'Keeffe: Works from Southern Collections*, September 8–October 20, 1985, checklist // Perth, Art Gallery of Western Australia, *America: Art and the West*, December 11, 1986–January 21, 1987, no. 62, also cited in essay by C.M. Adams, "The West as Metaphor in Twentieth-Century Art," p. 33, illus. (color) (exhibition traveled to Sydney, Gallery of New South Wales, February 6–April 5, 1987) // Zurich, Kunsthaus, *Georgia O'Keeffe* (cat. by B. Curiger et al.), October 24, 2003–February 1, 2004, no. 43, illus. pp. 112–113 (color).

77
Hans Hofmann
(American, born in Germany: 1880–1966)

*Abstraction of Chair and Miró,* 1943
Oil on canvas: 58 x 44 inches (147.3 x 111.8 cm.)
Signed and dated lower right: *HH 43* [inscribed in a circle] / *III 12*
The Muriel Bultman Francis Collection, acc. no. 1986.200

PROVENANCE
Samuel M. Kootz Gallery, New York; Muriel Bultman Francis (died 1986), New Orleans and (later) New York; bequeathed by her to the museum in 1986.

REFERENCES
P.N. Dunbar, *The New Orleans Museum of Art: The First Seventy-Five Years*, Baton Rouge and London, 1990, p. 348 // C. Goodman, "The Lives and Works of Eminent Artists: Hans Hofmann," *Portraits*, I, No. 4, 1991, n.p., illus. fig. 2 // *New Orleans Museum of Art—Handbook of the Collection*, New Orleans, 1995, p. 134 (entry by S.E. Stearns), illus. (color).

EXHIBITED
New Orleans, New Orleans Museum of Art, *Profile of a Connoisseur: The Collection of Muriel Bultman Francis* (cat. by E.P. Caraco), November 10, 1985–January 12, 1986, no. 38, also cited in essay by E.P. Caraco, "The New York School," p. 21, illus. p. 78 (color).

78
Max Ernst
(German: 1891–1976)

*Turtle,* modeled 1944, cast by the Modern Art Foundry, New York, 1962
Bronze: 10 x 10 ½ x 6 ½ inches (25.4 x 26.7 x 16.5 cm.)
Stamped under stand:
*To Bernard Reis Max Ernst 9/9*
Gift of Mr. Bernard J. Reis, New York, acc. no. 1964.39a.b.

PROVENANCE
Presented by the artist to Bernard J. Reis, New York; presented by him to the museum in 1964.

COMPARATIVE REFERENCES
W. Spies et al., *Max Ernst: Werke, 1939–1953*, Cologne, 1987, no. 2469,1, illus. (unidentified cast).

79
Jean Dubuffet
(French: 1901–1985)

*Paul Léautaud in a Caned Chair,* 1946
Oil, with sand, on canvas: 51 ¼ x 38 ⅛ inches (130.2 x 96.8 cm.)
Bequest of Victor K. Kiam, acc. no. 1977.287

PROVENANCE
Galerie René Drouin, Paris; Pierre Matisse Gallery, New York, as of 1958; acquired from them in 1959 by Victor Kermit Kiam (1896–1974), New York; bequeathed by him to the museum in 1977.

REFERENCES
J. Fitzsimmons, *Jean Dubuffet: Brève introduction à son oeuvre*, Brussels, 1958, illus. fig. 9 // M. Ragon, *Jean Dubuffet: douze reproductions*, Paris, 1958, pp. 23–24 // M. Loreau, *Catalogue des travaux de Jean Dubuffet*, Paris, 1966, fasc. III, *Plus beaux qu'ils croient (portraits)*, n.p., no. 90, illus. // J.G. Caldwell, *New Orleans Museum of Art—Handbook of the Collection* (ed. by B.N. McDermott), New Orleans, 1980, p. 85, illus. // London, Tate Gallery, *Paris Post War: Art and Existentialism, 1945–55* (cat. by F. Morris), 1993, cited in essay by S. Wilson, "Paris Post War: In Search of the Absolute," p. 27, illus. fig. 2 (erroneously listed as in a private collection) // *New Orleans Museum of Art—Handbook of the Collection*, New Orleans, 1995, p. 102 (entry by J.G. Caldwell), illus. (color).

EXHIBITED
Paris, Galerie René Drouin, *Les Gens sont bien plus beaux qu'ils croient: Portraits…Mr. Jean Dubuffet, peintre*, October 7–31, 1947, no. 7 // New York, Pierre Matisse Gallery, *Jean Dubuffet: paintings, gouaches, 1946–1948*, November 30–December 31, 1948, no. 5 // Koriyama, Koriyama City Museum of Art, *French Art of Four Centuries from the New Orleans Museum of Art*, February 27–March 31, 1993, no. 78 (entry by J.G. Caldwell), also cited in essay by M.R. Brown, "An Introduction to French Art of Four Centuries," p. 27, illus. pp. 120 (color), 181 (exhibition traveled to Yokohama, Sogo Museum of Art, April 21–May 23, 1993; Nara, Nara Sogo Museum of Art, June 9–July 4, 1993; and Kitakyushu, Kitakyushu Municipal Museum of Art, July 10–August 22, 1993) // Basel, Fondation Beyeler, *Face to Face to Cyberspace*, May 3–September 12, 1999, no. 24, illus. p. 43 (color) // Paris, Centre Georges Pompidou, *Jean Dubuffet* (cat. by A. Abadie et al.), September 13–December 31, 2001, p. 84, no number, illus. (color).

**80**
**Jackson Pollock**
(American: 1912–1956)

*Composition (White, Black, Blue and Red on White),* 1948
Casein on paper mounted on masonite:
22 ⅝ x 30 ½ inches (57.5 x 77.5 cm.)
Signed and dated lower right center:
*Jackson Pollock 48*
Bequest of Victor K. Kiam, acc. no. 1977.300

PROVENANCE
Acquired from the artist by Leo Castelli Gallery, New York; Mr. and Mrs. Ira Haupt, New York; their sale, New York, Parke-Bernet Galleries, January 13, 1965, lot 19, illus. in cat.; Victor Kermit Kiam (1896–1974), New York; bequeathed by him to the museum in 1977.

REFERENCES
F.V. O'Connor and E.V. Thaw, *Jackson Pollock: A Catalogue Raisonné of Paintings, Drawings, and Other Works,* II, *Paintings 1948–1955,* New Haven and London, 1978, p. 8, no. 189, illus. // J.G. Caldwell, *New Orleans Museum of Art—Handbook of the Collection* (ed. by B.N. McDermott), New Orleans, 1980, p. 147, illus. // C. Betti and T. Sale, *Drawing: A Contemporary Approach* (2ⁿᵈ, revised ed.), New York, 1986, p. 184, illus. fig. 254 // P.N. Dunbar, *The New Orleans Museum of Art: The First Seventy-Five Years,* Baton Rouge and London, 1990, p. 276 // *New Orleans Museum of Art—Handbook of the Collection,* New Orleans, 1995, p. 135 (entry by J.G. Caldwell), illus. (color) // New York, Solomon R. Guggenheim Museum, and elsewhere, *No Limits, Just Edges: Jackson Pollock Paintings on Paper* (cat. by S. Davidson), 2005–2006, no. 56, also cited in essay by S. Davidson, "The Gesture of Intimate Scale: Jackson Pollock Paintings on Paper," p. 17, illus. p. 100 (color).

EXHIBITED
East Hampton, N.Y., Guild Hall Museum, *Krasner / Pollock: A Working Relationship* (cat. by B. Rose), August 8–October 4, 1981, no. 45, illus. (exhibition traveled to New York, New York University, Grey Art Gallery and Study Center, November 3–December 12, 1981) // New York, C & M Arts, *Jackson Pollock: Drip Paintings on Paper, 1948–1949,* October 13–December 11, 1993, n.p., no number, illus. (color) // Chadds Ford, Penna., Brandywine River Museum, *Milk and Eggs: The American*

*Revival of Tempera Painting, 1930–1950,* March 9–May 19, 2002, no. 37, also cited in essays by R.J. Boyle, "The America Tempera Revival in Context," p. 77, and by H. Brown, "On the Technical Side," pp. 102, 117, illus. in color, pp. 76, 120 (exhibition traveled to Akron, Ohio, Akron Art Museum, June 15–September 1, 2002; and Lawrence, Kansas, University of Kansas, Spencer Museum of Art, September 21–November 17, 2002) // New York, Robert Miller Gallery, *Dialogue: Lee Krasner and Jackson Pollock,* December 8, 2005–January 28, 2006, no number, illus. pl. 19 (color).

**81**
**Pablo Picasso**
(Spanish: 1881–1973)

*Mask of a Faun,* 1949–50
Bronze, height: 15 ¾ x 7 ⅞ inches (40 x 20 cm.)
Stamped on base at right, front: *2 / 2*
Stamped with foundry mark on back edge, at left: *E. GODARD / CIRE PERDUE*
Bequest of Victor K. Kiam, acc. no. 1977.298

PROVENANCE
Collection of the artist; Galerie Louise Leiris, Paris; Victor K. Kiam (1896–1974), New York; bequeathed by him to the museum in 1977.

REFERENCES
W. Spies, *Sculpture by Picasso, with a Catalogue of the Works* (trans. by J.M. Brownjohn), New York, 1971, p. 307, no. 341, illus. p. 199.

EXHIBITED
New York, Museum of Modern Art, *The Sculpture of Picasso,* October 11, 1967–January 1, 1968, no. 99, illus. p. 118.

**82**
**René Magritte**
(Belgian: 1898–1967)

*The Art of Conversation,* 1950
Oil on canvas: 20 ¼ x 23 ¼ inches
(51.4 x 59.1 cm.)
Signed lower right: *Magritte*
Gift of William H. Alexander, acc. no. 1956.61

PROVENANCE
Consigned by the artist in January 1951 to Alexander Iolas (1908–1987), New York, but returned to him in August 1952; Peter De

Maerel, Brussels; acquired in 1953 by William H. Alexander, New York; presented by him to the museum in 1956.

REFERENCES
H. Haydon, *Great Art Treasures in America's Smaller Museums,* New York, 1967, p. 91 // H. Torczyner and B. Bessard, *René Magritte: signes et images,* Paris, 1977, illus. p. 201 // J.G. Caldwell, *New Orleans Museum of Art—Handbook of the Collection* (ed. by B.N. McDermott), New Orleans, 1980, p. 79, illus. // P.N. Dunbar, *The New Orleans Museum of Art: The First Seventy-Five Years,* Baton Rouge and London, 1990, p. 97 // R.R. Thomas, *Dreams of Authority: Freud and the Fictions of the Unconscious,* Ithaca, N.Y., and London, 1990, illus. p. 254 // D. Sylvester, *Magritte: The Silence of the World,* New York, 1992, pp. 180, 324 // *René Magritte Catalogue Raisonné* (ed. by D. Sylvester), III, *Oil Paintings, Objects and Bronzes, 1949–1967* (by S. Whitfield and M. Raeburn), London, 1993, pp. 169–170, no. 743, also cited pp. 15, 23, 35, 36 (under chronology), 171, illus. p. 169; V, 1997, p. 46 // *New Orleans Museum of Art—Handbook of the Collection,* New Orleans, 1995, p. 97 (entry by J.G. Caldwell), illus. (color) // New York, The Equitable Gallery, and elsewhere, *Dreams, 1900–2000: Science, Art, and the Unconscious Mind* (ed. by L. Gamwell), 1999–2001, p. 253, illus. p. 200, pl. 138 (color).

EXHIBITED
New York, Hugo Gallery, *Magritte,* March 20–April 11, 1951, no. 27 // Rome, Galleria dell'Obelisco, *Magritte,* January 19–February 2, 1953, no. 7 // Montreal, Museum of Fine Arts, *Magritte* (ed. by D. Ottinger), June 20–October 27, 1996, no. 104, also cited in essay by D. Ottinger, "The Spiritual Exercises of René Magritte," p. 24, illus. (color) // Düsseldorf, Kunstsammlung Nordrhein-Westfalen, *René Magritte: Die Kunst der Konversation,* November 23, 1996–March 2, 1997, no. 88, also cited in essays by D. Ottinger, "Die spirituellen Exerzirien René Magrittes," p. 18, and by T. Heyden, "Erinnerung an eine Reise," p. 166, illus. p. 170 (color) // Brussels, Musées royaux des Beaux-Arts, *Magritte, 1898–1967* (ed. by G. Ollinger-Zinque and F. Leen), March 6–June 28, 1998, no. 163, illus. (color).

83
Joseph Cornell
(American: 1903–1972)

*Radar Astronomy*, 1952–56
Mixed media: 13 x 19 ¼ x 4 ¼ inches
(33 x 49 x 11 cm.)
Signed in mirror script on back of box,
lower right: *Joseph Cornell*
The Muriel Bultman Francis Collection,
acc. no. 1986.174

PROVENANCE
Estate of the artist, inv. no. 2272; acquired from
them by Castelli Feigen Corcoran, New York,
as of 1984; Muriel Bultman Francis (died 1986),
New Orleans and (later) New York; bequeathed
by her to the museum in 1986.

REFERENCES
P.N. Dunbar, *The New Orleans Museum of Art:
The First Seventy-Five Years*, Baton Rouge and
London, 1990, p. 348 // *New Orleans Museum of
Art—Handbook of the Collection*, New Orleans,
1995, p. 138 (entry by S.E. Stearns), also cited
p. 19, illus. p. 138 (color).

EXHIBITED
New Orleans, New Orleans Museum of Art,
*Profile of a Connoisseur: The Collection of
Muriel Bultman Francis* (cat. by E.P. Caraco),
November 10, 1985–January 12, 1986, no 18, also
cited in essay by E.P. Caraco, "The New York
School," p. 22, illus. p. 58 (color) // Madrid,
Fundación Juan March, *Joseph Cornell*, April-
May 1984, no. 21, illus. (color) // New Orleans,
Contemporary Arts Center, *The Ghost of Cornell:
New Orleans Boxed Assemblage*, November 24,
1998–January 17, 1999 [CD-ROM only].


84
Alberto Giacometti
(Swiss: 1901–1966)

*The Studio*, 1953
Oil on paper mounted on canvas: 27 ¾ x 19
inches (70.5 x 48.3 cm.)
Signed and dated lower left:
*Alberto Giacometti 1953*
Bequest of Victor K. Kiam, acc. no. 1977.291

PROVENANCE
Galerie Maeght, Paris; acquired from them by
Victor Kermit Kiam (1896–1974), New York;
bequeathed by him to the museum in 1977.

REFERENCES
J.G. Caldwell, *New Orleans Museum of
Art—Handbook of the Collection* (ed. by B.N.
McDermott), New Orleans, 1980, p. 87, illus. //
P.N. Dunbar, *The New Orleans Museum of Art:
The First Seventy-Five Years,* Baton Rouge and
London, 1990, p. 276 // *New Orleans Museum
of Art—Handbook of the Collection*, New
Orleans, 1995, p. 104 (entry by J.G. Caldwell),
illus. (color).

EXHIBITED
Koriyama, Koriyama City Museum of Art,
*French Art of Four Centuries from the New
Orleans Museum of Art*, February 27–March
31, 1993, no. 80 (entry by J.G. Caldwell), illus.
pp. 122 (color) and 182 (exhibition traveled to
Yokohama, Sogo Museum of Art, April 21–May
23, 1993; Nara, Nara Sogo Museum of Art, June
9–July 4, 1993; and Kitakyushu, Kitakyushu
Municipal Museum of Art, July 10–August 22,
1993) // Montreal, Museum of Fine Arts, *Alberto
Giacometti*, June 18–October 18, 1998, no. 60,
illus.


85
Alberto Giacometti
(Swiss: 1901–1966)

*Standing Woman*, circa 1953–55
Painted bronze, height: 22 ¼ inches (56.5 cm.)
Bequest of Victor K. Kiam, acc. no. 1977.292

PROVENANCE
Acquired from the artist by Galerie Maeght,
Paris; acquired from them in 1955 by Victor
Kermit Kiam (1896–1974), New York;
bequeathed by him to the museum in 1977.

REFERENCES
J.G. Caldwell, *New Orleans Museum of
Art—Handbook of the Collection* (ed. by B.N.
McDermott), New Orleans, 1980, p. 88, illus. //
P.N. Dunbar, *The New Orleans Museum of Art:
The First Seventy-Five Years,* Baton Rouge and
London, 1990, p. 276 // *New Orleans Museum of
Art—Handbook of the Collection*, New Orleans,
1995, p. 105 (entry by J.G. Caldwell), illus.
(color).


86
Naum Gabo
(American, born in Belorussia:
1890–1977)

*Construction in Space: Suspended,* conceived
circa 1957, executed circa 1963–64
Perspex [a plastic], stainless steel, spring-wire,
phosphor-bronze (cradle) on aluminum base,
height: 22 x 22 x 16 15/16 inches (55.8 x 55.8 x 43 cm.)
Inscribed on base: *Naum Gabo*
Gift of Mrs. Edgar B. Stern, acc. no. 1964.13

PROVENANCE
Acquired from the artist in February 1964
by Marlborough-Gerson Gallery, New York;
acquired from them later that year by Mrs.
Edgar B. Stern, née Edith Rosenwald (1895–
1980), New Orleans; presented by her to the
museum in 1964.

REFERENCES
H. Haydon, *Great Art Treasures in America's
Smaller Museums*, New York, 1967, p. 91
// J.G. Caldwell, *New Orleans Museum of
Art—Handbook of the Collection* (ed. by B.N.
McDermott), New Orleans, 1980, p. 91, illus.
// C.C. Sanderson, "Catalogue Raisonné of
the Constructions and Sculptures of Naum
Gabo" (ed. by C. Lodder), in exh. cat.,
Dallas, Museum of Art, and elsewhere, *Naum
Gabo: Sixty Years of Constructivism* (ed. by
S.A. Nash and J. Merkert), 1985–1987, p.
248, no. 70.4, illus. // P.N. Dunbar, *The New
Orleans Museum of Art: The First Seventy-
Five Years*, Baton Rouge and London, 1990,
pp. 219, 233 // M. Hammer and C. Lodder,
*Constructing Modernity: The Art and Career of
Naum Gabo*, New Haven and London, 2000,
pp. 439, 442, illus. p. 439, fig. 9 // C. Lodder,
"Gabo, Naum," in *Saur. Allgemeines Künstler-
Lexikon. Die bildenden Künstler aller Zeiter
und Völker*, XLVI, Munich and Leipzig, 2005,
p. 539.


87
Richard Diebenkorn
(American: 1922–1993)

*Woman on Porch*, 1958
Oil on canvas: 72 x 72 inches (183 x 183 cm.)
Museum Purchase, National Endowment
for the Arts Matching Grant and Women's
Volunteer Committee Fund, acc. no. 1977.64

PROVENANCE
Poindexter Gallery, New York, 1958; acquired from them in 1964 by Mr. and Mrs. David Lloyd Kreeger, Washington, D.C.; acquired from them by the museum, via Richard L. Feigen & Co., in 1977.

REFERENCES
P. Cummings, *A Dictionary of Contemporary American Artists*, New York, 1966, p. xi, illus. p. 102 // H. Taubman, "Mrs. Johnson Making Additions to American Art in White House," *The New York Times*, February 3, 1966, p. 25 // H. Dorra, assisted by A.B. Weinshenker and C.J. Jaffee, *The Kreeger Collection*, Washington, D.C., 1970, p. 127, illus. // M.P. Sharpe, ed., *The Collection of Mr. and Mrs. David Lloyd Kreeger*, Washington, D.C., 1976, p. 88, illus. // G.J. Hazlitt, "Problem Solving in Solitude," *Art News*, LXXVI, January 1977, illus. p. 76 (color) // R. Hughes, "California in Eupeptic Color," *Time*, CIX, June 27, 1977, illus. p. 59 // J.G. Caldwell, *New Orleans Museum of Art—Handbook of the Collection* (ed. by B.N. McDermott), New Orleans, 1980, p. 152, illus. // T. Calas, "Four Modernists in the New Orleans Museum of Art Collection," *Arts Quarterly* [New Orleans Museum of Art], V, March 1983, pp. 10/12, illus. p. 11 // T. Albright, *Art in the San Francisco Bay Area, 1945–1980: An Illustrated History*, Berkeley and Los Angeles, 1985, pp. 66–67, illus. p. 67, fig. 58 (color) // *New Orleans Museum of Art—Handbook of the Collection*, New Orleans, 1995, p. 139 (entry by J.G. Caldwell), illus. (color).

EXHIBITED
San Francisco, California Palace of the Legion of Honor, *Recent Paintings by Richard Diebenkorn*, October 22–November 27, 1960, brochure, no. 14, illus. (lent by Mr. and Mrs. George Poindexter, New York) // Little Rock, Arkansas, Little Rock Art Center, *Six Americans*, February 8–March 29, 1964, no. 3 // Washington, D.C., Washington Gallery of Modern Art, *Richard Diebenkorn*, November 6–December 31, 1964, no. 29, illus. on front cover (color) (exhibition traveled to New York, The Jewish Museum, January 13–February 21, 1965; and Newport Beach, Calif., Pavilion Gallery, March 14–April 21, 1965) // Washington, D.C., The White House, Executive Wing, June 1965–July 1967, special loan (intermittent) // Washington, D.C., Corcoran Gallery of Art, *Past and Present: 250 Years of American Art*, April 15–September

15, 1966 (no catalogue) // Washington, D.C., Corcoran Gallery of Art, *Friends of the Corcoran: 10th Anniversary Exhibition*, October 23–November 21, 1971, no. 24, illus. p. 31 // Buffalo, N.Y., Albright-Knox Art Gallery, *Richard Diebenkorn: Paintings and Drawings, 1943–1976*, November 12, 1976–January 9, 1977, no. 36, also cited in essay by G. Nordland, "The Figurative Works of Richard Diebenkorn," p. 31, illus. p. 32, fig. 50 (color) (exhibition traveled to Cincinnati, Cincinnati Art Museum, January 31–March 20, 1977; Washington, D.C., Corcoran Gallery of Art, April 15–May 23, 1977; New York, Whitney Museum of American Art, June 9–July 17, 1977; Los Angeles, Los Angeles County Museum of Art, August 9–September 25, 1977; and Oakland, Calif., The Oakland Museum, October 15–November 27, 1977) // San Francisco, Museum of Modern Art, *Bay Area Figurative Art, 1950–1965* (cat. by C.A. Jones), December 14, 1989–February 4, 1990, p. 222, no number, also cited in "Chapter Three: Growth and Maturity of the Reluctant Movement," p. 61, illus. p. 61, fig. 3.31(color) (exhibition traveled to Washington, D.C., Smithsonian Institution, Hirshhorn Museum and Sculpture Garden, June 13–September 9, 1990; and Philadelphia, Pennsylvania Academy of Fine Arts, October 5–December 30, 1990).

## 88
## Sam Francis
(American: 1923–1994)

*White Line I,* 1959
Oil on canvas: 71 ¾ x 47 ⅞ inches
(182.2 x 121.6 cm.)
Bequest of Victor K. Kiam, acc. no. 1977.290

PROVENANCE
Martha Jackson Gallery, New York; Victor Kermit Kiam (1896–1974), New York; bequeathed by him to the museum in 1977.

REFERENCES
J.G. Caldwell, *New Orleans Museum of Art—Handbook of the Collection* (ed. by B.N. McDermott), New Orleans, 1980, p. 153, illus. // P.N. Dunbar, *The New Orleans Museum of Art: The First Seventy-Five Years*, Baton Rouge and London, 1990, p. 276 // *New Orleans Museum of Art—Handbook of the Collection*, New Orleans, 1995, p. 141 (entry by J.G. Caldwell), illus. (color).

EXHIBITED
New York, Whitney Museum of American Art, *Annual Exhibition of Contemporary American Painting*, December 9, 1959–January 31, 1960, no. 42, illus. (as "The White Line").

## 89
## Joan Miró
(Spanish: 1893–1983)

*The Red Disk,* 1960
Oil on canvas: 51 ¼ x 63 ⅜ inches
(130.2 x 161 cm.)
Signed lower right: *Miró*
Dated and inscribed on reverse of canvas:
*19 / 4 / 1960 Le Disque Rouge*
Bequest of Victor K. Kiam, acc. no. 1977.296

PROVENANCE
Pierre Matisse Gallery, New York; Galerie Maeght, Paris; acquired from them by Victor Kermit Kiam (1896–1974), New York; bequeathed by him to the museum in 1977.

REFERENCES
J. Dupin, *Joan Miró*, Paris, 1961, pp. 466/468, 552, no. 896, illus. p. 469 (color) [English trans., as *Joan Miró: Life and Work*, New York, 1961, pp. 482–483, 568, no. 896, illus. p. 489 (color)] // J. Dupin, "Peintures récentes du Miró," *XXe Siècle*, No. 16, May 1961, illus. p. 35 (color) // P. Volboudt, "Univers de Miró," *XXe Siècle*, No. 17, December 1961, supplement, p. 7 // S. Gasch, *Joan Miró*, Barcelona, 1963, illus. p. 59 // H.H. Arnason, *History of Modern Art: Painting, Sculpture, Architecture*, Englewood Cliffs, N.J., and New York, n.d. [1969?], p. 354, illus. fig. 563 // J. Perucho, *Miró y Cataluña*, Barcelona, 1969, p. 138, no. 98, illus. (color) // A. Cirici Pellicer, *Miró en su obra*, Barcelona, 1970, p. 105, no. 29 // R. Penrose, *Miró*, New York, n.d. [1970?], illus. p. 129, pl. 94J // J.J. Sweeney, *Joan Miró*, Barcelona, 1970, p. 106, illus. (color) // M. Tapié, *Joan Miró*, Milan, 1970, p. 21, no. 72, illus. pl. 72 // T. Okada, *Miró*, Tokyo, 1974, p. 81, illus. // *25 Great Masters of Modern Art: Miró*, Tokyo, 1981, illus. pl. 41 // R.M. Malet, *Joan Miró*, Barcelona, 1983, illus. fig. 70 (color) // P.A. Serra, *Miró i Mallorca*, Barcelona, 1984, p. 88, no. 104, illus. (color) // W. Erben, *Joan Miró, 1893–1983: The Man and His Work*, Cologne, 1987, p. 156, illus. (color) // P.N. Dunbar, *The New Orleans of Art: The First Seventy-Five Years*, Baton Rouge and London, 1990, p. 242 // Porto, Fundação

de Serralves, *Os Mirós de Miró*, 1990, illus. p. 175 ("Joan Miró, una cronologìa," by V. Llorca) // R. Penrose, *Joan Miró*, London, 1990, p. 129, no. 94 // J. Dupin, *Miró*, Paris, 1993, p. 306, illus. p. 310 (color) [English trans., New York, 1993, p. 305, illus. p. 310 (color)] // *New Orleans Museum of Art—Handbook of the Collection*, New Orleans, 1995, p. 101 (entry by S.E. Stearns), illus. (color) // J. Punyet-Miró and G. Lolivier, *Miró. Le peintre*, Paris, 1998, p. 98, illus. (color) // J. Dupin and A. Lelong-Mainaud, *Joan Miró: Catalogue Raisonné. Paintings*, Paris, 2002, IV, *1959–1968*, p. 66, no. 1084, illus.

EXHIBITED
Paris, Galerie Maeght, "Poètes, peintres, sculpteurs," July-September 1960 [for cat., see *Derrière le Miroir*, No. 119, 1960, no. 5] // Paris, Galerie Maeght, "Miró" [for cat., see *Derrière le Miroir*, Nos. 125–126, April 1961, no. 1] // New York, Pierre Matisse Gallery, *Miró, 1959–1960*, October 31–November 25, 1961, no. 22, illus. pl. 22 // Saint-Paul-de-Vence, Fondation Maeght, *Miró*, July-August 1968, no. 54 // Barcelona, Recinto del Antiguo Hospital de la Santa Cruz, *Joan Miró*, November 1968–January 1969, no. 57, illus. p. 112 // Munich, Haus der Kunst, *Joan Miró*, March 15–May 11, 1969, no. 71, illus. // Washington, D.C., Smithsonian Institution, Hirschhorn Museum and Sculpture Garden, *Miró: Selected Paintings* (cat. by C.W. Millard), March 20–June 8, 1980, no. 37, also cited p. 31, illus. p. 86 (color) (exhibition traveled to Buffalo, Albright-Knox Art Gallery, June 27–August 17, 1980) // Houston, The Museum of Fine Arts, *Miró in America* (cat. by J. McCandless), April 21–June 27, 1982, no number // Zurich, Kunsthaus, *Joan Miró*, November 21, 1986–February 1, 1987, no. 149, illus. (color) (exhibition traveled to Düsseldorf, Städtische Kunsthalle, February 14–April 20, 1987) // New York, Solomon R. Guggenheim Museum, *Joan Miró: A Retrospective*, May 15–August 23, 1987, no. 129, illus. p. 219 (color) // New York, The Museum of Modern Art, *Joan Miró* (cat. by C. Lanchner and L. Tone), October 17, 1993–January 11, 1994, no. 197, also cited in "Chronology" by A. Umland, p. 341, illus. pp. 292 (color), 427.

90
Pablo Picasso
(Spanish: 1881–1973)

*Woman in an Armchair (Jacqueline Roque Picasso),* 1960
Oil on canvas: 45 ½ x 34 ¾ inches (115.6 x 88.3 cm.)
Signed upper right: *Picasso*
Bequest of Victor K. Kiam, acc. no. 1977.299

PROVENANCE
Galerie Louise Leiris, Paris; Galerie Claude Bernard, Paris; Victor Kermit Kiam (1896–1974), New York; bequeathed by him to the museum in 1977.

REFERENCES
C. Zervos, *Pablo Picasso*, XIX, *Oeuvres de 1959 à 1961*, Paris, 1968, n.p., no. 217, illus. pl. 63, fig. 217 // D.D. Duncan, *Goodbye Picasso*, New York, 1974, pp. 205–207, illus. (photographs of painting as displayed in the artist's château de Vauvenargues, France) // J.G. Caldwell, *New Orleans Museum of Art—Handbook of the Collection* (ed. by B.N. McDermott), New Orleans, 1980, p. 84, illus. // *New Orleans Museum of Art—Handbook of the Collection*, New Orleans, 1995, p. 100 (entry by E.P. Caraco), illus. in color, pp. 19 (detail), 100.

EXHIBITED
Jackson, Miss., Mississippi Museum of Art, *With a Little Help from Our Friends*, 1978, no. 40, illus. // Orléans, Musée des Beaux-Arts, *Peintures françaises du Museum of Art de la Nouvelle Orléans*, May 9–September 15, 1984, no. 37 (entry by E.P. Caraco), illus. // Koriyama, Koriyama City Museum of Art, *French Art of Four Centuries from the New Orleans Museum of Art*, February 27–March 31, 1993, no. 63 (entry by E.P. Caraco), illus. pp. 102 (color detail), 103 (color), 170 (exhibition traveled to Yokohama, Sogo Museum of Art, April 21–May 23, 1993; Nara, Nara Sogo Museum of Art, June 9–July 4, 1993; and Kitakyushu, Kitakyushu Municipal Museum of Art, July 10–August 22, 1993).

91
Louise Bourgeois
(American, born in France: 1911)

*Female Portrait,* 1962–82
Marble, height: 23 ¾ x 17 x 11 ½ inches (60.5 x 43.2 x 29.2 cm.)
Museum Purchase, General Acquisition Fund, acc. no. 1982.165

PROVENANCE
Robert Miller Gallery, New York; acquired from them by the museum in 1982.

REFERENCES
New York, Museum of Modern Art, *Louise Bourgeois* (cat. by D. Wye), 1982–1983, illus. p. 115, fig. 27 (photograph by Allan Finkelman of the artist's West 20th Street studio, August 1982) // B. Gallati, "Louise Bourgeois [exhibition review]," *Arts Magazine*, LVII, March 1983, p. 34, illus. // *New Orleans Museum of Art—Handbook of the Collection*, New Orleans, 1995, p. 152 (entry by S.E. Stearns), illus. (color) // C. Meyer-Thoss, "Bourgeois, Louise," in *Saur. Allgemeines Künstler-Lexikon. Die bildenden Künstler aller Zeiter und Völker*, XIII, Munich and Leipzig, 1996, p. 375.

EXHIBITED
New York, Robert Miller Gallery, *Bourgeois Truth* (cat. by R. Pincus-Witten), November 23–December 30, 1982, illus. n.p. (color).

92
Romare Bearden
(American: 1914–1988)

*Jazz: Kansas City,* 1977
Collage and oil on board: 18 ¼ x 27 inches (46.4 x 68.6 cm.)
Signed upper left: *romare bearden*
Museum Purchase, Robert P. Gordy and Carrie Heiderich Funds, acc. no. 1996.28

PROVENANCE
Commissioned in 1977 by Warner Brother Records for an album cover for a boxed edition of Charles ["Charlie Bird"] Parker recordings; Michael Rosenfeld Gallery, New York; acquired from them by the museum in 1996.

REFERENCES
"Collage: Made in America," *The New York Times* [art review], July 21, 1995, p. 46, illus. //